THE WILLIAMSBURG AVANT-GARDE

THE

WILLIAMSBURG

AVANT-

GARDE

EXPERIMENTAL MUSIC AND SOUND ON THE BROOKLYN WATERFRONT

Cisco Bradley

DUKE UNIVERSITY PRESS
Durham and London
2023

© 2023 DUKE UNIVERSITY PRESS
All rights reserved
Printed in the United States of America on acid-free paper ∞
Project editor: Lisa Lawley
Designed by Dan Ruccia
Typeset in Untitled Serif and Trade Gothic LT Std
by Westchester Publishing Services

Library of Congress Cataloging-in-Publication Data
Names: Bradley, Francis R., author.
Title: The Williamsburg avant-garde : experimental music and sound
on the Brooklyn waterfront / Cisco Bradley.
Description: Durham : Duke University Press, 2023.
Identifiers: LCCN 2022036523 (print)
LCCN 2022036524 (ebook)
ISBN 9781478019374 (paperback)
ISBN 9781478016748 (hardcover)
ISBN 9781478024019 (ebook)
Subjects: LCSH: Avant-garde (Music)—New York (State)—New York—
History. | Underground music—New York (State)—New York—
History and criticism. | Avant-garde (Aesthetics)—New York
(State)—New York—History. | Williamsburg (New York, N.Y.)—
History—20th century. | Williamsburg (New York, N.Y.)—History—
21st century. | BISAC: MUSIC / Genres & Styles / Jazz | SOCIAL SCIENCE /
Ethnic Studies / American / African American & Black Studies
Classification: LCC ML3477.8.N48 B73 2023 (print) |
LCC ML3477.8.N48 (ebook) | DDC 781.6409747/1—dc23/eng/20221114
LC record available at https://lccn.loc.gov/2022036523
LC ebook record available at https://lccn.loc.gov/2022036524

Cover art: Little Women (Darius Jones, Travis Laplante,
Andrew Smiley, and Jason Nazary) performing at Zebulon.
Williamsburg, Brooklyn, New York, April 5, 2012. Photograph
by Peter Gannushkin. Courtesy of the artist.

To Juliette,
Who was with me on this journey,

and

to all of the people who made the
Williamsburg scene happen

CONTENTS

PART II

COMMERCIAL DIY
AND THE LAST
UNDERGROUND
VENUES

Acknowledgments

I began the earliest work on this book in 2012. Like any in-depth research project, it took many twists and turns before it found its way to stable ground. The core of the research involved conducting about 250 interviews with musicians, curators, club owners, and label owners about the Brooklyn music scene over the span of nine years, many of which have been published on the website Jazz Right Now (https://www.jazzrightnow.com), which I founded in 2013. Of these, 182 pertained specifically to Williamsburg, which became the focus of this volume. I wish to thank everyone who spoke with me about their work and trusted me to convey their perspectives about the music of which they were a part. It was an absolute honor to spend these years deeply engaged with some of the United States' most visionary artists.

I wish to thank all of the following people, whom I interviewed about the Williamsburg music scene: Tom Abbs, Mariano Airaldi, Jeff Arnal, Gregor Asch, Newman Taylor Baker, Andrew Barker, Mick Barr, Matt Bauder, Gordon Beeferman, Mike Bell, Louis Belogenis, Millie Benson, Tom Blancarte, Shanir Blumenkranz, David Brandt, Tyondai Braxton, Patrick Brennan, Matt Bua, David Buddin, Ras Moshe Burnett, Ken Butler, Taylor Ho

Bynum, Jason Cady, Adam Caine, Damian Catera, Anthony Coleman, Cooper-Moore, Chris Corsano, Jeremiah Cymerman, Tim Dahl, Steve Dalachinsky, Ward Dennis, Jon DeRosa, Harvey Diamond, Terry Dineen, Jesse Dulman, Virg Dzurinko, Marc Edwards, Harris Eisenstadt, Moppa Elliott, Shane Endsley, Brandon Evans, Peter Evans, Jaime Fennelly, Amnon Freidlin, Dan Friel, Tomas Fujiwara, Carlos Giffoni, Jeff Gompertz, Hilliard Greene, Jimmy James Greene, Admiral Grey, Jonathon Haffner, Ben Hall, Onaje Will Halsey, Mary Halvorson, Shawn Hansen, Ratzo Harris, Sam Hillmer, Anna Hurwitz, James Ilgenfritz, Jon Irabagon, Michael Irwin, Russ Johnson, Chris Jonas, Darius Jones, Galen Joseph-Hunter, Bonnie Kane, Ha-Yang Kim, Jake Klotz, Montgomery Knott, Frank Lacy, Andrew Lamb, M. P. Landis, Travis Laplante, Gabriella Latessa Ortiz, Matt Lavelle, Carol Liebowitz, Evan Lipson, Nick Lyons, Jon Madof, Eyal Maoz, Sabir Mateen, Eric Maurer, David McClelland, John McCutcheon, Jason Merritt, Dominika Michalowska, Matt Mikas, Alex Mincek, Seth Misterka, Ravish Momin, Jackson Moore, Mark Morgan, Matt Mottel, Aron Namenwirth, Jason Nazary, David Nuss, Eivind Opsvik, Matt Pavolka, Jessica Pavone, Ethan Pettit, Mike Pride, Reuben Radding, Jose Ramos, Ted Reichman, Tom Roe, Michael X. Rose, Harry Rosenblum, Heather Roslund, Sari Rubinstein, Angelica Sanchez, Lorenzo Sanguedolce, Ryan Sawyer, Ursel Schlicht, Tom Schmitz, Aaron Ali Shaikh, Kevin Shea, Matthew Shipp, Tamio Shiraishi, Aaron Siegel, David Simons, Andrew Smiley, Jocelyn Soubiran, Richard Tabnik, Hideji Taninaka, Chad Taylor, Weasel Walter, Bill Ware, Russ Waterhouse, Charles Waters, Fritz Welch, Matthew Welch, Sarah Wilson, Michael Wimberly, Kenny Wollesen, Andrea Wolper, Estelle Woodward, Nate Wooley, and Michael J. Zwicky.

The research for this book relied heavily on private archives maintained by musicians who were a part of the scene. I dug through many dusty boxes, binders, and collections of old posters, flyers, tapes, letters, fanzines, and other ephemera through the years I worked on this book. Special thanks in particular are due to Andrew Barker, Mike Bell, Ken Butler, Jesse Dulman, Ebon Fisher, Seth Misterka, Jessica Pavone, Ethan Pettit, Michael X. Rose, Harry Rosenblum, Aaron Siegel, and Kenny Wollesen. I also wish to thank Galen Joseph-Hunter and Tom Roe for their work in building and maintaining the Wave Farm Archive.

I received a small grant from the Faculty Development Fund at the Pratt Institute that helped pay for certain logistical costs. I received general support from the Department of Social Science and Cultural Studies at Pratt for indexing and other editorial expenses. Certain colleagues at Pratt provided comments over the years that helped challenge and advance my thinking:

Carl Zimring, May Joseph, Luka Lucic, Macarena Gómez-Barris, Ann Holder, and Zhivka Valiavicharska all deserve mention.

I also wish to thank a few other scholars and writers who have contributed to my thinking in this book. Rashida Braggs (Williams College) has given me feedback through the years that I found very helpful. I met her and a number of other scholars at the conference held at the Guelph Jazz Festival in 2016. Thanks are due to William Harris for his help with one Robert Hayden poem reference. In addition, I would like to thank three writers who contributed to Jazz Right Now who have had an impact on me: Gabriel Jermaine Vanlandingham-Dunn, John Morrison, and Jordannah Elizabeth. Thanks also to the artist No Land for assistance in curating some of the photos included in this book. Furthermore, I got feedback on specific chapters from Chris Williams and Sam Weinberg that helped me refine my thinking. I wish to extend a special thanks to Akira Saito, who has translated and published some of my interviews on JazzTokyo (https://www.jazztokyo .com) over the years.

And finally, I want to thank my wife, Jennie Romer, for supporting me through the writing of this book. I also wish to thank my eldest child, Juliette Bradley, who has a beautiful, creative mind and to whom this book is dedicated. I hope that they will never stop exploring and imagining.

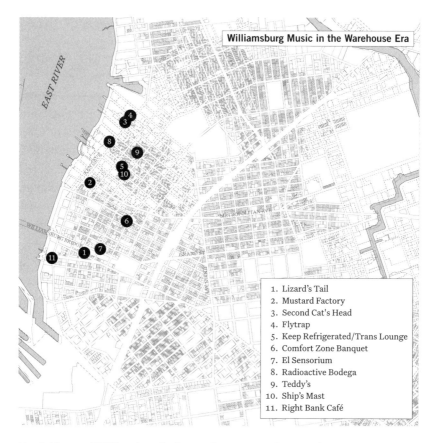

Williamsburg Music in the Warehouse Era

EAST RIVER

1. Lizard's Tail
2. Mustard Factory
3. Second Cat's Head
4. Flytrap
5. Keep Refrigerated/Trans Lounge
6. Comfort Zone Banquet
7. El Sensorium
8. Radioactive Bodega
9. Teddy's
10. Ship's Mast
11. Right Bank Café

Map 1 Venues of Williamsburg in the warehouse era, early 1990s (*designed by Korin Tangtrakul*)

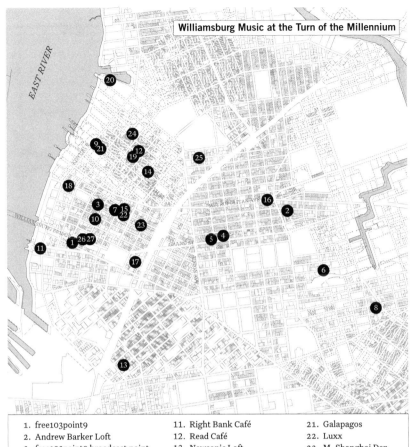

Williamsburg Music at the Turn of the Millennium

1. free103point9
2. Andrew Barker Loft
3. free103point9 broadcast point
4. 617 Grand
5. Artland
6. Brooklyn Free Music Festival
7. 220 Grand
8. Office Ops
9. Northsix
10. Sideshow Gallery
11. Right Bank Café
12. Read Café
13. Newsonic Loft
14. Williamsburg Art neXus
15. Lucky Cat Lounge
16. Pourhouse
17. Aaron Ali Shaikh Loft
18. Cave
19. The Charleston
20. Context Studios
21. Galapagos
22. Luxx
23. M. Shanghai Den
24. Momenta Art
25. Pete's Candy Store
26. Red and Black
27. Rubulad

Map 2 Venues of Williamsburg at the turn of the millennium (*designed by Korin Tangtrakul*)

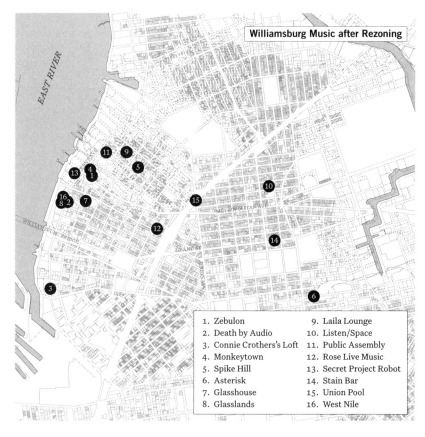

Williamsburg Music after Rezoning

1. Zebulon
2. Death by Audio
3. Connie Crothers's Loft
4. Monkeytown
5. Spike Hill
6. Asterisk
7. Glasshouse
8. Glasslands
9. Laila Lounge
10. Listen/Space
11. Public Assembly
12. Rose Live Music
13. Secret Project Robot
14. Stain Bar
15. Union Pool
16. West Nile

Map 3 Venues of Williamsburg after rezoning in 2005 (*designed by Korin Tangtrakul*)

Introduction

Locating the Williamsburg Avant-Garde

As I finished writing this book in 2020–21 during the COVID-19 pandemic, it could not have been a more unsettling time to be writing about the history of live music in New York City. With most live music canceled or broadcast remotely, communities like those described in this book were brought to a standstill in terms of live performances in formal venues. For some musicians, this was a moment of reckoning, compelling them to temporarily or permanently leave the city. Many bided their time, practicing, composing, and recording as they waited for live performances to be possible again. Others turned to performing outside in parks, in parking lots, and on rooftops because these were among the few safe places to gather as a community. This inventiveness in how music and communities relate to performance space has a long history in New York, inspired by the urban geography of a city that always seems caught in the throes of change.

From the late 1980s into the 2000s, one of the largest and most dynamic art scenes in the United States coalesced in Brooklyn. People from around the country and the globe found its inexpensive rents, ample space, and close proximity to Manhattan desirable as a launching point to take part in the arts cultures of the city. Fast-forward to the early 2020s, and Brooklyn has quickly become far too expensive for most artists to inhabit, its former arts hubs have been transformed into condominiums for the wealthy, and the arts community is being pushed further and further out from the center. Over the course of three decades, Brooklyn has witnessed a tremendous output of art across disciplines, despite mounting challenges that threaten its vitality.

Within this art scene, experimental music has been fantastically prolific and eclectic in Brooklyn since the 1990s. Nowhere was this more concentrated than in the north Brooklyn neighborhood of Williamsburg in the period 1988 to 2014. The Williamsburg avant-garde included a wide array of music, new and innovative in a variety of ways, and was situated in the most densely concentrated artist community in the borough. Improvisation was at the heart of many of these performances, and it is the single most unifying thread. Creative composition, aimed at creating unusual sounds or giving life to unusual ensembles, also was central to much of the activity. The use of new technology to create sounds, especially in the 1990s and early 2000s, spurred much of the noisier, electronic avant-garde. Experimentalists defied disciplinary and genre boundaries in these times and drew from an eclectic, global array of sources for their inspiration. At times, the avant-garde was a social experiment in bringing together people who might not otherwise gather or interact. And experimentation itself, in which the outcome was uncertain and the aim was to create something new, was at the heart of these performances.

The informal or do-it-yourself (DIY) nature of the community and of the spaces that musicians came to inhabit nurtured the creation of music that has been noncommercial, and the sounds themselves often seem to reflect back on the forgotten edges and broken seams of the city that fostered them. The DIY could take many forms but generally involved nonpublic, noncommercial venues, operated by artists or their collaborators, without public or private funding, and out of necessity often in direct violation of building codes and public safety standards. Thus, the vast majority of the musical performances discussed in this book occurred illegally. In postindustrial and abandoned residential pockets, the music community formed and blossomed, while still dealing with the harsh conditions, political opposition, and destructive moneyed interests that worked to displace them.

Occasionally, DIY art spaces went legit, but they catered to the same community of artists and generally did not have an apparatus for advertising their concerts widely. Even in licensed venues, police were still a regular threat to the survival of the scene owing to encroaching noise complaints. The struggle for access to and control of art space, having played out constantly since the inception of the Brooklyn art wave, has become its defining feature. This book examines the social and cultural tensions surrounding the making of the musical avant-garde, the spaces it has inhabited, the communities that have formed within and around it, and the forces that have sought to undermine, co-opt, or destroy it.

Over these twenty-five years, Williamsburg's primary role was as the workshop—a very necessary one—for the New York avant-garde and for world stages around the globe. Williamsburg was where experimentalists presented their ideas, sometimes without much of an audience and often in raw form, as they worked toward an objective of sound bold and new, confrontational and daring, eclectic and defiant of definition. Oftentimes, the Williamsburg DIY afforded artists places where they could *fail*. In an art form where experiment is at the center of striving for something new, having the freedom and space to try things, not all of which might succeed, was necessary and played a central role in the emergence of new sounds and ideas that have pushed the music forward into new territory. Things can happen on small, out-of-the-way stages that cannot happen in the limelight, or at least not right away. This book charts many of those experiments, some of which were never attempted again, while others were refined, altered, restarted, or evolved into works that were later presented on stages in grand concert halls in New York and across the world. Only in recent years, primarily in gentrified areas, has Brooklyn possessed well-funded stages for experimental performances. The genesis of the Williamsburg avant-garde generally occurred at times and in places when most people were not paying attention.

The critical importance of the Williamsburg avant-garde, as one of the foremost expressions of the broader American avant-garde, was that it extended the musical and sonic culture of the United States further into unexplored realms. Put more simply, the avant-garde of various kinds is where experiment happens. It is the sonic space where old rules are broken and new ones are made. It is where previously existing concepts and sounds that existed separately are brought together for the first time to stew together in a kind of sonic alchemy. The avant-garde has a fearlessness aimed at peeling back the layers of the unknown, step by step. Sometimes the experiments themselves are critical. Sometimes the experiments lead to something more conventional that could not have been arrived at without the experiment and the breaking of conventions in the first place. The avant-garde is new sound, new aural senses, new audiences and communities.

In the 1980s and 1990s, there remained a semblance of commercial venues for experimental artists in Manhattan, but by the 2000s these had receded into memory or became that elusive ideal that people chased but rarely found. That struggle stands in contrast to the immense artistic value that the music itself possesses. In fact, the struggle for the definition of value has plagued the avant-garde through its history. On the one hand, the avant-garde has broken into many new areas and explored concepts and trajectories never before pursued, but these new discoveries and innovations have rarely become any kind of commodity that could be packaged and sold. No dollar value may be placed on the utterance of a new sound, even a profound one, but at the same time musicians need to survive, pay rent, and eat. Pressure on musicians has mounted and continues to increase, as they seek to find a means to support their work in a world with limited grants, performance opportunities, commissions, and teaching positions. The aesthetic value of noncommercial music has regularly faced the accusation that it does not serve the capitalist machine.

This book is a social and cultural history of the Williamsburg avant-garde. While artist communities existed in numerous parts of Brooklyn, they were often more connected to Manhattan than to each other. Because of the structural layout of mass transit in the city via the subways, artists in central and southern Brooklyn often had more of a foothold in Manhattan than they did in North Brooklyn. The strongest affiliate was the South Brooklyn scene, which existed in the Park Slope, Kensington, and Ditmas Park neighborhoods during the same period, which I intend to write about in a subsequent study. The South Brooklyn community, although it shared a number of musical influences and interests, largely possessed its own character, more strongly informed by the early and mid-twentieth-century European avant-garde and some of the creative compositional practices that emerged out of it. Williamsburg's defining spatial characteristic was the postindustrial environment, which impacted on every level how the arts community was formulated and spatialized, and how artists presented their work to audiences.

This study traces the formation and dissolution of artist communities in Williamsburg over a span of twenty-five years. A distinct community possessing specific aesthetic influences and spatial orientations emerged in the neighborhood and evolved over time, with artists arriving in and departing from the social milieu throughout the period. My approach is to examine two related phenomena: art spaces and the communities that inhabit them. To accomplish this, I illustrate a series of sites around which scenes formed across a diverse array of art spaces, ranging from the back rooms of bars to artist lofts, galleries, rooftops, basements, warehouses, living rooms, stairways, backyards, wharves, street corners, subway platforms, balconies, and boats. Virtually every type of space, public or private, was a stage for performance during the two and a half decades I study here, but these spaces also impacted what was possible within them.

By examining the development of the music within the context of the physical transformations of the city, we are able to see how and why particular scenes emerged or disintegrated. Laws passed under the Rudy Giuliani and Michael Bloomberg administrations had catastrophic effects on the artist communities and led directly to their displacement. Certain neighborhoods in particular times became social centers for the communities of artists, lasting as long as financial and logistical conditions remained viable. But when one center collapsed, another soon sprang up, allowing us to see how scenes were reconstituted in new locations from the remnants of earlier dissolution or dislocation.

Gentrification has been the specter of artist communities, following like a shadow. Whereas it took developers more than a decade to respond to the emergence of an artist community in Williamsburg, at present developers are anticipating the transformation of Brooklyn neighborhoods before artists even arrive. The perceived hipness of musicians and other artists has been ringing the bell on the cash registers of developers, with no benefit for most artists. This process of displacement has affected many people outside of the artist community proper, and thus I examine the communities outside of the music scene, which sometimes formed relationships with artists, and the ways both groups have been displaced and dispossessed in this process. The story of the Brooklyn avant-garde is one of struggle and survival in the face of a development-oriented city government that has often offered little more than lip service to artists, despite New York's storied legacy as a city of art and music.

Hundreds of bands and thousands of performances resulted from the Williamsburg music wave. To have a scene, at its most basic level, one needs only two groups of people: performers and listeners. But in most cases music scenes involve vast networks of people who all play a role in their sustenance. To understand the communities that form around and inhabit art spaces— including musicians primarily but also curators, venue owners, critics, videographers, and audience members—I examine the social networks that maintain the scene. The manner in which artists formed social networks changed dramatically from 1988 to 2014, so I examine at each juncture how these relationships evolved, grew, and discarded old forms and took on new ones. Where possible, this book illustrates the series of human relationships that kept the vital heartbeat of musical creation going in Williamsburg.

The Evolution of Williamsburg

Williamsburg's memories are embedded brilliantly in its physical landscape. It has witnessed incredible change since the dawn of the twentieth century, with waves of immigrants from eastern Europe, the Caribbean, Latin America, and other parts of the world. Williamsburg has also experienced periods of incredible economic change, from the early twentieth century, when it was home to a broad range of chemical and industrial manufacturers, to the post–World War II era, when it contained munitions plants and other businesses. But like the rest of New York City, Williamsburg's economy collapsed in the 1960s and 1970s when deindustrialization swept through the area, leaving much of Brooklyn with crumbling buildings and a dwindling population. White flight to the suburbs left many urban neighborhoods like Williamsburg with few jobs, decaying infrastructure, and underfunded education.

To exacerbate an already difficult situation, the crack epidemic of the 1980s and 1990s tore through entire sections of Brooklyn, leaving thousands of inhabitants dead, communities fragmented and disintegrated, and property values destroyed. As economic rebirth has occurred since the 1990s, there has been gross inequality in its distribution, leading to extreme gentrification of neighborhoods and the displacement of many communities. Artists often dwelled and worked in the areas that were the hardest hit by gentrification, if even they were unwitting harbingers and ultimately victims of that transformation. The history of the musical avant-garde in Brooklyn is one of class and racial tension and of acute financial struggle placing working-class Brooklynites, artists of various means, and real estate developers into a contest that has resulted in profound transformation of the borough and the mass displacement of many residents, artists and otherwise, by economic forces far out of their control.

Today Brooklyn as a whole is New York's most populous borough; if it separated from New York City, Brooklyn would be the sixth-largest city in the United States and increasingly one of the youngest. This book examines how the flash points of Williamsburg's evolution from postindustrial landscape to hip trendsetter–created spaces of artistic experimentation. Or, in other words, I look at the people and the places where new ideas were born before they were distorted, diluted, stolen, or commodified by other social forces. Beginning in the late 1980s, Williamsburg became the site for the development of a whole range of innovative musical and sonic vocabularies in a shifting patchwork of communities.

Musical ideas never form in isolation, and they are never informed solely by other musical ideas. Much of the process is rather accretive, communally informed, and interdisciplinary. This book thus examines the social and intellectual context of musicians working in the avant-garde throughout the period. When possible, I zoom in and examine the specific locations of creation and presentation to see how these framed the music produced in such environments. I also see how the formation or dissolution of creative communities made its mark on the musical output of the participants.

A number of key cultural, aesthetic, social, and political elements contributed to the unique formation of the Williamsburg scene. In fact, the scene was constantly redefining itself. There was no single defining idiom but rather a diversity of communities and aesthetic influences, which shaped it over the twenty-five years covered in this book. The lack of unifying terminology is evidence enough of a scene that had no definitive center, though still connected through an array of influences, venues, community links, and a spirit of experimentation. Different elements, sometimes at war with one another, have worked to shape the music and the community of artists. Major streams of music coming from free jazz, noise, and postpunk bore the greatest influence on the Williamsburg avant-garde.

Free Jazz

Free jazz has been a monumental influence and has had a presence in the city since saxophonist Ornette Coleman (1930–2015) began recording with Atlantic Records in 1959 and released *The Shape of Jazz to Come*. Coleman did not adhere to the standard rules of twelve- or sixteen-bar blues, and he had a particularly spontaneous approach to playing. As one writer noted, Coleman's music was "described as raw, shrill, beautiful, repulsive, provocative, but rarely boring and always extremely personal."[1] His following two-and-a-half-month residency at the Five Spot club solidified his presence as an iconoclastic innovator. The work of Cecil Taylor (1929–2018), John Coltrane (1926–67), Don Cherry (1936–95), Albert Ayler (1936–70), Archie Shepp (b. 1937), and many others created a tidal wave of free jazz in the 1960s.[2] Despite this, the controversy that grew up around the music was something it would never shake. It would continue to be seen as outside the jazz mainstream despite generations of premier performers contributing to its legacy. Even the word *out* would come to describe the method of free improvisation or avant-garde sounds that challenged the listener to consider new musical possibilities, orienting listeners to view it as nonstandard or outside of the "jazz tradition."

The outsider characterization of free jazz, however, enabled it to be the repository for Black American political consciousness in the late 1960s and 1970s during the era of Black Power and the Black Arts Movement. Many of the key Black intellectuals who were articulating and defining Black consciousness at the time saw the music as central to the transformation of Black America. Amiri Baraka, then Leroi Jones, wrote that the "New Black Music," as it was then called, would be the "summoner of Black Spirit, the evolved music of the then evolved people."[3] Or, as saxophonist Charles Gayle characterized it:

> In the 1960s in the United States, there was a Black revolutionary spirit of breaking away from the mainstream of society for 30 million or so Black people. With the advent of Malcolm X we had the re-justification of the principles of Marcus Garvey and Harriet Tubman, and other people even in the times of slavery tried to help us gain our independence in thinking and in spirit, if not physically, from this particular land; and with other religions appearing, such as Islam and other African religions, the 1960s was an overwhelming period and it transferred itself to the music. It was a cry out and many people made music about revolution and indepen- dence and controlling our own destiny.[4]

A whole generation of musicians, just then coming of age, would give birth to an organic underground free jazz movement, though commercial con- straints would eventually slow its growth. When commercial opportunities were not available, free jazz would be self-organized and self-produced in downtown lofts throughout the East Village, the Lower East Side, and SoHo.[5]

By the 1980s the free jazz wave began receding in terms of its public per- sona, but a circle of dedicated musicians kept the scene alive in New York. Pianist Cecil Taylor was at the center of that movement; he had drawn a num- ber of musicians around him on returning to the city in 1973 and the following year presented his big band at Carnegie Hall, which showcased young and established talent. Taylor persisted through the 1980s by touring regularly in Europe, where he could get paid well at festivals, and cultivating new and innovative projects back in New York with dancers such as Dianne McIntyre (b. 1946) and his regular unit, which involved figures such as bassist Wil- liam Parker (b. 1952), saxophonist Jimmy Lyons (1931–86), and drummer Rashid Bakr (originally Charles Downs, b. 1943). Institutional forces rallied against free jazz in the 1980s, taking root in the music criticism of Stanley Crouch and later in the formation of jazz at Lincoln Center under the direction of Wynton Marsalis, which favored a fundamentalist turn toward the earlier bebop roots of the music. Documentaries such as Ken Burns's *Jazz* (2001) and many conservatories ignored or excluded free jazz in their work to build a jazz canon that was increasingly archaic.

From 1975 onward, the downtown loft the Kitchen became a space for experimental music in New York, but it was during George Lewis's tenure as music director there, 1980–82, that he shifted "the debate around border crossing to a stage where whiteness-based constructions of American experimentalism were being fundamentally problematized."[6] The scene struggled to survive through the early part of that decade, with outlets at the Public Theatre; loft or DIY spaces such as the Kitchen, Soundscape, and Judson Memorial Church; and a few jazz clubs like Lush Life that sometimes booked the more well-known figures.[7] White participation in free jazz also began to increase more visibly in the 1980s through the period of challenging economics, a trend that would continue to build momentum in the decades after.

The scene found a new home at the Knitting Factory by the late 1980s and eventually migrated to the club Tonic by the turn of the millennium.[8] Bassist William Parker, saxophonists Charles Gayle (b. 1939) and David S. Ware (1949–2012), pianist Matthew Shipp (b. 1960), guitarist Joe Morris (b. 1955), multi-instrumentalists Daniel Carter (b. 1945) and Cooper-Moore (b. 1946), and their associates carried on the free jazz scene into the 1990s and beyond. The annual Vision Festival, organized by dancer Patricia Nicholson each year since 1996, became the focal point of the New York free jazz scene, dedicated to featuring members of the community that had spent so many years maintaining it against financial, commercial, and social pressures. Saxophonist John Zorn's DIY club, the Stone, became another vital space from 2005 to 2018 and continues at the New School in recent years. The 2010s witnessed a resurgence of the Black free jazz tradition within a younger generation.

Noise and Postpunk

It is difficult to identify when exactly noise came into being and when it became a component in sound art and music. One theorist has argued that "in the nineteenth century, with the invention of machines, Noise was born."[9] In the twentieth century, cities and living spaces became louder, filled with noise of many varieties, and these sounds eventually came to inform the aesthetic of musicians in a wide variety of genres. To the present, much of the palette of noise music has retained identifiable industrial, metallic, or mechanical qualities. In 1954 John Cage's well-known investigation into sound, noise, and silence, *4'33"*, alerted listeners to all of the other sounds in the concert hall, including those from outside the room, blowing open the infinite possibilities of the musicality of the world in which we live. Cage later concluded, "Wherever we are, what we hear is mostly noise."[10]

The 1960s cast open the possibilities of noise in the musical palette, first in the form of free jazz and the avant-garde, as well as in the rock music wave that swept into popular music.[11] Lou Reed's *Metal Machine Music* (1975), though widely criticized at the time of its release, became a forerunner for noise as it developed over the following decades.[12] Punk rock would further explore many of the questions posed by the growth of noise and rock from the 1970s onward.[13] Punk featured stripped-down, fast-paced songs; hard-edged melodies; and often antiestablishment lyrics. Its full embrace of the DIY ethic became a defining feature and, like the contemporaneous lofts and self-run record labels of free jazz, would serve as an example for future experimentalists of how to create opportunities and interface with the general public. In New York the punk scene centered on CBGBs and Max's Kansas City, with a strong presence soon after in the East Village, where it continued to evolve in various forms until it began migrating across the river to Williamsburg in the late 1980s.

The conscious production of noise as part of a sonic experience in the pursuit of a broadly defined vocabulary began in earnest in the late 1970s.[14] In this context, one theorist described the phenomenon: "Noise is a negativity (it can never be positively, definitively, and timelessly located), a resistance, but also defined by what society resists."[15] That is, noise is culturally specific, defined by individual contexts; the cultures that create noise infuse it with meaning and value. What came to be known as industrial music emerged simultaneously with the decline of industry in manufacturing centers from London to New York. As one theorist characterized it, "Industrial music is music for the end of industry, the end of dreams of liberal softening of the capitalist machine."[16] Though the first industrial bands emerged in the United Kingdom, such as Throbbing Gristle, Wax Trax Records brought wider attention to the Chicago scene and bands from other parts of the United States in the early 1980s.[17]

Of importance to the development of noise, especially in New York, was the emergence of the No Wave movement in the late 1970s, which grew out of and in response to punk and postpunk. The venue Artists Space, located at 155 Wooster Street in Tribeca, was the inception point for a scene that included an eclectic array of artists such as the Contortions, DNA, Mars, Rhys Chatham, and Teenage Jesus and the Jerks (fronted by Lydia Lunch), among many others.[18] As one writer observed, "The music was spare but precipitously jagged and dissonant, with little regard for conventions of any sort; the basic idea seemed to be to make music that could never be co-opted."[19] Another writer argued that "No Wave groups defined radicalism not as a return to roots but as a deracination. They were united less by a common sound than by this shared determination to sever all connections with the past."[20]

As one scholar observed, "Many [No Wave] bands still used the instruments of rock—guitar, bass, drums, the occasional horn or keyboards—but forced sounds from them that were deliberately or obviously intended as confrontational acts. This was not music meant to offer people escapism or entertainment. In their various forms, one was offered disharmony, irregular tunings, static, sparseness, unmelodic and/or atonal vocals as well as re-petitive single-beat rhythms and single-note chords that were distorted into thudding white noise and drones."[21] The music bore a nihilistic worldview that was manifest in the apocalyptic, decaying, postindustrial New York of the late 1970s. No Wave crafted its sound in the live setting. As one writer noted, "It was in small clubs at overwhelming volume that No Wave was most effective."[22] The influence of No Wave was deeply felt in Williamsburg.

From the 1980s onward, a major movement in noise emerged in Japan. The roots of this movement date back to 1960, but it had gained momentum by the 1980s.[23] *Japanese noise* and *Japanoise* are both contested terms, since not all artists involved in the movement approve of the classification.[24] However, we can reasonably identify a number of key innovations among musicians from Japan through the 1980s that formally gave birth to noise as a genre of music. Paul Hegarty argues, "Japanese noise music is a loose, pleasingly futile and facile genre, grouping together musicians with enormously varying styles. With the vast growth of Japanese noise, noise music becomes a genre, a genre that is not one. It is not a genre, but is also a genre that is multiple, and characterized by this very multiplicity."[25] Placed in context, Japanese noise was "a resistance to conformity, a sort of extreme and messy combination of 1960s ideas and the more aggressive outlook of late 1970s and early 1980s music."[26] Figures such as Keiji Haino, Merzbow, and Hijokaidan pioneered these sounds, and many later bands expanded the possibilities of the music. As David Novak argues, "Over the last two decades of the twentieth century, Noise became a musical discourse of sounds, re-cordings, performances, social ideologies, and intercultural affinities. It connected a spatially and culturally diverse network of musicians and was embodied through the affective experiences of listeners. It was exchanged as an object of transnational musical circulation that touched down in par-ticular places and eventually came to be imagined as a global music scene."[27]

Shonen Knife, an all-woman band from Osaka, was one of the first noise bands to become popular in the United States in the late 1980s.[28] By the early 1990s, a wave of other noise units also gained in popularity, such as Hijokaidan, Incapacitants, Masonna, and the Boredoms, which received broad distribution and exposure through independent record stores and college radio stations, while appearing on a number of labels, including New York's Shimmy Disc and Tzadik.[29] Noise was to have an immense influence on the Williamsburg avant-garde by the late 1990s and early 2000s and has continued to be felt in the music community in various parts of the city up to the present.

The Demise of New York City's Downtown Scene

The New York downtown scene was a watershed moment for music in the city, a moment when many things came together between the mid-1970s and 1990s.[30] There seemed to be a shared interest in noise, distortion, high vol-umes, and dissonance, often presented as or within the context of a "breach of convention."[31] As one scholar theorized, "In disrupting common practice, outré musical language amounted to a kind of defamiliarizing syntactical noise. Artists downtown tended to manifest this interest by juxtaposing idioms that ostensibly did not belong together, tweaking the hierarchies of taste and disrupting the semiotics of style that often underlay judgments of artistic quality."[32] In other words, artists sought to undermine or destroy the method by which they were being judged in the first place and often to instill new senses of quality, taste, or value in their place.

Manhattan had long been home to the New York avant-garde. Brooklyn inherited key elements of Manhattan's music scene only as the city, and es-pecially the Lower East Side, no longer was a haven for artists. The period from the mid-1970s to the 1990s was the heyday of New York City's down-town music scene, with cutting-edge, forward-looking music finding its home at the Knitting Factory and other venues. With four stages and an eclectic mix of performers and audience members, "the Knit" was at once a cosmo-politan community center, a cultural vanguard, and a global epicenter for adventurous music. Situated on East Houston Street, the venue featured a variety of rooms with an array of different performers. The Alterknit was a closed black box theater, where musicians would often unveil new projects. The Tap Bar often had regular weekly performances featuring the most accessible music. Then there was the Old Office, which hosted innovative jazz-oriented and left-of-jazz types of music. And, of course, there was the main stage, which could accommodate bigger bands and the largest crowds. Innumerable performers played at the Knitting Factory, which managed to retain high standards while still making itself accessible to musicians who were new to the scene. Through the years it provided a stage for musicians ranging from free jazz players such as Cecil Taylor and David S. Ware to Steve Coleman and the M-Base scene to grunge rock stars like Vernon Reid, new and veteran proponents of No Wave, and unclassifiable figures like John Zorn. Music sometimes went as late as four in the morning on weekends.

The Knitting Factory scene has remained in the consciousness of all who experienced it. Its demise marked the end of the era when musicians playing new and experimental music could play with regularity at one hub. In addition to being able to offer well-attended gigs to musicians, the Knitting Factory also ran its own label and arranged tours for its artists. As trumpeter Russ Johnson noted, "If you were on their label, that meant you could instantly get gigs in Europe, and touring became easy. You could tour in Europe and make enough money there to support yourself for most of the rest of the year."[33] The cash flow allowed bandleaders to pay their musicians well and to envision ambitious projects with large groups or draw performers from beyond New York City.

One musician who arrived in 1994 said, "I started playing a lot of gigs that paid $50. If I did five gigs a week at different clubs, which was totally possible then, I could make $250 a week and more than $1,000 a month. Some months were better than others, but it worked because I was only paying $275 per month in rent. I wasn't making a lot of money, but I could at least survive." Then he reflected, "Today, if you had a gig every day of the year that paid $50, you couldn't even come close to paying rent."[34] Another artist recalled that up until 2001 there was "a spirit of artistic freedom that could exist because of cheap rent. An artist could survive on gig money or temp a couple days a week. The flexibility allowed artists to go on tour when the opportunity arose."[35]

The downtown scene was not to last forever. Already by the late 1980s, the structure of the scene was cracking. Rising rents for businesses and tenants were making the Lower East Side no longer as accessible as it had been a decade earlier. Many clubs in the area saw their rent go from $5,000 per month to $15,000 to $30,000 within the span of only five or ten years through the 1990s.[36] With such a massive increase in overhead costs, venues could no longer make enough money just from drawing crowds to hear music. With the landlords, venue owners, and musicians as the three groups of participants in this contest, we can see how the power dynamics resulted in musicians being the first to be disenfranchised through the process. Without labor laws that protected them adequately, compensation for their services either flatlined while the cost of living skyrocketed, or their income rapidly decreased altogether. Still, in the early 1990s, almost every venue paid musicians a cut from their bar till on top of a door fee. By the turn of the millennium, most venues stopped paying anything beyond the door fee. And in the early 2000s, it became increasingly common for venues to claim part of the door fee as well. The economics of live music was eroding at an alarming rate.

Then 9/11 happened. Thousands lost their lives. Lower Manhattan was cast under the shadow of industrial dust and the fear of another attack. The environment suddenly became unpleasant for both musicians and audiences. As one musician recalled, "A band that used to draw thirty to fifty people suddenly might only have four people in the audience. The whole energy downtown changed."[37] Another musician added, "A lot of musicians didn't want to perform there anymore. Everything south of Canal Street felt like a police state."[38] In the wake of 9/11, many people temporarily stopped going to hear live music.[39] The clubs could not survive without their patrons. In the span of a couple years, a huge wave of live music venues that had sustained the music scene for many years went bust, to the point that one artist referred to it as a moment of "oblivion."[40] One of the most cohesive and sustained music scenes ever to exist in the city quickly disintegrated. Though other Manhattan venues such as Tonic, the Stone, and Cornelia Street Café became important centers for music, a new but related scene emerged in Williamsburg, which increasingly became the place where musicians lived, created, and presented their work to whatever audience they could muster. As one musician described the shift, "It was a matter of survival."[41] Brooklyn was the workshop of the New York avant-garde, even as its participants fought an increasingly difficult battle to maintain art spaces and performance opportunities.

The years after 9/11 in Brooklyn were transformative. Many artists found opportunities, space, and community on an unprecedented scale. As one Pratt Institute art student recalled of the time, "In the wake of 9–11 we were free to do whatever the hell we wanted. The paranoia and overreaching authority hadn't settled in yet. Everyone sort of walked around like a celebrated survivor, like the little things didn't really matter because at any moment a true and massive tragedy could occur. Those first years after 9–11 really felt like we could do anything."[42]

The Internet Age

The internet made all kinds of musical connections possible. Certain facets of the internet would also lead to the destruction of the music industry, and all of this would happen over less than a decade. Up until the early 2000s, most events were advertised by word of mouth, in the *Village Voice* or other local newspapers, or via flyers and posters in areas where community members lived. In other words, physical media predominated in how the community managed its internal communication and how it related to the general public.

Changes to how music was consumed happened fast. iTunes was launched in January 2001, which made music more accessible to audiences, in theory, but began to sever the public's relationship with record stores. It was either an opportunity or an obstacle for musicians, depending on how they managed to relate to these changes; not all music was treated equally by these new platforms. The introduction of the iPod in November 2001 had a deeper impact on music consumption as it changed how the public related to each other—music became a more personal, less collective experience, and this also altered how the public related to live performances. The digitization of music has also completely alienated musicians from the fruits of their labor and creativity as it can be so easily replicated, which has deflated the value that musicians are able to get from recordings.[43] As one theorist described the process, "Once musical performances have been digitized they are in principle capable of being copied and disseminated in an infinite number at no extra production cost. It is at this stage of the whole process that it appears, in the consumer's perspective, that digital products are effortlessly and immediately duplicated and distributed."[44] This process of alienation has been taken to such an extreme that in many cases musicians now lose money producing records or choose to use physical media that cannot be so easily replicated. But as theorist Adolfo Sánchez Vásquez stated, "Under capitalism the artist tries to escape alienation, for alienated art is the very negation of art."[45] Musicians have been on the losing side of this struggle for two decades now, and if left unchecked, it will continue to undermine the well-being of music communities.

Method

This book relies on a combination of extensive ethnographic interviews, private archival collections, formal and informal music recordings, videos, photos, and other ephemera. I began preliminary research for this book in 2012, conducting extensive interviews with musicians who had worked the Williamsburg scene or had chosen to live there. I also attended hundreds of concerts in a variety of Brooklyn venues over the course of the 2010s.

In 2015, drawing from newspapers, websites, posters, flyers, recordings, and correspondence, much of which was located in private or informal participant-managed archives, I reconstructed a Brooklyn sessionography. The Word file was over nine hundred pages long and documented the live concerts that had occurred in the borough since the 1990s. Working from that resource, I shifted my interviews toward location-specific questioning, often with the curators of particular music series, to get a sense of the culture and social milieu of different art spaces and the communities that inhabited them. Over the course of this research, I have conducted over 250 interviews with musicians, curators, critics, venue owners, audience members, and others who have been active in Brooklyn since the late 1980s.

In 2013 I founded the website Jazz Right Now, which concentrates on "improvised and experimental music on the New York Scene" with a focus on Brooklyn-based bands and artists. The website has since accumulated the largest archive on that music scene ever assembled, including reviews, interviews, and artist features. The website has also built a repository of over a hundred artist profiles, as well as many hundreds of band profiles, discographies, concert listings, and press links.

I became directly involved in the DIY elements of the scene in 2014 when I began running my own loft shows in my home in the neighborhood of Bushwick, which I called New Revolution Arts, just as what remained of the scene that had once inhabited Williamsburg had fully shifted to the area. I drew direct inspiration from my research into the Williamsburg scene when curating bills and planning events. It should be noted, for the sake of understanding the challenges faced by artists, that none of the concerts that I produced there was officially licensed, and I sold beer and other alcohol off the books, turning over all of the proceeds to the artists themselves. Still, oftentimes this resulted in only a meager amount of money for the performers, though, on occasion, larger audiences crammed into the space such that I was able to pay bands better. From this experience I learned about the logistical and funding challenges that make the economics of the avant-garde difficult to maintain. It also gave me firsthand experience of how communities form around particular venues, as well as the inclusions and exclusions that arise through the curatorial process.

Chapter Outline

In Part I, the book examines the rise and proliferation of music venues in Williamsburg from the late 1980s through the early 2000s. Each of these interconnected experimental scenes had its own unique qualities and bore a unique mix of influences, including free jazz, rock, metal, punk, classical, noise, and various international musics. In each chapter the book situates the music in the physical landscape of the city and examines why these locations were initially conducive to attracting a community of artists, what communities took root in those environments, what cultural influences people exhibited, and how each of these had an impact on the music they produced. The book notes key venues and performers in each of the scenes and the influence they had on the music. Maps detail the proliferation of music venues and the way their emergence was facilitated by the existing urban landscape.

Chapter 1 examines how, with the shift to Williamsburg, music began appearing in settings ranging from warehouses and lofts to squats and neighborhood bars. These spaces had been home to a punk and noise rock scene since the 1980s, which bore considerable influence on this phase of experimental music as it began to germinate. The art spaces of the early Williamsburg waterfront scene, almost all of them unlicensed, were no longer tenable from the mid-1990s onward as some were forced to close and the community began to be pushed inland and away from the largest spaces.

Chapter 2 examines how the Williamsburg music scene shifted from waterfront warehouses to inland lofts, cafés, clubs, rooftops, and house concerts. The catalyst for much of this was the pirate radio station free103point9 and the community it fostered via microbroadcasts in 1997–2004. In this rebellious atmosphere, experimental music thrived. The organization Jump Arts also worked to bridge the musician communities of Williamsburg and the East Village together through a dozen festival events. Toward the end of the period, large festivals situated in East Williamsburg marked the shift of the community further east and south into other parts of postindustrial Brooklyn in future years.

The music also began to take root in cafés and bars as the community of artists grew. Chapter 3 examines the work of a wave of students who arrived in Brooklyn having previously studied with Anthony Braxton at Wesleyan University. They came with an eclectic training in composition and improvisation and an avid interest in the DIY possibilities of Brooklyn in 2001–6. Most established series in bars and cafés, while the community's most vibrant social center was at Newsonic Loft. The continued intermingling of such music with rock, noise, and electronic music, as well as visual art and film, made these spaces particularly vibrant for music aimed at exploring new sound.

Part II examines the period after the dissolution of most of the artist lofts, although some unlicensed DIY venues managed to persist. A few licensed venues came to cater to the scene, though they retained much of their DIY feel. The number of spaces that featured experimental live music in Williamsburg began to decline after 2005. However, some former loft spaces acquired legal certifications and became dynamic spaces for the music. Zebulon, more than any other space, became the new home for the scene in Williamsburg as other spaces closed. Chapters 4 and 5 look at the experimental music that occurred at Zebulon in two phases. From 2004 to 2006, Zebulon drew elements of the downtown scene to its stage. During its later years, up to its closing in 2012, Zebulon also issued a new generation of younger performers who made the scene their home.

Chapter 6 examines how the final DIY venues and a few licensed places persisted in Williamsburg up until 2014. Death by Audio was the last great venue of Williamsburg and was a key piece in a nationwide scene that followed experiments along the improvised music–rock–punk–metal–noise continuum. The chapter also discusses late artist lofts such as the one run by pianist Connie Crothers, as the scene itself became more and more fractured. Ultimately, neighboring Bushwick inherited much of the scene as musicians migrated inland and southeast to its cheaper rents. And during the later stages of the writing of this book, parts of the Bushwick scene have subsequently relocated eastward into Ridgewood, Queens. The voracious appetite of developers to further gentrify North Brooklyn has been stalled in recent times only by a global pandemic.

PART I

UTOPIAN SPACES FOR SOUND

CHAPTER ONE

The Emergence of the Williamsburg Scene

Warehouses, Squatter Parties, and Punk Roots,
1988–1994

Williamsburg was working-class cool as opposed
to rich pseudo-hip.
      —*Ray Brazen*

I was looking for community, and I found it in Williamsburg.
      —*Anna Hurwitz*

The Williamsburg neighborhood of Brooklyn has a long and diverse history. The population of nineteenth-century Williamsburg was predominantly German. At the beginning of the twentieth century, when the bridge bearing its name was completed, it experienced an influx of Jewish residents fleeing the ghettos of Lower Manhattan.[1] After a subsequent migration carried many of them further out onto Long Island, the South Side of the neighborhood, between Grand Street and Division Avenue, became the home of primarily Puerto Rican and Colombian populations after World War II.[2] Further south still, between Division Avenue and Flushing Avenue, Hasidic Jews settled, having fled eastern Europe before and during the war. Poles, migrating south from Greenpoint around the same time, inhabited much of the area between North Fifteenth Street and Grand Street; their numbers were rejuvenated with a fresh wave of migrants coming after the fall of the Iron Curtain in 1989. East Williamsburg—so named only after the construction of the Brooklyn-Queens Expressway, which split the neighborhood in two—was almost entirely Dominican, Italian, and Puerto Rican. In addition to this diverse mix, the late 1980s also witnessed a shift of people from overcrowded Chinatown settling in various parts of Williamsburg and establishing businesses.[3]

The Puerto Rican and Dominican South Side of Williamsburg, because it was one of the poorest areas of New York, had a particularly vibrant street culture.[4] "There were gangs and a lot of drugs in Williamsburg at that time, but it was not dangerous for us because we were from the neighborhood and we knew everyone," one longtime Puerto Rican resident, now a union sheet metal worker, observed. "We were all poor together, so we knew how to survive together. When I say 'poor,' I mean relying on public assistance, going to church food pantries, eating government-issued cheese, wiring electricity in from a neighboring apartment or building. We were all suffering together, while our parents struggled to give us a better life."[5] Kids and teenagers had the streets as their playground, and when they ventured into the mostly abandoned North Side of Williamsburg, they explored buildings and played on rooftops, rollerblading and biking to get around and playing in streams from fire hydrants, amid burned-out cars and broken bottles.

Latinx residents of South Williamsburg called that part of the neighborhood Los Sures (the South Side). The streets were the repository of history, communal memory, and consciousness.[6] Informal musical performances regularly happened on stoops and street corners, which kept folk songs alive in the community. Salsa and merengue could be heard from shops and stoops, coming from radios and boom boxes, and sometimes live, and were a common part of the social fabric of the area, loud and ever present. On weekends the music would often go late into the night. Friendly dance competitions among rival youths were common. In the 1980s breakdancing came to replace traditional folk dances as the primary form. The annual Los Sures Cultural Festival bridged generations with music, dance, food, and other cultural practices. The month of June was particularly festive with weeks of parties and preparations leading up to the annual Puerto Rico Day, with the climax being the parade with flags, food, music, cars, and bicycles. Writer Jesús Colón (1901–74) and poet Lydia Cortés (b. 1942), who both had roots in the neighborhood, illustrated the life and culture of the area in their writings.[7]

Journalist Brad Gooch, writing for *New York Magazine* in 1992, provides a different, outsider view of Williamsburg: "Its low nineteenth-century brick houses with their steep stone staircases and rickety shutters rarely rise more than four stories. Shades are pulled down in ancient pharmacies, and parking is never a problem along the deserted streets that unravel toward the river."[8] Gooch hearkened back to authors Henry Miller and Betty Smith for a period when Williamsburg was culturally vibrant, unaware of or uninterested in its present inhabitants, and lamented its previous industrial glory. Most of the industry had indeed left, with only a few factories—such as the Domino Sugar Factory, a few metalworks, and furniture knitting and spice factories—still scattered throughout the area.[9]

The arrival of artists in the neighborhood created immediate anxieties among the existing residents of Williamsburg, even as early as 1980. Some local Puerto Rican real estate agents and lawyers were directly involved in appealing to artists because the area had so many abandoned postindustrial buildings, many of which were in a state of intense decay.[10] One longtime business owner whose family had run a paint-manufacturing firm there since 1917 stated, "The artists have given [Williamsburg] a new lease on life."[11]

But the local dynamics of Williamsburg were complex. Even though property values had collapsed in the 1970s, the Puerto Rican, Colombian, and Hasidic communities were expanding to the point of creating a housing shortage.[12] So, in many cases, low-income residents were concerned that they would be displaced as more artists came from Manhattan.[13] One estimate showed that the prices of homes sold in Williamsburg increased 200 percent between 1983 and 1987, and commercial rents in some parts of the neighborhood tripled during the same period.[14] The "abandoned" warehouses also had a function for nonartists; that is, they played a role in the shadow economy of the area. By the mid-1980s, many of the empty Williamsburg warehouses served as storage for banned substances or even hideouts for drug dealers.[15] Sex workers sometimes squatted in buildings or worked out of postindustrial spaces throughout North Williamsburg. South Second Street was the site of one particularly active cocaine and heroin market in the late 1980s.[16] Rival Colombian and Puerto Rican gangs, including the Latin Kings, often contended for control of territory along the waterfront and throughout the warehouse district of the North Side.[17] Some early artists in the area recalled local businesses employing gangs to protect their property in what was otherwise a rather lawless environment.[18]

From the early 1970s to the late 1980s, Williamsburg served as a bedroom community for artists who commuted to Manhattan to take part in the gallery activity in SoHo and the East Village.[19] The early 1970s witnessed Black and Latinx artists first taking up residence in Williamsburg.[20] White artists, primarily from SoHo, began arriving by the mid-1970s.[21] By 1980 an estimated two hundred artists were living on the South Side of Williamsburg, with smaller numbers of artists living in Italian neighborhoods along Graham Avenue as well as in Polish Greenpoint.[22] Approximately 650 artists settled in Williamsburg between 1979 and 1983, most of whom had been displaced from SoHo, NoHo, and Tribeca.[23]

In the 1980s Williamsburg artists were primarily art school–trained painters. The first commercial art gallery to serve the North Brooklyn community, Minor Injury, opened in Greenpoint in 1985, and others began to proliferate down into Williamsburg in the years that followed.[24] The nonprofit Association of Williamsburgh/Greenpoint Artists was formed in 1985 to advocate for artists and arts organizations and counted a number of musicians among its members.[25] Brooklyn gained notice within the Manhattan art scene, especially in the East Village, by around 1987.[26] Grassroots artist publications also emerged in the form of the *Brooklyn Nose* and *Word of Mouth* in late 1987.

Things then suddenly changed around 1989 when a whole new, younger community of artists who were "more performative and musical," commonly described as *freaks* or *punks*, settled in the neighborhood.[27] This new community had its origins among the squatters who had been evicted from Tompkins Square Park and nearby areas of the East Village during police raids in 1988. A punk movement called Squat or Rot had resulted in many people reclaiming and inhabiting abandoned and empty buildings throughout the East Village, often installing their own plumbing and wiring in electricity from the street. "On the night of the Tompkins Square riots," punk rocker Michael X. Rose recalled, "I was running the box office at a cabaret called the Bottom Line, and from the club I could see a surge of people running away from the police down Fourth Street. There were cops with electrical tape over their badges beating people with clubs. There were no cell phones at that time, so cops could get away with anything."[28] Many of the evicted squatters took refuge in Williamsburg.[29] This new wave of artists had a more intimate relationship with the environment around them in that they occupied space, built homes in squats, brought their art outside into the streets, and began to use the empty warehouses as staging sites for their work.[30]

As one art critic wrote rather innocently in 1990:

In the last few years, the public signs of artistic life have increased particularly in the Williamsburg and Greenpoint neighborhoods, an area of low buildings and factory-framed river views bordered by the semicircle of the East River and [Newtown Creek]. It would be rushing things to say that Brooklyn, or North Brooklyn in particular, is an art scene waiting to happen. It may in fact be an art scene waiting not to happen, with natural geography and the gaps in the New York transit system enabling the area to maintain its grass-roots status. But those roots are healthy, and the sense of artists taking things into their own hands palpable.[31]

A music critic wrote in the same year that "the East Village scene that drowned in hype and high rents has washed up on the shores of Williamsburg."[32]

By 1991 or 1992, Williamsburg had developed a reputation as the go-to destination for aspiring young artists and musicians coming to the city. The character of the neighborhood began to change, symbolized by growing numbers of artists adorned in trench coats moving into the area.[33] In 1992 an estimated two thousand artists lived in the area.[34] Galleries proliferated, along with health-food stores, art-supply retailers, and performance spaces. The buy-sell-trade clothing movement also emerged, which informed the emerging Williamsburg fashion aesthetic.[35] Earwax Records opened just off of Bedford Avenue in 1990 and became a haven for musicians and DJs searching for cutting-edge or hard-to-find records.[36] Posters and flyers advertising poetry readings, art openings, and film screenings, stapled or taped to lampposts or bus stops, became commonplace.

But still there was a certain sense of lawlessness in Williamsburg up until even the early 2000s. Sex workers frequented areas from Metropolitan Avenue all the way north and east to the water.[37] Banned substances like LSD, cocaine, and other narcotics were easily acquired both on the streets and in the back rooms of nightclubs or bars. As one music critic noted, "You could go into any bodega and buy weed."[38] Crack and heroin had hit the neighborhood in the early to mid-1980s but by 1988 were beginning to be pushed south into neighboring Bushwick.[39] Memorials littered sidewalks and the sides of buildings throughout the area, in memory of people killed in drug-related fights or other street conflicts.[40] Fires were a constant threat and claimed many buildings in the area.[41] Along the edge of the East River, sofas, televisions, tires, refrigerators, and gutted cars could be seen bobbing in the water amid liquor bottles and crack vials. At any given time, packs of aggressive wild dogs roamed through the postindustrial areas, especially along the waterfront.[42] Every surface was covered in graffiti.

In the 1990s a number of musicians recalled playing their first gigs in Williamsburg squats; some did not even have power and were lit entirely by candles.[43] Drummer Mike Bell recalled setting up jam sessions with other drummers right out on the piers "with all of Manhattan as our backdrop."[44] Informal homes existed even at the turn of the millennium, as saxophonist Charles Waters remembered: "There were people living in Winnebagos on the East River. I saw old Italian guys skinny-dipping from the piers at the end of North Fifth Street."[45] Old Polish men from Greenpoint would sometimes go swimming off of the docks near North Seventh Street, even though there were smashed bottles along the shoreline and old cars submerged in the water.[46] Puerto Ricans would fish for eels and various kinds of fish in the water there, right off of the piers. In this unregulated environment without gentrifying financial pressures, noncommercial music that was explicitly experimental in form and content was allowed to germinate and grow. It did not take long for this music to find a home in the burgeoning warehouse and loft scene. Activity generally occurred along two lines: large-scale events that took up entire buildings and smaller lounge or pop-up events called *chill outs* in more intimate settings such as living rooms, lofts, or clubs.

The Williamsburg Warehouse Movement

The beginnings of the Williamsburg art and music scene along the waterfront took root in postindustrial spaces, mostly warehouses that had been abandoned for decades, which attracted artists because they could accommodate significant audiences; were big enough to hold ambitious, large-scale projects; and, for a time, staved off interference from police or other authorities. Such events were generally conducted without any official license and were done via squatting in the buildings, sometimes in spaces where artists also lived, or at other times in temporary takeovers of buildings for the purpose of staging performances. As one participant characterized the phenomenon at the time, "There is a strong sense of community and collaboration in Warehouse art; there is a dimension of ritual and mythology; and there is an element of science fantasy and futurism."[47]

The Williamsburg warehouse movement flourished in 1988–94.[48] The activities hearkened back to the SoHo loft era of the 1960s or the jazz loft era of the 1970s, though the Williamsburg lofts differed in some key ways. For one, they were more removed from the center of New York City and thus managed to avoid official interference for a time, but they also were outside of Manhattan and thus drew mixed reactions from the New York art intelligentsia, who either downplayed them or sometimes misunderstood what was happening there.

Some theorists have characterized the period as one of immersionism, a kind of "total artwork, a complete experience that brought together installation art combined with baroque postmodern LARPing, or installation art without minimalism, taken to excess, saturated with symbolism."[49] As Ebon Fisher stated in 1988, in reference to the first use of the term, "You are the SUB MODERN. You live in a million tribes and burrows, beneath the illusion we call the real world. While the Party passes over your heads you see its abject nakedness. You never believed in modernism and you aren't fooled by its vain reflection, postmodernism. . . . Without proclamation you have integrated yourself into the endless folding of spectacles. You found that to immerse yourself was the thing, sensing that objectivity was only another dream."[50] Fisher further elaborated, "Postmodern deconstruction was over. Immersionism was about biological congealing and the vitality born from such convergence."[51]

In many ways, immersionism was the next stage of evolution of the New York art scene, which had evolved from the rationalist works of figures like conceptual artist Joseph Kosuth (b. 1945) or minimalist Donald Judd (1928–94) to the postmodern rebellion of the 1980s, which reasserted expressionist forms. The Williamsburg art scene in some ways combined these earlier trends, going back to environmentalist installation art, earth art, and conceptual art but inflected with the expressionist component of postmodern symbolism and allegory.[52] Many of these trends were informed by the environment in which the artists worked. The rationalism of the 1970s emerged from large postindustrial art spaces in SoHo, while the East Village scene of the 1980s was confined to small storefront galleries.

Williamsburg had ample space, which allowed immersionist forms of art to take root in huge postindustrial spaces.[53] The spaces were considerably larger than the jazz lofts had been and could accommodate a scale of projects and audiences not seen since the first SoHo artist lofts in the 1950s and 1960s. Such installations staged things unthinkable elsewhere, like giant spiderwebs, waterfalls, or huge marionette puppets hanging from a ceiling. As some of the early theorists of immersionism stated, "[Immersionists] helped to shift cultural protocols away from cold, postmodern cynicism, towards something a whole lot warmer: immersive, mutual world construction."[54] As a reaction to the postmodernism of the 1980s, immersionism rejected the idea that deconstruction was going to change the world. As painter and performing artist Ethan Pettit stated, "The people involved were dedicated to taking the world as it is and transforming it into something else."[55] Or, as DJ Olive (Gregor Asch), another Williamsburg-based artist noted, "Post modernism was cool but we'd had enough of it. We wanted to build something pure and forward-looking, something positive."[56] Music was an integral part of this all-encompassing experience, as the conduit to our most intimate sense.

The Lizard's Tail

One of the first underground venues that emerged in Williamsburg that was to give life to the music scene was the Lizard's Tail, opened by an Irish-Belgian couple, Terry Dineen and Jean François Pottiez, at 99 South Sixth Street, right under the Williamsburg Bridge, in 1988, which they rented for $600 per month.[57] Dineen and Pottiez had met at Café Bustello (which had been on Avenue B and later on East Houston Street), which had also sparked their interest in opening their own art space. Their building in Williamsburg had previously been a manufacturing center for industrial oil paints and was located next door to an old opera house that had been abandoned for many years.[58] A music critic for the *New York Times* described it in 1990: "The Lizard's Tail in Williamsburg is an avant-garde club that is mining the recent past. It is pure bohemia, reminiscent of the Lower East Side in the early 1980s." He added, prophetically, "The club is unpretentious and serves the neighborhood which is on the verge of staking a claim for itself as an art scene."[59]

The Lizard's Tail was constructed from scraps that the owners gleaned from the neighborhood. Pottiez renovated the place, doing carpentry, electrical work, and other fixes to make it functional.[60] A narrow rear stairway led to a small backyard shaded by two trees; the back of the lot was demarcated by the eastern support tower that held the J and M subway lines above, which "cast a pale green light over the scavenged sofas, chairs, and other furnishings that were arranged there."[61] As one art critic described it at the time, "To get to it, you first have to find it in the maze under the Williamsburg Bridge, then walk down a skinny little alley lined with radiators, then plunge through the door, which is made of a loose sheet of reflecting plastic. Benches line the walls in one of the two rooms."[62]

Pottiez sold bottles of beer and wine behind an old "rickety" bar he had made himself, though when his stock ran out, patrons were free to obtain their own from nearby stores and bring it back to the Lizard's Tail.[63] Parties ran there from Wednesday until Sunday every week and quickly became a magnet for the artist community. The Lizard's Tail developed a very loyal following, and when they drew audience members from Manhattan, "they often stayed for the night" because, unlike in the East Village, there were no other competing establishments in the area. The cover charge was $5, which went to pay the artists.[64]

The Bread-and-Puppet-type stage, only four feet by six feet, was adorned with a small curtain. Pottiez had crafted a six-dimmer light board, which he operated, and artist Anna Hurwitz designed a backdrop out of glitter for the stage.[65] "The ceiling is low, the atmosphere casual, and somebody with a beret might just pick up a guitar and play a bit before the acts go on," one critic observed.[66] A stove from a local junk shop heated the place. The one thing the owners invested in was a sound system. The main event room could seat thirty people.

Dineen curated and emceed most of the events, usually split among short performance pieces, poetry readings, visual art exhibits, and music, often with three-act bills. "The shows feature everything from poetry to performers from Peru, dancing to the sound of an electric guitar, whirling around, eyes glazed. This club is a place where younger musicians and performers, perhaps bound for the stardom of the Knitting Factory, can hit a stage without having to worry too much; it has a friendly atmosphere open to experiment and works in progress."[67] Most music occurred on Friday and Saturday nights, with an open mic and backyard barbecue on Sunday afternoons.[68]

The Lizard's Tail soon sparked a music scene in Williamsburg. From the very beginning, the music scene there was eclectic, though certain elements began to solidify over time. Antifolk, which shared certain aesthetics and sensibilities with punk and noise rock, found a home in the antiestablishment underground of Williamsburg. As a movement, antifolk was largely sparked by the singer-songwriter Lach and took root at the Chameleon Club, the Sidewalk Café, and other spaces in the East Village in the early 1980s.[69] One figure from the antifolk scene, Brenda Kahn, had some of her key early concerts at the Lizard's Tail around 1990, just before the release of her critically acclaimed debut record, *Goldfish Don't Talk Back*.[70] Another figure with roots in the antifolk scene, Billy Syndrome (1963–2017), soon emerged as one of the leaders of the noise rock scene at the Lizard's Tail.[71] Singer-songwriters Dina Emerson and Roger Manning each played some of their first shows there. Rock and noise rock bands like the Living Guitars, Jet Screamer, Fly Ashtray, and Uncle Wiggly also played some of their early concerts there.[72] A Hasidic performer from the neighborhood known as Curly Oxide joined space rock singer Vic Thrill at the Lizard's Tail, and the two were propelled to near stardom.[73] Poets, playwrights, and dancers added to the eclectic mix of arts presented at the small club. Punk rocker Ray Brazen referred to the Lizard's Tail as "the greatest performance space ever" because it was generally open to new artists, and anything was allowed to happen in the space.[74] After each show the performers were invited to write their names on the wall, which was completely full after just one year of being in business.[75]

Some figures from the downtown scene soon learned of the Lizard's Tail. Guitarist Elliot Sharpe played there in 1989.[76] Pianist and noise artist Anthony Coleman played there several times, once in August 1989.[77] He introduced an element there that had been stirring in Manhattan at the Knitting Factory over the preceding two years.[78] Within the musical milieu of Chris Cochrane, David Weinstein, David Shea, Ikue Mori, and others, Coleman had pioneered the use of samplers in improvisatory and experimental music settings. Their music possessed much more influence from rock than free jazz. Coleman had been profoundly impacted by the No Wave band DNA, which he first encountered after he, a native Brooklynite, moved back to the city in 1979.[79]

For the gig at the Lizard's Tail, Coleman asked percussionist Jim Pugliese to join him. Coleman was playing on an Ensoniq Mirage sampler, creating drum and sampler patterns. Coleman aimed to use the sampler as an improvising instrument, trying to break out of the trope of it being merely a loop maker.[80] Innovations in technology made samplers increasingly agile and informative around that time.[81] Coleman drew from all manner of sources—including Romanian traditional music, Radio Moscow broadcasts, the early jazz cornetist King Oliver, and other sources—to create landscapes, reconstruct pieces, or do covers of existing tunes. The type of material that he presented at the Lizard's Tail was later recorded and released on several different records.[82]

Tragically, in March 1990, the same weekend that the Lizard's Tail received a complimentary review in the *New York Times*, an unlicensed nightclub in the Bronx named Happy Land Social Club was burned down, killing eighty-seven people.[83] The authorities immediately began cracking down on such informal and unlicensed venues, so the Lizard's Tail was forced to close down after operating for only about a year and a half.[84] The Lizard's Tail had already been fined regularly by the police for selling beer and liquor without a license, so things just escalated further after the Bronx fire.[85] Dineen called a meeting and fundraiser for April 19–20, stating, "The Lizard's Tail will no longer be open every Friday and Saturday night. It will, however, continue to function as a vital nerve center for the production of independent projects, recordings, performances, informalities. . . . From the Lizard's

Tail will spring the Cat's Head. Come hear talk of the Cat's Head. Come to the benefit at the Lizard's Tail for the premiere of the Cat's Head. Together we will be born into the future."[86] The benefit featured many of the artists who had been central to the Lizard's Tail, such as Ken Butler, Uncle Wiggly, and Billy Syndrome, though the second night also featured the music of trumpeter Wadada Leo Smith.

The Sex Salon

Before the Cat's Head events took place, and about a month and a half before the Lizard's Tail closed, another event became a flash point for the Williamsburg community, an event known as the Sex Salon. The three-day festival was held at the warehouse space Epoché, near the Williamsburg Bridge. A coalition of artists, groups, and organizers came together to plan the event. Brand Name Damages, Epoché, the Lizard's Tail, Minor Inquiry, Nerve Circle, the band Verge, Kit Blake (who edited the local arts magazine *Word of Mouth*), and the collective of writers who put out *Waterfront Week* created the event through a process of discussion and consensus.[87] Many of these organizations traced their origins to the early or mid-1980s, some even being formulated in Manhattan or outside of New York entirely and coalescing in Williamsburg later.

The theme as advertised was "sex . . . the great glue. The method? Total salon. All media."[88] Media theorist Sam Binkley wrote at the time, "The Sex Salon brought together more people with more energy and more focus than any other event" up to that time. He added, "People seemed to be actually inventing a new sense of community as they experienced it."[89] As one of the artists involved, Ebon Fisher, noted, "The playful title was an early indication of the Immersionists' interest in corporeal connection. The Sex Salon celebrated gender-bending performances, anatomical diagrams of lesbian, gay, and heterosexual intercourse, and evocative sculptures and films celebrating a range of sexual orientations."[90] This process set the tone for future events, queered the social expectations, and sparked much of the community that followed.

The Cat's Head

The Cat's Head events evolved into "really big parties" held by "young artists not finding success"—or not seeking commercial success—"in the commodity-driven art market of SoHo," but they began rather secretively owing to the trouble Dineen and Pottiez had encountered with the police at the Lizard's Tail.[91] Nobody controlled the spaces of operation of the Cat's Head, which heightened, for a time, the sense of community and participation by artists, audience members, and revelers. At the first event, on July 14, 1990, they occupied an old mustard factory, where they built a thirty-two-foot stage, and Anna Hurwitz designed another stage backdrop similar to the one she had made for the Lizard's Tail, though now involving six panels, each five feet by ten feet.[92] It was a catalytic event for the music and arts community, and some have argued that this event marked the formal beginning of Williamsburg as a "scene," drawing together many previously disconnected groups into one space.[93]

The Cat's Head events took on a kind of utopian and collaborative mode of operation "both in art- and decision-making, stressing human relationships" in interactive public performances.[94] "What we were doing at the time was quite unique. Raves came later. We were trying to create art that people did not just look at, but they could play with and interact with as part of the experience. That was quite new in terms of what artists were doing," Dineen noted.[95] The building still contained two-story vats circled by stairs, around which people danced. Art installations that invited audience participation were situated throughout the space. As artist Anna Hurwitz, who helped organize the event, stated, "[Pottiez] had experience doing lighting, tech, and sound, and [Dineen] had experience stage managing and performing. I don't think any of us had [any] idea what we were doing. They brought in a lot of people that had no previous background but had a lot of energy. It was like playing a huge trust game. We could do it without skills because we trusted each other and worked really hard."[96]

In terms of practical funding, the organizers each put in different amounts of money according to their means and were then paid back with the proceeds from the event.[97] This was generally how many of the Williamsburg warehouse arts events were financed, which at times led to tensions between participants. They rented generators, lights, a sound system, and portable toilets and bought wood for stage construction and insurance for the event. They charged $6 at the door, paid each band $250, and barely broke even.[98] All of the equipment and other costs had to be financed on credit cards by a few of the organizers.[99] The Cat's Head and later warehouse events were mainly publicized through phone chains and via posters and flyers distributed in the East Village and throughout Williamsburg.[100]

The bill headlined the Reverb Motherfuckers, a punk band that had emerged at the legendary punk club CBGBs in 1988, described at this event as "ugly guys, ugly fuzz guitars, catchy riffs, an homage to Manson. The Reverbs lurch and rumble like an exploding diesel train."[101] The party went until five in the morning and drew 750 people. Artist Anna Hurwitz recalled, "After the first Cat's Head, we were all stunned by what had happened. How did we do that? How did that happen? Jean François [Pottiez] was an incredible leader and a visionary. The Cat's Head changed what we thought was possible."[102]

The second Cat's Head event, on October 6, 1990, was nearly canceled by police and fire inspectors who had safety concerns about the spaces—two adjacent warehouses at Kent Avenue and North Tenth Street totaling twenty thousand square feet—but ultimately permitted it to occur.[103] The organizers squatted in the buildings without any communication with the owner. As one critic noted of the event, "Renegades from performance space the Lizard's Tail staged the Cat's Head—an irreverent romp in a Macy's-sized abandoned shipping terminal that defied the cops, the fire department, monster rats, and resurgent club laws."[104] The fire department's main concern was a hundred-foot-long fabric tunnel draped over a rope skeleton suspended from above, though the organizers had also set up emergency exits and lighting, as well as fire extinguishers, as precautions.[105] The critic added that the gathered crowd successfully intimidated the authorities into allowing the event to occur, with a man shouting, "We're squatting this space and they can't stop it!" while others used various blunt objects to bang on the junked cars that littered the area outside. One of the police officers later returned, in civilian clothes, and sat and had a pint with the organizers as the sun came up the next morning.[106]

The first performance featured drag queen Medea de Vice playing a guitar-like light board outside that projected "wild spectrums of color" into the warehouses.[107] Next, a butoh performance occurred amid a heap of abandoned cars in a lot nearby. Many artists who had attended the first Cat's Head event were now involved in presenting installations or performances of their own.[108] Inside, twenty participatory installations drew 850 audience members, with Frank Shiffren's *Spider's Memory*, a floor-to-ceiling web of ropes that accommodated several climbers at a time, as the most impressive feature. It also included an unflattering life-size figure of Senator Jesse Helms of North Carolina, who had notoriously led the fight to defund federal arts programming in the United States, as a form of protest.[109] Roving performance artists moved through the space throughout the evening, taking on a particular character and interacting with the audience and other installations. Every artist performance or exhibit was interactive, compelling the audience to directly involve themselves in the act of creation and performance.

Punk bands headlined the event, including Cop Shoot Cop, Chemical Wedding, and the Colored Greens, along with psychedelic rock band Laughing Sky, and Billy Syndrome DJ'd the event.[110] Within this rebellious setting, experimental music took root as part of this total experience. At the other end of the ten-thousand-square-foot space, opposite the main stage, Michael Zwicky's Scrap Metal Music project was suspended on cables and arranged on tables, composed of pieces of scrap metal he had gleaned from the nearby area (see figure 1.1).

Zwicky's Scrap Metal Music had been seven years in the making. Zwicky had been trained as a sculptor and painter at the University of Wisconsin and had moved to New York in 1983.[111] He also played saxophone, guitar, and other instruments. Soon after his arrival, he participated in the movement that became known as the Rivington School, a circle of sculptors, metalworkers, performers, and painters who forged the massive public art piece in the Rivington Sculpture Garden. Zwicky was further inspired by a street performer, violinist Mike Mason, whom he had encountered in Madison, Wisconsin. Mason made bows by wrapping horsehair around tree branches, and he would build fires down by the railroad tracks and fashion gongs, using the fire to temper and shape the metal. Mason sparked Zwicky's interest in scavenged and self-designed instruments and the idea that one could draw sounds from all manner of natural or found objects. After moving to New York City, Zwicky noted, "My work became more and more abstract as my psyche became permeated by the pulse of the city. Graffiti art was a big influence."[112] Zwicky also considered an array of downtown Manhattan influences to have made their mark on him, including saxophonist Jemeel Moondoc's Jus Grew Orchestra, the free jazz–noise rock band Borbetomagus, and Sun Ra.[113]

Zwicky first conceived of the idea for Scrap Metal Music in collaboration with saxophonist Steve Hagglund when they met in Lower East Side Manhattan soon after Zwicky's arrival.[114] They went around the neighborhood in what they called "scavenging," to put together "a rig" that could be used to create metallic percussive sounds. Zwicky's rig was composed of an oil drum that he cut in half, to which he affixed a bass drum pedal. There was a piece of rebar in the middle of the rig, on which he placed myriad other pieces of metal that collectively resembled a Christmas tree. The duo began to workshop Scrap Metal Music at Nada Gallery, which was around the corner from the Rivington Sculpture Garden, an experimental space where,

Figure 1.1 Scrap Metal Music, first performance, Nada Gallery, 1985 (*photo by Michael J. Zwicky*)

through successive presentations, they were able to develop the project considerably (see figure 1.1).[115] More than just a band playing metal trash, they developed a sophisticated vocabulary of rhythms and tones from the various metal pieces they incorporated. Zwicky had become aware of the Cat's Head organizers after he moved into an apartment a few doors down from the Lizard's Tail in early 1990 and immediately felt accepted by the arts community there. He soon placed one foot in the punk scene and became the drummer in the Billy Syndrome for a few years.

To present Scrap Metal Music at the second Cat's Head event, Zwicky took advantage of the ample space and spent the week prior gathering pieces of scrap from the site itself, including pieces from abandoned cars, stainless-steel sinks, a five-hundred-gallon tank, and oil drums. He suspended a number of metal pieces from cables that were hanging from the ceiling, arranging them to allow for an array of different tones, and assembled the remainder of the pieces on tables and on the floor for people to use (see figure 1.2).

From the very beginning, "audience members naturally wanted to take part in scrap metal events. People feel apprehensive about playing a guitar in front of other people if they have never trained with it, but there was

Figure 1.2 Scrap Metal
Music with bystanders,
Cat's Head II, 1990
(*photo by Anna West*)

no such anxiety with these found objects. So the audience-as-performers experiment developed quite naturally."[116] Indeed, one observer described the project as "a riotous cacophony of rhythm and noise. The players were the audience, watched in fascination by more audience who in turn took to the metal themselves. The unleashed energy was electrifying."[117] The rhythms evolved and changed as between ten and twenty people played at any one time. "Everybody was an equal in that performance," Zwicky reminisced. For the entire evening, from ten o'clock until the early hours of the morning, audience members coaxed different tones from the assembled metal mass, often in concert with one another.[118] It was the last time Zwicky ever presented the project, feeling such a level of catharsis that he did not want to revisit it again. Zwicky's performance situated environmental sound-noise art within the milieu of the Williamsburg avant-garde, foreshadowing much that was to come.

Most of the artists who presented their work at the Cat's Head events regard them as a kind of utopian experience. This was possible for a number of reasons. First, the work to present them was collective, without any single authority making decisions. The spaces were rented or squatted and were likewise not controlled in the same way that a gallery with a single curator is. Transforming the space itself was a central part of the artistic act. "Having the whole buildings just allowed everything to go because space does that," Dineen reflected.[119] Because they were self-funded, there were no stipulations from a grant, for instance, that demarcated what could and could not happen. Furthermore, none of the artists who might later emerge as stars had yet made names for themselves, and the events, in many ways, were not about developing fame but about taking over a space and providing attendees with an interactive experience. Artists made virtually no money from the event, but it was also possible because rents were relatively low. "Generally, there was not much animosity or competition between the artists," Dineen said.[120]

Flytrap

Soon after the second Cat's Head event, Dineen and Pottiez moved to Berlin, but what they had sparked continued, as many of the other organizers had witnessed what was possible in the warehouses of the waterfront. The scene shifted to Flytrap for an event on June 15, 1991, in a building at Kent Avenue and North Eleventh Street, just north of the second Cat's Head event. Artists Anna Hurwitz and Myk Henry were the main organizers of the event. Their aim was to have "experiential art that would really change attendees" and to get people to explore the space, performances, and the senses in their own way, allowing for different kinds of individual experiences.[121] Another aim was for the interactive nature of the event to break down some of the traditional barriers between art and audience, to get people to relate to art in new ways. Again, ambitiously large installations, including Lauren Szold's *Medea's First Period*, a monumental display of menstrual spills, appeared there, along with a full bill of bands that involved over two hundred artists and drew an audience of between 1,200 and 2,000 people.[122] Yvette Helin installed a floor-to-ceiling marionette puppet of which attendees could pull the strings and make it dance.

Michael J. Zwicky opened the night with the noise band Fihi Ma Fihi.[123] He interspersed his own vocals into the raw squeals and searing abrasions, which called for people to rise against the capitalist establishment that forced them to endure a postapocalyptic setting imposed by the world order of the time.[124] The headliner was the Voluptuous Horror of Karen Black, fronted by Kembra Pfahler, a punk band with a horror-infused performative element.[125] It was the biggest stage she had performed on up to that point. Pfahler described the band's concept at the time: "We've created this genre of voluptuous horror in our concerts using props and creating sick little B-movie characters for each song."[126] Pfahler and other members of the band performed mostly naked, adorned with demonic makeup and covered in body paint, for a uniquely confrontational musical performance. At the pinnacle of her performance, Pfahler did a handstand, spread her legs, and cracked an egg full of paint into her vagina, while abrasive guitars cut through the air of the huge warehouse. By the time of Flytrap, putting on a warehouse party had been professionalized to a certain degree, directed by people who had gained the technical knowledge needed to arrange, organize, fund, and advertise the events along the waterfront.

Organism

Ebon Fisher and Megan Raddant produced Organism on June 12, 1993, in the Old Dutch Mustard Factory on Metropolitan Avenue. Organism was intended to be a "web jam" in which "participants are asked to conceive of a project which interacts with the entire space."[127] As critic Suzan Wines noted, "Unlike a traditional gallery exhibit where each object only engages the cube of space it occupies, the collaborators in a 'web jam' create work that engages the entire space, the body and mind of the audience and through the process ultimately integrates with the community at large. A layering of system upon system whose interactions spawn unique accidental places created out of temporary conceptual cohabitation."[128]

In terms of sonic explorations, there was an installation designed by Myk Henry where attendees could light a fuse that exploded watermelons. Sasha Noë and Bradford Reed designed a machine that would smash bottles for recycling, emitting the sounds of breakage. There were a number of sonic environmental pieces, especially some that played with the sound of water. Some installations explored the sounds of the human body. Roving rapper Doc Israel moved through the space and amid the audience, offering his words and rhythms intermittently throughout the event.

The band Thrust, which included Kelly Webb, Viva, Theresa Westerdahl, and Julie O'Brien, performed an orgasmic climax associated with a crawl-in womb structure that they collaborated on with sculptor James Porter. Additional women working with the piece operated as "talking clits throughout, expressing their genital pride," as part of a sex-positive performance piece.[129] Together, all of these intermixing performances "amalgamated into a pulsating Organism."[130] Or as Webb wrote, this meant "every individual realizing their vision to create a thriving pulsating very alive whole."[131] As Wines wrote of the event, "Organism became a kind of symbolic climax to the renegade activity that had been stirring within the community since the late eighties. It exploited the notion of architecture as living event, breathing and transforming for fifteen hours in an abandoned mustard factory."[132]

Over two thousand people attended Organism. The event led to a regular series in the same space that continued until the Old Dutch Mustard factory burned down in late 1994. The end of that space led to a lull in activity in the mid-1990s, before a brief resurgence later in the decade in spaces such as Floating Point Unit Wild Child Productions and Federation of Ongolia, just before the real estate boom made it impossible for such spaces and events to survive.[133]

The Omnisensorial Arts Movement
Keep Refrigerated

Keep Refrigerated began at 110 North Sixth Street in 1991, founded by Mariano Airaldi, visual artist Jeff Gompertz, and DJ Tom Schmitz, the last of whom named Keep Refrigerated and was also the founder of the community record store Earwax. Airaldi, the son of the Argentinian ambassador to the United States, had previously lived in the East Village and had started a short-lived venue called Ex-Funeral Home on Twelfth Street between First Avenue and Avenue A, which joined a milieu of venues where the installation and experimental music scene was hatching—places such as Generator Experimental Music Gallery, the Gas Station, and Gargoyle Mechanique.

Ex-Funeral Home closed by 1991, and Airaldi moved to Williamsburg, where he joined Gompertz and Schmitz in a new venture.[134] The area around the building on North Sixth Street, which formerly served as a meatpacking warehouse, was completely abandoned.[135] Inside the space there were three floors. On the ground floor, they had the techno and DJ scene, and running it was a collaborative venture by all three of them; this coincided with the rise of rave culture, which was sweeping through New York at that time.[136] The basement housed a punk music series and was consequently barebones, with a concrete floor, illuminated by one lightbulb. Schmitz booked the bands, though it was a pretty open process of curation.[137] On the top floor, there was the "technorganic cave" with installations of plants and environments, tape loops playing recordings, smells, flashes of light, temperature changes, machines, smashed glass, wobbly floors, and even live chickens, all curated by Airaldi.[138] They also sometimes hosted a free Argentinian barbecue that could fit twenty guests there, running from nine thirty in the evening until three in the morning. All three floors were active when the space was open, and could hold up to three hundred people.[139] One journalist described Keep Refrigerated as "a Berlin-style underground club" that "featured tiny space heaters, pyramids of smashed TV sets, washes of blue light, Disney cartoons projected on the wall, and tapes playing everything from Moroccan chants to techno-industrial noise."[140] They held parties in the space every Friday and Saturday for nine or ten months until the fire department forced them to close.

Lalalandia

After the demise of Keep Refrigerated, Airaldi joined together with Maria Alejandra Guidici, Gabriella Latessa, and Once 11 (Ignacio Platas) to organize a new space. Airaldi and Latessa had met in art school at Parsons School of Design in the mid-1980s but had only recently become reacquainted after a chance encounter in the East Village that also included Platas. Latessa fronted the money for most of the collective's projects throughout its existence.[141] The four of them formed Lalalandia in February 1992 and were soon afterward joined by Kurt Pryzbilla and Gregor Asch (DJ Olive).[142] The events were to achieve a much grander scale than those at Keep Refrigerated. In a way, their vision came as a reaction to the Cat's Head events. They did not want to have the feeling of a gallery because that would create an environment where artists felt comfortable but where others might feel alienated. Instead, they aimed to have their events be a meeting place for artists, nonartists, and the array of ethnic groups who were present in Williamsburg and connected parts of New York City at the time. This alienated some of the artists of the warehouse scene who wanted to bring their work into the Lalalandia events or to take part directly, though quite a few artists from that scene still attended the events.

The group that formed Lalalandia considered their project an entertainment research company, and the venue quickly became the avant-garde of the DJ, party, and dance scenes in New York through a unique kind of social experiment. Like at the Cat's Head events, there was a sense, among the organizers at Lalalandia, of a kind of utopian collective, which some have interpreted as a reaction to the "egocentric 'art star' mentality"; many contributors did not use "their own names and many had shifting pseudonyms within collectives that had pseudonyms."[143] As DJ Olive, also trained as a painter, articulated it, "If I were to sell my paintings in SoHo, nobody I knew would be able to buy them. I felt like art space was much more powerful than anything that could be put inside of it. So I went to Williamsburg with the idea 'I want to make the container, I want to make an environment.'"[144] Latessa viewed Lalalandia as a direct rebellion against the art gallery world and self-conscious, pretentious "artizoid" personalities.[145] Airaldi added at the time, "We would like to see Lalalandia as a whole city, a place where everything is different."[146]

As one writer theorized, Lalalandia "rel[ied] on sensory stimulation as opposed to a language of icons as catalyst for interaction," setting them in contrast to the visual or performance art scenes taking place in other warehouses on the waterfront. She added, "These young entertainment researchers were pushing the limits of media technology, and more importantly its social and perceptual implications, well beyond mass media applications. As architects of spatial experience rather than space proper, they used immaterial elements like data, light, color, wind, temperature, touch, and odor to build experiences able to traverse time and space through memory."[147] The Lalalandia collective thus considered themselves to be omnisensorialists, where they would choose the medium after they had already conceived of the project.[148] It was aimed at making people more aware of and alert to their senses. Many of the events were called "omnisensorial sweepouts," or as DJ Olive described it, "We worked in all of the senses all of the time."[149]

The founders had many conversations just observing the communities that existed there at the time and aimed to create a space where "everyone would feel like a foreigner. If you came from the East Village, or were Polish from Greenpoint, or Puerto Rican from South Williamsburg, it was aimed to take everyone out of their comfort zone."[150] One of the taglines they used was "Lalalandia conspiring against Normalandia since 2077." Airaldi explained, "It was a retro-futuristic, third world kind of thing."[151] The explicit goal was to break down social barriers and through this experience get people talking and interacting who otherwise would not normally do so.

On a grander scale, Lalalandia emerged at the time of the fall of the Berlin Wall, which came with great hope for fundamental social change, and the First Gulf War, which represented one of the great problems in the minds of many artists of the time.[152] At the time, one of the prevailing feelings was that techno music was not a culturally specific music and therefore represented a certain kind of utopian universalism that was supposed to unite the diverse audience drawn to Lalalandia events.[153] As DJ Olive put it, "With the rave scene it wasn't like you sat and talked a lot, it was just a feeling. It was contagious. You got really positive after going out and dancing with a few thousand people. It was political without being overtly political."[154] As one writer noted, "Lalalandia also transposed the virtual notion of place as collective experience to the warehouses of Williamsburg in the form of interactive environments to stimulate and nourish the senses and the mind."[155]

Lalalandia's first attempts at realizing their vision were conducted at Comfort Zone Banquet with a series of chefs beginning in March 1992; they offered an eleven-course meal beginning at eleven at night and running to four in the morning for $9.99.[156] They ran an old school bus around the neighborhood to pick people up and drop them off so that they could attend easily. The flyer for the events described them as "succulent futurology banquets" that often involved a fusion of elements from Asian, French, Argentinian, and other cuisines, which Airaldi described as "experimental cooking."[157] Every meal was different. Vocalist Dina Emerson, who attended, described it as a "lush, stylized, visceral, cabaret quality."[158] The cook was on a stage, and they amplified the sounds of the frying pans and projected images of the food preparation.

"There are microphones, so the sound of cooking starts getting mixed with opera," Airaldi explained. "There's a video camera focusing straight on [the chef's] cutting."[159] As DJ Olive described it at the time, "An overhead projector shows jiggling frog legs in quail eggs. On stage a bizarre drama starring our food unfolds. Even the pans are mic'd. The chopping block is a favorite instrument. Quiet Village, Taboo, and Caravan Cycle [can be heard] quietly from dangling tape decks."[160] One menu featured quail eggs, fried Chinese eggplant, octopus, duck, squid, beef ribs, celery, walnuts and cream, plums, big red peppers, and unique salads. One attendee perceived Comfort Zone as a "radical re-imagining of an art space as confrontationally immersive restaurant. The participant was assaulted by sounds, smells, feels, and flavors."[161] It was the first attempt at creating a larger-scale sensorial experience. The banquet events soon evolved into regularly scheduled social gatherings on Friday and Saturday nights.[162]

El Sensorium

Having taken steps into omnisensorialism at Comfort Zone, Lalalandia found their vision most fully realized at a space they named El Sensorium. They rented a space at 141-155 South Fifth Street, where they had eight thousand square feet for just $800 per month.[163] After spending the first half of 1992 preparing the space through extensive building projects to create a futuristic aesthetic, they unveiled their first events in the summer of that year.[164] They had painted the entire interior silver, and artist Kit Blake shone light through large plexiglass disks to create a water projection onto surfaces in the space, and created other displays that ran water through pressed sheets of Mylar illuminated by lights.[165]

DJ Olive described walking into the space one night: "We emerge to a blinding light obscured by a vertical wall of falling water, trip over a pile of chopped logs, land at the feet of someone in scuba gear. Vertical plains of water slip down while intense pointed beams of light project it running across a ceiling of sloppy silver pipes and beams."[166] To add to the aquatic theme, "the bartender served drinks through a curtain of raining water which followed the contours of the bar."[167] Lalalandia often hired Dennis Del Zotto, a designer who crafted huge inflatable objects, to build items for the space, sometimes big enough to incorporate a performance itself, such as one that involved soon-to-be Finnish techno star Jimi Tenor and other artists with drum machines and a couple of chickens, to create otherworldly sonic landscapes.[168] In various ways, El Sensorium bore traces of influence from surrealism, Dadaism, and performance artists such as Laurie Anderson.[169]

At El Sensorium they began to develop "a new, decentered form of entertainment, where rather than going to an event and having performers onstage, the party itself was the entertainment and the attendees were actively involved in participating in the production."[170] Latessa described the involvement of organizers and attendees as a kind of "social sculpture."[171] At the time, DJs were often hidden in a booth and focused on making beats and keeping the crowd working, rather than being positioned as the visible director of the entire party. DJ Olive added, "It was a space aimed at freeing people from feeling like they needed to judge a 'performance'" and blurred the lines between audience and performers.[172]

It often took weeks or even months to plan the events. As one attendee characterized it, Lalalandia's events at El Sensorium were "more dangerous, dirty, weird, unearthly, sexier, and definitely more illegal than any themed-out nightclub anyone could remember in Manhattan. It was a movement that produced objects and environments of unearthly beauty, as well as unforgettable experiences for thousands of young people of that era."[173] Another writer simply stated, "The true 'art object' was the experience of the audience and participant."[174]

DJ Olive assembled a bunch of old turntables on the wall of El Sensorium with all of the speakers next to each other in an array.[175] He tethered the tone arms so that each turntable would create a particular repetitive sound and mixed them through two guitar amps with pedals so that the sounds could be manipulated. He also experimented with playing records at sixteen revolutions per minute (rpm) instead of forty-five. Then he would skip them, using multiple records at the same time. "Once you got five going, it was pretty psychedelic," he stated.[176] He would create collages and layers of sound through this process, with each performance delving into new territory. Ethan Pettit considered DJ Olive to have "constructed the soundtrack for the physical environment of that time period."[177]

Other members of the collective developed similar innovations with pre-recorded tracks, loops, or effects that could be called on through an array of new electronic devices to create sonic collages and soundscapes at El Sensorium.[178] Then two or more of them would often collaborate for a particular performance, improvising in the moment and drawing on music that ranged from tango to funk to new wave and other genres. Elements of the techno, dance, and rave scenes all had a place in the space. In effect, this made DJing at the time an art of found "objects"—in this case, sound—as a form of live, in-the-moment performance. The DJs challenged each other if they sensed that one of them was falling into patterns or clichés, with the aim of retaining a cutting edge to their work.

Embedded within the broader events, Lalalandia often had smaller performances cued by a particular track or music that would prompt, for example, "a person wearing a scuba outfit to descend along a wire through an array of fluorescent tubes" or some other visually stunning act.[179] Such a moment would then be followed ten minutes later by some other kind of performance, like a set of actors spontaneously performing a section of William Shakespeare's *Hamlet*, for example. They also would hire street musicians whom they met in the subway to play from inside the installations they set up.[180] Experimentalist Ken Butler sometimes played the events, using instruments he had invented.[181] These moments always happened within the party, amid the attendees, rather than separated on a stage. It may not be necessary to state that these events were ephemeral, but as one participant stated, "Many of the definitive statements happened at one-off events that left no trace behind the next morning."[182]

These types of events were possible only in underground loft spaces because the organizers controlled the space; they were impossible to re-create in bars or clubs because of logistical barriers. Similar to the Lizard's Tail, Lalalandia was targeted by Mayor David Dinkins's social club task force, which sent undercover firefighters to infiltrate the Lalalandia events.[183] The mayor's task force also used the cabaret law that prevented dancing in bars as further justification to close down Williamsburg's experiential arts events and open the area to real estate development.[184] El Sensorium had avoided being closed for a while by maintaining good relations with many officers from the local police precinct.[185] They had a system of signals they would use to shut things down if police did come during an event, and the entire thing was done under the guise of a film shoot. Despite these attempts to conceal their activities from the authorities, El Sensorium was forced to close after a police raid in early 1993.[186]

After they lost their home base, Lalalandia began to operate Trans Lounge back in the space on North Sixth Street where Keep Refrigerated had first operated, continuing to put on occasional events through 1993 until the organization disintegrated owing to internal disagreements.[187] After they disbanded, DJ Olive, Once 11, and Rich Panciera, a DJ who had performed many times at Lalalandia and had been integral to the innovations developed there, went on to form the band We. We was one of the defining forces behind New York's "illbient" sound of the mid- to late 1990s, which melded elements of "dub, ambient, and hip hop aesthetics, and found kinship in sounds emanating from Europe (namely jungle and trip hop), as well as the downtown music scene."[188] Much of the omnisensorial arts scene moved back to Manhattan to places such as the Gas Station and Save the Robots on Avenue B in the East Village, though We did present some of their material at another Williamsburg loft, the Federation of Ongolia, in the late 1990s.[189] Among other things, the illbient movement was instrumental in bringing electronic music to the stage. Many of the techniques they pioneered had been developed during the Lalalandia parties in Williamsburg.[190]

Postpunk on the Waterfront

While warehouse parties raged in squats along the waterfront, painter, punk rocker, and filmmaker Michael X. Rose started a new series in 1991 that eventually came to be known as Radioactive Bodega.[191] The series took its name from Radiac, the nearby processing facility that worked with radioactive waste but that was eventually closed down owing to consistent activism, especially within the Puerto Rican community.[192] The events "took the music fests out of the abandoned warehouses and literally into the streets," one participant stated; they generally took place outside of a warehouse between North Seventh and North Tenth Streets at Kent Avenue that had once been an old munitions factory, which has since been torn down.[193] The loading docks were about four feet off of the ground and very wide, so they functioned as ideal stages for musical events.

October Revolution

Rose had often wandered down along the waterfront by himself to escape the oppressive summer heat, and it occurred to him then that it would be a nice place to hold concerts. He later wrote, "It was a place of post-apocalyptic loneliness and desolation right smack dab in the throbbing chaos of New York City. It was anyone's who was punk enough for the using."[194] In another way, it began as a response to the warehouse movement, which Rose perceived as focused on "art school and trust-fund kids"; although he had studied painting at an art school himself, he did not identify with what he viewed as an elitist arts culture that often emanated from such institutions.[195] His events featured punk rock more than any other venue had up to that time. The series began under the provisional name of October Revolution, and he used images from communist propaganda posters, intended as tongue-in-cheek humor. After it drew disconcerted reactions from the predominantly Polish population of nearby Greenpoint, however, he changed the name to Radioactive Bodega.[196]

An ethnically diverse squatter community dwelled inside the warehouse and outside along the waterfront north of Kent Avenue, from around North Fifth to North Tenth Streets. This large-scale shantytown occupied areas that now constitute several public parks.[197] They lived in a collection of tents or other temporary structures made from plywood with tarp or zinc roofs, cooked over fires, and traded junk or fished out of the river. Some people hollowed out cavelike enclosures within mounds of trash and debris to create other living spaces. Spontaneous music often happened within the community on old guitars and other instruments. Crack vials littered the sidewalks throughout the area. The shanty communities survived until about 2003.[198]

Street photographer Ralph Baker, a key figure who was working to create amenities for the squatter residents, played a key role in the squatters' interfacing with artists and the community in the area.[199] He notoriously drove around the neighborhood in a car with four spare tires; worked to create an outdoor movie theater, beds, and shelters; and unsuccessfully attempted to legally acquire the property. Some of the squatters had figured out how to tap electricity from the light poles on Kent Avenue, so Rose powered the outdoor concerts using bootleg electricity.[200] Rose brought free food for attendees as well as the homeless community, as compensation for the use of their space. He felt that offering free food at such an event was itself an act of resistance. Rose sold beer from kegs he brought with him to pay the bands gas money for performing.

Describing his vision for October Revolution and Radioactive Bodega, Rose wrote, "Our conflict is with job-wardens and consumer-keepers of a permissive looney-bin. Property, credit, interest, insurance, installments, profits are stupid concepts. Millions of have-nots and drop-outs in the U.S. are living on an overflow of technologically produced fat. They aren't fighting ecology, they're responding to it. Middle-class living rooms are funeral parlors and only undertakers will stay in them. Our fight is with those who would kill us through dumb work, insane wars, dull money morality. A store of goods or clinic or restaurant that is free becomes a social art form. Ticketless theater. Out of money and control."[201]

The first October Revolution event, held on October 12, 1991, featured a number of local punk bands. In the flyer for the event, Rose wrote, "Not street-theater, the street *is* theater. Parades, bank-robberies, fires, and sonic explosions focus street attention. A crowd is an audience for an event. Release of crowd spirit can accomplish social facts. Riots are a reaction to police theater. Thrown bottles and overturned cars are responses to a dull, heavy-fisted, mechanical and deathly show. People fill the street to express special public feeling and hold human communion. To ask, 'What's Happening?'"[202]

One of the main bands featured at the first event and also at most subsequent shows was Rose's own band, the Astro-Zombies (see figure 1.3). Another musician described them as "a horror film come to life," a perceptive analysis since the band had actually taken its name from the 1968 American horror-film cult classic *The Astro-Zombies*.[203] Having begun their experiments in 1989 while students at the Pratt Institute, the Astro-Zombies were a guitar-bass-drums trio with Rose on bass and lead vocals. Their initial experiments began with a particular process. "We lived together and we used to rent videos, turn the sound off, turn on the strobe lights and make a soundtrack to these '60s B-horror movies with drums, bass, and a lead feedback guitar."[204]

By the time of the first October Revolution event, they had a rotating cast of DJs who performed with them "on anything other than a real instrument," such as drills, saws, or a blender, as part of the set. The intention was to "bring about the end of music, to deconstruct it in the form of collages."[205] Rose felt that the world already had all of the pop and love songs it needed, so he wanted to write "primitive" antisongs. The Astro-Zombies sometimes created songs with only one line of lyrics that simultaneously combined existing songs, such as one that pitted the traditional "I Want Candy" with the lyrics from "The Devil Went Down to Georgia" and called it "The Devil Wants Candy." Another song called "Sweet Home Alabama Avenue," in reference to the street in East New York, Brooklyn, laced Lynyrd Skynyrd's original "Sweet Home Alabama" over noise rock riffs.[206] The first October Revolution event also included the bands Chicken Scratch, from New Brunswick, and Vertebrae, from Albany, as well as Brooklyn bands Formaldehyde and the Pleasures, in addition to the Astro-Zombies.[207] Later bills reached farther out of New York.

Figure 1.3 The Astro-Zombies (*from left*, Michael X. Rose, Cleve Lund and DJ Drunken Pat) at the Radioactive Bodega loading docks, 1991 (*private collection*)

Radioactive Bodega

After the second October Revolution concert, held in March 1992, Rose and the Astro-Zombies joined with another punk band, the Colored Greens, to organize future Radioactive Bodega shows.[208] These were performative concerts with musicians dressed in costumes or using creative stage props as part of the shows. One of the biggest events was a two-day weekend event on July 4–5, 1992, featuring punk bands from up and down the eastern seaboard from Georgia to Maine that drew between three thousand and four thousand people to the North Seventh Street waterfront.[209] The bill included familiar acts like the Astro-Zombies, the Billy Syndrome, and the Colored Greens but also the local band Yuppicide, which was just then emerging and would go on to become a significant hardcore band of the mid-1990s. The band Public Nuisance, which had been integral to establishing the hardcore scene on the Lower East Side since 1987, and the street punk band Blanks 77 also helped draw fans from across the river. One of the most widely known acts from beyond the city was Pittsburgh's Submachine. Rose occasionally included free jazz bands on the bills he organized because he felt they shared a similar aesthetic.

The Billy Syndrome was Williamsburg's most well-known noise rock band of the era, formed in the 1980s and shifting in personnel every few years (see figure 1.4). Syndrome played bass, and Jim Sherry, commonly called "Evil Jim," was the singer, with various guitar players involved through the years. Syndrome attended his first punk shows at CBGBs in the early 1980s but appreciated music across the spectrum from soul to Paul McCartney, but especially obscure garage rock. His own music formed, at least in part, as a

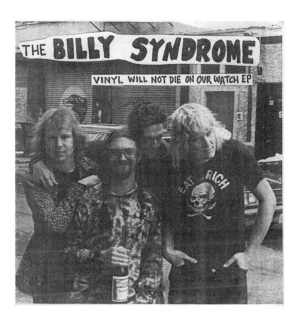

Figure 1.4 The Billy Syndrome (*from left*, J. Z. Barrell, Jim Sherry, Mike Bell, and Billy Syndrome), ca. 1992 (*photo by Jim McPherson*)

rejection of the mainstream culture of the 1980s. "Creativity flowed out of him," drummer Mike Bell noted of the bandleader. "He was constantly writing, coming up with new ideas, working it out on his guitar."[210] He worked as a foot messenger in the World Trade Center for many years, working on his ideas while moving about in the bustle of the city. He self-released most of his music on his own label, Slutfish Recordings, and despite his prolific recordings and centrality to the Williamsburg scene, he remained a mostly underground figure beyond New York.[211] Billy Syndrome was the charismatic leader of the punk–noise rock community in Williamsburg through the period. Studio and live recordings of his band, the Billy Syndrome, document his unique and important work in forming the early Williamsburg sound through the 1990s.

On June 11, 1994, Rose organized a particularly ambitious event: an all-day festival right along the "trashy East River waterfront" that was a "large, but informal affair featuring all local bands, artists, good friends, and personalities."[212] The bill featured the Colored Greens, the Billy Syndrome, and Nice Undies but also lesser-known acts like the all-woman noise rock band Mongrel Bitch and antifolk underground legend Paleface. Radioactive Bodega was famous for the way that they would incorporate the remains of whichever abandoned space was being squatted in creative ways, turning every room into a conceptual art piece. The pinnacle of this at the June 1994 event was an installation aboard an abandoned ferryboat in the East River.[213]

That was the last event put on by Radioactive Bodega, but the mark it made on the punk and broader music community was formative and long-standing in how performers occupied space, made it public and free of charge, and embodied a working-class sensibility.

The Bar Scene
The Ship's Mast

The social life of the waterfront community revolved around "the holy trinity of bars": the Ship's Mast, Teddy's, and the Right Bank Café. Each had its own personality. Old-school bohemian types hung out at Teddy's, which had been holding performance art events since 1985.[214] The Ship's Mast, opened in 1981 at North Sixth Street and Berry Street, is where people went for party-oriented, late-night revelry in a space with a nautical theme. The interior was a "*Deer Hunter*–style wood-paneled club," which on the weekends also served lasagna, meatballs, and knishes and also offered people free hot dogs as long as supplies lasted.[215] The owners, John and Nora Gallagher, sometimes featured antifolk, punk, jazz, and various kinds of experimental music, developing a reputation as supportive of artists, though the owner admitted, "I don't think the people born and bred in the area feel very comfortable around the artists, so they stay away."[216] A back room of the bar that had no chairs but a small stage could accommodate twenty-five people and was "always a full house."[217]

Michael Zwicky's new band, Dem, which he formed with alto saxophonist Matt Seidman and bassist Hideji Taninaka, played at the Ship's Mast regularly after first assembling for a jam at a house party.[218] Taninaka described the music as full of "rage and passion."[219] Dem was one of the earliest fully improvised acoustic free jazz units to play the scene on any kind of regular basis, though it would take a few more years before it built a strong presence on the scene. Ken Butler also played there in different formations with drummer Michael Evans and others, performing improvised sets as well as pieces from Miles Davis's electric period.[220]

Saxophonist and flutist Bonnie Kane also played frequently at the Ship's Mast and at the Right Bank Café. She was originally from Philadelphia and had grown up with two primary musical influences: psychedelic rock, including Jimi Hendrix, Pink Floyd, and Captain Beefheart; and free jazz, such as that of Albert Ayler. Seeing the Sun Ra Arkestra playing in parks in Philadelphia was particularly impactful.[221]

In 1989, while living in the East Village, Kane organized the band W.O.O. and played their debut show at CBGBs on a bill with White Zombie. She liked to vary the lineups and included a range of musicians, eventually settling on trio or quartet formations. Her most consistent bandmate in the Williamsburg period was drummer Glenn Sorvisto. She focused on the group's live sound primarily.[222] Kane liked rock players who could also improvise, and the band explored the aesthetics of a rock sound in an improvised setting, consciously trying to avoid blues riffs, "to see what they could bring to the moment." Kane added, "It was a guy's scene then, with very few other woman instrumentalists."[223] She led the band at the Ship's Mast and at the Right Bank Café regularly in the early 1990s, and the band toured Europe three times during that decade. The band W.O.O. evolved into several iterations, the final being MaMbo ManTis with Blaise Siwula and Chris Welcome after Kane became enmeshed in the improvised music community surrounding the venue ABC No Rio. Kane has continued to lead other bands and perform solo up to the present.

The Ship's Mast was also where the *Waterfront Week*, the scene's community bulletin board in the form of a newspaper, was produced.[224] Writers would leave clippings of their contributions in a shoebox there, and then once a week an informal circle of organizers would gather the pieces without exerting editorial control and use Scotch tape to assemble them onto a tabloid card. (Medea de Vice served as the managing editor for the first three years.) Then they would go to Kinko's to print five hundred copies, before finding drop locations and passing the paper around personally. The paper featured reviews, concert listings, announcements for art openings, editorials, and advertisements for local businesses.

Right Bank Café

One of the waterfront buildings, at 409 Kent Avenue, eventually came to house the Right Bank Café, a "home away from home" and "welcoming watering hole."[225] Opened by ex-firefighter Kerry Smith in 1989, the café immediately became one of the major social centers of the waterfront Williamsburg community. One local resident, on first seeing it, supposedly remarked, "Who in the hell would build a bar in the middle of nowhere?"[226] At first, it was an oasis in the urban desert that surrounded it, but the café quickly became one of the epicenters of a whole new community just then forming along the waterfront. Firefighters, many of whom, like the proprietor, were Irish, always drank for free at the Right Bank, giving the place a fraternal camaraderie.

Smith bore a typical rough Brooklyn exterior but was a kindhearted, open-minded free spirit who welcomed everyone to his establishment and was particularly supportive of artists and musicians. The Right Bank gained a reputation as a kind of art gallery and event space.[227] Soon after the café opened, punk rocker Billy Syndrome convinced Smith to start hosting concerts there. Punk bands including the Billy Syndrome, Thundering Lizards, Thai Raid, the Astro-Zombies, and Nice Undies began to play there.[228] Folk singer Amanda Pollock worked at the Right Bank as a bartender and also played regularly there. Smith also hired a Baltimore native, artist Bonnie Bonnell, as a bartender and concert booker, and there soon developed a whole community of Baltimore transplants, bands, and musicians at the place.[229] Smith even accommodated their tastes by regularly going to Baltimore to acquire their local brew, National Bohemian, aka Natty Boh, to serve at the Right Bank.[230] Most of the shows either occurred outside or on the second floor, where Smith also allowed band members to sleep after gigs.[231] Though punk was at the center of the scene, many other forms of music began filtering into the music scene, such as psych, surfer rock, country, rockabilly, and even zydeco and merengue.[232] Bassist Reuben Radding and other experimental musicians at the time also played occasional shows in the space in the mid-1990s.[233]

At many of the warehouse events and others that were occurring in lofts, bars, and cafés nearby, MDMA (Ecstasy) was the substance of choice for both artists and audience. Some of this may have emerged from rave culture, which was a contemporary and had originally popularized it.[234] Some who employed MDMA referred to how it "expanded their capacity for creativity" or how "it opened channels of perception," enhancing sensorial experience. Individual use of the drug varied considerably: some did not use it all, and others used it frequently. Numerous participants in the warehouse events also referred to MDMA playing a role in enhancing the feeling of community and connectedness, a claim that has many parallels in other art and social scenes.[235]

Decline of the Waterfront Warehouse Era

By 1994 the waterfront warehouse arts boom was receding.[236] Social and political forces were coalescing to destabilize the unusual availability of art space in Williamsburg. The Happy Land fire had instigated a political reaction against unregulated spaces. The use of fire codes to evict squatters from the East Village in 1988 had been a test case for legal displacement, and the same approach was then used in Williamsburg. Though there were only hints of real estate prospecting at the time, the motivations eventually became clear: the waterfront properties and locations were far too attractive not to gain the attention of developers. These forces crept into Williamsburg by the mid-1990s, and the crumbling warehouses were eyed for renovation or full-scale demolition and replacement.

There was also local resistance to the intrusions of white artists into Williamsburg. These tensions manifested in numerous ways, from community self-segregation to occasional protests or community events aimed at countering what many Latinx residents saw as an intrusion into their neighborhood. In 1993 one of the most visible acts occurred when a Puerto Rican artist from the neighborhood began stenciling "90 Days" on the walls of some DIY music venues and art galleries, declaring that they must close and reinforcing the demand with bomb threats. These demands were accompanied by a manifesto that the Taino peoples of Williamsburg, referring to their indigenous ancestry, were under attack. The entire action was orchestrated by a high school student who viewed the movement he was trying to inspire as his own art project. As Tom Schmitz, owner of Earwax Records, stated, "I used to engage with them in debate. They knew what was coming and saw the artists for what we were. Trailblazers for the investors to follow. They left me alone because I engaged them seriously and I had opened before gentrification really took off. But we all failed to see the big picture clearly. The local community and the artists should have been natural allies. The artists failed to see how vulnerable they were too."[237]

The effects of gentrification on a grand scale were gradual over the course of about a decade, though in particular areas of Williamsburg they had dramatic effects.[238] The Rent Regulation Reform Act of 1997 weakened the rent-control laws as well, leading to an immediate increase in rents for many of the artists who inhabited the waterfront; this had even more of an impact on the South Side.[239] Also, as Schmitz reflected many years later, "If I look back now, I see the mistakes we made as a community. Of not taking our role in the gentrification process more seriously."[240]

Artists began to be pushed inland, south and east, by evictions and rising prices. Communities formed and dissolved in places like Kent Avenue, South Fifth and Sixth Streets, North Seventh to Tenth Streets, Bedford Avenue, sections of Grand Street, Graham Avenue, and eventually farther away.[241] Newcomers arriving to take part in the still-vibrant art scene also could not expect to find affordable housing in the heart of Williamsburg, and thus the community naturally shifted into East Williamsburg and Bushwick over the years that followed. The most dramatic changes came to the waterfront itself. The large-scale, warehouse-sized events were no longer possible. But still, the memory of Williamsburg in its raw and untamed glory would remain as a powerful example of what a community of creative artists could accomplish in the intense urbanity of New York if afforded ample space in which to work. Police closures and real estate prospectors combined to make such spaces no longer tenable.

The legacy of the Williamsburg waterfront music scene was to outlive the spaces it inhabited. Most of the key elements of the Williamsburg avant-garde were present there from the beginning: improvisation, noise, post-punk, free jazz, and electronic music, all in various degrees. The influence of both the well-known and lesser-known Williamsburg sonic experimentalists was felt via the legacy of the sonic culture they had played a principal part in generating. These sounds would continue to reverberate in clubs, lofts, basements, and backyards, where the experimental sounds of the scene would continue to gestate, intermix, and take on new forms in the years to come.

CHAPTER TWO

Pirate Radio and Jumping the River

The Williamsburg Loft Scene, 1997–2004

The idea of synchronicity, of just being free in the streets, that whole idea of having the time and the space to get bored, that existed in Brooklyn then.

—*Tunde Adebimpe*

The identifiable Williamsburg sound crystallized fully at the turn of the millennium. Elements of the early 1990s scene persisted, while it absorbed a great deal of transformative experimental ideas, aesthetics, and communities. New waves of free jazz soon arrived, reverberating out from the Knitting Factory scene of the 1990s but carried forward by a generation that had absorbed hip-hop, grunge, and early 1990s alternative rock. Whereas the early 1990s music scene drew its noise aesthetic primarily from a punk and postpunk world, the noise of the late 1990s shifted dramatically toward an aesthetic heavily influenced by Japanese noise bands. The result was an increasingly systematic examination of the possibilities of noise and a gradual codification of both concepts and techniques to produce the sounds in a full embrace of electronics as a chaos factor, rhythm maker, and noise palette.

The other major new development in the Williamsburg sound was the meteoric rise of Brooklyn as a major center of indie rock music. The impact was not solely one of sound but also one of attitude and independence. The cross-pollination of music and sound in Brooklyn was perhaps never richer than during the years immediately straddling the millennium. Rent was still relatively inexpensive, young artists from around the United States were coming to New York City in unprecedented numbers, and Williamsburg was the epicenter for their creativity, imagination, and yearnings to invent something new. The scene achieved a critical mass of artists and ideas. Counterculture was the Williamsburg mainstream. A generation that had witnessed their airwaves and their music taken over by the drab conservativism of media conglomerates was rebelling; they demanded art that was more relevant, shocking, and outspoken. Reflecting record producer Steve Albini's prophetic 1993 manifesto, "The Problem with Music," in which he decried an industry that stifled self-expression, exploited musicians, and sanitized music for the sake of marketability, this new generation was less compromising and more overtly rebellious.[1] In those years much of the Williamsburg scene felt like a fascinating, unpredictable, creative Hydra-like organism of DIY projects, spaces, collectives, and other communities yearning to spread its wings and breathe free.

Pirate Radio: Free103point9

On the evening of September 18, 1999, a crowd gathered on South Sixth Street, between Bedford Avenue and Berry Street. The bodega in the middle of that block drew unprecedented numbers of people for "the Fight of the Millennium" between Oscar De La Hoya and Felix Trinidad.[2] Latecomers elbowed their way through the crowd, trying to catch a glimpse of the fighters as they flickered on a fuzzy black-and-white television that someone had carried out onto the sidewalk. With regularity, people in the gathering toasted with cans of Presidente, made bets, and draped flags over their shoulders as a few roosters skittered about among the onlookers.[3] It was a strongly partisan crowd. A chorus of voices shouted "Viva Puerto Rico!" as Trinidad entered the arena with his entourage. The island's native son raised his gloved fists to show that he, the underdog, was ready to face the Golden Boy. Unlike De La Hoya, who entered with the characteristic hood, hiding his eyes, Trinidad had elected to come with a straw hat, occasionally chanting lyrics to Puerto Rican folk songs and smiling to the many thousands who filled the arena. This was more than a fight; it was a cultural moment.

It was a tense fight. De La Hoya seemed to have the edge from the beginning and dominated a majority of the first nine rounds. By the fifth round, one of Trinidad's eyes was swollen, and his nose was bleeding. By the eighth round, Trinidad's eye had worsened, and his trunks were stained with blood. It looked as if Trinidad was destined to lose, and many viewers on that Williamsburg street corner muttered a desperate hope that their star would just avoid the humiliation of a knockout. Then, in the last half of the ninth round, as De La Hoya grew more conservative, Trinidad rallied. He threw down flurries of punches, knowing that the scorecard up to that point did not favor him. Then, in the final round, as De La Hoya was losing energy, Trinidad sprang at the chance to steal the fight and landed enough punches to win over the judges. The exhausted, yet elated, crowd exploded.

Mingling in the gathered crowd was a smaller contingent of tensely smoking musicians and radio technicians, who also casually drank beer on the street while curiously observing the fight. There were no police around to enforce open-container laws. This was Brooklyn, unregulated before nearly two decades of gentrification and physical transformation violently recast parts of the borough in a new image of wealth and extravagance. As TV on the Radio front man Tunde Adebimpe described it, "The idea of synchronicity, of just being free in the streets, that whole idea of having the time and the space to get bored, that existed in Brooklyn then."[4] In Brooklyn—culturally rich, diverse, and free from the watchful eye of the authorities—boxing and gambling, art and music, still occurred unabated.

While the world watched the two fighters, the radio techs were preparing another broadcast, one reaching only half a dozen blocks in any direction, which they projected from the building next door. Free103point9, a Williamsburg pirate radio station, had been broadcasting for over two years by that point, led by the journalist and DJ Tom Roe, musician Greg Anderson, and painter Violet Hopkins.[5] Before arriving in New York, Roe, DJ Matt Mikas, and others had launched 87X, a pirate station in the Ybor City neighborhood of their native Tampa Bay, Florida, in reaction to gentrification and the disintegration of an alternative artist community there in 1994.[6]

Free103point9 and the Williamsburg Loft Scene

Free103point9 was deeply rooted in the DIY Williamsburg culture of the time. At the turn of the millennium, DIY cultural events featuring art and music were so commonplace that one artist and regular concert attendee stated, "If we were not already invited to a party, we would just walk down the street and listen for music. If we heard music, we would press as many buzzers as we needed to get into the building and then find the party." The scene was incredibly eclectic, "always involving music and visual art in the same spaces," including a range of different kinds of music and sound, installation art, performance, film, graffiti, and live painting.[7] Most people living in the area were artists, musicians, filmmakers, designers, or independent contractors, so few people worked a day job in the traditional sense, leaving them free to conform their schedules to the social scene that had grown up around art and music. If there was any tension in the lofts, it was between older punks raising children and the wave of younger, more affluent residents that arrived around the turn of the millennium. "Sometimes the older punks would get upset with us for throwing parties, which we found ironic and hilarious because they were the ones that were supposed to be antiestablishment!" artist Jason Merritt recalled, "though I can see from their eyes they saw us as more privileged."[8]

Lofts were ideal for hosting live music in a large-party atmosphere. In the last years of the 1990s, the loft scene began moving away from the waterfront and gained momentum in neighboring postindustrial areas. Lofts are unique spaces for artists in that they serve as homes, community centers, workspaces, galleries, and performance venues, often all at once. The usually wide-open, high-ceilinged rooms appealed to the DIY mindset of their new inhabitants. They wanted to move in, transform every aspect of the space to their liking, and then forge a world of creativity. The lofts of Williamsburg were, in some ways, inspired by the jazz loft era of the 1970s and the Brooklyn art loft trend that had been growing since the late 1980s.[9] In a city like New York, where physical space was gradually getting scarcer and more expensive in the 1990s, such places were absolutely vital for aspiring artists. But as one musician and venue owner explained, "There was nothing special about Williamsburg other than it was close to Manhattan and there was cheap rent. That's why people were flocking there at the time."[10] Creating a community was just as important as producing the art itself, and in this environment the Williamsburg loft scene became the most dynamic center in the city for a broad range of arts at the turn of the millennium.

Roe found a loft space at 97 South Sixth Street (right next door to where the Lizard's Tail had been) between Bedford Avenue and Berry Street in September 1995 and by May 1997 was broadcasting from his living room. The station had emerged as part of a proliferation of pirate radio stations across the country in the 1990s. Roe recalled, "At the time there were two to three thousand micro radio stations across the country, working together and committing civil disobedience because the FCC [Federal Communications Commission] laws were unjust at the time." He further explained, "There was very little public access to the airwaves that we regarded as akin to park land and [that] should be available to the public."[11] This movement aimed at defying the increasingly corporate takeover of radio stations in general and reclaiming the airwaves for an intended local audience.[12]

Roe noted that "the easiest way to get public access to the airwaves was to allow small stations to broadcast to neighborhoods in towns and cities," but there was no functional way for individuals to apply for these rights with the FCC.[13] These micro radio stations needed a landmark case to justify their existence. In 1997 the Ninth Circuit Court in California ruled, in a case against the FCC, that Radio Free Berkeley, one of the most prominent stations of this kind, was allowed to remain on the air.[14] Pirate radio continued to proliferate in the wake of the ruling, though after 2000 federal laws were passed that inhibited micro radio broadcasting.[15] Still, many stations continued to commit acts of civil disobedience against the system that was meant to support corporate stations while drowning out small-scale operations.

Aside from the politics, an artistic drive also compelled some to seize the public airwaves. Roe recounted, "We thought that the airwaves were incredibly boring and not being used in an artistic way. So we became an art radio station within the pirate radio movement."[16] One journalist described the medium as "a newly emerging form of sound-art based primarily on manipulation of the live airwaves."[17] In 2000, when the floor above Roe's apartment opened up, he expanded into the space with the aim of hosting larger public performances. According to oral legends, a biker gang had taken over the first floor for a few years in the early 1990s, until they got kicked out and supposedly threw a firebomb over the back wall. Evidence of the blast remained when Roe moved into the space a few years later.[18] Roe intended to revive its legacy as an underground performance venue, making it a place for "free jazz, noise, experimental sound, and electronic music."[19]

Free103point9 lent out transmitters like a library, and when they hosted their own events, they broadcast them live.[20] In the beginning the audience was no doubt small, as news of the station passed via word of mouth. When they broadcast from a tall building, such as one on North Eleventh Street, they could reach all of Williamsburg. From the station's home base on South Sixth Street, the broadcast reached only from Grand Street in the north to just past Division Street in the south, and over to the Brooklyn-Queens Expressway to the east. "We put flyers up on telephone poles locally around where we thought people could actually tune in to the broadcast," Roe recalled.[21] The focus on the microcommunity in their initial scope is telling; they attempted to build bridges across the local area and gather artists together who were inhabiting those spaces for a series of cutting-edge cultural experiences. Radio listeners thus shared the experience alongside those who attended the concerts in person, an audience that one musician noted was, "in terms of gender, an unusually balanced audience, in a room that could hold a hundred people."[22]

The increased mobility of transmitters was itself a product of technological innovations from earlier in the 1990s. Equipment got cheaper, and people got better at making smaller kits and making their own antennae, led by peace activist Stephen Dunifer of Radio Free Berkeley.[23] Dunifer produced a number of instructional videos and affordable kits for people interested in micro radio or in building their own equipment. These innovations paved the way for a generation of mobile pirate radio practitioners who saw reclaiming the airwaves as an increasingly necessary form of cultural expression.[24] To avoid police raids and seizures of equipment, and also to make the transmitter a kind of communally owned social centerpiece, free103point9 lent out its equipment regularly.[25] Events at free103point9 most commonly occurred on the weekends, when both performers and audiences were available to take part. Broadcasting from the mobile transmitter sometimes began on Fridays, with Saturday night as the climax. Using the mobile transmitter as both a tool of broadcasting and a focal point for live performance allowed free103point9 to bridge audiences along the Brooklyn waterfront.

Expanding Operations

In 2000 experimental DJ Matt Mikas, who had worked with Roe in Tampa Bay, followed the latter north and moved into the upper floor of the building where Roe was already working. Mikas's apartment became known as "the project space" for the radio station, and he came on board as its operations manager.[26] Mikas built a stage to give the space more of the feeling of a venue than it had previously had on the lower floor. Earlier that year, the FCC had begun issuing licenses for short-range broadcasting, limiting

Figure 2.1 radio techs broadcasting from free103point9, late 1990s (*photo by Galen Joseph-Hunter*)

them to a 3.5-mile range and to noncommercial educational programming, so free103point9 was able to become a licensed radio station.[27] With the opening of the project space, free103point9 was able to host live music more consistently and to accommodate larger gatherings (see figure 2.1).

From that point until it stopped functioning as a performance venue in late 2004, the space hosted multiple live performances each week. There was a spirit of rebellion and resistance in the air, and free103point9 sometimes threw pot parties as a way of setting the tone for the events. As saxophonist Charles Waters recalled, "One night they pulled the rolling papers out of the Cheech and Chong record *Up in Smoke* and lit up a foot-long joint that they passed around. That was the aesthetic there."[28] The owners also sold beer off the books.[29] Another musician recalled that in the late 1990s he had felt that there was no grassroots music space in the New York area, "but I was wrong, because as soon as I walked into free103point9 for the first time in June of 2001, I knew, this was it!"[30]

The synthesizer player Matt Mottel, who grew up in Upper West Side Manhattan, recalled being drawn to the space in 1998, when he was just seventeen, because "it was a definitive choice against mainstream culture." It was a space for people "choosing to consume culture and life in a way that was antithetical to mass culture."[31] Having yearned for an alternative cultural center ever since reading Jack Kerouac's *On the Road* one summer in Central Park, Mottel also found it a welcome contrast to many of the premier Manhattan clubs then booking free jazz shows, such as the Knitting Factory, Tonic, or the Cooler. It cost only $5 to enter, patrons could bring their own alcohol, all ages were welcome, and artists were in charge of the space.

The atmosphere of the space and the opportunity to have performances broadcast live drew many musicians involved in the experimental jazz and improvised music scene. The booking process was simple and open; as Roe recalled, "A number of bands at the time preferred to play underground shows rather than at clubs in Manhattan. So those bands began contacting us to play."[32] At the time only a few other venues were doing regular underground concerts in Williamsburg, so the demand for performance space was high. As Williamsburg transitioned to being the go-to place to hear live music in New York City, free103point9 came to define the cutting edge of the grassroots musical revolution that was then taking place.

Gold Sparkle Band

One of the key ensembles to emerge from this scene was Gold Sparkle Band, led by drummer Andrew Barker, saxophonist Charles Waters, and trumpeter Roger Ruzow.[33] Waters and Ruzow had been roommates at Appalachian State University, where they both studied the music of John Cage and Karlheinz Stockhausen, and soon afterward met Barker, who had studied film at Georgia State University.[34] Together, they established themselves in Atlanta, a place that did not really have a free jazz scene, finding their niche with "experimental, left-of-center rock-oriented acts such as Smoke, Flap, the Jody Grind, and Seely."[35] Gold Sparkle Band's first widely publicized gig was opening for John Zorn's Masada during the latter's US tour through Atlanta in 1994. By the time the band left for New York in 1998, they had already released several records and played US tours and were thus capable of contributing to a music scene teeming with innovators.[36] They took their name from Barker's vintage 1965 Ludwig drum kit.[37] Williamsburg became the ideal setting for them to play.

From the beginning the band had a rebellious attitude and a sense of mission. As Ruzow declared, "American children are not going to be introduced to music of substance unless a parent, friend, or teacher introduces them to it. The airwaves are controlled by the corporations, and they need a product they can package and market. The vast majority of good new music doesn't fit into that."[38] In terms of their own music, Waters noted that their third record, *Downsizing* (1997), "is angry. Anything is expendable at a certain level in terms of capitalism. But that's not true, music isn't expendable."[39] A later piece, "Promises of Democracy," on *Nu-Soul Zodiac* (1999), originated in the idea that "democracy is an unrealized idea. There's a big façade that goes on and we're trying to make sense of it with our music. That requires us to improvise and improvisation creates a certain need for freedom and I think that necessitates a questioning of what goes on in the status quo."[40] Gold Sparkle Band fit quite comfortably into the anticorporate, civilly disobedient atmosphere of pirate radio at free103point9.[41]

Waters referred to their music as "NuZion," a new fusion of "structured and improvised music that has many influences not just Ornette [Coleman] and Don Cherry; but [Olivier] Messian, [John] Coltrane, and Elliot Carter."[42] The music was designed to give ample room for individuals to improvise, while maintaining an evolving identity through compositional structures.[43] But the band also looked outside of the free jazz genre for ideas. Waters expanded their list of influences, noting, "The Atlanta hip-hop scene had a bigger influence on us than people know," pointing to a band like Goodie Mob, as well as the house party, DJ, and rock scenes in their native city in the early to mid-1990s.[44] As Tom Roe observed, "They took the energy they found alluring in punk rock sounds, and applied it to the jazz they were schooling themselves in at the time."[45] Barker had also previously been in a cover band of the Melvins called the Melts, so he brought in a certain kind of rock influence.[46] Waters observed, "We try to sculpt a record in terms of its architecture, and I think that comes from rock."[47]

In Gold Sparkle Band's early years in New York, Waters composed about half of the band's material, and they actively played at free103point9 and other postindustrial spaces along the Brooklyn waterfront. Many of the events they were a part of featured electronic, punk, noise, or indie rock music as well, placing Gold Sparkle within an eclectic mix of performances in the Williamsburg scene. In 2000 they embarked on a US tour, making key stops in Atlanta and Chicago—extractions from which formed their 2002 release, *Fugues and Flowers*, which one critic referred to as their "definitive statement" up to that time.[48] Because the record drew from live performances, it featured extended solos by the band members, with Barker serving as "both the applecart and the upsetter."[49] Soon after, Gold Sparkle also did a European tour, primarily in France.

Gold Sparkle Band's record *Thunder Reminded Me* captures the kind of music they were playing in Brooklyn at the time.[50] Taped at one of their greatest concerts ever, a Vision Festival performance at the Knitting Factory in 2001, the record illustrates the creative fire they could muster in the live setting.[51] One critic wrote of it, "The trio, who manage to walk the finest line between composition—both highly and loosely structured—and free improvisation, are at their level best here, walking a tightrope of tension where their naturally lyrical improvisational style is juxtaposed against their innate desire to push the envelope."[52] One of the tracks was written as an ode to their neighborhood, "Williamsburg Concerto 1 and 2," featuring "edgy scalar structures that are at the heart of the mismatched angles," which epitomized Williamsburg itself. The critic added, "Intervals are introduced and extrapolated upon in a thematic manner and discarded in favor of complete disintegration."[53]

Still, as doors opened to Barker and Waters, a deep connection with the scene on the Lower East Side remained somewhat elusive. Both musicians noted that even though they knew many of the figures on the downtown scene well—Waters recalled spending hours at bassist William Parker's apartment on East Sixth Street—they nevertheless felt a bit of separation from that community because they lived in Williamsburg, where rents were less expensive. "We went and saw the downtown guys play all the time—we didn't have families, or jobs, or anything else going on really, just the music, and we played with them sometimes, but being in Williamsburg we felt a bit separated from that whole Vision Festival scene."[54]

Legitimizing Brooklyn: Jump Arts Festivals

In 1999, however, conscious attempts were made to bring the East Village and Williamsburg artist communities together, in the form of a collective called Jump Arts, led by recent New School graduates bassist Tom Abbs and drummer David Brandt.[55] The explicit goal was to get musicians from the East Village, some of whom had lived and worked there for decades without ever playing in Brooklyn, to attend or perform at events in Williamsburg. Jump Arts also organized events in Manhattan that featured musicians from both communities and at times organized tours for these musicians outside of New York City.[56] Some of the demand for these connections came as the Knitting Factory was beginning to become less the center of the scene, first moving to Leonard Street on the Lower East Side in 2000 and then closing altogether two years later. Tonic would soon emerge as the new center, but for a time the community was searching for other venues and specifically for opportunities in Williamsburg.

Jump Arts put on a series of twelve festivals, drawing the downtown scene and the emerging Williamsburg scene together in 1999–2003. Abbs specifically aimed to bridge the two scenes, incorporating Gold Sparkle Band into much of what was happening in the downtown scene, and fuse them in Williamsburg. Abbs sensed that "there was nothing for emerging artists, very few opportunities for the up-and-coming generation to get gigs to play their own music, so I formed the Jump Arts collective nonprofit."[57]

One of the earliest events, Jump over the River: Liberation Music Festival, took place on July 2, 1999. The bill featured a number of bands, including the Triple Threat Sextet, which was essentially an expanded Gold Sparkle Band lineup with Abbs and others. The same evening, multi-instrumentalist Daniel Carter (b. 1945) and Williamsburg-based drummer Randy Peterson played in their first-ever duo performance. Carter had been a pivotal figure on the downtown scene since the 1970s.[58] Peterson, a close associate of renowned saxophonist Joe Maneri (1927–2004), has remained more of an underground figure, despite appearing on a number of records.[59] Carter's involvement, though it was not his first time playing in Williamsburg, sparked a string of innovative performances by the multi-instrumentalist at free103point9 in the years that followed.

Butch Morris

The success of the event convinced the Jump Arts organizers to continue with a series of festivals through the following years that continued to build bridges between the communities. For example, in April 2001 the organization invited Lawrence "Butch" Morris to convene a big band called the Jump Festival Orchestra at the Brecht Forum (in Manhattan), which included a broad range of players from both sides of the river.[60] It was an intergenerational ensemble, in addition to bridging geographies, including more established figures such as Steve Swell (trombone) and Assif Tsahar (bass clarinet) but filling out its ranks with many of the up-and-coming musicians of the time, such as Okkyung Lee and Shiau Shu Yu (cellos), Charles Waters (clarinet), Oscar Noriega (bass clarinet), Andrew Barker (drums), John Blum (piano), Chris Jonas and Brian Settles (saxophones), Reut Regev (trombone), Matt Lavelle (trumpet), Tom Abbs (tuba), and Jessica Pavone (viola), among many other performers.[61]

Morris's theories of "improvised duet for ensemble and conductor," or "conduction," as he termed it, were boldly innovative in that he aimed to improvise as a conductor with the ensemble in the moment.[62] "I teach a vocabulary to the ensemble but we don't rehearse the music we are going to perform. The conduction is an instant composition. I started doing this in the first place because I realized there was a great divide between what is notated and what is improvised." By *vocabulary*, Morris meant a range of signals that indicated actions such as repeat and sustain, as well as graphic information and melodic directions, "but each musician was able to interpret" that vocabulary.[63] Morris would return with slightly altered lineups of the big band at future Jump Arts events.[64] Many of the figures in the Morris conduction projects would figure prominently in the development of the Brooklyn scene; for violist Jessica Pavone, it constituted one of her first gigs in the city and helped her connect with the community of artists at an early stage of her career.[65]

The April 2001 bill included many other key encounters, such as pairing veterans Paul Flaherty (saxophone), Steve Swell, and Wilber Morris (bass) with the younger Brooklyn-based drummer Chris Corsano for a fully improvised set.[66] Daniel Carter returned and played with the younger figures Tom Abbs, tenor saxophonist Brian Settles, and drummer Chad Taylor. As Abbs, the organizer, stated, the events were intergenerational, "to include our mentors on the stage next to us."[67]

The festivals were also multidisciplinary, with bills that included dance, poetry, live painting, or gallery shows, paired with or integrated into the musical performances. In 2003 the festival had reached a point of exhibiting interdisciplinary works such as saxophonist Patrick Brennan's Transmedia Band. Brennan's goal with the group was to form an ensemble "of disparate activities who would be able to interact with the intensity and intersubjective responsiveness of an improvising musical ensemble." The strategy was to try "to make visually evident the internal dynamics of what was going on in dialogical music via the common kinetic-rhythmic potentials shared by gestural painting, dancing, and sounding."[68] The painter, in this case, was calligrapher Lan Ding Liu, from Beijing, whose images were projected onto a wall so that the audience could see them, while dancer Patricia Nicholson brought her many years of improvisational knowledge to dance, and Brennan coaxed the sounds of the piece out through his saxophone.[69]

TEST

The festival also included TEST, which comprised members who lived on both sides of the river: Daniel Carter (many instruments), Matthew Heyner (bass), Sabir Mateen (reeds and woodwinds), and Tom Bruno (drums).[70] The band was steeped in the free jazz tradition of groups like the 1970s loft band the Music Ensemble and the band Other Dimensions in Music, which was first convened by trumpeter Roy Campbell in 1989; both of these bands also included Carter.[71] Mateen had grown up singing in church choirs before studying and playing saxophone and flute in the air force band. Before coming to New York, Mateen had lived in Los Angeles for more than a decade, where he played in Horace Tapscott's Pan-Afrikan Peoples Arkestra, which expanded his understanding of the possibilities of an ensemble.[72]

TEST was one of the great freely improvised bands of the period and had honed their craft playing in the streets and subways of New York City (see figure 2.2).[73] Carter and Bruno had regularly been playing duo on the streets a few blocks away from where Mateen was playing solo; they eventually fused, and that was the beginning of TEST.[74] Heyner joined later, having studied with bassist William Parker and developed as a player in the No-Neck Blues Band. Mateen explained that the name came from the idea that "everything we go through is a test—how we live, how we survive. What we are doing at the moment is a test."[75] Carter said, "It really surprises me that other musicians haven't decided to do that, especially considering the economics of this music."[76] The band finally cast light on the considerable talents of Mateen, who until the late 1990s had been chronically underdocumented.[77]

One critic described TEST's music: "The group constructs a succession of peaks from its disparate elements, bridging all dynamic [possibilities] along the way. As it is created entirely of-the-moment, the music of TEST determines its own form—attesting to the individual and collective abilities of Bruno, Carter, Heyner, and Mateen."[78] With both Carter and Mateen as multi-instrumentalists, the timbral and textural possibilities of the group were vast. Their released live recordings capture the kind of music that they presented at Jump Arts.[79]

Jump Arts Goes on the Road

Jump Arts also organized tours for the artists. After the 9/11 attacks, the organization was motivated to reinvigorate American culture and put together a tour that launched from Galapagos Art Space in Brooklyn; then

Figure 2.2 TEST: *from left*, Sabir Mateen, Tom Bruno, and Daniel Carter at Astor Place subway station, 1997 (*photo by Michael Wilderman*)

swept through Tritone in Philadelphia, the University of North Carolina in Chapel Hill, and a restaurant gig in Winston-Salem, North Carolina; and climaxed at the two-night Jump to the Eyedrum improvisational music festival in Atlanta.[80] The artists traveled together in a caravan of cars.[81] They returned to Tonic in New York and were disappointed by low attendance after encountering enthusiastic crowds at most of the other tour stops.[82]

Many of the featured groups on the tour shared members, allowing for different lineups and personnel within the larger group of touring artists. Gold Sparkle Band reunited with trumpeter Roger Ruzow, who had remained in Atlanta, and played at the Eyedrum.[83] Afterward, Waters remarked about the show and the reunion with Ruzow, "The real missing part is his voice and understanding of how the group works. He is very responsible for Gold Sparkle Band's aesthetic—and that's what Barker and I miss most."[84]

The performance opportunities at the Eyedrum anchored the entire tour.[85] Ruzow was the local organizer for the festival, which also included regional acts such as the Flakes, Konx, Chattanooga's Shakin' Ray Lewis, and the Erik Hinds Trio alongside the Jump Arts performers.[86] Of the Jump

Arts participants, Barker also played in a fiery free jazz trio with Daniel Carter and Sabir Mateen that was released on record.[87] Poet Steve Dalachinsky often performed solo but also paired with Charles Waters in a duo. The Transcendentalists, a group comprising Carter, Abbs, Steve Swell, and percussionist David Brandt, performed with Mateen as a special guest, having recorded and released a record a few months prior.[88] Carter and Brandt formed trios with Swell or Mateen on different nights. Cellist Okkyung Lee played duo with Abbs in a group called Dichotomy. Lee and Mateen both played solo on the bills as well. To conclude each night, all of the performers would appear onstage together for an improvised large ensemble.[89] The concerts ended up lasting three to four hours each night. Jump Arts sold a CD-R compilation recording from the tour that contained work by each of the artists.[90]

The music often incorporated nonsonic elements. Dancers Jessica Kjos, Heather Kravas, and Jessie Gold improvised with different groups on each of the bills. In a different vein, M. P. Landis did live painting, using primarily household latex paint and acrylics, either onstage, if there was room to accommodate him, or immediately offstage.[91] He would paint through the entire evening of performances, with two wooden panels covered in paper on which to work. One panel was covered by one large piece of paper, while the other panel had multiple smaller pieces stapled to it. Landis described his process: "I painted the whole board, not thinking about where one piece of paper stopped or started. I liked how it gave the work a sense of being midstream, like capturing a sound in time." He added, "The intensity of the music made the painting intense. It felt like I was doing months' worth of painting within a few hours."[92] Poet Steve Dalachinsky presented his work every night, often with the Transcendentalists, while also working as the emcee for the events. Dalachinsky composed several poems during the tour that tell of their travels and of the people and places they encountered.[93]

Abbs eventually got burned out organizing festivals and raising funds, after organizing a dozen of them over the span of four years. Some of the scene moved to the Pink Pony, on the Lower East Side, for a year or so afterward.[94] The festivals and events had a lasting impact. For a time, Jump Arts forged a strong link between the established downtown scene and the burgeoning scene in Williamsburg and provided a stage for established, underground, and just-then-discovered figures who would have an impact in the years to come.

Continued Development of the Free103point9 Scene
The SB

While the electronic, noise, sound art, and free jazz scenes often existed as separate entities in Manhattan, at free103point9 all of these vibrant scenes collided.[95] Most bills included bands from across that spectrum, and soon bands emerged that consciously drew from a similarly eclectic array of influences. No band epitomized the creative possibilities of such encounters more than the SB, which had gradually formed between 1996 and 1999 while doing regular sessions at Night Owl Studios on Thirtieth Street in Manhattan. After Night Owl closed, they shifted their regular operations to Context Studios on Avenue A and East Second Street. The band included a concentration of individuals who worked in computer-generated imagery at postproduction houses in Manhattan, and they combined their aesthetic appreciation for small or unusual sounds with an appetite for improvisation. They also bore influence from an eclectic array of musicians ranging from electric Miles Davis and Spacemen 3 to percussionist contemporaries such as Tatsuya Nakatani and Chris Corsano.[96] When they performed, they created soundscapes drawn from an array of instruments and devices such as a micro-Moog, a homemade noise generator and other electronics, vintage analog synthesizers, didgeridoo, ocarina, voice, a computer fan, five-string guitar, microcassette recorder, theremin, hand drums and other percussion, electric or upright bass, shakuhachi, and various other wind instruments. This incredibly diverse mix of instruments and sound-producing objects was aimed at "experiments with audio intermodulation and sympathetic resonance, alternately producing strange attractors, unstable drones, standing waves, and complex fields of interference."[97]

The SB played entirely improvised music with little to no discussion beforehand, though they did talk about techniques or strategies for interactions that occurred live. For example, they sometimes used mics or splitters to manipulate each other's signals as sound or modulation sources. Or, as one of the band's members, Eric Maurer, recalled, they might begin a show with a simple concept such as "Let's start with a drone to balance our levels."[98] From there, they drew from myriad electronic, noise, rock, fusion, and everyday sounds; as one critic depicted it, "It's delicate and benevolent, rather than cracked and hostile. . . . [T]hey sound like standard improv moves, but they always resolve into something else, something better."[99] As member Russ Waterhouse described it, "We never tried to sell the audience on a feeling or implied a message. We didn't always offer catharsis or a narrative arc; we conjured an atmosphere instead."[100]

Fritz Welch

One significant noise artist to emerge at free103point9 was percussionist Fritz Welch. Welch had been a student of Dada, surrealism, Fluxus, and situationism who blended those ideas with late 1960s radicalism.[101] Throughout his career he has been an eclectic artist and a polymath working in a range of media from experimental noise to illustration, sculpture, book design, installations, and performance.[102] After moving to an old carriage house at 10 Bushwick Place, in what would be dubbed the Morgantown area of the Bushwick neighborhood in 1991, just a block from where the Brooklyn Free Music Festival would later take place, he began inventing and building instruments.[103] As a sculptor, he brought an interest in and understanding of physicality to the objects with which he created sounds. His range of inventions included myriad "rudimentary percussion devices utilizing springs and vibrating elements augmented by homemade contact mics, as well as simple cut and shaped pieces of sheet metal."[104] Welch considered the poet and inventor Stefan Weisser, known as Z'EV (1951–2017), to be a major source of inspiration. Z'EV was a significant figure in the American avant-garde from the late 1970s onward, playing a key role in the development of industrial music.[105]

Seeing many concerts at the Knitting Factory and other venues pushed Welch down the road of free improvisation; percussionist Han Bennink led him to explore Dutch free jazz, and percussionist Tony Oxley expanded his idea of the possibilities of the drum kit.[106] Having a laboratory of sorts where he could practice and experiment at any time of the day or night was crucial to his ability to develop his work and was the launching pad for his autodidactic approach to sound. Employing DAT recorders and digital multitrack recorders, both technological innovations at the time, helped push his work to the cutting edge.[107] The Berkeley-based experimental noise rock band Caroliner Rainbow opened up a whole new palette of performance possibilities to Welch that ranged across sound, noise, colors, movement, costumes, and myriad abstractions; this was then further expanded by exposure to Japanese noise bands, such as the early work of the Boredoms, including *Soul Discharge*, described as "a Dadaist cut-up of pop music styles, performed at top speed with an absurdly aggressive, over-the-top energy" drawn from "vocals over warped guitar, bass, electronics, and two drum sets in a montage of hardcore and *musique concrète*."[108] Their influence even went beyond music, with the performative elements of their work involving absurdist, multicolored fluorescent costumes.[109]

At a show that Welch organized at free103point9 on May 12, 2001, he featured Irritating HorseEye, which, in addition to himself, included painter and noise artist Matt Bua and electric guitarist David McClelland, which was an "organic placebo for transmuting electro-acoustic detritus."[110] Welch and Bua had forged an immediate understanding of each other through their interdisciplinary work; McClelland joined soon afterward and brought elements of improvising at low volumes.[111] Welch's fascination with British drummer Tony Oxley had him experimenting with a "mutated" drum kit setup that he used for shows. In addition to the standard kit, he used various found elements, including "a steel turntable platter, [the] lid of an old-fashioned twenty gallon milk jug, a drum core roller out of a photocopier, and an assortment of rich-sounding wood."[112] In addition, he customized broken cymbals by cutting and shaping them or adding rivets for "sizzles." The setup was always in flux. For Welch, the music constituted a kind of sonic sculpture.[113]

Matt Bua

Matt Bua also quickly became a major fixture of the free103point9 scene, having been inspired by downtown figures such as Fred Frith, John Zorn's Naked City, and Borbetomagus, as well as Japanese noise bands, even before arriving in New York.[114] He had begun experimenting with noise, while also working as a painter. He had moved from his native Wilmington, North Carolina, to live with his grandparents in the Bronx in 1994, before settling in Williamsburg and eventually setting up a loft at 338 Berry Street, near the corner with South Fifth Street.[115] He would often borrow the free103point9 transmitter and broadcast shows from his own loft and soon became integrated into that scene.[116] Bua joined with DJs Tom Roe and Matt Mikas in recording *Of the Bridge* in the summer of 2001, part of which was microbroadcast from the Williamsburg Bridge itself.[117] Bua played his self-designed suitcase orchestra (a suitcase packed with a mixer, small motors, and circuit-bent toys) and various field recordings, while the other two worked beats. It was an ode to the bridge, to Williamsburg, and to the formation of public gatherings and the claiming of public space at a time when such acts were beginning to be difficult.

Figure 2.3 Brent McCoy (*left*) and Matt Bua, warehouse on Kent Avenue, late 1990s
(*photo by Kiyoharu Kuwayama*)

At the Irritating HorseEye gig in May 2001, Bua played his suitcase orchestra. Other components, such as compact Fred Frith–inspired tabletop guitars, constructed from strings affixed to a two-by-four piece of wood and contact microphones for percussive techniques, became central to the suitcase orchestra.[118] Contact microphones augmented small or subtle sounds from whatever surface they were affixed to and allowed Bua to manipulate them in the live setting. He often aimed to create the sound of a "herd of animals" or a "swarm of insects" in his noisescapes.[119] He had intended it to be primarily a solo project, but in Irritating HorseEye, he evolved it to work in an ensemble, working well with Welch and McClelland.

Ras Moshe Burnett's Music Now! Festivals

Tenor saxophonist Ras Moshe Burnett appeared at least half a dozen times at free103point9 around 2003, where he organized a series of one-night festivals (see figure 2.4).[120] He had begun his concept of curation in 1999 with a series of events at the Orange Bear and the Brecht Forum in Manhattan that featured free jazz and occasionally experimental performance art.

Figure 2.4 Ras Moshe Burnett, live at Downtown Music Gallery, 2003 (*photo by Peter Gannushkin*)

"The festivals that I put together were an extension of what I grew up with culturally in the Black community," Burnett explained.[121] As a child, he spent a lot of time at the East, a critically important cultural center for peoples of African descent in Bedford-Stuyvesant, where he saw saxophonist Pharoah Sanders and pianist McCoy Tyner play, among many others, in a Black-owned and -run space. "At that time, cutting-edge music was right in the community," Burnett recalled, having grown up in the East New York neighborhood of Brooklyn. "Sanders, Tyner, Alice Coltrane, early Norman Conners, some of the avant-garde also included African concepts and rhythms as well. . . . [I]t was practically on the level of Malcolm X in terms of the reverence that people had for the music and the musicians." But Burnett considered his events "multinational while not at all negating the Black presence."[122] Burnett was also inspired by other eras, such as Bill Dixon's October Revolution in Jazz in 1964, the loft era of the 1970s, and the Sound Unity Festival of 1984, the last of which he attended as a teenager. "The festivals that I organized were a child of that spirit of self-determination," Burnett added, "and I have always been motivated by the concept of *umoja*," one of the principles of Nguzo Saba, the seven principles of Kwanzaa, "drawn from an African concept that advocated for unity of community."[123]

For Burnett, the events were an act of community, drawing together musicians to play different forms of creative music in one event. Burnett would typically include his own group alongside three or four other sets that covered a range of musical expressions. For his own group, the Music Now! Unit, he rarely featured the same lineup twice, inviting a rotating cast of people drawn loosely from a circle of musicians whom he had become involved with since the early 1990s.[124] In late 2002 he saw flyers for other events happening at free103point9 and then inquired about setting up his own shows at the loft.

"I witnessed a lot of factionalism at that time," Burnett reflected, "and so I wanted to organize shows that brought in people from every musical grouping. Over time, some people began to be involved more often, but it was never closed to new people from participating. I also used it to put together ensembles of different musicians who I had played with individually in different contexts."[125] Burnett's groups included a range of people, including multi-instrumentalists Matt Lavelle, Daniel Carter, and Sabir Mateen; trombonists Steve Swell and Reut Regev; guitarist Tor Snyder; bassist Matt Heyner; drummer Jackson Krall; and many others, sometimes experimenting with multiple drummers. All of the music that the Music Now! Unit played was fully improvised.[126]

The No-Neck Blues Band

One other band that had a great deal of influence on the free103point9 scene was the No-Neck Blues Band, which drew inspiration from Japanese noise bands such as Merzbow, late 1960s Krautrock experimentalism, the musical primitivism of bands such as the Blue Humans, and the improvisation of free jazz–noise bands like Borbetomagus.[127] In 1997–98, when the Lower East Side was gentrifying, members of the band were pushed out of their studios and apartments; instead of following the trend of moving to Brooklyn, they relocated to 638 West 131st Street in Harlem, where they founded Hint House, originally intended as a rehearsal space. They had 2,500 square feet over three floors of the building and soon began holding regular concerts there in a room that could fit two hundred people.

All of No-Neck Blues Band's early records, up until about 2001, were recordings of loft shows, many of them at Hint House, often recorded on a room microphone. As one of the leading figures in the group, David Nuss, described it, "Everything before *Sticks and Stones* [2001] sounds like it was recorded in a garbage can, but it has a vibe, right?"[128] As critic Peter Gershon described their music of the time, "Sculpted bits of guitar feedback and extraneous mechanical-sounding whirrs and blips over steadily-chugging low-fi drum beats. Interesting things happen at a glacial pace: waves of sound crest and slowly decay, rhythms elasticize, then layer with opposing beats as ambiguous sonic items dart in and out of frame."[129] Another critic described their work: "Eschewing both standard melodic conventions and the easy button-pushing approach of computer-generated electronic noise, NNCK [No-Neck Blues Band] gets down and dirty, finding anything they can scrape and bang on, setting up in warehouses and rooftops."[130] Their ability to build narrative tension and to keep that going over a piece that might reach forty minutes in length became one of the hallmarks of their sound, especially their work in the late 1990s and early 2000s.

For one critic, the No-Neck Blues Band embodied the contemporary economic struggle that many people faced at the turn of the millennium, as embodied in their sounds. "For those of us who want to dig for the grubs under the rock that is capitalist culture, we inevitably turn to the devices available to us to create an alternative," one critic wrote. "Few entities have done this as resolutely and successfully as the variable-member noise-improv collective known as the No-Neck Blues Band."[131] The No-Neck Blues Band put its energy into the experience of the DIY live scene, trying to create an atmosphere and a community feel for all who attended their shows. In this regard, they also fit well at free103point9, where they first played in October 2001. Their involvement in that scene proved that links forged on the Lower East Side in the 1990s had survived the splintering of the community, even as some of the artist diaspora settled in Harlem, while others were pushed even further into the Hudson Valley, Connecticut, and New Jersey, in addition to Brooklyn.

Ryan Sawyer

One final figure to first emerge at free103point9 was drummer Ryan Sawyer. Originally from San Antonio, Texas, he had roots in punk rock but discovered improvised music when he happened to attend a duo concert in nearby Austin by pianist Matthew Shipp and bassist William Parker on March 14, 1997, when he was nineteen. Sawyer managed to interview them about their work for a local publication and learned about the music scene in New York.

"They made a huge impression on me, so I immediately began seeking out that music as much as I could," he stated; he soon discovered the music of John Zorn.[132]

Between Parker, Shipp, and Zorn, Sawyer was so inspired that he moved to New York in 1998 and began attending concerts at the Knitting Factory regularly. During his first year, he studied regularly with Bobby Previte and also took a few lessons with Susie Ibarra and Thurman Barker, while consuming music by all of the free jazz drummers that he came across. Rashid Bakr and other drummers who played at the Vision Festival were also an inspiration, along with figures such as Joey Baron with Zorn's Masada. "The great thing about Bobby Previte as a teacher is that he was more invested in teaching me to play music, not how to play drums," Sawyer explained. "He began with an idea and wanted to see if I could convey that to the drums. It was consciously not technique-based drum education, and that played a direct role in me finding my own voice. I'm deeply indebted to him for his wisdom."[133]

By 1999 he had become aware of the Williamsburg arts community, especially the scene that surrounded free103point9. "I originally had thought that playing at the Knitting Factory was going to be an amazing experience," Sawyer explained, "but by that time, it was not very vibrant. It felt like the same people were coming to see the same music by the same people every week. The scene at free103point9 was so exciting in comparison. It was younger, it was a party, people were dancing. It wasn't just free jazz, it was all kinds of expressions. People were free to create there."[134]

Rather than form a steady band, for the most part, Sawyer played with many different formations at the space to push himself as an improviser and to expose himself to many different possibilities and situations. Big Numbers was the one band that Sawyer played with often at free103point9 in 2001–3; they toured clubs and squats in Europe, including a Communist Party fundraiser in Italy, though they did not necessarily endorse its specific political platform. Big Numbers was an angular punk rock band heavily influenced by the Dutch anarchist punk band the Ex, and Sawyer self-released all of their records. "We were all looking for an alternative to capitalism," he recounted, "and I thought that anybody who was okay with how the world worked were fooling themselves."[135]

Sawyer also led his own band with tenor saxophonist Brian Glick and bassist Matt Heyner at free103point9 on numerous occasions, which played fully improvised music. Sawyer also played with multi-instrumentalists Daniel Carter and Sabir Mateen, "because they were down to play anywhere, anytime, sometimes even multiple times per week. In many ways, they mentored a whole generation of players who were arriving at that time as they were so gracious with their time. What they were doing in TEST was the guiding light for so much else that was happening."[136]

Sawyer developed his ideas and approaches in collaborative improvisational settings in these early years at free103point9. He developed a unique and sophisticated vocabulary on drums. "Most of my playing of the period was high energy, really going for it. Sometimes I would compose graphic scores that were aimed at high energy, fast and dense sounds. The aesthetic had a touch of punk mentality to it as well."[137] In the beginning Sawyer felt that he did not play well enough, but over time he grew to value his own sound. "I realized that I should just play all of the unusual or weird stuff that I had been thinking about or experimenting with, to develop what felt most natural, and work on that. I like to swing in the music sometimes, but I know that so many people have done that at such a high level for so long. I realized I needed to do what I can do that others can't do and focus on that. Everyone has something like that, and I just needed to focus on mine. And I learned that it is okay to fail in what you are attempting to do and that there is something to learn in that process, too."[138]

Brooklyn Free Music Festival, May 17–19, 2002

The scene that revolved around free103point9 gained greater visibility during one of the largest-scale concerts put on during the whole history of the Williamsburg avant-garde. This came in the form of the Brooklyn Free Music Festival in May 2002, the first significant event in the scene to occur in East Williamsburg. The show was conceived of in the months following the September 11, 2001, attacks on the city when many people in the community had a prevailing sense of despair. While traveling in Chile together, artists Jake Klotz and Josefina Blanc Mendiberri decided they wanted to do something positive for everyone to lift spirits and bring the community together. Klotz had a loft at 300 Meserole Street in East Williamsburg with eight thousand square feet of space on the second floor and ten thousand square feet on the silver-painted roof.[139] Klotz was a builder, and so after getting the place in 1996 for $1,400 per month, he had built it out with walls and had previously held several concerts there but nothing on the scale of a festival. His vision was bold: a free festival lasting three days with a wide range of genres of music that would have a significant impact on the music scene itself.[140]

The event took six months to plan. Rather than curate the entire thing himself, Klotz selected one influential person from a number of different music scenes, allotted them blocks of time over the three days, and basically ran a venue on each of the two floors through the course of the festival. The music store Main Drag donated back-line equipment, including amplifiers and soundboards, for the event. Free103point9 broadcast all of the performances. The radio station WFMU announced the event in their broadcast during the week prior, which compelled Klotz to hire a bouncer as he prepared for an even bigger audience than he had originally envisioned.[141] Klotz built a stage on each level, several bathrooms, and three bars spread throughout the space where attendees could buy drinks. The musicians played for free, but Klotz got local restaurants such as Enid's, Black Betty, and Pete's Candy Store to contribute food for meals for all artists. Klotz, who was originally from Chicago, invited a couple of his well-known hometown DJs, Dante Carfagna and Ronnie Defries, to spin records on the final night. The result was nine different curators setting up fifty different acts and eleven DJs over the course of the event, generally running from four in the afternoon until two in the morning each night with music on the rooftop extending until four in the morning.[142] The music began in the heat of the afternoon, moved through sunset, and then the party grew all the way past midnight. The music ended up including indie rock, experimental music, free jazz, country, techno, rock, and other kinds of unclassified music that were common in Williamsburg at the time.

Klotz gave the loft venue Rubulad, which was run by vocalist Sari Rubinstein and guitarist Chris Thomas, the rooftop for the entirety of Friday. Rubulad had started near the Williamsburg waterfront in 1993 and were just in the process of being gentrified out; this was the first time they presented a bill in another venue.[143] As a prelude to the music, Rubulad organized an array of displays, exhibits, and activities on the roof, including a miniature carousel ride and a booth where they sold absinthe.[144] At one particularly provocative exhibit, participants were allowed to photograph their own genitalia and post the pictures anonymously on a wall as a kind of antiauthoritarian rejection of insecurities, expectations, and social norms.

For the music, Rubulad booked five bands, with a headline performance by the rock unit Fly Ashtray. Fly Ashtray had formed in the Bronx in 1983, were known for "fractured pop songs that buried their hooks under heaps of lo-fi noise," and grew out of "warped pop eccentrics working in similar territory as Pavement," as well as some shared sound with R.E.M., art punk bands like Television, and New York avant-garde rock groups such as Red Krayola and the Residents.[145] By that time, Fly Ashtray had built a reputation as one of the defining voices of the Williamsburg indie rock scene through the release of four records, though they had also developed a distinct following with regular exposure at Rubulad. At this performance Fly Ashtray headlined the night, featuring its characteristic edgy guitars and searing vocals ringing out over the postindustrial landscape that sprawled in all directions.

Downstairs, on Friday night the experimental percussionist Fritz Welch curated the entire evening. His goal was to represent a broad range of musicians that he had presented elsewhere, especially in affiliation with the Good/Bad Art Collective, which put on one-time shows that often drew together music, art installations, and performance art into one space and, commonly, one set.[146] That expansive bill included a wide range of experimental music, such as that of David Simons, an eclectic musician who worked with a range of mediums including percussion, theremin, electronics, and homemade instruments. On that particular night, Simons performed on a theremin, whereby his movements and proximity to the antennae triggered and altered the samples he had prepared, and he simultaneously used effects to alter the sound of the theremin.[147] The samples featured irregular rhythms, field recordings, operatic tidbits, and piano, often establishing rhythmic structures alongside other percussive explorations.[148] The audience was entranced.

One of the other acts on the bill was Bat Eats Plastic, fronted by guitarist Millie Benson, which employed unusual time signatures with melodic pop songs that often began from a point of familiarity and then grew louder, noisier, and more distorted as they were played, with nods to grunge punk, giving them a kind of otherworldly feel.[149] Or as Fritz Welch described it, Bat Eats Plastic "unwound pop music."[150] Benson wore a garbage bag for the performance, delivered a very physical vocal performance, and led with the song "City Beat," which later received a rave review in the *Village Voice* on release in 2003.[151]

One of the common threads of Welch's bill was pitting experimental music with body-movement pieces. The greatest example of this was a piece pairing the electrifying bodily movements of dancer Miguel Gutierrez with Jaime Fennelly performing intense improvisation with electronics and noise in a project called Sabotage.[152] Fennelly had moved from Washington, DC, to New York in 2000 to study upright bass with William Parker but soon after had begun exploring the possibilities of noise and electronics.[153] Fennelly had first met Gutierrez at the American Dance Festival a few years earlier, but after meeting again in New York in August 2001, they got a loft together at 249 Varet Street in the Morgantown area of north Bushwick, called Aqui the Bushwick, where they began working intensely together.[154] Gutierrez introduced Fennelly to Welch, who had a loft a few blocks away, and the two musicians performed with Gutierrez in the latter's twenty-four-hour performance on New Year's Eve that year. Gutierrez was blindfolded with earplugs for the entirety of the work, titled *Freedom of Information*, in protest of the United States' propaganda campaign to justify its later invasion of Iraq.[155] Welch provided wall drawings for the performance and played drums, while Fennelly elevated the intensity through noise as it reached its ecstatic conclusion.

After the New Year's Eve performance, Gutierrez and Fennelly collaborated in Sabotage, developing a number of pieces together, often working in queer imagery, with improvisation as the method bridging dance and noise together in a series of groundbreaking performances.[156] Their performance at the Brooklyn Free Music Festival was one of the earliest in this series, when they were still developing much of their vocabulary. Fennelly provided an environment of foreboding electronic drones matched by an extended opening section during which Gutierrez used a clothes iron, which occasionally emitted steam, as a way of creating tension and the suggestion of danger as he kept it close to his face and other body parts. But over the final thirty minutes, Gutierrez began taking the stage apart as a way to actively deconstruct the performance space.[157]

The Convolutionist Orchestra also played on Welch's bill at the festival; it comprised electronics and found-object instrumentalist Matt Bua, dancer and keyboardist Michiko (Mico) Takahashi, alto saxophonist Tamio Shiraishi, tubist Jesse Dulman, and Welch himself (see figure 2.5).[158] Bua first met Shiraishi in 1995 playing outside amid the ruined buildings near North Seventh Street and the East River (see figure 2.3). Bua discovered a piano soundboard that had been installed there, and the two began making music together.[159] Takahashi joined them the next year. The authorities began clearing the area out, and the band had to cease playing there in 1998. Welch joined the group around 2001. Added to this complex milieu was Naval Cassidy, who used tapes and a sampler with which he looped "sounds appropriated from popular music," often distorted, fractured, or cut up.[160] The group's sound was an eclectic mix of harsh noise, squealing saxophone, and distorted samples set against the rich, aqueous tones of the tuba.

On the first night of the Brooklyn Free Music Festival, an intense thunderstorm forced the music to move downstairs prematurely, so Rubulad left their equipment set up overnight with the goal of disassembling it in the

Figure 2.5 Michiko Takahashi dancing with the Convolutionist Orchestra as Andrew Barker (*standing*) and others look on, Brooklyn Free Music Festival, 2002 (*photo by Montgomery Knott*)

morning. One of the bands, the soulful electro-funk band Chin, had even been forced to move down and played on the twenty-by-fifteen-foot landing in the stairwell to a jam-packed crowd.[161] Drummer Andrew Barker, who curated the roof on the second night, was the first one up on the roof the next morning to get his part of the festival set up, and his first thought was "This is not going to happen" because everything was in disarray and the weather was still very windy.[162] The tents were mangled, lopsided, and twisted together. The carousel was hanging halfway off of the roof. Klotz called a number of metalworkers that he knew, and they worked to clear the roof and get everything back in order to allow the event to go on. By the time the No-Neck Blues Band took the stage, the sky was shimmering with a beautiful sunset as the backdrop. The band unveiled one of their most theatrical performances, dressed in exotic costumes, with dancer Michiko Takahashi putting on a particularly riveting show.[163]

Figure 2.6 Gold Sparkle Duo (drummer Andrew Barker and saxophonist Charles Waters) with Thurston Moore on guitar, Brooklyn Free Music Festival, 2002 (*photo by Montgomery Knott*)

Barker featured his own band, Gold Sparkle Duo with Charles Waters, on the rooftop and on this occasion they were joined by Sonic Youth guitarist Thurston Moore (see figure 2.6). Moore had had one foot in the downtown scene for a number of years, playing in a number of bands and giving artists such as Don Dietrich, Arthur Doyle, and the No-Neck Blues Band exposure on his label, Ecstatic Peace![164] The Knitting Factory had provided for a lot of crossover and synthesis between music scenes, and so Barker approached Moore for the gig. The original intention was to play mellow soundscape pieces, as a kind of somber atmosphere hung over the roof owing to the storm, but by the evening the roof was overflowing with energy, and this propelled them into a fiery post–Albert Ayler noisy free jazz set with Waters playing amped saxophone and Moore improvising on his electric guitar while Barker played furiously on his kit. Moore said to the duo after the set, "I didn't mean to go blitzkrieg!" and they all laughed.[165]

Barker also decided to include the trio Irritating HorseEye, which at that time also included noise alto saxophonist Tamio Shiraishi. He had become familiar with free jazz and rock music while working as a software engineer. But "because office work is a restrained and boring business," he sought another life.[166] Then he went to the club Minor in Tokyo around the same time, where he encountered other musicians; after buying a saxophone from a friend, he "started creating sounds by himself." It was at Minor that Shiraishi first encountered noise artist Keiji Haino (b. 1952) and played with the latter's band, Fushitsusha. After a few months, he quit the band and formed his own unit, Taco, a noise group with performance artists including Ryo Goitsuka and Toshi Tanaka. After being offered a job in New York City in 1990, he began playing at ABC No Rio around 1995 but remained an underground, almost mythical figure.[167] His work with Welch served to draw him a little more out into the community of musicians in Williamsburg.[168]

Sightings also played on the rooftop that night, a band that included guitarist Mark Morgan, drummer John Lockie, and electric bassist Richard Hoffman in an explosive set of high-octane improvised, rock-tinged noise experiments. The wind had picked back up, and it had been raining off and on, adding to the hectic and intense atmosphere of the music itself.[169] Morgan and Lockie had formed the band in March 1997 and played together for about a year and a half before they met Hoffman.[170] One of Morgan's first connections with the community of musicians happened at free103point9. He had been inspired by postpunk bands such as the Birthday Party and Gang of Four as well as the eclectic work of Keiji Haino, especially the latter's explosive and angular solo record, *Execration That Accept to Acknowledge*.[171] Sightings got more improvised and psychedelic as it developed and the players became more comfortable with each other, often working from pieces or sections that they had hashed out in practice and in a number of performances at free103point9 and some underground clubs such as Mighty Robot, the Rock Star Bar, and Warsaw.[172] The band's records *Michigan Haters* and *Absolutes* contain material that they presented at the Brooklyn Free Music Festival as the closing band before DJs took over on the roof with a torrent of searing guitar riffs, explosive noise, and occasional vocals delivered at high speed and intensity.[173] Sightings grew to become an influential postpunk-experimental-noise band of the period until they disbanded in 2013, having done numerous US and European tours and leaving behind more than a dozen records documenting the growth and development of their work.[174]

To stave off any problems with the police, Klotz contacted them in advance, and they gave him tacit approval to run the festival in the space.[175] He also invited all of the neighbors he knew in the area to attend the event to avoid any noise complaints. An estimated three thousand people attended the event, including many artists, giving rise to the idea that the festival was "the weekend that Williamsburg shut down."[176] At midnight on Sunday, the police arrived, and Klotz punctually ended the festival without incident.

Though the Brooklyn Free Music Festival was the biggest event in the era to bring the North Brooklyn music community together and to connect them with an audience, it was exemplary of many smaller events that had been happening over the previous five years. These kinds of events cut across genre, resulting in a tremendous amount of cross-pollination of musical ideas. As one participant in the free103point9 scene noted, "The poly-idiomatic nature of the scene, with no stylistic boundaries, was really exciting. People were drawing from all kinds of music."[177] The near erasing of genres was "a conscious effort," Andrew Barker recalled. "People were not making the divisions so much then. And people were borrowing from across the spectrum of music, so you had rock bands or electronica using improvisational techniques, for example, or free jazz-ers incorporating electronics or electric guitars. We threw the doors wide open to possibility."[178] Genre was in decline, people were hearing things that challenged them and opened new doors, and this, together, resulted in the Williamsburg sound: an eclectic array of sounds, origins, styles, rhythms, and instruments melded together into a coherent whole with an eye for experiment, newness, surprise, and futuristic visions.

Not all musical events were able to work as well with the local authorities as the Brooklyn Free Music Festival. Eventually the police became increasingly aware of the public performances that were happening in unlicensed venues in Williamsburg. While they sometimes turned a blind eye, an event in 2004 changed the atmosphere entirely. A performance by the experimental pop band Animal Collective at Mighty Robot drew approximately five hundred people and resulted in substantial crowds outside in the street.[179] In response, police and fire marshals began to regulate Williamsburg art spaces with greater scrutiny. They sent a warning to free103point9 and other underground venues in the area that they could no longer host shows. In December 2004, after attempting to close down another show a few blocks away in the neighborhood and getting their dates wrong, the police raided free103point9. Faced with fines and possible eviction, free103point9 ceased hosting public concerts.

220 Grand

Grand Street, between Driggs Avenue and Roebling Street, formed another vital corner of the burgeoning Williamsburg experimental music scene present in artist lofts, bars, and nightclubs. Right in the middle of the block, there was a Cuban bodega where people would sit and drink outside while playing dominoes. The owner, who made his own guitar-like instruments, would often sit outside and play music in the afternoons. The main loft that hosted the music was 220 Grand, named for its address.[180] It was an old storefront that had formerly served as a bar in the 1970s and 1980s and had subsequently been gutted.[181] Then, in July 1999, Mike Burke and Harry Rosenblum took over the lease from a friend who had built one bedroom in the back in an otherwise raw space.[182] The 1,400 square feet of space rented for only $1,200 a month, and after they acquired three additional room-mates, they could all live there very cheaply. By the following year, having built two additional bedrooms on either side of the entrance, added a pool table, and lined the walls with record shelving, Burke and Rosenblum began hosting concerts in the space.[183]

In the beginning the two curators invited friends to play and charged $5 at the door. They advertised via word of mouth and by flyers hung on light poles on the walk to the subway. They also distributed flyers at cof-fee shops on Bedford Avenue such as the Verb or at Earwax Records, and in Manhattan at Academy Records and Kim's Music and Video.[184] An av-erage night attracted about twenty-five audience members, but the room could fit as many as seventy.[185] Guitarist Jon DeRosa described the place as "a great alternative for people who did not want to play in a club. It had a low-key, friendly, community vibe. A lot of us in that circle of musicians knew that we could play gigs there, and it was fine, even encouraged, to be experimental."[186]

There was not as much drug consumption at 220 Grand as at many of the other lofts, but there was a bar down the street where people occasionally bought low-grade cocaine on their way to the show. Guests were expected to bring their own alcohol to the shows if they were planning to drink. Over time, however, 220 Grand attracted some of the same performers and cli-entele as free103point9. Burke and Rosenblum were going out to eight or nine concerts a week at places like the Knitting Factory and the Continen-tal in Manhattan and at lofts in Williamsburg, as well as late shows at the Charleston on Bedford Avenue. In all of these spaces, they built connections that would shape the types of musicians they invited to play in their space. If the bands were from out of town, the musicians often slept on the floor after the show ended. During the first concert, with a honky-tonkish rock band, the guitarist cut his hand while playing and left a bloody handprint on the wall that remained.[187]

Figure 2.7 Dan Friel live with Tyondai Braxton (*far left*) and others looking on, ca. 2002 (*private collection*)

Dan Friel

The music at 220 Grand was an eclectic mix of free jazz, guitar loop improvisation, and experimental rock. Dan Friel, of the experimental rock band Parts and Labor, played his first concert at 220 Grand on June 21, 2001, at which time he was also living in the space part-time.[188] Friel had met Mike Burke when both were involved in founding Flywheel Arts Center in western Massachusetts in 1998, and Burke was involved in producing some of the early records by Friel, Tyondai Braxton, and other figures in the emerging experimental rock scene on his label, JMZ Records.[189]

Friel's early solo work was primarily influenced by Amps for Christ and the Boredoms (see figure 2.7).[190] He was interested in exploring the noisier edges of rock and had developed a number of pieces over the course of 2001, some of which were documented on his first solo release.[191] Building from that, he chose to collaborate with bassist B. J. Warshaw, whom he had met while working at Knitting Factory Records two years prior. By the fall of 2001, the two of them were transforming Friel's solo pieces into more elaborate songs for a rock trio and joined with drummer Jim Sykes through the following year.[192] By that point, their influences had expanded to include more Japanese noise bands, such as Melt Banana and Ruins, as well as punk and alternative rock bands such as Hüsker Dü, Sonic Youth, and the Minutemen.[193] The aim was to expand beyond these initial influences by incorporating electronics and using the resulting dynamics to establish a new sound. They also employed electronics to mimic sounds from instruments such as bagpipes or a hurdy-gurdy. One critic described the process on the band's first record, *Groundswell*: "Keyboardist/electronics manipulator Dan Friel creates dense, aggressive textures with what sound like simple tone generators and oscillators . . . and the rhythm section then has their way with them, carrying the squealing cloud of melting drones . . . on an epic ride."[194] These explorations continued through a rotating cast of subsequent drummers until Parts and Labor disbanded in 2012.

Tyondai Braxton

On the same bill at 220 Grand with Friel in June 2001, multi-instrumentalist and composer Tyondai Braxton also played solo (see figure 2.8). The two had been college roommates at the Hartt School of Music in Hartford, Connecticut, where they had both studied guitar. Braxton moved to Williamsburg in 2000 and tapped into a community of experimental rock artists who played at a loft space at North Fifth Street and Kent Avenue. One of the centers of the community was the Verb Café on Bedford Avenue, where musicians would congregate and discuss their projects. That "was a really vibrant, healthy, exciting moment in the city at the time," Braxton recalled.[195]

When Braxton first arrived in the city, the indie rock community was swiftly coalescing, with bands like the Yeah Yeah Yeahs and the Strokes being just then discovered by producers and record labels. Two years later, when Braxton cofounded the band Battles, they had a practice space in the same building with other key emerging indie or experimental rock bands such as TV on the Radio, Black Dice, Animal Collective, Interpol, and Gang Gang Dance. "There was a sense of momentum at the time," Braxton observed, "like we were in dialogue with one another. We were alone together, each person isolated in their own universe, but communicating with each other. There was a lot of deconstruction and reimagination happening around what a band could be and how to use the technology that we had access to at the time. The music was filled with texture; some of it was primal, even minimalist at times."[196] In another interview, Braxton stated, "I feel like the

Figure 2.8 Tyondai
Braxton performing
at Chester Fest, outside
151 Kent Avenue,
2002 (*photo by Harry
Rosenblum*)

artist's role is to be in dialogue with their time, whatever that means, and
to translate complicated ideas simply . . . to create clarity out of something
that isn't clear, or that has disparate elements."[197]

Despite taking part in a music scene that was teeming with innovators,
Braxton already had a well-developed musical concept that dated back to
his first year in college, when he recorded and self-produced cassettes of his
solo project.[198] He was interested in using "crude electronic devices to do
something interesting compositionally," all at a time before laptops made
this kind of work easier in later years. Whether in the studio or on a stage,
Braxton employed a PS3 Boss Pitch Shifter Delay pedal to create "dense
electronic tapestries," which at the time was novel.[199] For the work that
he presented at 220 Grand, Braxton used these techniques and gear, which

allowed him to create a two-second-delay loop that he used to create counterpoint to himself instantaneously.[200] "This allowed me to not just think horizontally on the time scale," Braxton noted, "but to also think vertically as far as stacking sounds on top of one another. This opened up possibilities in texture, force, and noise," and he began using additional, more complex pedals to further develop his work.[201] "It completely changed my life," he confessed. "It opened an entire new door for me." In the years that followed, Braxton would experiment with pedals to manipulate his voice and other pedals for the electronic sounds, building out his "rig" so that he had a lot of options with which to improvise "and focus on world building in the sound."[202]

Following the solo performances that Friel and Braxton did at 220 Grand, the two set off on a double solo tour through the Midwest, playing in Cleveland, Columbus, Minneapolis, Madison, Milwaukee, Chicago, Ann Arbor, Rochester, Pittsburgh, and Buffalo. The following year Braxton cofounded Battles, one of the key experimental rock bands of that decade, utilizing techniques, concepts, and technology that he had developed in his solo project, like the material he had presented at 220 Grand and other venues in Williamsburg in the early 2000s.[203]

Jon DeRosa

Another figure who received early exposure at 220 Grand was Jon DeRosa, with his band Aarktica. Originally from New Jersey, DeRosa had moved to New York in 1998 to attend New York University. DeRosa's sonic world came into being shortly thereafter when in the winter of 1998 he had a rare ear infection that resulted in the total loss of hearing in his right ear. In the wake of developing this disability, he began the project Aarktica to "re-create my version of hearing."[204] DeRosa's deafness was accompanied by a series of aural hallucinations, a "really weird aquatic sensory feeling," and his body equilibrium was thrown into disarray. "It was therapy for me, trying to re-create sound as I heard it," DeRosa explained, with music that included ambient drones that often transformed in front of the audience very slowly.[205]

By the time he was playing at 220 Grand, DeRosa was beginning to incorporate other elements, especially free jazz concepts (see figure 2.9).[206] He often used his gigs at the space as an opportunity to debut new works. These projects eventually evolved into a larger ensemble version of Aark-

Figure 2.9 Jon DeRosa (*left*) and Molly Sheridan at 220 Grand, 2002 (*photo by Harry Rosenblum*)

tica that included trumpeter Nate Wooley, saxophonists Seth Misterka and Harry Rosenblum, and drummer Mike Pride. The group released *Bleeding Light*, a tone poem to New York City that, according to DeRosa, "captured the present moment at that time, the darkness and the alienation of the city and the music of that time."[207] Aarktica also played at other venues on the scene, such as the Right Bank Café and Rooftop Films, and eventually played across the river at the Mercury Lounge and the Knitting Factory.

While many of the musicians at 220 Grand became better known later for working in experimental rock, during their early years in Brooklyn, they played improvised music or worked in genre-crossing contexts that defied definition. The relaxed, intimate atmosphere of 220 Grand was perfect for musicians who were just beginning to launch their careers in an environment where experimentation was encouraged.[208] The space hosted well-established musicians such as Cooper-Moore, who played in a duo with keyboardist Matt Mottel, and figures such as saxophonist and flutist Arthur

Doyle. Sabir Mateen's band TEST also played the space at the peak of their abilities, coming off of several years of being very active on the scene. And a number of figures active elsewhere in the early Williamsburg scene, such as Andrew Barker, Charles Waters, Tatsuya Nakatani, and Mike Pride, all performed with their working bands or in new, one-off formations as they were working to get their footing in the music scene. Two days after the 9/11 attacks, 220 Grand hosted a concert as a memorial to the tragedy and a gathering of the community.[209]

Another venue, the gay bar Luxx (later the Trash Bar), just down the block at 256 Grand Street, hosted music in the same rooms that formerly served as a Dominican nightclub, still equipped with head mirrors and dancer poles. The music at Luxx was, in many ways, an extension of the free103point9 and 220 Grand scenes, with bands like the SB and Fear and Trembling (Harry Rosenblum, Casey Block, and Noelle Dorsey) playing there with some regularity.

Free103point9 at Office Ops

After the Brooklyn Free Music Festival, the first major concert in a scene removed from that of Bedford Avenue, took place at Office Ops in East Williamsburg in 2004. It was "a building in the early phases of gentrification that developers intended for startup companies, but free103point9 just rented it for the event."[210] The first two events were two free103point9 seventh-anniversary concerts held in March. The first night featured People, comprising guitarist Mary Halvorson and drummer Kevin Shea, and Jessica Pavone's solo viola alongside avant-noise indie rock bands Japanther and Parts and Labor.[211]

The second night had an even more eclectic bill, including "completely improvised" movement and dance by Tony Eaton, who drew from "surfing, rock climbing, breaking, contact improvisation, the martial arts, Buddhism, butoh and yoga."[212] This performance was immediately followed by Seth Nehil, who created sound art "using found objects and instruments, old records, reel-to-reel machines, discarded magnetic tape, and other detritus." Nehil was interested in the "sensual surface of found objects, materials, and spaces, and the inner dynamics of their acoustic properties. Without altering those properties, the possibilities of the studio are explored as a means of transforming sounds into dense interactions—meditations on physicality, germination and disorientation."[213]

The peeesseye

The peeesseye, formed in Brooklyn in 2002, comprised percussionist Fritz Welch, guitarist Chris Forsyth, and electronicist Jaime Fennelly. It added the component of lowercase minimalism to the diverse range of performances.[214] The peeesseye was a departure from the downtown scene that was so pervasive at the time. They were inspired by contemporary music happening in Berlin and other parts of Europe, such as Perlonex, Alex Dörner, Kai Fagaschinski, and Andrea Neuman, as well as Japanese Onkyo and a range of music from folk to minimalism to hardcore.[215] Japanese Onkyo was a kind of electronic minimalist music that was "predominated by silences and pauses between sparsely placed singular sounds."[216] It had only just emerged in Tokyo around the turn of millennium, led most prominently by Yoshihide Otomo.[217]

After meeting for a session at Welch's loft, there was an immediate connection between the members of the peeesseye; they began to distill their sound rapidly, "and it just mutated from there as we experimented," Welch explained.[218] Fennelly saw their music as developing right from the soundscape of the city: "It came from the experience of living down the street from a garbage dump, a wonton factory, a meat distribution plant, the trucks coming and going, the filth, but also humanity in those spaces."[219]

Fennelly was exploring no-input feedback with a mixer and pedals, by sending the output into the input on the mixer, "creating many threads of feedback channels that I then was harnessing. It is chaotic, but there are ways to control it. It is also very sensitive to micromovements, so it is ideally suited to improvisation."[220] The techniques had been pioneered by Toshimaru Nakamura, a Japanese noise artist, in the late 1990s, "turning a mixer into a bank of oscillators," but had spread to the United States, and the techniques were quickly taking on new forms and were being employed in new environments.[221] Fennelly opened up a full range of possibilities with the no-input mixer at the time, which was a key innovation.

Forsyth employed Brillo pads, sandpaper, and pieces of metal for a prepared guitar, focused on understated melodies. Welch threw open the possibilities for drawing all manner of noise sounds by using many different percussive devices on all surfaces of the drum kit. Welch also saw a clear connection to his visual art. One perceptive critic noted, "It really feels like [the peeesseye's music] is more like a sculptural form with a particular kind of mass and structure, like this thing that gets built as it's played."[222] Welch also wore a brightly colored costume for the performance, stating,

Figure 2.10 The peeesseye: (*from left*) Chris Forsyth, Jaime Fennelly, and Fritz Welch, live at Cave12, Geneva, Switzerland, 2006 (*photo by Marion Innocenzi*)

"It's important for a little bit of humor to enter into a really serious realm like improvised music."[223]

The peeesseye's performance was a slowly evolving experiment in collective improvisation, exhibiting a sound that was "all stretched out and low volume with vast sheets of texture and units of sound that shifted with sharp stops and starts rather than any type of call-and-response or emotive interaction more typical of free jazz improvisation."[224] The band's sound often included multiple layers of texture and abrasive ambience tinctured with sparse, irregular percussive intrusions (that sometimes swelled to thunderous explosions), distorted human voicings, and bits of guitar, the last of which served as the tether that kept it loosely grounded as experiments unfolded (see figure 2.10). "The urgency of the live setting was an important part of the band's musical output," Fennelly added.[225] The band diligently developed over the course of more than a decade, demonstrating breakthroughs in group sound with *Pestilence and Joy* and their final record, *Sci Fi Death Mask*, a masterful statement as a culmination of their many years of work.[226] In total, the first concert at Office Ops inhabited four rooms in the postindustrial loft type of space and drew together some of the most cutting-edge experimentalists working in a diverse array of genres and media.

Then, in June 2004, free103point9 put on one of their last festivals, "Assembled: Free Jazz + Electronics," again at Office Ops, "featuring free jazz musicians interacting with electronic performers."[227] The event lasted only one night but inhabited three rooms and the rooftop of the space. Pianist Matthew Shipp, well established on the downtown scene, and percussionist Guillermo E. Brown played on the ground floor, where they worked on material that would later be recorded for their album *Telephone Popcorn*, and featured Brown experimenting with electronics when not playing drums.[228] Shipp and Brown had met while playing together in the David S. Ware Quartet, and Shipp had hired Brown as a drummer for two of his own recordings, *Nu Bop* and *Equilibrium*, before they began working as a duo. Also of significant influence was Shipp's work with DJ Spooky, FLAM, and Anti-Pop Consortium, who really opened his eyes to the possibilities of recording improvisations over prerecorded beats that served as "raw material" that could later be cut up, distorted, mixed, or otherwise manipulated as part of the production process.[229] Though *Telephone Popcorn* witnessed Brown working primarily from a laptop, electronics, and Zendrum, instead of drum kit, Shipp observed that his collaborator "was a part of DJ culture, he was of a younger generation than me, and that whole world seemed to come to him as naturally as jazz." Reflecting on his own development, Shipp noted, "Doing all of that work in that period, working in the studio, definitely gave me a different sense of resonance and placement."[230]

The set also included the debut of Acid Birds, led by Andrew Barker, who had written a graphic score for Charles Waters and Jaime Fennelly. This was a jumping-off point for this new band that would later tour widely in Europe and release a series of records. Barker described the music as "psychedelic free jazz" in which Fennelly's electronics, harmonium, and tape echo enabled the other two musicians to amplify themselves. The band also explored the possibilities of harmonium drones mixing with "jittery electronics and extended techniques."[231]

In another room, well-known multi-instrumentalist Daniel Carter improvised alongside DJ Matt Mikas. Mikas used an interactive audio response kit to create a sonic environment in which Carter improvised. Mikas described the project as "a functional collaborative composition conceived as an analogous representation of theme and repetition based on acknowledged consent to experimentation and re-appropriation." It involved "themes of contemporary political paranoia and cut up techniques," and Mikas used

Figure 2.11 Tom Roe (*left*) and Charles Waters (Andrew Barker not pictured), Office Ops, 2004 (*photo by Peter Gannushkin*)

vinyl records of manipulated computer beats that worked with Carter's sounds.[232] Mikas had developed the project in other settings, adding drumbeats or analog synth sounds.

Carter and Mikas were followed by Jaime Fennelly and Chris Forsyth working with keyboardist Shawn Hansen and saxophonist Chris Heenan in a band that later became known as Phantom Limb and Bison.[233] The band exhibited a mixture of rock, jazz, and noise concepts and aesthetics. Hansen played an EMS Synthi AKS, a 1970s-era modular synthesizer, or used radio feedback loops, and Fennelly sometimes put sine wave inputs into his mixer or used his usual no-input mixer at the gig. The band improvised off structures. "We focused on long-form improvisations, usually ranging from forty-five to ninety minutes," Hansen later noted. "Fennelly and I both used electronics, so we worked in the bass quadrant. Heenan switched between also saxophone and contrabass clarinet, so we had to give him space since the rest of us were amplified." The aim was "to reach some kind of elation by the end of each performance."[234] In other contexts around that time, Phantom Limb and Bison played to French New Wave director Chris Marker's short film *Le Jetée* (1962), a postapocalyptic depiction of time-travel experiments, using the images as springboards for their improvisations.[235]

Later that night, N.R.A., a band made up of percussion master Tatsuya Nakatani, Vic Rawlings on cello and open-circuit electronics, and Ricardo Arias playing a balloon-bass kit, took the stage as they continued to refine their booming, edgy, metallic experimentation. The concert served as a pivotal moment for many of the artists involved, as they began or deepened their interest in combining free jazz with electronics and noise. The long evolution of the eclectic improvised–free jazz–noise scene in Williamsburg had reached a new peak, and this community played a direct role in the making of the Bushwick music scene in the years after the Office Ops concerts.

No Fun Festival

Another festival that also happened in 2004 was crucial for drawing together disparate elements of noise into one venue and event. The No Fun Festival at Northsix, at 66 North Sixth Street, was a three-day event on March 19–21 and bore national significance.[236] As keyboardist Matt Mottel observed, "Up until that point, bands from the American underground that were explicitly connected to the noise, industrial, and hardcore scenes did not have a single event that codified the scene and identified it as one. No Fun Fest did it."[237] The festival was organized by Carlos Giffoni, a Venezuela-born American noise artist who had moved to the city from Miami in 2000, who felt "there was no broad festival for experimental music that was oriented toward noise at the time and lots of international bands that I had met through touring, so I wanted to bring all of that together in one place with the No Fun Festival."[238] In addition to the international acts, the festival included many bands that had gotten recognition through being asked by Thurston Moore to open for Sonic Youth in the early 2000s. Some of the connections were explicit, such as Sonic Youth guitarist Lee Ranaldo's collaborations with free jazz drummer William Hooker, and Moore's electric improvised set with Jim O'Rourke, drummer Chris Corsano, and saxophonist Paul Flaherty.

Juxtaposing the New York experimental scene at Tonic at the time, the No Fun Festival proposed a different kind of avant-garde, one focused on noise and drawn from around the country, especially from the Midwest. Michigan's Wolf Eyes, one of the premier bands on the festival bill, had just signed with the Sub Pop label, which one observer said was for noise what the signing of Nirvana with DGC was for postpunk.[239] Wolf Eyes and some of the other bands treated their audiences to abrasive walls of sound as they represented a fusion of Japanese and European noise with American hardcore.

Bringing these bands to Williamsburg at that moment connected the New York avant-garde to the national and international underground. One attendee recounted the moment: "Wolf Eyes' set was striking, it was all fist pumps and mayhem led by John Olson onstage, with the crowd responding in mosh pit hardcore-style action; harsh electronics, Iggy snarl'd vox from Nate Young and Aaron Dilloway."[240] Giffoni, in reflecting on the festival years later, stated, "Some of the people on the festival did not know each other before and were coming from different parts of the country and the world, but it felt like we all belonged together in that space. It was a special moment for experimental music with multiple generations who felt connected to each other."[241] The No Fun Festival ran annually in New York through 2009, with the final event held in Stockholm, Sweden, in 2010.[242]

End of the Free103point9 Scene

Free103point9 was forced to close, along with many other lofts, as policing and gentrifying pressures were used to create an atmosphere that was increasingly hostile to practicing artists as well as longtime residents. "I noticed the changes in Williamsburg around 1999–2000," Jose Ramos, a Puerto Rican union sheet metal worker noted. Buildings in the neighborhood started getting fixed, new people were moving into the area and buying property, what was left of the factories and warehouses were all closing, and white people were moving into Williamsburg in much greater numbers. The changes were slow but steady. There was an increased police presence. Then bars began popping up here and there, large residential buildings began going up, the dynamics of the streets and neighborhood changed. Most of the Latinx residents who were able to stay in the neighborhood were those who lived in co-op–owned buildings. The people who were displaced moved to Pennsylvania, North Carolina, Florida, and elsewhere. "For those of us who remained here," another resident stated, "we encountered the attitude of, 'You are poor, why are you here?' even though we had been here all of our lives. The street culture and the parades really diminished."[243] Real estate developers and Wall Street bankers followed closely on the heels of the artists flocking to Williamsburg.

As saxophonist Seth Misterka observed, "Circa 2002, I remember walking by the old Gretsch Building on Broadway, which was one of the first loft buildings that was converted into luxury condos, and thinking, 'Why would rich people want to live in this neighborhood?' It was, and still is to a certain extent, really polluted, loud, and just not very nice. I lived and worked there because the affordability allowed a great deal of freedom for myself as an artist, not because it was a nice neighborhood."[244] Another artist and writer on the scene wrote in 2002, "No one can pin an exact date on when [Williamsburg] became such an atrocious quasi-trendy arthood with all the 'one stop to the East Village' pretensions" after the area had become "a living museum of hipster Gen-X dotcom irony."[245] As Sabir Mateen, who moved there from Manhattan in 2001, reflected, "Most of the people living there in 2015, the gentrifiers, could not have set foot there back in those days without getting robbed or beat up."[246] It was not a very hospitable place, but it worked for those artists who were willing to forgo everyday comforts for the opportunity to be a part of an increasingly dynamic and prolific art scene.

In the early years after the turn of the millennium, art in Williamsburg was getting increasingly commodified. Williamsburg had been discovered by the New York arts intelligentsia, and they were descending on it to anoint the stars and to drive a profit. Small DIY galleries turned into crowded Friday nights with cameras flashing. Graffiti artists, who just a few years previously had been outcasts plying their trade in the shadows, were now getting reviews in elite magazines and drawing huge crowds to their openings.[247] When spaces were available, the DIY could and did flourish, but as these spaces became increasingly valuable in the voracious New York real estate market, it became more and more difficult to find spaces where these music scenes could germinate, grow, and serve as the focal point of the community. The loft era had mostly come to an end, and the music would now shift to galleries, cafés, bars, and clubs as the face of Williamsburg itself began to change rapidly.

CHAPTER THREE

Art Galleries, Clubs, and Bohemian Cafés

The Williamsburg DIY, 2001–2006

It's all about each individual discovering their own potential and the power of being curious.

— *Anthony Braxton, in Koenig, "Anthony Braxton: Between the Quadrants" (2002)*

By the turn of the millennium, Bedford Avenue between South Sixth and North Ninth Streets had become the social center of the bohemian arts community in Williamsburg. Whereas at the beginning of the 1990s a majority of the storefronts along the avenue were boarded up, small galleries had given way to cafés, bookstores, and small grocery stores amid Polish delis, pawn shops, a Salvation Army outlet, and family-run pharmacies.[1] Many commercially zoned storefronts that had served as makeshift residences over the previous decade were now being converted into retail stores, restaurants, and bookstores, especially on Grand Street, Bedford Avenue, and North Sixth Street. One resident recalled suddenly feeling as if one could stay in the neighborhood on a Friday night to socialize because there were places to go, whereas previously there had been only a couple of bars in the entire North Side.[2]

Musicians and artists lived throughout the neighboring blocks in lofts and run-down apartments. The Bedford Avenue L train stop at North Seventh Street became synonymous with the art scene at the time, still bringing people from the Lower East Side and other parts of Manhattan. It also set the foundation for the North Brooklyn arts community to be interconnected along the postindustrial L train corridor, eventually spreading and moving into East Williamsburg and Bushwick, with an offshoot eventually appearing along the M train line in Ridgewood, Queens, in the late 2010s.

At the dawn of the new millennium, a new community began to form that would grow and evolve the music scene in new directions and in new spaces. In some ways, they were a different socioeconomic class of musicians: private university-trained musicians who had studied with some of the highest-profile figures in music. As a whole, this wave of musicians benefited from the support of foundation grants more than any group that had operated in Williamsburg before that time.[3] The emphasis on creative composition, a hallmark of many of these figures, allowed practitioners to draw financial support aimed at European classical music, which did not exist in the same amounts for improvised or experimental music. In other words, the experiments of this new wave were more successfully legitimized by connecting them to a musical lineage that was institutionally recognized than those of the musicians operating in earlier phases of the Williamsburg scene.

This wave also began the geographical scattering of the community of musicians, even if Williamsburg remained the epicenter of activity. Some musicians began to live in areas removed from Williamsburg proper, moving down the G train line into the Fort Greene neighborhood and adjoining parts of Clinton Hill and Bedford-Stuyvesant, an area that had an extensive history as a Black cultural center, having been home to a wide range of artists and entertainers in the 1980s, 1990s, and 2000s, ranging from filmmaker Spike Lee and saxophonist Branford Marsalis to comedians Chris Rock and Dave Chapelle.[4]

This transformation of the music scene brought a heavy influence that could only have been born in music school, making its imprint on the character, purpose, and substance of the music. "Creative music" that wedded the improvisation of jazz with the compositional structures of classical music, as well as many other, sometimes international influences, became the new vogue. It was not that this had never happened before, but the approach increasingly became the lingua franca of the avant-garde, reflecting a union that was primarily forged in music schools.

Anthony Braxton and the Wesleyan University Community

This new wave of musicians came primarily from Wesleyan University in Middletown, Connecticut, where they had studied with multi-instrumentalist visionary Anthony Braxton. Braxton was an early member of the Association for the Advancement of Creative Musicians in Chicago in the 1960s; has been a singular innovator, improviser, and composer over the decades since; and has recorded prolifically. Braxton's influence on the Wesleyan graduates was immense, though not in the traditional ways a teacher might make their mark. Braxton was to not committed creating clones of himself but rather sought to open his students' eyes to themselves and the possibilities of their own musical ideas.[5] As one student noted, Braxton "would find whatever aspect of a student's work was most unusual or striking and encourage the student to expand that aspect."[6] Braxton explained his teaching philosophy as "I teach fifty percent, but I also learn fifty percent," meaning that he saw education as a bilateral exchange between teacher and student.[7] Commenting on his own music, he stated, "My music is just like my life: in between quadrants. Not [exclusively] in the black or white or jazz or classical communities. I have found a life that moves between the spaces and has given me the possibility to take from various idioms and integrate them into my formal schemes."[8]

The ability to defy easy categorization is something that Braxton passed on to all of his students. He stated, "It's all about each individual discovering their own potential and the power of being curious."[9] All of his students spoke of his enthusiasm and limitless imagination when it came to conceiving of new compositions or unusual ensembles, or delving into musical territory never before explored. Braxton worked regularly with graphic scores, geometric grids, performative cues, and other signals and experimental types of notation that challenged the traditional vocabulary of conduction and orchestration.[10] Some of his theories and ideas are explained in his multivolume *Complete Tri-Axium Writings*. Braxton instilled a kind of self-confidence in his students that enabled them to discover their own voices, aesthetics, and talents, which directly countered the approach most music schools took at the time.[11] Multi-instrumentalist Matthew Welch recalled

Braxton getting wide-eyed when he first told him that he played bagpipes in addition to alto saxophone, and they immediately sat down and made a list of over fifty ideas that Braxton had for the bagpipes.[12] Other students recounted similar experiences.

In Middletown in the late 1990s, graduate students Chris Jonas and James Fei, along with undergraduates Jackson Moore, Seth Misterka, and Seth Dellinger—all saxophone players except the last, who was a bassist—worked with Braxton.[13] Matthew Welch also studied with Braxton in 1999–2001. Alto saxophonist Brandon Evans, who had first encountered Braxton's recordings and writings while living in San Francisco, eventually relocated without formally enrolling at Wesleyan and attended Braxton's classes there in 1993–94 and was thus affiliated with that scene.[14] Taylor Ho Bynum did his undergraduate degree at Wesleyan in 1994–98 and then returned to work further with Braxton in graduate school in 2003–5. Guitarist Mary Halvorson studied with Braxton from 1998 to 2002.

Misterka, Moore, Dellinger, and Bynum were all part of the Middletown Creative Orchestra, which soon drew in violist Jessica Pavone, who attended the Hartt School at the nearby University of Hartford.[15] Pavone had become alienated by the orchestral focus of her program and yearned to do something creative and more aesthetically interesting. She began to find her path while experimenting with improvisation during her final semester at Hartt in 1998. A friend invited her to see a Braxton concert in Middletown at that time, which opened her eyes to the possibilities of creative music. Soon afterward, Pavone joined the orchestra, composing her own music and improvising, which she found to be a "liberating experience after the conservative atmosphere of the conservatory."[16] The Middletown Creative Orchestra was prolific in 1997–99, releasing five records that documented live performances, all of which appeared on DIY labels run by its various members. It was a staging ground for much of what was to come, as members of the orchestra had the opportunity to present their own compositions within a supportive creative and experimental community, as well as benefiting from the self-production process that brought the works to the general public.[17] Key members of the orchestra would soon after play a role in the emergence of the next phase of the Brooklyn avant-garde.

In 1999 and 2000, Fei, Moore, Misterka, Dellinger, and Pavone all moved to Brooklyn, some sharing apartments in locations concentrated around Fort Greene.[18] Chris Jonas had been living in Carroll Gardens since 1995, while commuting to graduate school at Wesleyan.[19] Brandon Evans had moved to

New York in 1995, and though he never lived in Brooklyn, he built ties with many of the other post-Wesleyan musicians as they began to grow the DIY presence in the early years of the new millennium.[20] Other Braxton students followed, including librettist Jason Cady and multi-instrumentalist Matthew Welch in 2001, guitarist Mary Halvorson in 2002, and multi-instrumentalist Taylor Ho Bynum in 2005.

In 2003 Braxton remarked about this generation of students, "My hope is that more opportunities will be given to this new group of creative people who are here now in New York, but they're not getting any play from the media because there's so much misunderstanding about music that is neither 'jazz' nor 'classical.'"[21] Despite these obstacles this post-Wesleyan community would form a major wave in the emergence and evolution of the Brooklyn avant-garde, with its firmest imprint on music happening in Williamsburg in the early 2000s.

One other major point of Braxton's influence on all of his students was his encouragement of DIY practice, especially in terms of organizing concerts. Seth Misterka organized long-running music series at the Right Bank Café and Newsonic Loft.[22] Jackson Moore founded a series at the Pourhouse that outlived his involvement.[23] Jessica Pavone and Mary Halvorson were actively involved in renting performance spaces and organizing many one-time shows.[24] It was as if this wave of students had been primed to participate in the Williamsburg DIY before even arriving there.

Many of Braxton's students also created their own record labels.[25] Brandon Evans cofounded Parallactic Records in 1997, which was incredibly active in documenting his own work and that of his post-Wesleyan contemporaries as well as Braxton and Sonny Simmons until around 2005.[26] He explained his motivations by stating, "The idea of self-production comes back to the desire to document the music without it being a commercial affair."[27] Misterka founded Newsonic Music, which released the early recordings of the Middletown Creative Orchestra, as well as many records by Misterka, Brian Glick, and other Wesleyan graduates, after he moved into his studio loft in Williamsburg in 2000, where he also recorded many sessions.[28] Jessica Pavone founded Peacock Recordings, which released her early recordings and those of Jackson Moore.[29] Taylor Ho Bynum cofounded Firehouse 12 Records, which, though based in New Haven, became a major label that played a key role in drawing attention to his own work and that of his contemporaries.[30] James Fei and Brian Glick also founded labels that released a few recordings each.[31] Significant advances in recording technology in the mid- to late 1990s made much of this possible.[32]

Sideshow Gallery

One of Bedford Avenue's many emerging art galleries, the Sideshow Gallery, occasionally booked music to coincide with art openings and other events. One particularly propitious encounter there took place on October 30, 2002, when guitarist Mary Halvorson and violist Jessica Pavone played their first concert as a duo in the space.[33] Trumpeter Peter Evans, who happened to meet Halvorson at a weekend jazz program when they were both teenagers, remarked how certain key elements of her distinct sound had formed fairly early: "She would play these very pretty voicings and melodies, but her solos were really twisted and angular with huge interval leaps and jagged rhythms."[34] After having met the previous summer, Halvorson and Pavone had developed an instant connection and had been rehearsing several times a week for several months.[35] They would meet informally, each bring a composition, make dinner, and then practice the two pieces. In the beginning the songs were usually short instrumental pieces, but they began to lengthen and evolve as they added vocals, sometimes laced with humor or irony.[36] Pavone observed of their duo, "The music . . . in some ways feels like the closest thing I have to a diary."[37]

The concert at the Sideshow Gallery did not garner a significant audience. Pavone happened to record the session on a room mic, revealing that though their ideas were not yet refined, the buds of many of their ideas were present, ready to bloom.[38] It was the beginning of one of the 2000s' most prolific and innovative duos, which over the following ten years would evolve and grow, putting out four highly praised records (see figure 3.1). Their music was a searching, sometimes almost meditative exploration that drew the audience into their intimate improvisations and compositions. Soon after, Halvorson and Pavone began making their way through the Brooklyn scene in a series of concerts at the Pourhouse, the Read Café, Barbès, and the Right Bank Café, where they workshopped their material, some of which would eventually appear on their debut record, *Prairies*.[39] Pavone later stated, "I didn't think about it much back then, but looking back, we were almost always the only women on most of those bills. It was a very male scene, but we made our music and were proactive in making opportunities for ourselves since they didn't come easily."[40]

By September 2003 they were prepared to present their work at Tonic, which had inherited much of the Knitting Factory scene since the latter had closed the previous year, and now was the premier stage for the New York avant-garde.[41] Critic Kurt Gottschalk characterized the music as "string

Figure 3.1 Jessica Pavone (*left*) and Mary Halvorson, Tonic, 2006 (*photo by Peter Gannushkin*)

puzzles, variations on cat's cradles and owl's eyes that are curious and delicate. The short tracks, precisely played, are reminiscent of [Anton] Webern, instrumental lines that suggest larger worlds without elaborating or even repeating. A couple of vocal tracks add to the feeling of peeking in on something, glimpses of very personal musics. What to Halvorson and Pavone might seem like prairies come off to the listener as teeny patches of grass in forests unseen for the trees."[42]

Fellow guitarist Elliott Sharp, meanwhile, detected a kind of daring aesthetic fused with an intense studied approach in their music and music composition.[43] Critic Peter Margasak noted the difficulty in categorizing the work of the duo, while noting their "jagged counterpoint, extended harmony, dynamics that dissolve notions of foreground and background, composition and improvisation."[44] Pianist Matthew Shipp, who recorded them for the Blue Series, which he managed for the Thirsty Ear label a few years later, wrote, "The way the music is shaped is unpredictable but sounds familiar, even though you would be hard put to figure out who or why there is a familiarity to it. And it is beautiful. They push the envelope but are not afraid to just be musical when that is what is called for."[45] Fittingly, Halvorson and Pavone described their work as "the American prairie sound rebuilt with modernity."[46] Halvorson, in describing her process, wrote of instrumental techniques that she enjoyed, "repetition, the balance between symmetry and asymmetry, familiar and unfamiliar, direct and circumvented, and the absurd and the nonsensical."[47]

The early concerts and the release of *Prairies* allowed Halvorson and Pavone to set up a tour through the southern United States and the Rust Belt in January 2006, playing at the Red Room in Baltimore; an unspecified venue in Richmond; Church of the Covenant in Greensboro, North Carolina; the Flicker Theatre in Athens, Georgia; the Eyedrum in Atlanta, Georgia; Rivoli Art Mill in Chattanooga, Tennessee; the Firebird Studio in Lexington, Kentucky; ACME Art Company in Columbus, Ohio; and Garfield Artworks in Pittsburgh, Pennsylvania.[48] Their goal was to play in New York about once per month and to organize two tours per year, but opportunities opened up quickly. A tour of the Northeast and Midwest soon followed, visiting Boston, Northampton (Massachusetts), Buffalo, Ann Arbor, Chicago, and Philadelphia in May and June. They played at the Other Half Festival at Tonic in New York in August and had their first European date at the Unlimited 20 Festival in Wels, Austria, on November 10.[49]

Three records followed in 2007–12, as well as numerous domestic and international tours and festival performances.[50] By 2008 they were playing the majority of their concerts outside of New York, and in October and November 2009 they did a European tour that began in Brussels and then played extensively in Italy.[51] They also performed at the Experimental Arts Festival in Athens, Georgia, in April 2010.[52] Halvorson, in particular, was heralded as a star on the rise, making singular breakthroughs on guitar.[53] Both eventually began to focus on other projects.

Right Bank Café

The Right Bank Café was one of the few venues from early 1990s Williamsburg that survived to the turn of the millennium. By that time the second floor had evolved into an art gallery, and by late 2001 saxophonist Seth Misterka began booking "avant-garde jazz and experimental music" there on Tuesday nights.[54] It was a pretty small space, so that a crowd of thirty people made the place feel packed, making it ideal for the kind of experimental music that Misterka featured there. The close confines allowed dedicated listeners to immerse themselves in the sounds of any given night. The café was eager to allow performers space in which to experiment as the audience

Figure 3.2 Mike Pride Trio (the MP3 or MPthree): (*from left*) Mary Halvorson, Mike Pride, and Ken Filiano, at Freddy's Backroom, 2003 (*photo by Scott Friedlander*)

looked on. Behind the stage where the bands played, there was a beautiful backdrop of the Manhattan skyline across the river.[55]

Transit

One band to emerge from the Right Bank scene was Misterka's collaborative project Transit, which included drummer Jeff Arnal, trumpeter Nate Wooley, and bassist Reuben Radding. Misterka and Arnal had been performing in the city for a few years, and Radding for much longer, but the Right Bank was one of the first places in the city where Wooley played live.[56] Radding recalled getting a call from Arnal on the day of the gig in March 2003 and just showed up to play with them, but it all coalesced into something, and the band quickly took off.[57] In the beginning they rarely talked about what they wanted the music to be; rather, they just met and played sessions together, and a chemistry formed among the musicians. They would take turns starting a piece with a seed of an idea and see how the others responded. Not long after the first gigs at the Right Bank, the four musicians met at Misterka's loft and recorded a record together. Arnal was the organizing force behind the band, and Misterka's procedural efforts behind the recording made things happen. The band later played at Barbès and a few other venues in Brooklyn, including the Clean Feed Records Festival in September 2006.

Employing "graphic scores, harmonic predeterminations, and conceptual systems of rules and signs," Transit created sophisticated interchanges among musicians that would then build and recede in intensity.[58] The sounds themselves were deeply rooted in the Brooklyn of that time, featuring odes to trains, canals, neighborhoods, and the distinct cultures and peculiarities that inhabited those spaces. At times metallic and industrial, at other times lonely and mournful, their music contained myriad moods and often evolved from one phase to another quickly. The sounds they produced captured the changing Brooklyn, caught in its postindustrial, not-yet-gentrified moment.

Dynamite Club

To add to the eclectic mix of music, Dynamite Club, a rock band with improvisational leanings led by drummer Mike Pride and guitarist Kentaro Saito, played some of their first Brooklyn gigs at the Right Bank.[59] The two musicians had encountered one another while both attending the New School in 2001. Saito was from Japan. Pride was originally from Maine but moved to New York in 2000 to study. He had previously studied film at the University of Southern Maine and had also pursued painting, but an encounter with trombonist David Baker spurred his interest in jazz.[60] After one semester at the New School, he had had enough and turned instead to establishing himself on the New York music scene. He played in a number of bands, including leading his own group, the MP3. Their record, *Sleep Cells*, is one of the earliest to feature guitarist Mary Halvorson, whom he had met during their brief time together at the New School (see figure 3.2).[61]

According to Pride, Saito was "an amazing bebop guitar player." But their music became anything but bebop as it developed. Originally, Pride recalled, "I used to write a bunch of duo music for the two of us. We would do twenty compositions in twenty minutes or something like that. That was called Be More Naked. And after every short composition was finished, we would take off an article of clothing. But I would bundle up and wear layers upon layers of clothing. He would show up in shorts and T-shirts. So, by the third song, he's naked. So we did that, and then that became Dynamite Club."[62] Their approach made them shred insecurities and become vulnerable in order to delve into the musical ideas they possessed.

Like much of what happened in the free103point9 scene, the presence of Dynamite Club at a place like the Right Bank was an example of the eclectic music series in Williamsburg at the time. Rock, improvised left-of-jazz, noise, electronic, and other types of experimental music from across the spectrum could all be found intermingling, with many musicians taking part in a number of different genres. A night might open with an improvised trio, follow that with an electro-noise set, and then close with a rock band, or some other combination. The evenings were open to personal expression in a wide array of forms, and this variety naturally bred a great deal of fusion and cross-pollination.

Like many series, however, the live music lasted only as long as the venue was able to support it. In 2003 Kerry Smith sold the building. Intent on going out with a bang, Misterka organized one final bill. On the closing night, Saito, "who was notorious for his wild performances, was literally bouncing off the walls and accidentally kicked a hole in the wall," Misterka recalled with a laugh. "It was a fitting end to the series and to the Right Bank."[63]

Read Café

Over on Bedford Avenue, near the corner of North Eighth Street, the "book-strewn" Read Café emerged as another dynamic center for music beginning in late 2000, having only opened its doors the previous year.[64] The Read had a "slew of odd books and highbrow magazines to flip through" and was equipped with "a sweet backyard."[65] Percussionist and electronicist Aaron Siegel, newly arrived from Ann Arbor, Michigan, curated the Eggwolf Series at the café.

Siegel referred to the music at the Read as a "neighborhood scene," which featured mostly Williamsburg-based artists and also drew its audience primarily from the local area.[66] Building an audience was fundamentally different before the advent of social media. Siegel listed some of the shows in the *New York Press* and occasionally emailed a small list of people from the community of musicians that he knew in New York, but much of it was still generated face-to-face and by word of mouth.[67] Just fifteen or twenty people filled the café. Participants also recalled that many audience members just happened to be walking by on a given evening and curiously poked their heads in the door after catching a glimpse of a particular performance from out on the street.[68] Once inside, onlookers found the space to be "informal and intimate" and were welcome to "listen, eat, or read."[69] Siegel joked that it was like welcoming people to his living room; they moved tables out of the way, and some people sat in the large windowsill to watch.

Siegel's vision for the Eggwolf Series was "a performance opportunity for improvised, quiet, or otherwise neglected music performed by musicians from New York and elsewhere."[70] Like many DIY series, the participants involved in the Eggwolf Series often came from Siegel's own social network. He invited people he had met while a student at the University of Michigan in the late 1990s who had followed him east or people he had met since moving to Brooklyn. He also tapped into networks of musicians he had met at festivals or while on tour. Regardless, a trio was the largest group the room could accommodate, and most of the performances were solos or duos. It was also common to have just one set per night, so the performances were relatively short and focused on one ensemble or solo set.

Nate Wooley

Other than making sure no music was particularly alienating to the café audience, Siegel kept the curation of music pretty open. Trumpeter Nate Wooley, who performed regularly in the series, regarded it as "good for doing more experimental music."[71] In May 2002 Wooley played duo with Aaron Siegel at the Eggwolf Series, which marked a new stage of his development as a musician. He was already exhibiting the noise scene's aesthetic influence on him. By this point Wooley had spent a number of months enmeshed in the lowercase scene in particular and had been playing "very quiet and minimal sound-based improvisation" with figures such as Tim Barnes, Margarida Garcia, members of the peeesseye, Alessandro Bosetti, and Jack Wright.[72] But Wooley came up pretty hard against the dogma of reductionist music fairly quickly. He wrote:

> By the time I was finding my place in lowercase music, the limits of it had been stretched to their furthest point by the people I was most interested in. There is only so far you could go with minimalism and there were people within and outside of that scene that, because of a need to codify and limit the language for whatever reason, were pushing that music to its logical conclusion, which is, I think, what is now loosely called the Wandelweiser crowd. I love that music. I'm a huge fan of it, but it isn't fulfilling for me to make it.[73]

In the summer of 2002, Wooley and Siegel did a dual solo tour through the Midwest, where Wooley played trumpet with a close microphone, often in long drones. For the tour he purchased a large speaker and microphone that formed the beginning of his work with amplification, feedback, and related extended techniques. "The amp really started as a way to use the softest parts of the musical vocabulary in a group that may not always want to play soft. I just figured that it would be a way to get those frequencies heard," Wooley explained.[74] Some of Wooley's aesthetic seemed rooted in a phrase he attributed to Ralph Waldo Emerson, "listening to the still, small voice." Explaining what that meant to him, he wrote, "The voice is that slight quickening of the heartbeat that tells me that what I'm doing is honest and, more importantly, specific to who I am as a human being."[75]

By the conclusion of the tour, Wooley noted, "I started to find that I was less interested in just amplifying small sounds and more interested in the different areas I could explore, like pure rhythmic or frequency stuff, or the manipulation of voice and feedback. I really think of it as a different vocabulary at this point; not just a solo vocabulary, but like a doubling instrument." Or put another way, "The amp basically went from being a speaker to a chaos generator to another horn for me." Reflecting on that period, Wooley remarked, "That kind of playing seems to have informed a lot of artistic decisions that I have made since."[76]

Blue Collar

Another of Wooley's projects to emerge from the Read Café scene was the trio Blue Collar. The band featured Wooley on trumpet as well as flugelhorn, Steve Swell on trombone, and Tatsuya Nakatani on drum kit and other forms of percussion (see figure 3.3).[77] Nakatani's percussion work with the group was unique; as one critic noted, "Nakatani works more with the suspension of time than its division."[78] Another critic speculated that the band's name was intended as a reference to "the machine shop, the factory, or the garage, all repositories of heavy tools and equipment," the result being a mixture of shifting metallic drones, scrapes, explosions, and recesses.[79]

Wooley himself described it differently, stating that the band was a "free improvising trio that explores the possibilities of stopping time. The group's goal with each piece of music is to subtly change the listening environment, to infuse silence with specific meaning."[80] And though the instrumentation left room for "brash, jazz-oriented interjections," Blue Collar focused most closely on "the smallest and subtlest of sonic details," creating music that

Figure 3.3 Blue Collar: Nate Wooley (*left*) and Tatsuya Nakatani (Steve Swell not pictured), Downtown Music Gallery, 2003 (*photo by Peter Gannushkin*)

drew from "speech, silence, and the everyday sounds that are taken for granted."[81] As another critic noted, the music "explores the textural, using sounds and vibrations for improvisation."[82] In addition to the Read, the band played its early gigs at CBGBs and at emerging Brooklyn series such as those at the Pourhouse, the Lucky Cat Lounge, and Barbès, culminating in a show at the Improvised and Otherwise festival in 2005.

One critic noted that Blue Collar's music shared some characteristics with trumpeter Bill Dixon's work, "but with a more industrial bent."[83] Each of the three players would make sudden or unexpected entrances, proceed with concise, unadorned-yet-expressive statements, and then withdraw to make room for one of the other players. Nakatani's bowed percussion often added the feeling of a third horn or an atmospheric gong that gave buoyancy to Swell and Wooley as they moved above or within it. The music contained greater doses of silence than sound, which had the effect of intensifying even the slightest sonic gesture.

Memorize the Sky

A third band to emerge from the Read Café scene was Siegel's own Memorize the Sky, a group that he co-led with saxophonist Matt Bauder and bassist Zach Wallace. The three had met as undergraduates while attending the University of Michigan in the late 1990s; after each had moved elsewhere, they eventually reconvened in Williamsburg. Bauder was then a graduate student at Wesleyan University, where he studied with Anthony Braxton, and Siegel would later follow him there. Siegel described the band as "at the crossroads of European free improvisation, American free jazz, independent songwriters, and electronic music." Or, to put it another way, the band's aesthetics were situated in "static textures, combinations of electronic and acoustic music, melody, and noise."[84]

At the Read, Memorize the Sky played about once every other month, using a method of free improvising that, while unplanned, often settled on "pieces" that they developed through years of playing together.[85] Memorize the Sky thus relied on a base comfort level exhibited through remembered textures toward which the players naturally gravitated. Siegel recalled that the group initially hung onto its "Midwestern romanticism," which sometimes felt awkward in Williamsburg, where there was such an emphasis on harsh noise or progressive rock–influenced improvised music.[86] But the group then began gravitating toward harsher sounds and incorporated more electronics into its sound, which allowed them to expand the dynamic range of the music.

Memorize the Sky exhibited an interest in drones, "sound by itself, but with heart," and "finding environments to sit in," where they could express themselves through the spontaneous energy of improvisation.[87] Still, Siegel admitted, "All of our improvisations came from a defined space, so we weren't as much freely improvising as we were making new articulations of a common value."[88] Bauder described the music as "moving slowly and involving a lot of repetition." He added, "To me it was like a secret language, but not human language, more like a rainforest where sounds had a connection but not a linear one."[89]

The Eggwolf Series ended when Siegel left to study with Anthony Braxton in graduate school at Wesleyan University, but Memorize the Sky continued to evolve.[90] Siegel later confessed, "Braxton really helped us feel more confident in our vision."[91] Most of Memorize the Sky's recorded work came in later years but was based on an aesthetic and common understanding among the performers that had been refined at the Read Café.[92]

Newsonic Loft

One loft space that was particularly connected to the post-Wesleyan scene managed to survive well into the 2000s: Newsonic Loft, located at 76 Rutledge Street in South Williamsburg. Seth Misterka and some friends discovered it in the classified ads of the *Village Voice* in 2000. "It was a completely raw 2,500 square feet and rented for just $1200 a month when we first moved in," Misterka described it. "Interestingly, the back part of the space was elevated about a foot higher than the rest of the loft," a remnant from its days as a factory. "The first time I saw it, I immediately thought it would be a perfect stage, and a great place for shows," he recalled.[93] Misterka and his roommates moved in shortly thereafter, and he began booking experimental jazz and rock shows there about once a month, beginning in 2001. Other musicians, such as guitarist Tyondai Braxton, lived in the space in the early 2000s.[94]

Situated in Hasidic Williamsburg, Newsonic seemed in many ways to be out of place. As one journalist observed, "On any given Friday night, South Williamsburg, with its stately brownstones, vinyl-sided walk-ups, endless apartment complexes and sagging warehouses, is a virtual ghost town. The only people on the corner of Rutledge Street and Bedford Avenue are two Hasidic men in mid-discussion, dressed in black overcoats. Tonight is Shabbat, and so this neighborhood, heavily populated by Orthodox Jews, sleeps."[95] It was almost unthinkable that one of Brooklyn's wildest live music parties was going on just a few hundred feet away.

"Further down Rutledge, toward the East River and the imposing Manhattan skyline, a group of scruffy friends loiters outside of a nondescript warehouse, smoking cigarettes," the journalist continued.[96] Once the music began inside, sounds would tumble out through the windows and shake the walls, but there was never any real problem with the authorities or the other residents of the area. For one, phone usage for the Jewish population was generally off-limits. But as one of Misterka's collaborators, Jenny Electrik (of the band Dynasty Electric), said, "Our neighbors support us. They are a mystical people and they see us as mystical, too."[97]

Venturing inside and up a rickety staircase, one found "smaller, incongruous rooms haphazardly stitched together and packed with strangers, artists, freaks, slummers, and revelers."[98] Having full control of a performance space was a rare opportunity for young musicians, so Misterka took advantage by transforming the entire space. Tropical plants in the main room gave the place an exotic feel, and Christmas lights strung from floor to ceiling outlined the stage. "My strategy with these shows was to give them a loft party vibe with cool lighting, projections, and a speakeasy bar." With large crowds indoors, the space often got hot and sweaty, so many attendees relaxed with a cold beer, Pabst Blue Ribbon being the most popular. Absinthe, vodka, whiskey, and wine were also commonly available. As Misterka recalled, "After bars and clubs banned smoking, people seemed to get a kick out of being able to smoke indoors."[99]

"We were marijuana friendly as well," Misterka added. "So you could easily stumble upon a joint or bowl being passed around."[100] Occasionally they also served marijuana bong hits from the bar. One observer described an evening: "A group of burly stoners wearing sunglasses are plopped on a couch watching a distorted video of what looked like a nightmare about ballroom dancing, as imagined by Chuck Close. The light prances, refracted through clouds of cigarette and marijuana smoke."[101] Misterka added, "Psychedelics were also fairly common with the most popular being MDMA, followed by mushrooms and LSD. I occasionally saw signs of cocaine being used, but it wasn't common." Parties often went until four or five in the morning. "One time, I went into my room (which doubled as the backstage) and some guys were doing lines of coke on my bandmate's theremin. At first I was upset, but they apologized and one of them said 'I just came in from Cali, let me make it up to you' and he proceeded to break off a big piece of hash to appease me," Misterka said.[102] It is not surprising that Nonsense NYC, an email list that publicizes these kinds of underground parties, once dubbed Newsonic "one of the best parties this side of the cosmos."[103]

The parties themselves were designed to be welcoming to people of all kinds, and any given night might be billed as "beautiful vibrations, cosmic people, an all night harmonic love fest."[104] Certain annual events elevated the feeling to another level, such as the Valentine's Day parties or the annual 4/20 pot-smoking parties. The most anticipated events, however, were the annual Halloween costume parties that guests could attend for free if they dressed up. Those parties attracted the largest crowds, and creativity was on display from wall to wall.

Misterka publicized the shows mainly by word of mouth, but Newsonic quickly developed its own following. Avoiding publicity in print media was a conscious decision to avert potential problems with the police. Such parties, which commonly swelled to more than a hundred attendees, were the epitome of Williamsburg culture at the time. Young people from across the city (and even from New Jersey, Connecticut, or elsewhere) would flock to Newsonic to take in the latest that the underground experimental music scene had to offer. It was particularly important for the post-Wesleyan community, who

Figure 3.4 (*from left*) Matthew Welch, Brian Chase, and Seth Misterka, Newsonic Loft, ca. 2003 (*photo by Jennifer Deveau*)

often hung out there, including Mary Halvorson, Jessica Pavone, Jackson Moore, Taylor Ho Bynum, Jason Cady, and Matthew Welch.

The music at Newsonic was about as eclectic as one could find in the burgeoning Brooklyn music scene. Typically, music began around ten o'clock in the evening. People could get in for free before eight o'clock, so attendees would sometimes arrive early, but most people trickled in later as the party began to grow in energy. Misterka curated the concert lineups specifically to challenge listeners. "I would book a metal band right after a dance DJ, or an experimental jazz group right next to a rock band," he recalled. "Sometimes it completely backfired and the whole room would clear out. I never worried about it though, because I was interested in exposing people to new music."[105] New, of course, was relative, since the crowd's tastes were as diverse as the musicians who played there. Misterka remarked, "I recall one time I booked Mike Pride's Drummer's Corpse, which was a band of all drummers, very intense and very loud. They took over the stage and dance floor and put on the most visceral performance. Most people there had not heard anything like that before."[106] As critic Nate Chinen later wrote of the band's recorded work, "The title track—three minutes of anticipatory rustle on gongs and cymbals, followed by half an hour of percussive hailstorm—feels like Mr. Pride's precise definition of catharsis."[107]

Blarvuster

Matthew Welch's band Blarvuster also played at Newsonic.[108] Blarvuster was an eclectic mix of sounds, approaches, and styles.[109] In reference to the band, one critic wrote, "New avant-gardes are often a hybrid of many musical languages."[110] Indeed, by Welch's own description, the band merged "Scottish bagpipes, Balinese gamelan, minimalism, improvisation and rock into a textural labyrinth of ecstatic sound."[111] Or, as critic Vivien Schweitzer noted, in Blarvuster "bagpipes meet Bali in an Indonesian-hued Highland jig."[112] Welch experimented with drones and pentatonic modes, especially on the extended piece "Blind Piper's Obstinacy."[113] As the performances went on, sometimes they grew into all-encompassing sonic experiences with the bagpipes taking hold, but the music also had quiet moments and always featured Welch's unique compositions.

Welch also took part in a large ensemble led by drummer Harris Eisenstadt named Ahimsa Orchestra. It was an assemblage of other people who were part of the Newsonic-Wesleyan scene. Jessica Pavone, André Vida, Nate Wooley, and cellist Loren Dempster played in the big band, for example. Stuart Bogie and J. D. Parran bolstered the clarinets, and Jordan McLean expanded the trumpet section. Other musicians also played with the group at Newsonic in a kind of community orchestra led by Eisenstadt.

Mary Halvorson and Kevin Shea

The mix of music naturally had an impact on musicians, too. One evening, Misterka organized an improvising trio with Mary Halvorson and Kevin Shea. Halvorson remembered, "It was my first time meeting Kevin and I was struck right away what an original drummer he is. I've never heard anyone like him. This definitely sparked my interest in working with Kevin more." New encounters in such an eclectic setting pushed Halvorson to expand her musical horizons. "There were a lot of indie rock bands playing at Newsonic around the time, too, and I remember thinking it would be cool to try composing for a band with vocals. This sparked the whole idea of forming the band People with Kevin. He started showing me lyrics, short stories, and poems that he was writing, too, so the pieces fell into place. Newsonic was at the center of it."[114]

Halvorson's involvement in People pushed her to explore untapped areas of her creativity. She described Shea's lyrics as "super weird, like bits of philosophy text" that often pushed the music into another world. Halvorson enjoyed moving away from jazz, too, which she had burned out on while in college. "I made up my own exercises, working on weird things on guitar, stretching the possibilities," she observed of her own playing.[115] So in People, Halvorson gave voice to Shea's lyrics, while they improvised over unusual time signatures.[116] "I thought of more complex music, especially rhythms, like complex thinking or philosophy," Shea explained. "I wanted to challenge audiences to think more about what they were hearing instead of just being on autopilot. I am sometimes amazed at people who spend their day reading [Jacques] Derrida, but then they listen to techno."[117]

Shea had first emerged as a player in Pittsburgh, occasionally visiting and playing in New York in the early to mid-1990s, but it was an encounter with guitarist Ian Williams that led to his involvement in the experimental rock band Storm and Stress, which in turn brought him to greater notice with gigs at the Knitting Factory and touring opportunities in Europe.[118] After Storm and Stress broke up in 2000, he joined another experimental rock group, Coptic Light, and in that milieu learned of Mary Halvorson through future Battles guitarist Tyondai Braxton. Shea had at times felt constrained in the more rock-oriented work he had done and had been seeking greater freedom in those environments.[119]

The duo Talibam!, consisting of Shea and keyboardist Matt Mottel, also emerged around the same time, crossing genres and drawing from the eclectic mix of music then happening in Williamsburg, which has resulted in the band creating records across a broad spectrum of rock, electronic without drums, free jazz, noise, rock opera, collage with different cityscape sounds meshed together, and numerous other ideas, involving collaborations with a shifting array of musicians, totaling over thirty records to date (see figure 3.5).[120] As Shea stated, "Each record was a different genre. It's not good for branding since we constantly ostracize our audience and bring new people in. This band exists because we want it to exist, and the point is to experiment as broadly as possible."[121] This kind of cross-genre exploration was one of the enduring hallmarks of the Williamsburg scene.

The encounter with Shea had the inverse effect on Halvorson. She began delving into experimental rock music of the time, a practice that had a lasting impact on her sound. She later remarked, "People always feels like a different form of expression than what I do in my other work." Halvorson would eventually return to her improvising, jazz-oriented roots, but she would rarely be regarded as a jazz guitarist along the lines of Wes Montgomery or Joe Pass. "I care about jazz probably more than any other kind of music, but I had to investigate other areas, [and] then once I began to combine different elements of what I learned, combined with chord changes, scales, and

Figure 3.5 Talibam!: (*from left*) Matt Mottel, Ed Bear, and Kevin Shea, 2005 (*photo by Peter Gannushkin*)

the feel of jazz, integrating that into my own thing, my later development wouldn't have happened without that."[122] People soon played the local scene at the Cake Shop, Luxx, the McKibben lofts, and especially the basement at Northsix before going on some US tours.[123] The imprint of rock's harder edge, driving riffs, and pedal effects has remained a feature of her music in the years since, having first crystallized on the live scene in the unique environment of Newsonic. Halvorson would emerge fully in the late 2000s and 2010s with her trio, quintet, septet, and octet, which would propel her to considerable praise and eventually a MacArthur Foundation grant.

Dynasty Electric

Most evenings at Newsonic featured as many as five bands, one or more DJs, and a veejay (video jockey), each set growing in intensity as they built toward dance music, which often closed the night. Dynasty Electric, Misterka's electronic avant-rock duo with Jenny Electrik (voice), was commonly featured in the series and emerged to prominence from the scene.[124] Dynasty Electric sometimes performed Sun Ra's "Space Is the Place," though they generally worked with their own original tunes.[125] Other mainstays at Newsonic included Brooklyn Raga Association, Optimus Tribe, Namaste, and Navegante. Further, veejays such as Suit Machine, Larry Carlson, and other artists specializing in psychedelic projections often brought their work, adding a significant visual element. Combined with the mind-altering drugs some performers and attendees ingested, the psychedelic visuals expanded the possibilities of sensory experiences at Newsonic. "Once, Jenny [Electrik] thought she was taking a cold-remedy pill but it ended up being acid," Misterka recounted. "Right before we were about to go on, she was nowhere to be found. I found her wandering around outside, disoriented and totally tripping. I managed to get her back inside, and she actually ended up giving a great performance. She was totally in the zone."[126]

The rowdy atmosphere sometimes spilled over. "One time I was sitting in my room backstage with some friends and I could hear someone banging on the door," Misterka recalled. "All of a sudden this drunk fellow came crashing through the door, knocking it off its hinges. I was furious and about to kick him out of the party, but everyone yelled, 'He's the bass player of the next band!' so I forgave him and let him stay to play his set."[127] Despite the noise, however, Newsonic managed to avoid major problems with the authorities. The neighboring buildings housed an auto mechanic, a supermarket, and a Hasidic Jewish social hall for weddings and other events. Since most of the nearby residents were home with their families for Shabbat, "no one was really around to be bothered by a party. However, one time a private Hasidic security patrol came in, and Misterka recalled suddenly worrying that they were there to shut down the party. Instead, one of them said, 'We just want to listen to some music!' So they came in and hung out for a while and left without incident. Hasidics love music and a good party as much as anyone else!"[128] The closest scrape with the law came when a New York Police detective arrived one quiet day when no party was happening. The officer mentioned to Misterka that they were aware that they were having parties there, "but it looks like you have a good thing going, so watch yourselves, because I'd hate to see you get shut down." Newsonic closed for a couple of months but later resumed their activities.

Zs

Zs was not as integral to Newsonic as some of the other bands but did have an important early moment there and a significant impact on the broader music scene. One of the hallmarks of the band is that it often performed outside of the standard set of experimental venues, pushing its music into a broader cultural conversation. Saxophonist Sam Hillmer was from Washington, DC, where he grew up studying music formally while also participating in the vibrant punk scene in the city from the age of thirteen onward. "Those early years informed my own long-standing interests and informed part of the DNA of what Zs was to be about," he stated.[129] Hillmer moved to New York to study jazz saxophone at Manhattan School of Music in 1996–2001. The other cofounder, saxophonist Alex Mincek, came out of a "Young Lions–infused orthodox jazz" scene in Jacksonville, Florida, having arrived at the school two years earlier.[130]

At one point in his sophomore year, Hillmer had gotten into a routine of practicing eight to ten hours a day, "living a hermetic existence," and was pushing himself to learn the jazz idiom when he had an epiphany that it was not what he really wanted to do in music. "As impressive as the program was," Hillmer commented, "it was not feeding me in terms of what I wanted to do. I worked hard with some of the classical music professors, especially Renaissance and seventeenth-century music and a lot in contemporary music."[131] He began checking out all of the other kinds of music that fascinated him and began to grow in other directions, especially reconnecting with the punk scene.[132] At that moment, Hillmer and Mincek met. "We were both disillusioned with the jazz department and wanted to do something else," Hillmer recalled, reacting to the conservative approach in the classical and jazz curriculum there.[133] Mincek added, "We didn't really like the jazz scene at the school, the learning of the vernacular, a pretty traditional approach. We were looking for other scenes in the city and how to connect with them. Plus, as a white person, I felt uncomfortable being part of a preservationist mission for Black American music that was then happening within straight-ahead jazz and wanted to avoid that process of appropriation. It made sense to go in another direction in search of my own musical voice."[134]

A wide range of mid-twentieth-century composers such as Pierre Boulez, György Ligeti, Alvin Lucier, David Tudor, and more recent composers—especially the New York school of John Cage, Morton Feldman, Christian Wolff, and Earle Brown—were among the mutual inspirations that drew the two musicians closer together, and they even worked directly with Wolff. They were also becoming aware of the music scene that was just then beginning to emanate out from Wesleyan as students of Braxton began to move down to New York City. In particular, when Mincek witnessed a duo of Seth Misterka and Brandon Evans play, he was blown away by the possibilities and their radical, unconventional approach, which pushed him to think about creating a band where Hillmer and he could workshop their budding compositional concepts.

Spending nearly every day together one summer, Hillmer and Mincek "conceived of a band together that had an alignment with jazz but had the capabilities to address twentieth- and twenty-first-century compositional practice as well as an electroacoustic dimension and that all together it should be an amorphous, flexible band that was multistable in these different musical universes."[135] The first step was assembling a community of like-minded musicians, so Hillmer and Mincek began to organize brief or one-time ensembles with musicians they knew who they thought might be interested in participating in the experiment, first at a studio on Bethune Street and later at the Pink Pony.[136]

Hillmer felt strongly at the time that he wanted to do something relevant to the present time and avoid "drowning in academia pursuing some dusty bookish project that was out of touch with the present."[137] With one foot in the punk scene and the other in technical training, he was insistent on not being typecast as just one thing or being marginalized while making experimental music. So the circles that he and Mincek moved in grew to include the punk scene, free jazz, the post-Wesleyan scene, and a variety of non-genre-specific music that was then emerging in the early 2000s.

As Hillmer and Mincek began to work out material for Zs, they aimed to compose pieces that pushed the members of the ensemble "to the absolute limit of what they were capable of."[138] In particular, they employed difficult time changes and unusual meters, but as Hillmer described the band, "Zs is this group that has a bombastic, caustic quality of a fierce noise ensemble and at the same time has this restrained, austere quality you would associate with a chamber ensemble."[139] Drawing from compositional ideas from figures like composers Iannis Xenakis and Brian Ferneyhough, they "had access to complexity that would register as new in the world of complicated rock music and at the same time fit in the world of new composition."[140] Mincek admired Xenakis in particular because his work managed to combine "hyperformalistic, statistical modeled sound with a feeling that was visceral and direct." For the piece "Slalom," for example, Mincek worked with "brutal blocks of sound" where the durations were all minutely different, taking seemingly repetitive pulse- or groove-based frameworks of time and having them be "off" by little amounts to produce a different calibration of how timing was happening. "Mimesis" used the opposite approach, taking time out of the piece with almost no pulse. "Thus, together the pieces were varied surface representations of a similar goal of looking at how we perceive the passage of time."[141]

As they assembled the personnel for the band, it quickly evolved into a double trio that included guitarists Matthew Hough and Charlie Looker and drummers Brad Wentworth and Alex Hoskins. "There was an attitude at the time on the rock scene that if someone had trained in music school, they were soft," Hillmer explained. "We were there playing in rock clubs reading sheet music from music stands. Sometimes the audience was adversarial, often at the beginning, but we won over a lot of those rooms because it was something that people had not experienced before."[142] For Mincek, one of the things that Zs did was "to completely eject the surface identity of rock music and instead take the essence of rocking and put that into practice. It was a provocation. Sometimes we would play a hardcore show with the essence of fragility, humor, and restraint that might be more expected of a string quartet. We created a melting pot of ideas, though we tried not to make the sources obvious. We were trying to create our own language to communicate humanly."[143]

Meanwhile, Zs challenged expectations by "obliterating the hierarchy of lead and rhythm guitar"; for instance, there was no bass, and the rhythm section, in this case two drummers, was not subordinated to the rest of the ensemble.[144] This freed up the guitars to be more fluid in how they related to the other instruments in the band. Mincek considered the Paul Motian Trio with guitarist Bill Frisell and saxophonist Joe Lovano to be an antecedent for this, such that "Zs was the double version of that concept. Without bass, it does not sound like rock or jazz because bass is so quintessential to both of those musics, whereas it is not the underpinning of Western classical music, where there are often more equal voicings."[145] Mincek added, "We were bringing together math-y, overly composed material and playing that in hardcore or punk venues. It felt contrarian, and I never really was fully comfortable with the spectacle of it."[146] As a social experiment, Mincek theorized that he saw it as an accusation directed at the scene they were playing in, while for Hillmer it was more of an affirmation of a scene that he had roots in already. This division would eventually pull the band apart in later years, but in the meantime they encountered a lot of success.

The band really coalesced at a gig at Newsonic Loft on September 9, 2002, where they first used the band name Zs. Soon after releasing their self-titled debut record on Troubleman Unlimited, a punk and hardcore label, they were able to go on a national tour to showcase their work.[147] Todd Patrick, known professionally as Todd P, became a major concert organizer around that time and booked them many times in a variety of Williamsburg venues such as the Kingsland Tavern, Luxx, the Right Bank, and many others, as well as DIY places such as free103point9 and 220 Grand. As one observer noted, "[Todd P] got interns, paid cops to do security and built an infrastructure that allowed [the scene] to get bigger but keep its purity. Every band in the country that had any sense of a punk aesthetic, no matter what the music was, wanted to play a show with Todd."[148] Todd P booked thousands of concerts over the years and is still active in Brooklyn today.

The first Zs record release in 2003, at Lucky Cat, featured Tyondai Braxton playing solo and TV on the Radio as the opening acts. They later booked shows and toured with Braxton, as well as bands such as Animal Collective, Orthrelm, Black Eyes, and Coptic Light. The tour went west from Philadelphia through Kentucky to Oklahoma and Texas, then through the Southwest to Albuquerque and Phoenix, before going up the West Coast to Sacramento.[149] From there, they cut back through Salt Lake City, Colorado, South Dakota, and back through the Upper Midwest. "I didn't want to remain in obscurity in experimental music or free jazz, so to me it was about insisting on being relevant and stepping into circles that were not the normal circles for musicians who were working in new composition," Hillmer explained.[150]

Around 2006, after considerable activity playing and touring, the band withdrew from public performances for about a year to write a new body of work. The band also experienced a considerable personnel change, with Mincek, Wentworth, and Hoskins leaving the band. Hillmer hired drummer Ian Antonio, so the band shrank to a quartet, which facilitated touring more affordably. Mincek had grown tired of touring and was increasingly interested in the contemporary classical music scene.[151] Vocals, which had first been added to the band's sound by Looker a few years previously, also became featured slightly more on *Arms* and other recordings from that time period.[152] With a new book of music adapted to a smaller unit, Zs organized another national tour in 2006 and a subsequent tour in 2007 with guitarist Ben Greenberg replacing Hough.[153]

Looker had a transformative presence in the band, and after Mincek departed, he became the other principal composer and molder of the vision along with Hillmer. "He had a related but different vision than me, so we complemented each other in developing the music," Hillmer stated.[154] "B Is for Burning" and "Nobody Wants to Be Had," both composed by Looker, were among the most accessible pieces that the band created at that time. After Looker left the band in late 2007, the band effectively became a trio. By that point

Zs had numerous performance opportunities, having inserted themselves into a broader conversation. The band has continued to be prolific in the years since, continuing to show an eclectic range in their recorded output.

The End of Newsonic Loft

After 2005 Newsonic began to orient itself more toward the indie rock and warehouse party scenes, though it would occasionally include experimental bands. The loft managed to survive several waves of gentrification that closed most of the other major lofts, most notably in the wake of the 2005 rezoning under Mayor Michael Bloomberg.[155] But eventually the pressures became too much. In March 2011 Misterka received a notice of eviction giving him sixty days to vacate the building so that it could be converted to offices. Misterka was determined to bring the party scene to a fitting end and hosted events every weekend until a final two-night event on May 27–28. These final bills included an array of pop and rock music, video projections, and DJs, each themed in a different way, including the Brooklyn Experimental Music Festival on May 7. That bill included fierce performances, driven by a sense of urgency and endangerment of the community, from figures such as drummer Mike Pride, saxophonist Jackson Moore, Talibam!, and Brooklyn Raga Association, as well as Misterka with drummer Brian Chase and Matthew Welch (see figure 3.4). Showcasing some of the hottest talent and drawn from an eclectic pool of performers, the festival was a fitting homage to the era.

Improvised and Otherwise Festivals, 2002–2006

One cohesive force—in terms of both building community between Williamsburg and other parts of New York, especially South Brooklyn, and offering a brilliant display of interdisciplinarity—was the series of festivals called Improvised and Otherwise that ran from 2002 to 2006. "At that time, there were fewer opportunities to present dance that was improvised and experimental, so I was aiming to change that," one of the cocurators of the events, choreographer Estelle Woodward, stated.[156] She was joined by drummer Jeff Arnal, guitarist Chris Forsyth, and pianist Dan DeChellis in founding and organizing the festival series, inspired by their mutual attendance of the Big Sur Experimental Music Festival in Big Sur, California, in 2000. Woodward and Arnal had met attending graduate school at Bennington College, where they were also inspired by the collaborative music and dance work of trumpeter Bill Dixon and dancer Judith Dunn. Work by composer

John Cage, pianist David Tudor, and dancer Merce Cunningham—especially *Variations V* (1964), which explored how music, the visual, and movement could share the same language—offered a model for what Woodward and Arnal envisioned for the festival. "From the beginning," Arnal stated, "we were thinking of how music and dance could occupy the same space."[157] A lot of dance performance spaces were also closing in Manhattan in the early 2000s, so Woodward and the other artists were aiming to build a base for dance in the burgeoning art scene in Williamsburg.

For the first four years of the festival, beginning in 2002, the organizers booked the Williamsburg Art neXus (WAX) at 205 North Seventh Street, which was a converted garage that also had a gallery but functioned primarily as a dance space. The first festival featured more music than dance and did not mix the two art forms as much as subsequent versions did, but established the festival as an entity in the community. From the second festival onward, the organizers also chose a visual artist to curate the gallery to expand the interdisciplinary prospects and invited international music and dance acts, though they were always constrained by a small budget.[158] Each artist who performed at the festivals was paid equally. "One of the unique features of the festival," pianist Gordon Beeferman observed, "was that it avoided the mistake that many curators make by presenting a particular subgenre of music or one particular artist clique. Jeff Arnal had such a wide range of interests that he managed to draw together a lot of different communities in one space. And beyond that, it brought together different mediums and art practices as well."[159]

Located just a block south of Bedford Avenue, WAX was in the heart of the Williamsburg art scene at the time. "It was an amazing space, but on the tech side of things, it was just the bare minimum in terms of lighting and sound system," Woodward explained, "so artists had to bring in their own gear, and we would rent a baby grand piano for the stage, which was our biggest annual expense." Donations from Brooklyn Brewery were critical to making the event viable and allowed them to sell beer to further pay artists "and actually break even as organizers."[160]

Improvised and Otherwise included a range of music from free jazz to electronic. By 2003 the festival was one of the most innovative annual arts events in the city, catering to younger performers and openly embracing video and other visual elements in live sets. The final festival, in 2006, combined music and dance in every set and even included Gordon Beeferman's new opera, *The Rat Land*. The music of the later years also began to include more noise-oriented bands, which also evolved the overall aesthetic of the festival.

The festival brought elements of the Williamsburg scene into contact with other aspects of New York City's music scene as well as artists from around the United States and Europe. Many of the artists already discussed in this book were present at the festival. In 2002 Daniel Carter, Tatsuya Nakatani, and Chris Forsyth all appeared in different groups. The MP3, led by Mike Pride and including Mary Halvorson, played one of their earliest gigs that year as well. The peeesseye appeared the following year, as did Dynasty Electric, and in 2004 Miguel Gutierrez and Jaime Fennelly's duo Sabotage closed the second night. HorseEyeless, the duo of Halvorson and Pavone, Triptych Myth, Phantom Limb and Bison, and Blue Collar all appeared in 2005. Dance and music elements from Berlin and other parts of Europe were also included. Contrasting the annual Vision Festival at the time, Improvised and Otherwise featured more improvised music from outside of the jazz idiom.

For the time, the bills also had surprising gender parity and featured openly gay performers, even though it was still a heavily male and heteronormative scene in Williamsburg overall. "The bills had way more female performers than any other venue, series, or festival at the time," percussionist Ben Hall, who attended all five festivals, observed. "And unlike so many other events that were all men, the audience correspondingly had far more women attend. It was unusual for the time and exhibited the untapped potential to grow the audience that most concerts or performances at the time ignored."[161]

One example of a group that combined music and dance was Loophole in 2003. The group included dancers Estelle Woodward, Corrina Kalisz, and Alison Richardson and musicians Gordon Beeferman and Jeff Arnal. The material they developed for their set was fully improvised in terms of dance and music but was based on weekly rehearsals they conducted in the months before the festival. Structures to their interactions emerged organically from the improvisations as they grew accustomed to each other over time, which allowed them to anticipate and better understand each other's artistic vision as they worked together. "It really allowed me to see how music and dance could go together," Beeferman noted. "There was a feedback loop. It was highly interactive. We were constantly communicating with each other regardless of the medium. It worked particularly well because Jeff encouraged us to use silence or stillness as an additional element in the performance alongside sound and movement."[162]

In 2005 the building where the Williamsburg Art neXus was situated was sold and torn down by a developer to make way for a condo building, so the organizers of Improvised and Otherwise moved their operations to BRIC in Fort Greene for the final year of the festival. At BRIC they were able to more fully bridge Brooklyn's two experimental music and arts communities, drawing greater numbers of performers from South Brooklyn and connecting with their audiences.

"The process for every collaborative group we worked with at the festival was different," Estelle Woodward observed.

> That was one of the amazing things. The heart of experimentation is exploring a new process and reaching new territory that is unknown for you as a creative practitioner. Reaching the unknown. Some people came in with set structures they were working within their pieces, others were fully improvised. Many groups were also working with media other than music and dance, such as video and electronics. One of the things that happened at Improvised and Otherwise was that the action was generally not initiated by one discipline for the others to follow. It was a true collaboration where each discipline was represented equally and informed the outcome of the work equally. Two or more things were happening simultaneously with artists creating in the moment.[163]

No festival or other event has fully filled the void left behind by Improvised and Otherwise in the years since.

Other Spaces

Over on Grand Street was the Lucky Cat Lounge, a festive, often-crowded place with a roughly painted red interior. Drummer Jeff Arnal and pianist Gordon Beeferman chose the space to curate Under the Radar, a monthly series of "free jazz and other experimental forms of music" on the third Tuesday of the month, beginning in 2004. The Lucky Cat became an intersection between the community of 220 Grand and the Read Café and the series had been started by the pair of curators explicitly to "provide a forum for artists to exchange ideas and create a dialog between the various ideologies of experimental music."[164] Arnal featured bands such as Nate Wooley's Blue Collar, Chris Forsyth's Dirty Pool, and New Math (a duo of multi-instrumentalist Mick Rossi and trumpeter Russ Johnson), as well as figures such as percussionist Satoshi Takeishi, keyboardist Shoko Nagai, and drummer Michael Evans. Takeishi and Nagai's duo, for instance, "explored the possibility of sound sculpting through twentieth-century music, free improvisation and real-time audio processing with the goal of extracting, magnifying, and modifying past musical events to make the passing of time a visual experience."[165] The Lucky Cat continued to occasionally host similar music until it closed in 2008.

Taylor Ho Bynum

As the Williamsburg scene began to splinter and be displaced, a vital new voice with strong connections to the post-Wesleyan scene emerged who would serve as a cohesive force for a time: trumpeter Taylor Ho Bynum. Fresh from graduate work with Braxton at Wesleyan, this young, versatile player arrived with an already well-developed artistic vision. Known as a particularly expressive player displaying an impressive emotional range in his music, Bynum set his sights on the frontier of what the instrument had to offer, building a vocabulary as he went. In live performances he managed to combine a great number of experimental techniques and sounds bearing a "bring music to the people" attitude.

Red Hook, 2005

Like many artists of that time participating in the North Brooklyn scene, Bynum lived outside of Williamsburg, nearest to the G and F train lines, settling in remote Red Hook. "One of the things the scene struggled with at that time was that for the first time it didn't have a geographical base," Bynum recounted. "It was very dispersed. Some musicians lived in Red Hook, and we did sessions there. Some lived in Greenpoint or Williamsburg. Some were further away, in Jersey City, Queens, or Washington Heights. But no one lived in Manhattan proper because no one in our generation could afford to live there!"[166]

To overcome the dispersed nature of the community and the many obstacles that faced artists at the time, Bynum joined with others to form a short-lived musicians' collective. "I don't remember the name of it, but it included Miya Masaoka, Matana Roberts, Vijay Iyer, and Salim Washington. We did a night or two at the Jazz Gallery," Bynum remembered. "We were specifically thinking about artists of color of our generation within the creative music spectrum. There was also a scholarly focus, with an interest in raising the discursive standards of the music. Basically we followed the George Lewis model that there is a role for people who are both practitioners and scholars. We also wanted to set a standard for diversity and inclusiveness."[167] The group met a number of times and put on a series of concerts. Though it didn't last long, the ideas generated through their discussions have been put into practice by the individuals involved in the years since.

The collective was difficult to replicate and maintain at the time. "With working day jobs, everyone was pulled in different directions."[168] Muhal Richard Abrams and others involved in the early Association for the Advancement of Creative Musicians (AACM) days produced many of their own shows. But Bynum noted, "It was nearly impossible to self-produce in New York because it was too expensive to get space. There was a different geographic, social, cultural, and economic reality in New York, but we still looked at AACM as an idea of how to do things." The AACM was not only an organizational model but also one of the primary aesthetic touchstones. "There wasn't one identifiable AACM sound. Anthony Braxton sounded totally different than Art Ensemble of Chicago, which sounded totally different than Henry Threadgill and Muhal Richard Abrams. There was a transidiomatic embrace of sound. It wasn't about genre, it wasn't about definition. It was about an experimental creative process of engaging composition and improvisation in revolutionary ways."[169]

Brooklyn in the first decade of the twenty-first century was changing rapidly, becoming younger, and the gentrification that had already swept Manhattan was beginning to spread there. Bynum noted:

> I think by our generation one of the things we lacked was that we didn't have that political consciousness or cultural drive that existed in the all-Black organizations of the South Side of Chicago in the late 1960s. But on a purely creative level, we drew inspiration to push the standards of technical excellence and investigation higher even as we had a wholly open-minded embrace of any kind of influence or approach. You could be in a band that freely improvised or played something that was composed or one that had a graphic score. A lot of us had come up under Braxton, and there were some people who studied with Wadada Leo Smith and Roscoe Mitchell. In some ways, I would say our generation of artists was the first to emerge as products of the AACM founders as our primary mentors, so the influence they had upon us as working musicians was quite natural.[170]

Before Bynum formed his sextet, he had always been the youngest member of the bands he had been involved in professionally. Thus, he explicitly decided to form a band that "would include close friends from the same generation." He wanted to create a band where "there wasn't a revered elder,

Figure 3.6 Taylor Ho Bynum Sextet: (*from left*) Evan O'Reilly, Jessica Pavone, Mary Halvorson, Matt Bauder, Tomas Fujiwara, and Bynum, at Barbès, 2006 (*photo by Scott Friedlander*)

where the musicians had grown up with similar experiences, all part of one generation. It was also meant to represent the scene we had in Brooklyn at the time."[171] Bynum chose well. A number of the members of his band later emerged as significant leaders for the new generation of creative musicians in New York and beyond.

At the time Bynum arrived in Red Hook in 2005, he was fresh off of a tour with the Anthony Braxton Quartet, where he had gotten to know guitarist Mary Halvorson. So, as Bynum moved toward forming his own working band, he originally envisioned a quintet with Halvorson as well as friends he had known for a bit longer: Jessica Pavone, drummer Tomas Fujiwara, and guitarist Evan O'Reilly. "I remember reading in the biography of Ornette Coleman," Bynum reminisced, "that he started Prime Time with two guitarists and two electric bass players because he really wanted to have a string quartet and couldn't afford one!"[172]

Bynum also had been focused on his group Taylor Ho Bynum and the Spidermonkey Strings, which was a large ensemble and more of a chamber group than a jazz band. He needed a band that was more mobile (and affordable). "I was never an Allman Brothers fan, but I liked the idea of twin guitars, I wanted back-to-back solos! I liked that I had this group Spidermonkey that leaned more classical because of the instrumentation, and I wanted to have a group that leaned more rock. Evan was explicitly a rock player, and Mary had a lot of rock influence in her playing."[173] Not much later, he added tenor saxophonist Matt Bauder, whom he had crossed paths with during his first year at Wesleyan. The band played its first gig at the Jazz Gallery in Manhattan in March 2005 and was soon winning over crowds at Zebulon in Williamsburg and at the Stone on the Lower East Side (see figure 3.6).

The Middle Picture (2007)

At the same time, Bynum was also leading a trio with Halvorson and Fujiwara with the aim of having a more mobile, modular touring group. Bynum soon took the sextet on a tour of the Northeast, while booking a trio tour out to Oberlin, Ohio, and back to New York City. All of the accumulated experience compelled Bynum to take the band into the studio to record by October of that year, laying down the sextet pieces on the record *The Middle Picture*.[174] The album also affords attentive listeners two tracks drawn from a concert in Philadelphia performed just two days before the studio takes, documenting how the band sounded in the live setting. The hallmark of the record is Bynum's emotional range, from somber, even mournful lines to great ecstatic bursts. It is also a record that insists on big ideas, while grounding them in the immediacy of Bynum's surroundings—the specific musicians in the band, the environment in which he grew up, all with a strong sense of community.

In a certain sense, the record bore a political, even spiritual message. "In terms of the big picture, the situation is dire," Bynum wrote in the liner notes for the record, pointing to the disastrous foreign and domestic policy of the US government under the George W. Bush administration, rising fundamentalist violence, and a world still in denial of impending climate catastrophe.[175] He juxtaposed this with artists' day-to-day frustrations with New York City's rising rents and declining opportunities. "There is much in between the pressing issues of the world and the mundane toils of the everyday," he notes. "I call it the middle picture: pursuit of one's life goals, the search for one's true calling, the cultivation of one's personal relationships. I try to focus on the middle picture, and hope that some of that positive energy and inspiration can influence the pictures on either side. The music on this album grows out of that middle picture, and is dedicated to that hope."[176] Bynum gave voice to the anxieties of an entire generation just then emerging and attempting to establish themselves as working artists in a city and an era that seemed to regard them with growing ambivalence.

Bynum took the opportunity to display his growing talents as a composer, arranger, and performer, while paying homage to many musicians he held in high regard. The inaugural record for the band displays a wide range of influences. He dedicated "Woods" to trumpeter Bill Dixon and opened the piece with solo cornet in a manner that explored the latter's language via a semigraphic score. His cover of "In a Silent Way" revealed another strong trumpet influence—Miles Davis. That piece had sparked some of Bynum's interest in jazz as a kid.[177] He also included a Duke Ellington–Billy Strayhorn piece.

A string quarter by Béla Bartók inspired "3V2," though Bynum admits, "I don't think anyone would hear that connection! I was consciously playing with the juxtaposition of composed trio sections with duo improvisation."[178] The piece serves as an introduction to Bynum's often-intricate sonic geometry in which relationships among musicians (and often physical location in relation to each other) play a central role in the overall structure of a piece. The centerpiece of the record is the two-part "JP and the Boston Suburbs," written before Bauder joined the band, serving as a tribute to the origins of four of the band's original five members—everyone except Jessica Pavone. So "JP" was a reference to both Pavone and the Boston neighborhood of Jamaica Plain, where Bynum had lived earlier. The second part of that piece contained another pun, subtitled "Knit and Swim," as a tribute to Henry Threadgill, another artist Bynum admired greatly. Specifically, he drew on an intervallic logic from Threadgill's Very Very Circus Band, with two bass lines moving simultaneously to build an expanding melody.[179]

Bynum then began shopping the record around but was plagued by the nagging feeling that it was still missing something. In the following year, as he gained notoriety, Bynum managed to take the trio part of the band on the road quite a bit and by late 2006 had recorded two more tracks to bookend the record. "Before I added those trio tunes," Bynum remarked, "it didn't feel quite right. I would like to think of each record as a novel. You want the right chapters and things to fit together correctly. Even though everyone listens to music on iPods and other mobile devices, I still think of each album having a narrative and a flow to it."[180] Unhappy with the various offers he received to produce the record, Bynum joined together with longtime friend Nick Lloyd to found the Firehouse 12 Records label, and the record was their inaugural release. At that time, Lloyd had put together a studio and concert series and managed a bar, all in the same space in New Haven, so the label served as the finishing touches on a vital music space well situated between the New York and Boston scenes.

Back in Brooklyn in 2006, even before the first record had been released, Bynum was already working on new material. He unveiled this work on September 28 of that year at Issue Project Room on a shared evening with choreographer Rachel Bernsen. Alto saxophonist Loren Dempster had been added to the lineup, making the band, at least temporarily, a septet. The focus of the evening was a suite titled "whYeXpliCitieS." The piece was written so that it featured material for duo, trio, quartet, quintet, sextet, and septet. Drawing from compositional techniques engineered by Anthony Braxton and Charles Ives, Bynum created the piece to function in a modular fashion in which multiple ensembles existed alongside one another within the same piece. He managed to produce "different complexities through the juxtaposition of different melodies and ensembles" or, rather, "creating complexity through the layering of simple materials as opposed to creating complex material through linear complex form."[181]

Issue Project Room at that time existed in an old circular silo space along the Gowanus Canal, with the audience situated at the center. So Bynum had his band move around and within the audience, choreographed to physically form duos, trios, and so forth along the different sides of the room. Bynum described the process: "There might be a duo happening on one side of the circle while there was a trio on the other side, with one musician moving from one group to the other."[182] For each ensemble that formed, there were two parts, one simple and one complex. The capitalization of X and Y in the suite title also revealed that Bynum was thinking about space and movement on an axis; C and S stood for *complex* and *simple*. Bynum was able to draw from his trio work with Halvorson and Fujiwara as base material for some of the compositions and then elaborate on them with the larger group. On a compositional level, this suite introduced structural ideas that he explored further on his later album, *Navigation*.[183]

By February 2008, with a great number of performances and tours under his belt, Bynum took the band back to the studio to record. Again, Bynum gave considerable thought on how to round out his second record. He bracketed the sextet suite with trio tunes and then, in turn, bookended each of those with a solo improvisation.[184] So the overall structure of the record reflected much of his thinking on sonic geometry and compositional layers. With the recording finished, he approached Werner X. Uehlinger at Hat Hut Records, hoping that the Switzerland-based label would give the band more visibility across the Atlantic. After its release Bynum began getting gigs in Europe as a leader for the first time and brought the band there to tour.

Vision Festival 13, June 10, 2008

Back home, Bynum had also gained the respect of older generations of players and festival organizers. He was invited to play at Vision Festival 13 on June 10, 2008.[185] Bynum and others in the band agree that they reached their climax as a musical unit that night.[186] The band continued to play, going to Europe that summer, but Bynum began to get restless. During the latter half of 2008 and into the following year, Bynum began experimenting with other ideas, bringing in Nate McBride on bass in place of Pavone, and, together with Fujiwara, doing an event in Chicago with trombonist Jeb Bishop, flutist Nicole Mitchell, and guitarist Jeff Parker. For another gig at the Jazz Gallery in November 2008, he brought in Jason Kao Hwang on violin. But these new directions eventually compelled Bynum to write a new book of music for mostly new musicians. In 2010 he started a new sextet, retaining Halvorson and Fujiwara but also bringing in alto saxophonist Jim Hobbs, bassist Ken Filiano, and tubaist Bill Lowe.[187] While the generational band idea had made its mark, Bynum consciously returned to something intergenerational. "For my music and what I am interested in as a composer, I think I like the energy that comes from different backgrounds, different generations. With my sextet now, I have someone born in the 1940s, 50s, 60s, 70s, and 80s."[188] Bynum had also had enough of New York. In 2009, after spending nearly five years in the city, he moved his base of operations to New Haven so that he could participate in both the New York and Boston scenes. Nevertheless, he left a deep imprint on his generation of players, both through his musical ideas and through the people he brought together in the process.

Pourhouse

In the spring of 2003, alto saxophonist Jackson Moore started the Overground Improvised Music Series at Pourhouse, a bar with a back room for performances situated at the corner of Metropolitan Avenue and Humboldt Street in East Williamsburg. The bar was situated just a block off Bushwick Avenue, so the appearance of the series there marked the first weekly events in the scene to occur at the east end of the neighborhood. Moore sent out an email to "everyone he knew," pooling together musicians he had met since moving to New York City, as well as the community he had been part of while studying with Anthony Braxton at Wesleyan University in the late 1990s.[189] Moore was not particularly exclusionary about whom he booked in terms of the aesthetics of the music.[190] He often had more straight-ahead jazz on the same bill as some very experimental music. The aim was to have a neighborhood series for the community. Moore kept it accessible by charging only $5 at the door, attracting a range of musicians, Pourhouse regulars, and passersby who came in to check out the music.

Each bill at Pourhouse featured three bands. Moore's personal impetus for founding the series was to create a weekly gig for himself, the primary feature of which was his trio with bassist Shanir Blumenkranz and drummer Kevin Zubek, though he also played with other groups there.[191] The trio had come together after Moore had witnessed SATLAH, Danny Zamir's trio, and decided to hire the rhythm section for his own band.[192] Moore began writing music for the trio and, aside from practicing with them regularly, invited them to be the mainstay of the scene at Pourhouse. Their music featured melodic yet exploratory or, at times, mournful alto lines that simmered above a turbulent undercurrent of rhythmic volatility.[193] Moore generally split the door fees between the other two bands and usually paid his band out of his own pocket.[194]

The other reason Moore started the series was to build a creative space for his generation of musicians, who were just then coming of age. "If I had been five or ten years older, maybe I would have been part of the neoclassical jazz movement, but people my age, at that time, were more interested in the 1980s downtown scene and with the ideas of figures like Albert Ayler . . . rather than trying to copy Miles Davis." Ayler (1936–70) was one of the most influential saxophonists of the 1960s free jazz era. According to Moore, the spirit of the time was "Has it already all been done, or can we do something new?" Moore had a natural inquisitiveness in relation to the music. He remarked, "To me, creative music is almost like a scientific field, and each decade brought new discoveries of how the music-making process worked in terms of cognitive and performative constraints. Or to put it another way, jazz history is analogous to different and evolving expressions of human nature."[195] Moore's generation was not bound together by a certain musical structure, practice, or procedure but rather attracted to a common spectrum of concepts, drawing influence from myriad sources and genres both within and outside of jazz. Following the energy music of the 1990s, Moore cited "rigorous composition" as one of the hallmarks that the younger

Figure 3.7 James Ilgenfritz's Anagram Ensemble: (*from left*) Nate Wooley, Joe Tomino, Jonathan Moritz, and Ilgenfritz, ca. 2005 (*private collection*)

generation began to employ, while retaining significant room for free improvisation.[196] The Overground series was one of the primary spaces for experimentation for the post-Wesleyan generation in Brooklyn at the time.

Among the bands that emerged at Pourhouse was bassist James Ilgenfritz's Anagram Ensemble. Ilgenfritz had studied at the University of Michigan and thus had connected with figures such as Matt Bauder and Aaron Siegel before arriving in New York. The first version of the band had been founded in Ann Arbor, but after moving to the East Coast, Ilgenfritz hired trumpeter Nate Wooley, saxophonist Jonathan Moritz, and drummer Joe Tomino for the new iteration of the group (see figure 3.7). "Anagram Ensemble," Ilgenfritz remarked, was "a working band for my compositional strategies" at that time, working on music that was situated in the space between jazz and new classical music.[197] In particular, Ilgenfritz focused on investigating the relationship between "odd meters and fluid time," especially meters that were "focused on feeling awkward," as inspired by bands such as Secret Chiefs 3 and the Balkan-inspired Pachora.[198]

On a compositional level, Ilgenfritz drew from guitarist Derek Bailey, as well as more contemporaneous figures such as John Hollenbeck's The

Claudia Quintet, Tim Berne's Bloodcount, and Tomino's own band, Birth, and the way the musicians in these groups managed to form grooves while playing free over the unusual meters and rhythms.[199] The final ingredient that tied it together was from the work of Greg Kelley and Bhob Rainey's experimental and improvisatory duo Nmperign and percussionist Sean Meehan, whom he had encountered at ABC No Rio. One particular performance organized by Kurt Gottschalk with Meehan, James Fei, and John Butcher, "where they were each in different rooms, but playing together, because the walls were low and sound bled," sparked additional conceptual ideas for Ilgenfritz. Thus, "Anagram Ensemble was about integrating those interests: awkward grooves, ecstatic melodies, fluid integration of odd meter time and free rhythm, and increasingly an emphasis on ambiguous sound worlds."[200]

Performances at Pourhouse in December 2003 and April 2004 helped launch the Brooklyn version of Anagram Ensemble, and they also played at South Brooklyn clubs such as Freddy's Backroom and Barbès before embarking on two tours through the Midwest and New England in 2004 and 2005. Unfortunately, the band never recorded any studio material. Nevertheless, the band provided Ilgenfritz with an opportunity to explore musical concepts he found intriguing and was a journey in itself, though he concluded, "One thing that led me to moving on from that band was more fully embracing the Joe Maneri–influenced sense of freedom and gesturality," which he explored with Jonathan Moritz in Trio Caveat in subsequent years.[201]

By 2004 Jackson Moore found it difficult to keep up with booking a weekly series and invited young alto saxophonist Aaron Ali Shaikh to share the task with him. Shaikh was still an undergraduate at the New School but lived in the neighborhood and was "a very social, garrulous kind of guy who was great at organizing and getting people to support the series."[202] Shaikh had some experience organizing concerts at his apartment at 283 South Fifth Street in Williamsburg.[203] One of Shaikh's interests in the series was to offer musicians who were not getting gigs at Tonic or other Lower East Side venues a place to present their music.[204]

Moore and Shaikh eventually produced a series of bigger events called New Languages Festival at other locations, such as a basement room at Anthology Film Archives in Manhattan or at Rose Live in Williamsburg, but these were directly connected to the series at Pourhouse.[205] The aim was to feature the music of their generation and developed in response to the fact that the Vision Festival, which had been running since 1996, focused on an older generation of musicians and thus did not afford opportunities to Moore and Shaikh's contemporaries.[206] The first festival featured Shaikh for a set that doubled as his senior recital show. At another of the festivals, Moore presented work that "featured a series of meter modulations" and other experiments in rhythm, structure, and time.[207] Bassist Eivind Opsvik's band Overseas also explored rhythmic possibilities that were "abstracted, inflated or deconstructed" while maintaining a pop-like feel to the music.[208] With Akoya Afrobeat Ensemble and Burnt Sugar on the bills, they aimed to present a spectrum of music to challenge the audience on multiple fronts each night.

By late 2005 Moore withdrew from the series, and soon after, Shaikh asked fellow saxophonist Will Jones to help with the booking. Jones came from a more straight-ahead jazz circle, and he began drawing from that community for many of his contributions to the booking.[209] Shaikh and Jones bartended at a different bar down the street, so they would publicize events there, hang up posters in the area, and advertise them by word of mouth. The two continued curating the series until the owners sold Pourhouse in 2006.

The Scene Finds a New Home

Major rezoning passed by the Michael Bloomberg administration in 2005 led to the swift decline of Williamsburg's arts wave. In anticipation of the neighborhood's rezoning from manufacturing to residential, buildings had been converting in small numbers, month by month, since the late 1990s.[210] These conversions represented an earlier wave of neighborhood transformation but precipitated the massive wave in 2005–6. Also, the group Neighbors against Garbage (NAG) led a movement that advocated for more residential areas, affordable housing, access to the waterfront, and mixed-use zoning; the plan was approved by the City Planning Commission in 2001 but had no force of law.[211] Community-based planning champion and activist Jane Jacobs, famous for building an opposition movement to city planner Robert Moses's infrastructure projects in Greenwich Village in the 1960s, voiced her support for NAG's plan and attacked the city's plan in an open letter in the *Brooklyn Rail*, stating:

> The proposal put before you by city staff is an ambush containing all those destructive consequences, packaged very sneakily with visually tiresome, unimaginative and imitative luxury project towers. How weird, and how sad, that New York, which has demonstrated successes enlightening to so much of the world, seems unable to learn the lesson it needs

for itself. I will make two predictions with utter confidence. 1) If you follow the community's plan you will harvest a success. 2) If you follow the proposal before you today, you will maybe enrich a few heedless and ignorant developers but at the cost of an ugly and intractable mistake. Come on, do the right thing. The community really does know best.[212]

The city government ignored most of the community's demands and pushed for much denser redevelopment on the waterfront to incentivize developers' involvement.[213] Ultimately, 186 blocks were marked for rezoning, which had a major impact not just on the waterfront itself but deep into the interior of the neighborhood.[214]

The rezoning was catastrophic. Within a year Williamsburg was undergoing full-scale physical transformation and displacement of existing residents and businesses. Lofts and garages, like the one that had hosted the Improvised and Otherwise festival, and many other venues were almost universally sold off to developers, who displaced the community wholescale. Artist evictions were especially acute around McCarren Park but happened across the neighborhood. As Pratt Institute's urban planning professor Ward Dennis stated, "No block north of Division Avenue went untouched by the rezoning. Virtually every block has witnessed new construction. It changed everything."[215] The rezoning also set the clock for commercial districts, many of which were on ten-year leases with a five-year option. When those leases began to expire in the mid-2010s, commercial districts changed dramatically as monthly rents went from around $5,000 at the turn of the millennium to $30,000 or more.[216] No music venue survived this escalation.

The cafés, galleries, and bars of Bedford Avenue and other parts of Williamsburg were soon replaced by upscale restaurants and apparel stores frequented by hipsters and fashionistas. This swept out the cafés and bars that had catered to the music. Many owners were incentivized to sell their buildings or businesses to developers because of rising real estate values. Much of the DIY scene was pushed out overnight, while spaces that managed to resist the 2005–6 wave gradually closed as their leases expired in the years that followed. What remained in Williamsburg proper coalesced around the club Zebulon and the unlicensed space Death by Audio, the last major music venues in Williamsburg that provided stages for the avant-garde. The Williamsburg community of artists found it increasingly difficult to live in the neighborhood, and they were rapidly pushed east and south. East Williamsburg was the first stop on the way to the Bushwick music scene that was then beginning to coalesce further along the postindustrial L train corridor.

Nevertheless, the post-Wesleyan music scene that arose at the Right Bank Café, the Read Café, Newsonic Loft, and Pourhouse had an enduring legacy. Many of the figures that had emerged not only were getting opportunities to play at Manhattan clubs but were also featured on the European festival circuit. It was a breakthrough for a generation of creative musicians bringing their innovative sounds to new audiences, first in the DIY venues of Williamsburg and then on a world stage.

PART II

COMMERCIAL DIY AND THE LAST UNDER- GROUND VENUES

CHAPTER FOUR

A Point of Confluence

The Downtown Scene Comes to Zebulon, 2004–2006

Their priority was to present music.
—*Louis Belogenis*

Fortunately for the Williamsburg music scene, its most visible, public, fully licensed venue appeared just before the rezoning laws were set to push out the artist lofts. In June 2004 Zebulon Café Concert opened at 258 Wythe Avenue in Williamsburg, having legalized a former loft, the Green Room, as a public venue. Zebulon quickly became the epicenter of the music for the neighborhood and for other parts of Brooklyn and Lower Manhattan.[1] Founded by three French proprietors, Guillaume Blestel and brothers Joce and Jef Soubiran, Zebulon came into being from their collective desire to feature music, film, and art they admired. With a rustic, yet welcoming interior with a familiar DIY feel, the club quickly drew artists and audience members alike to its doors. Just as the loft scene was about to be dealt a death blow by Mayor Michael Bloomberg's rezoning bill, Zebulon became the main place to play. In August 2004 Zebulon began hosting live music. The club took its name from a beloved 1960s character from the French television series *Le Manege enchanté*, which Jef Soubiran explained was "full of energy, jumping everywhere."[2] Rather quickly, the music scene concentrated at Zebulon unlike at any other venue in the history of Williamsburg.

The atmosphere at Zebulon was part of its allure. As one music critic described it, "Only a few blocks from the art-school monoculture of Bedford Avenue, Zebulon Café Concert is a dark, glittering, entirely different world—an authentically bohemian *boite* better suited to the Boulevard St. Germaine."[3] Another writer described the entrance into the club: "Sweeping aside the velvet curtain that hangs inside the doorway, helping to keep the winter air out, you emerge into a homey café where votive candles in glass holders flicker above the tabletops."[4] One artist who attended concerts there regularly described it as "beautifully bootleg. It was always dark inside with a few candles. When it was full, it was super cramped with people, practically sitting on top of each other; you had to look through the mass to see the stage, which was small, with chairs and tables positioned around it."[5] Meanwhile another observer described the interior ambience: "Orange orbs, suspended on rods from the high, tin-covered ceiling, added a soft glow to the dark wood surfaces. Across the ceiling beam that bisects the airy room hung album covers: Bob Dylan, John Coltrane, Jimi Hendrix, Rahsaan Roland Kirk, Babatunde Olatunji, the Beatles, Charles Mingus."[6] During the breaks between live sets of music, recordings by the likes of Don Cherry or Pharoah Sanders could be heard through the house speakers.[7]

From the very beginning, Zebulon featured eclectic bills, proudly ignoring genre classifications, from one night to the next, with music beginning every night at ten o'clock. The club emerged after the Knitting Factory had closed and the Lower East Side scene had gravitated to Tonic. The Soubiran brothers had also connected with the community on the Lower East Side through their years of running Jules Bistro on St. Mark's Place and Casimir on Avenue B, where they also booked live jazz.[8] But at Zebulon they were able to have more adventuresome acts. Many of the people they booked in the early years of Zebulon came from their connections to the Lower East Side community, such as Lawrence "Butch" Morris, Charles Gayle, and Billy Bang. In another way, the union of the Manhattan and Brooklyn scenes that Jump Arts had envisioned just a few years before was finally coming to full fruition at the club. Beyond music, the club was the site of the filming of Jonas Mekas's 365 Day Project, and it was where Sun Ra Arkestra leader Marshall Allen played a legendary concert until three in the morning "with such intensity that his hand was bleeding," and where poet Ira Cohen celebrated his seventieth birthday with a deep reading.[9] Zebulon was one of New York's vanguard art spaces during the years of its operation.

But a club like Zebulon functioned much differently than the loft or warehouse spaces that had littered Williamsburg in previous years. For one, it was a public venue, so it had greater visibility both within and outside of the communities of artists who presented their work there. Its public persona also allowed Zebulon to attract more established artists to their stage than the lofts ever could. This visibility, of course, had multiple outcomes for the community. For one, it meant that lesser-known artists who were still trying to establish a name for themselves were able to interact with the more established acts. As time went on, though, and Zebulon became more popular, it began attracting a different crowd and shifted its focus to cater to their interests, which were less experimental. And, of course, while the owners of Zebulon generally had a good reputation with artists, the club was not community run like a loft, and the bills tended to be more eclectic, rather than drawn through the collective social networks of a particular curator. Some artists and other residents even viewed Zebulon as part of the new wave of gentrification that was then sweeping Williamsburg, moving the scene away from the loft era.

Nevertheless, whichever artists took the stage brought with them accumulated histories of their work, varied years of experience, and various types of artistic output that made their mark on the collective cultural milieu of the venue itself. Collectively, the artists represented a vast network, drawing aesthetic influence from deep within avant-garde jazz but also tinctured with myriad other influences, local, regional, and international in their origin. This chapter and the following one explore some of those global networks and accumulated histories and the ways they interacted, coalesced, and contended with one another.

Zebulon never had a cover charge, and every band was paid the same base rate. The aim was to make the music "accessible to everyone."[10] Bands were paid by a portion of the bar till, supplemented by passing the hat. That meant that on good nights a band might make approximately $500, though at other times the money was much lower.[11] Every night was different, but Zebulon developed such a trusted reputation that musicians and audience members alike often said, "You did not have to look at the bill on any given night. If you wanted to see music, you would just drop by on the assumption that it was going to be great."[12] In musician slang, Zebulon was "a hang," where the community would gather from night to night, sometimes regardless of who was performing; at the same time, it was more relaxed than Manhattan venues like Roulette or the Stone. The Soubiran brothers seemed to have a deeper interest in the music than most venue owners, so their relations with musicians were generally marked with fewer tensions than in most club settings. The owners gave a lot of license to musicians. Bands got to decide the structure of the evening, such as three shorter sets or one long set, as long as the music began around ten o'clock and did not go later than three in the morning. "They put the music first, and they did whatever they had to do to stay alive financially, but their priority was to present music," one regular performer at the club stated.[13] "Zebulon was a busy bar run by people who loved music," trumpeter Peter Evans described it. "I much preferred to play there, even if it was a little DIY, than at some more well-known club in Manhattan because they let me do what I wanted as an artist."[14] Zebulon's owners often recorded the sets and at the end of the night handed a CD to bandleaders as they departed. A handful of those live recordings were subsequently released by individual artists, as well as a Zebulon sampler compilation.[15]

Zebulon's initial strategy to build an audience was to invite established figures of the downtown scene to play. The first major event the venue featured was a residency by violinist Billy Bang in August 2004. Though the event did not garner big crowds—perhaps fifteen people per night—it established the venue as a place committed to bringing masterful figures to the stage.[16]

Downtown Sound in Brooklyn: Charles Gayle's Residency

Soon after, tenor saxophonist Charles Gayle (b. 1939) began frequenting the club's bills on an extended residency from late 2004 to August 2005, presenting his fiery trio with bassist Hilliard Greene and drummer Jay Rosen. Gayle was and remains an immense figure, one of the most expressive and original tenor saxophonists ever to play the instrument, and his stature raised Zebulon's profile and legitimized it as a venue for serious music. This particular trio had been a long-standing project for Gayle, who had been playing with Greene since 1987 with various drummers over the years, including David Pleasant, Michael Wimberly, and others.[17] This extended musical relationship between Gayle and Greene fostered a deep understanding of each other and enabled Greene to react to Gayle in the live setting adeptly. The two had met when Gayle was homeless, dressed in an overcoat, playing at Grand Central Station, and Greene, who was working as a foot messenger, passed by. Greene was so impressed with Gayle's playing that he stopped, and the two struck up a conversation.[18] "After hearing him, I thought, he is really an extraordinary player," Greene recalled.[19] One critic in the mid-1980s described Gayle's playing as "forthright, speechlike lines," adding that Gayle "plays everything from deep subtones to whistling high notes with controlled clarity; he uses the upper register, in particular, as smoothly as a soul singer uses falsetto."[20] After the initial chance encounter, Gayle invited Greene to play with him soon after, and the two musicians became friends. "He was more of a mentor and a father figure to me, in a way," Greene recounted.[21]

Gayle had been playing for many years by the time the trio came together and had been an innovator but had received no attention in the press. He had begun playing piano at age nine and later undertook an autodidactic study of trumpet, bass, drums, harp, and, at the age of nineteen, saxophone, which he described as "my first love."[22] He grew up in Buffalo, New York, first in the Willert Park housing projects and then in the middle-class neighborhood of Hamlin Park. He described it as a community in which all businesses were Black owned and operated, where "you could walk all over the city and feel like you were coming home to something that belonged to you."[23] Gayle had been brought up on boogie-woogie blues ("not to learn it, but because everyone was playing it in the area"), European classical music, Black church music, and jazz. Gayle described his work as "personal music with all of those other forms of music included." He added, "To develop what I have, I had to stay away from playing like John Coltrane, Ornette Coleman, Eric Dolphy, Freddie Hubbard, or whoever, I had to break the influences to keep me in tune with myself. It has to be developed from inside. Good music, I don't care what you call it. The only reason I say mine is avant-garde is because I am not consciously using somebody else's principles, form, or thoughts."[24]

After attending college on a basketball scholarship, Gayle worked in the Westinghouse factory warehouse in Buffalo while he played locally.[25] He soon entered the ranks of bank management and seemed, for a time, destined for a life in the finance industry, before the call to the music became irresistible. Buffalo had an active jazz scene, and the avant-garde of the time included saxophonists Joseph Ford and Andrew White III; bassists Buell Neidlinger, Ray Combs, and Sabu Adeyola; and percussionists Nasar Abadey, Ameer Alhark, and John Bergamo.[26] The real springboard for Gayle's earliest public performances came through a series of Black arts festivals sponsored by the city.

Gayle's earliest known performance in New York dates to 1967, at Neidlinger's invitation, but he returned to Buffalo, where he taught at the

University of Buffalo from 1970 to 1973. During that period he led a number of bands and was considered by many of his contemporaries as the leader of the free jazz movement there. Still, he left no known recordings, and beyond the university, he found no consistent outlets for his music "unless you wanted to play in attics somewhere."[27] After he voiced public support for Black students engaging in school boycotts, the Superintendent of the Buffalo schools conspired with university administrators to have him fired from his position.[28] He basically disappeared from Buffalo, aside for a few gigs with Julius Eastman in 1976. In 1973 he moved to New York City, where one of Gayle's first gigs was with drummer Rashied Ali.[29]

Gayle spent much of the period from 1973 to 1987 homeless in New York City, residing in a squat on East Ninth Street, Manhattan, as well as in various locations in Bedford-Stuyvesant or Crown Heights in Brooklyn.[30] "I came to this city broke and I'm still broke," Gayle stated in 1985.[31] "I was on the streets—I walked out one day and that was it. That was one of the greatest experiences I had in my life, though I didn't do it for that reason. You have nothing and you're not asking anybody for anything."[32] Gayle maintained his musical practice throughout his years on the streets:

> Not to evaluate everything through money, I've lived in abandoned buildings. I've lived outside, inside, in the cold. There were a couple times when I was living in these conditions that I thought I was going to die. Every year hundreds of people freeze to death in New York, especially in the ghetto. Black men have the highest mortality rate in this country. But I like the streets, I grew up in them to a degree, and I'm still up in there, and I live in a neighborhood that is beautiful to me. The energy is there. The hard times become bearable. The hard times I think are necessary. To know joy on this earth is to know sorrow. As opposed to someone coming out of college or a conservatory eating good every day, I've had to eat off of the sidewalks and out of garbage cans, but I have maintained practicing. It doesn't harden your heart, but it hardens you to be able to do this, to get through.[33]

During his time living homeless, he experienced a profound calling to Catholicism, which has been a major guiding light for his life since that time.[34]

Gayle was one of the free jazz players who led the resurgence of the scene in the late 1980s, creating a "street-level buzz" unlike any other unrecorded figure of the time. He played duo with German bassist Peter Kowald in 1984 as well as at the Sound Unity Festival that year, but it was at the Knitting Factory from 1987 on that he really drew attention, leading one critic to describe his work as "unrepentant free jazz."[35] Labels took note, with the Swedish label Silkheart leading the way, releasing three records by Gayle in 1988–89. The Knitting Factory became a haven for Gayle, and he released six records with the club's label between 1992 and 2001, as well as making numerous appearances on FMP, Black Saint, and other labels of the era. Through these years Gayle established himself as one of the great voices on tenor saxophone and one of the most influential players since Coltrane and Albert Ayler. One enamored critic wrote, "Mr. Gayle plays contours and textures rather than melodies, using a different range and technique for each composition. He gets a huge saxophone tone, whether he's playing wide-open low notes or shrieking overtones—a different quality, steadier and steelier, than the overblown notes of Albert Ayler and Pharoah Sanders—and he holds the stage with calm dignity while generating a fusillade of music."[36]

On the New York scene, Gayle was propelled from a relatively unknown figure on the underground to suddenly being at the forefront of the music with a series of groundbreaking records under his own name. One critic praised his solos on *Homeless*, which "rivet you with their energy, control, and endless ripple of ideas."[37] Gayle remarked of his work at the time, "I want to play good music. I want it to happen, to be there, and I work on this every day, just staying in the spirit of it."[38] Gayle's monumental body of work from the 1990s documented the artist at the height of his powers, after many years of being ignored by the recording industry. Yet, when asked in 1999 about his success, Gayle replied, "I can only get by. This is not the rich man's music. And that's fine."[39]

Religious imagery and symbolism pervaded much of Gayle's work throughout his career and was evident in all of his preacher-style free playing of the late 1980s through the mid-1990s (see figure 4.1). The names of many of his pieces were drawn from biblical passages or embedded with religious symbolism. He also sometimes preached his views in between pieces during live sets, such as a now-famous moment at the Knitting Factory when he criticized the manipulative control white people exerted over the jazz industry.[40] He also expressed religious views, such as his opposition to abortion. These public pronouncements alienated some audience members, but that did not matter to Gayle. Some Black musicians appreciated his courage in speaking of issues about which most people were silent.

Over the years Gayle rarely talked with his bandmates about the music, though he had clear ideas of where he wanted to take it. The idea was for each of them to use their intuition and sensibilities to generate something. Gayle was the catalyst at the beginning of most pieces, but then the others

Figure 4.1 Charles Gayle, Vision Festival, 2005 (*photo by Peter Gannushkin*)

would "just go." Hilliard Greene described the process: "We would get locked in, and the energy waves would come, and we would just let it carry us, latch onto it. Each time we played, it was a different episode of the music."[41]

The Zebulon concerts in 2004 and 2005 stand out in the Gayle corpus in that they took place during a rare period when he was playing jazz standards (see figure 4.2). This part of Gayle's work, often ignored, began in a gig with his trio in the mid-1990s. "I had been playing with him for years and out of the clear blue he went into 'Giant Steps' at a faster tempo than I had ever played the tune," Greene recalled.[42] During the Zebulon residency, the band was exploring other standards, such as "I Remember April," but expanded and adapted significantly.[43] For one, Gayle did not adhere to the form of the piece. But the open format of the trio also allowed Greene and Rosen to reimagine the pieces and abstract them far more than would be done in most jazz contexts. Greene remarked around that time, "Working with him recently, we play standards mostly but in a different way. On the gig he jumps right into a standard and it will be, most of the time, one I have played for years. It's fun for me because I get to do stuff with the tunes that

Figure 4.2 Charles Gayle Trio: (*from left*) Hilliard Greene, Gayle, and Jay Rosen, Vision Festival, 2005 (*photo by Peter Gannushkin*)

I don't normally get a chance to do. The tempo range is wide. We will play ballads at Jimmy Scott tempos and some of the up-tempos at Oscar Peterson speed."[44] Greene later reflected, "Charles always had a clear idea of what we wanted to do and where he intended to go with the music, but he would not write it down. He would start, and we would follow and react. He was relentless and brilliant in his vision."[45] Musician Ken Butler commented with regard to Gayle's performances at Zebulon that the latter "never played a note that was not fully impassioned."[46]

The music the trio presented during the Zebulon residency was similar to material that appeared on a live recording that was done at Vision Festival in June 2005, though it did not include any of the standard variations.[47] At the time Gayle described how he imagined his audience as "desiring the fiber of their very existence to be deeply touched and carried to places unknown."[48] Gayle continued to perform regularly in New York until the early 2010s, before moving back to Buffalo, though he continues to play and record. Through this he has been guided by a strong personal drive, perhaps best encapsulated in a statement he made back in 1991: "It's just something in me. It's a fate that challenges you until it becomes very natural. You have to dig inside your soul and keep creating. You have to fight your memory, because it's easy to recapitulate. You keep pushing, because it's there, and you don't know what it is. You just keep going."[49]

Kalaparusha's Return

One musician who had largely disappeared from the music scene in the 1980s and 1990s but experienced a rebirth at Zebulon was saxophonist Kalaparusha Maurice McIntyre (1936–2013), who had a four-month residency there in late 2004 and early 2005. He was a player with an incredible array of influences ranging from hard bop to free jazz to Indian classical music and displayed this breadth in his recordings and live performances. And though he played free, he had an appreciation for musical structure and blending of different sounds and concepts, while maintaining a resolute identity as a musician.

Born in Clarksville, Arkansas, McIntyre grew up "in the ghetto" on the South Side of Chicago, the son of a pharmacist and seamstress, in a community that he described as "the side of town where all the Black people lived."[50] By the time he was in high school, his family had moved closer to Hyde Park. He played music during his youth, but he solidified his musical voice while serving time in a federal narcotics prison in Lexington, Kentucky, in 1959–62 "for abusing heroin." There he encountered pianist Tadd Dameron, who led him in a band that also included, at different times, reeds player Sam Rivers, trumpeter Chet Baker, pianist Kenny Drew, bassists Wilbur Ware and Charlie Haden, and an otherwise unknown saxophonist, Bobby Miller from Dayton, Ohio, whom Kalaparusha described as "phenomenal."[51] Kalaparusha realized in those prison sessions, "When I first got there . . . I couldn't play. I did two years and nine months, and all that time I stayed in the practice room all day long. When I got out . . . I was a professional musician."[52] Rivers served as his mentor, and the two of them jammed together, working out standards like "All the Things You Are," among other tunes.[53] Kalaparusha later considered him to be "very influential. Sam was there when I passed the barrier from not being able to play to being able to play."[54] Kalaparusha experimented with the baritone saxophone in addition to the tenor, working hard to impress the parole board in "learning a trade" so that they eventually released him early.[55] From his early days, Kalaparusha learned by playing bebop charts but also could play free. The fusion of composition and improvisation guided him through his musical life.

Kalaparusha got his bearings on the Chicago scene playing in Muhal Richard Abrams's Experimental Band every Monday night for a period in the early 1960s. "I could just see that something new was happening there," he later recalled thinking at the time. He lived with saxophonist Roscoe Mitchell and bassist Malachi Favors in the Chatham neighborhood, "where well-to-do Black folks lived at the time," and one time Mitchell caught Kalaparusha trying to play some Hank Mobley licks on his horn. He asked him, "Why are you trying to learn that? Why don't you play your own stuff? So I began to play my own stuff. At first, it felt like I was jumping into an empty elevator shaft. Nothing to stand on. But then I began to find my sound. That was right as AACM was starting. It brought about the music of expression."[56] Kalaparusha developed a competitive rivalry with Mitchell.

One night, after rehearsal, Kalaparusha was playing with Mitchell and some other musicians at a bar on Seventy-First Street. When people in the crowd were talking, Mitchell told them that the music was serious and asked them to be quiet. When the musicians resumed, they played "an old blues," and Kalaparusha "heard the sound of his own horn and he broke down crying like a baby" such that Mitchell had to come help him off the stage. "It was a spiritual awakening for me, a moment of great magnitude," he recounted many years later.[57] At that same time, Eric Dolphy's record *Out to Lunch!* was very inspirational for Kalaparusha.[58] But unlike many of his contemporaries on the scene there, Kalaparusha was not really interested in moving in the direction that the Art Ensemble of Chicago was going, further into the realm of creative music, and preferred his own aesthetic, "not quite as revolutionary and closer to the music that had come before."[59]

McIntyre appeared on some of the key early recordings led by members of the AACM, such as Roscoe Mitchell and Muhal Richard Abrams, as well as his own, *Humility in the Light of Creator*, receiving critical acclaim for his work.[60] Trumpeter Taylor Ho Bynum wrote that these early recordings "introduced a new kind of sonic world, where delicate overtones and harmonics are intimately examined, where extended silences are juxtaposed with found sounds and stately melodies, where traditional instruments are pushed to their breaking point to discover new timbres."[61] McIntyre adopted the name Kalaparusha Ahrah Difda in 1968. The name came from Sanskrit, *kala* (black) and *parusha* (male), with the final *a* going unpronounced, though he also considered it to have the meaning "spirit consciousness" or "never-ending spirit."[62] Ahrah was his own creation, meaning "elemental sonic energy," and Difda is an orange giant star, generally placed in the Cetus constellation.[63]

In 1974, at the suggestion of drummer Jack DeJohnette (b. 1942), and urged by his girlfriend, Gladys "Sita" Horton, whom he later married, Kalaparusha moved to Woodstock, New York. He taught at the Creative Music Studio, which had been founded by Ornette Coleman, Karl Berger, and Ingrid Berger two years prior.[64] Though he did meet musicians that way, he was alienated by the wealth of many of the Woodstock artists and community members, which eventually drove him out after a year and a half; he then moved to Brooklyn.[65] On arriving in the city, he took part in the burgeoning loft scene at places like Studio Rivbea and Studio WIS and played in the Sam Rivers Big Band, which performed in France in 1977.[66] He worked with DeJohnette and bassist Dave Holland (b. 1946), among others, and even auditioned with Miles Davis (1926–91).[67] He joined other AACM-affiliated colleagues there, such as multi-instrumentalists Muhal Richard Abrams (1930–2017) and Henry Threadgill (b. 1944), drummer Steve McCall (1933–89), pianist Amina Claudine Myers (b. 1942), and trombonist George Lewis (b. 1952), and they eventually founded a New York chapter.[68] He presented concerts with the organization until at least 1982.[69]

In 1981, after plans to take Horton with him on tour to Europe collapsed, their relationship deteriorated. She eventually "threw him out" of the nice apartment they had in Park Slope, Brooklyn, and his financial and personal situation rapidly deteriorated. She had effectively been working as his manager, arranging gigs for him, applying annually for grants from the National Endowment for the Arts, and taking care of the money. Without that support, Kalaparusha, who admitted he "did not have much business sense," became homeless by the following year.[70] He turned to the subways to make money on a daily basis so that he could survive, feeling too ashamed to ask for more support from his friends.[71] Then, after years of struggling in obscurity, he redeveloped an active addiction to heroin in 1994, after being free of it for over thirty years, when a friend shared some with him. He often thought that it would help him make better music.[72] Kalaparusha reemerged to notice in the late 1990s, busking on the streets and in the subways of New York.

Some elder members of the community tried to help him out, with fellow AACM members Professor George Lewis paying for dental surgeries and reeds player Roscoe Mitchell also contributing, while bassist William Parker gave him a better-quality horn to play.[73] Kalaparusha commented around that time, "If I wasn't dealing with music, I don't know what I would do to get any money. I don't know how to do nothing else but play the horn. My father didn't want me to be a musician. He called my horn a starvation box. I ain't ever starved, but I ain't had any money either."[74] In one of those many performances, Kalaparusha met tuba player and fellow busker Jesse Dulman, who was just nineteen years old at the time.[75] Dulman had grown up in a working-class family in Chelsea and by playing in the streets and subways was able to pay rent, making about $50 per day. In their first encounter, Kalaparusha walked down the stairs onto the mezzanine at the Broadway-Lafayette subway stop in Manhattan and asked Dulman if he could sit in with him. "Wow, you have a big sound," he told the tuba player after a few minutes of playing, though Dulman still did not know the identity of the mysterious saxophone player.[76] Eventually Dulman asked him his name and was shocked to find that he was playing with someone he regarded as a living legend. The two struck up a musical collaboration and began to play together, practicing at Kalaparusha's apartment in the South Bronx. They played their first duo shows at the Internet Café and at a barbershop at 211 Smith Street in Brooklyn.[77]

In 2001 multi-instrumentalist Will Connell Jr., a notorious matchmaker in the music scene, introduced Kalaparusha to drummer Ravish Momin because of their common interest in Indian music, and soon the group became a trio with Dulman called Kalaparusha and the Light, reviving a band name that Kalaparusha had used briefly in Chicago in 1969.[78] Dulman had studied with Bob Stewart, Marcus Rojas, and Charles McGee but claimed, "Where I really developed my chops was playing for hours on end in the subway."[79] Momin had previously worked with Connell, Sabir Mateen, and others, having arrived in New York the previous year. Momin was impressed that even though Kalaparusha was in his mid-sixties at that time, he still had a hunger to explore new areas of music, ranging from experimental Indonesian gamelan to Indian ragas. "He always had a sense of humor and sometimes would break into dancing during rehearsals or smile or laugh if music really gripped him," Momin recalled.[80] Kalaparusha remained a deeply spiritual and religious person throughout his life, and he often commented that God had brought the three of them together to do musical work.[81]

One of the rare qualities of the band was the substitution of tuba for bass. It had been done before, of course, and Kalaparusha felt some inspiration from the Sam Rivers Quintet, which included Joe Daley (b. 1949) on tuba, though he executed it differently in his own band.[82] At the core, this transformed the inner workings of the trio and the way the rhythms were formed. The kind of ostinato vamping that the bass might maintain was not possible, or at least not for the same durations, but the tuba created a more fluid, darker center. Sometimes Dulman's sound, when he and Kalaparusha played the melody together, formed a kind of "melodic foil," while at other times the tuba's undercurrent added texture as he delved into multiphonics.[83] At times, Momin and Dulman traded roles back and forth to maintain the underlying energy. Momin added Indian rhythms and techniques, such as hand drumming on the snare or other drums, as well as more common jazz rhythms, to the sonic palette. "Kalaparusha had played with some of the great drummers, like Jack DeJohnette and Warren Smith," Momin observed, "so I didn't try to compete with that. I just brought in my own energy and approach, and he seemed to appreciate what I was doing."[84]

For their first gigs, Kalaparusha and the Light played at various Lower East Side clubs and art spaces, eventually appearing with some regularity at the Knitting Factory. They also recorded material for their first record in May 2001, which appeared the following year on the CIMP label, which at that time was documenting a lot of the free jazz scene.[85] Kalaparusha still had a recognizable name in the jazz world, so he was able to book gigs elsewhere, too, so they soon played in New England and the Midwest and eventually at Vision Festival in 2002. By March 2003 they embarked on their first European tour, playing three dates in Poland; in Warsaw numerous billboards advertised Kalaparusha's visit, and ecstatic audience members lined up outside the venue to have their aged copies of his earlier records signed.[86] He commented on his popularity, "I think very deeply when I play my horn. People must be picking up on that, it must be coming through. After all I have been through to play this music, when I see people react like that, it makes it all worth it."[87] In August 2003 Kalaparusha received top billing at the Chicago Jazz Festival, returning to the city for the first time in decades.[88] Still, he was shocked at how much the city had changed, especially the South Side, where he had grown up, and commented, "Life pushes you forward. You can't go home. You gotta keep looking ahead."[89]

Kalaparusha had remained addicted to heroin through these years. The band was largely held together by Momin, who managed all of the booking, contacted agents, worked with promoters, made travel plans, organized rehearsals, and kept Kalaparusha focused on the work.[90] Because of his earlier success, Kalaparusha expected that he would be able to make the same kind of money he had in the 1970s, but the scene had changed so dramatically that he was often surprised that long residencies and major money from festivals were not as forthcoming as they had been earlier in his career. Because of his addiction and the unpredictability that came with it, he had undermined many of his relationships with his peers through the years. A key component of Kalaparusha's comeback was that eager younger musicians were willing to work with him despite the limitations that his heroin addiction sometimes imposed on the band. "I did a lot of extra work for him because I was young," Momin explained, "and I was just excited to be able to play and tour with him."[91] Dulman added, "I did not understand the magnitude of it at the time, I was only nineteen, touring with a living legend."[92] Sometimes Kalaparusha would arrive late, or he would nod off during a gig if he was tripping, but he also had plenty of cogent moments that showed every bit of the creative spark still persisting within him.

By the time of his performances at Zebulon in 2004–5, Kalaparusha and the Light had recorded three additional records' worth of material, some of which expanded the band to a quartet with Adam Lane on bass.[93] The most highly touted of these was *Morning Song*, partly because it appeared on Delmark Records, a mainstay for the AACM since the 1960s, but the recording released by Entropy and the second CIMP recording reveal a consistent exploration in his sound.[94] In 2004 Kalaparusha stated, "*Morning Song* is the best record I have made in my life."[95] One critic at the time stated that Kalaparusha "produces a comparatively light tone, his lithe phrasing, nimble technique and translucent timbre pointing to a player who has veered far afield from his more celebrated Chicago contemporaries."[96] The band debuted some of the work to an extensive audience at the Guelph Jazz Festival in Ontario in early September 2003, just a week after laying down the tracks in the studio. A US tour through Michigan, Illinois, Kentucky, and Washington, DC, followed in 2004.

By that time the band was rarely playing in New York since the best-paid work was elsewhere, so when they took the stage at Zebulon for a monthly residency between November 2004 and February 2005 in front of full audiences, it would have been difficult to predict then that these would be the band's last live performances in the city. The Soubiran brothers were aware of Kalaparusha's historical importance and were excited to have him play at the venue. They would have liked him to continue, but Kalaparusha still had unrealistic expectations that he would get paid more and eventually turned down an extension of the residency.[97]

The Zebulon performances prepared the band to perform at the Sons d'Hiver Festival in Paris for the fortieth anniversary of the AACM in February 2005. Those audiences witnessed some of Kalaparusha's most elevated playing of the period. He maintained a stalwart respect for his contemporaries from the organization and still composed homages to them, such as the piece "Hangin' by a Threadgill," written for multi-instrumentalist Henry Threadgill, the only recording of which is preserved from a live session.[98] He often structured pieces around composed riffs, sometimes based on os-

Figure 4.3 Kalaparusha and the Light: (*from left*) Ravish Momin, Kalaparusha Maurice McIntyre, and Jesse Dulman, Israel, 2006 (*private collection*)

tinatos, and the band would rehearse around those, and then he would build them out from there. He would also often vary pieces considerably, playing one up-tempo at one gig and as a ballad at the next performance, such as the piece "Antoinette," allowing pieces to grow, evolve, and fluctuate as he refined the ideas.[99] "When he was on, he was really on," Momin observed, "in full control of the band and with specific ideas of where he wanted the music to go. He would think about the shape not just of a song but of the whole set and how it all fit together. And he was always looking forward."[100]

Following these momentous performances in 2005, Kalaparusha's health began to decline. At the same time, Momin's own bands took off, and he began to put less work into maintaining Kalaparusha's band. The band rarely practiced after March of that year; aside from one performance at the University of Massachusetts in October, they did not have any other gigs through that year. Their final performance was at the Tel Aviv Jazz Festival in Israel in February 2006 (see figure 4.3). Normally, Kalaparusha medicated with methadone when he could not get access to heroin, but he did not have any during the tour and was experiencing significant withdrawal symptoms. Despite being the headline band, they played only a twenty-minute set, and then Kalaparusha left the stage. A critic wrote of the performance that "the group lacked any visible chemistry." He added that the bandleader "has a recognizable warm, deep tone and he can still manage to outline some beautiful and clear solos, but he could not compete with Momin's energetic mastery."[101] The audience uttered "a roaring vocal protest" that brought back the band, which eventually did several encores, but each one was all that Kalaparusha could muster without a break. Momin no longer felt that he could keep the band going.

When the band dissolved, Kalaparusha returned to playing on the streets and in the subways of New York. "Despite being one of the great tenor saxophonists, he was plagued with self-doubt, which is one reason why he continued to play in the subways," Dulman observed.[102] At the time of his death in 2013, Kalaparusha had numerous compositions that remained unrecorded, and many of them were never performed even in sessions, other than aspects of them that appeared in solo performances.[103] He recorded tracks for a subsequent record with a different band in 2010, but it was never released. Kalaparusha spent his final years living in public housing in the South Bronx, busking in the subways and streets of New York with a decaying saxophone held together with rubber bands.[104]

A New Approach to Order:
Conduction and the Butch Morris Orchestras

No figure was more ever present at Zebulon in its early days than composer and conductor Butch Morris. Morris lived on East Seventh Street on the Lower East Side and had a well-known public persona in the neighborhood, so much so that despite his gruff demeanor some jokingly referred to him as "the mayor of the East Village."[105] Morris met the Soubirans at their restaurant Casimir, which was around the corner from his apartment, so when the brothers opened Zebulon, they invited him to lead his groups there. Morris quickly became a pivotal figure in reaching out to other musicians on the scene who also began to present their music at the venue.[106] Morris was an immense figure who bridged the most potent elements of the East and West Coast creative music scenes together with his own brand of music making. His formulation of his unique musical ideas may be traced back to his early years as a musician.

Morris grew up in the Avalon Gardens housing projects of south-central Los Angeles, a few blocks away from Central Avenue, which was the locus of a Black cultural district during his youth.[107] The many jazz luminaries who were active playing in the neighborhood included vibraphonist and bandleader Lionel Hampton, drummer Chico Hamilton, bassist Charles Mingus, saxophonists Dexter Gordon and Art Pepper, pianist Hampton Hawes, and numerous others.[108] There was also a growing musical avant-garde within the Central Avenue music scene that fostered figures such as saxophonists Ornette Coleman and Charles Brackeen; reeds player Eric Dolphy; drummers Ed Blackwell and Billy Higgins; clarinetist John Carter; pianists Andrew Hill, Horace Tapscott, and Carla Bley; trumpeter Don Cherry; and bassists Gary Peacock, Scott LaFaro, and Charlie Haden in an increasingly racially integrated music scene.[109] The music of this period was deeply influential in forming Morris's sonic sensibilities and his appreciation for jazz as well as other music, and in inspiring him to pursue his own musical work.

As a teenager, Morris witnessed the machinations of Los Angeles politics, hostile policing, and a declining economy for Black residents there, which caused the once-vibrant community to erode, resulting in the Watts Rebellion of 1965.[110]

Morris began studying trumpet in 1961, in some ways following in the footsteps of his older brother, bassist Wilber Morris (1937–2002). Butch Morris worked as a music copyist after graduating from high school and served in the military as a medic in the Vietnam War in 1966–69. After his military service, he was nurtured by a community in Los Angeles that included Horace Tapscott, trumpeter Bobby Bradford (b. 1934), saxophonist Arthur Blythe (1940–2017), and a community that revolved around the Underground Musicians and Artists Association, which would later become Tapscott's Pan-Afrikan Peoples Arkestra.[111]

The Ark, as the group was colloquially called, was the center of the Los Angeles creative music scene with a monumental legacy in shaping the music of the city and the many members that passed through the band's ranks. As Tapscott explained, "'Pan Afrikan' because the music would be drawn from Afrikan peoples around the world, and 'Arkestra,' building off the word ark and Noah using it to save different parts of the world, as told in the Bible. We would preserve the music on our Ark, the mothership, and it will be around for people to listen to and enjoy."[112] Tapscott's focus was on developing the musical talents and sensibilities of the poor young people of the community, and the Ark taught music, theater, poetry, visual art, and dance to people from the communities of Watts and Compton.[113]

For Morris, joining the Ark was a turning point in his life that left a lasting impact.[114] At least some of Morris's later interest in Conduction may be traced back to his time playing with Tapscott. As French horn player Wendell C. Williams observed of Tapscott, "We'd play avant-garde, and he could direct that and just take it up and out. We'd sound like birds all of a sudden. We didn't rehearse that; he'd just direct it. He'd stick his hands up in the air, and we knew what he meant. He'd wiggle his fingers, and we'd start sounding like rain. We knew what he meant. We knew the hand signals."[115] Morris himself noted, "Horace had certain signs and everybody knew what those signs were just from having been in his band and playing with him. Those signs were sort of intuitive."[116]

During his time working with the Ark, as well as other groups from that milieu, Morris met saxophonists Charles Brackeen (b. 1940) and Will Connell Jr. (1938–2016) and reeds player David Murray (b. 1955), all of whom had an influence on him.[117] Morris soon moved to Oakland, in 1971, where he met two additional people who would exert a direct impact on his early ideas that would eventually coalesce around Conduction. The first was drummer Charles Moffett (1929–97), who was most famous for playing with Ornette Coleman but also led his own groups. "We played compositions," Morris recalled, "but from time to time Charles would literally conduct the compositions and ensemble improvisations; I say literally because he would slow them down or speed them up or give accents for the band to play. I had never seen anyone conduct this way before. The sign I use for 'sustain' and the gesture I use for 'literal movement' come from Mr. Moffett's vocabulary."[118] The other person of critical importance to Morris's development was his conducting teacher, Jackie Hairston. Though she approached it in a traditional way, it compelled Morris to ask himself, "If the composer was the conductor, and it was me, how could I alter the music in the moment? I'm looking for flexible music." A third influence that sparked some of his early ideas was encounters with Charles Brackeen, because Morris saw the former as "really being in charge, where there's no notated music. I told Charles, 'I want to carry this on because I've always been looking for that line that separates improvisation from composition or interpretation from improvisation.'"[119]

Morris sought to build a vocabulary for changing the music in the moment. "History has it that once it's written down, that's the way it goes," Morris wrote.

> I was never keen on an enforced tradition that would dictate history, especially when it came to culture (art). To redefine must mean that somewhere down the line you must have believed in something you no longer believe in, so you redefine it—or something was defined for you, so you came to believe that definition. My definition of musician is someone in the service of music and/or someone who has surrendered to a sound or sounds that make that person tick. I am not here to redefine music but to define what music is to me.[120]

Morris continued to incubate his ideas until he moved east to New York City in 1976, where he became involved with the jazz lofts of that time.[121] The "energy orchestras" that would meet and improvise together for hours at a time provided ideas for Morris. He found himself wishing, at times, that he could capture certain moments and re-create them later in performances. Experiences teaching, leading workshops, and conducting in Rotterdam, the Netherlands, and at the Conservatoire Royale in Liège, Belgium, helped Morris further develop his vocabulary and his yearning to "make music" as a conductor. "Even if I was working from notation," he later recalled of the time, "I was looking to make it a new work every time."[122] He employed numerous techniques at the time, including the use of what he called "ryth-notes," where hc would compose a rhythm and let the improviser choose what notes to play. "This directly relates to the way I give rhythm figures tapped out in midair to the ensemble," he observed.[123]

By the early 1980s, Morris began to develop his Conduction system in earnest, which first started with the Presto in Ludwig von Beethoven's Opus 130 for string quartet, for which he designed the signals for repeat, sustain, and improvise, as well as tempo modifiers and rehearsal numbers to direct the musicians to particular sections.[124] Morris then debuted his first work on record with violinist Billy Bang's mini–big band record, *Outline No. 12*.[125] Bang wrote in the liner notes for the record that Morris "faithfully conducted and interpreted the compositions. From the beginning of the recording, Butch was in complete control, inserting all the appropriate dynamics, to better accentuate the character and colors of the music. Butch spiritually brought out the virtuosity of all the musicians, in both written and improvised sections."[126] In his reading of books about physics, Morris finally settled on the name "Conduction" as a reference to combustion or heat, while stating, "It's the sound, lyricism, heat, and organization of [bebop, postbop, and rhythm and blues] that are fundamental to what I call 'Conduction.'"[127]

By the time that Morris presented at Zebulon, he had been refining his Conduction system for over twenty years. He began organizing and recording his own orchestras, with his first public performance occurring at the Kitchen in Manhattan on February 1, 1985.[128] It was the first public performance where Morris used the gestural vocabulary of Conduction without notation with the goal "to further develop an ensemble music of collective imagination" and "to have the ensemble featured at all times. I felt strongly then that collective improvisation must have a prime focus, and the use of notation alone was not enough for the contemporary improviser. For this music I look and listen for ensemble players who can make a decision for the good of the music and its direction."[129] One observer who witnessed the performance later stated, "I was astounded that all of these [musical elements] could go on in this organic way in the same performance. It was unabashedly beautiful, tortured, and strange all at the same time."[130] Or, more simply, guitarist Brandon Ross, a member of the band, said, "Everyone was playing their individual expression and Butch was sculpting it into this piece."[131]

Other concerts soon followed, first in New York and eventually around the globe in places such as Amsterdam, London, Montreal, Istanbul, and Tokyo from 1987 onward.[132] Through this process Conduction became a system of hand signals that could be employed to lead a band in a live setting. Morris defined the system as "a vocabulary of ideographic signs and gestures activated to modify or construct a real-time musical arrangement or composition."[133] Or, put another way, the "Conduction vocabulary/lexicon makes it possible to alter or initiate rhythm, melody, harmony, form/structure, articulation, phrasing and meter of any given notation."[134] While such signs and gestures do prescribe certain paths, forms, or structures for the music to take, they are also open to interpretation in how individual musicians respond in real time. "In traditional conducting, they don't create music, they interpret music," Morris explained. "I'm making music, they are not."[135]

Morris's Conduction system required group focus on particular concepts, ideas, charts, melodies, and, most of all, in-the-moment spontaneous creation. "If even just one person strayed away while the rest of the group was focused on going somewhere else, it would fall apart," reeds player Jonathon Haffner explained. "We couldn't break eye contact for even a second when playing in his orchestra."[136] The group might begin with particular melodies or rhythms, go away from them through Conduction, and then return to them later, or vice versa. Conduction allowed for considerable structure and depth, a more focused exploration than was often possible in free improvisation while Morris molded melody, harmony, and various musical phrasings.[137] Yet, because it was performed in the moment, it could never be replicated. "As a practice," cellist Ha-Yang Kim said, "it was useful to get us to collectively listen and to be very present in the music."[138]

By the time of Morris's performances at Zebulon in 2005 and later years, he had developed a complex array of signals, controls, and signs that allowed him to masterfully manage the output of his orchestras. To feature his work, Morris organized a momentous month-long festival in 2005 called Black February, during which he staged forty-four concerts and four workshops at nine different venues, involving eighty-five musicians in New York to celebrate the twentieth anniversary of his first Conduction performance. In reference to the event, he stated, "It's not swing that I am after, it is the essence of swing that I'm after, the very thing that makes swing. The thing that musicians create between each other is what I am after."[139] Morris appeared at the Knitting Factory, Nublu, Bowery Poetry Club, and many other venues during the festival and also led his Butchlandband at Zebulon during that run.[140] Butchlandband was a mini–big band that included Duane Eubanks (trumpet), Art Baron (trombone), Christof Knoche (soprano saxophone), J. D. Allen (tenor saxophone), Jonathon Haffner (alto saxophone), and Newman Taylor Baker (drums).

Morris would often isolate an idea and focus on it or "germinate it," as he described the process. Or he would take a composition and direct different instruments to play separate parts of the work simultaneously, then bring them back together. The system relied on Morris being an adept listener, and some musicians who played in his orchestras noted that he listened and heard music differently than most people. "Morris has such a romantic, lyrical streak as a composer," guitarist and writer Greg Tate described him. "He's such a gifted melodist."[141] Morris sought something personal from the musicians, "a human feeling, which is confrontational because I am asking people to give me something that is quite close to them."[142] Violinist Mazz Swift noted that the process "was like practicing getting the essence of me out and also communicating with other people."[143] Morris told the musicians in his ensembles, "You provide the content for the performance and I provide the context."[144]

Morris, Wollesen, and Haffner organized a group, Orchestra SLANG, that played several residencies at Zebulon with flyers that bore the statement "Challenge Your Perception."[145] The band was composed of Christof Knoche (tenor saxophone, bass clarinet), Kirk Knuffke (cornet), Ron Caswell (tuba), Angelica Sanchez (piano), Eyal Maoz (guitar), Cornelius "Neal" Dufallo (violin), Nicole Federici (viola), Ha-Yang Kim (cello), Jay Foote (bass), Bill Ware (vibraphone), and Kenny Wollesen (percussion).[146] Thus, it was a fusion of a big band and a string quartet, which was difficult because the unamplified strings had to contend with the volume of the horns.[147] But the aim of the music was always to achieve a high level of energy. The pieces were constructed in a modular fashion, and since the group had rehearsed so much, they could draw on a sophisticated vocabulary in the live setting. In reference to the innovations of Conduction, Henry Threadgill stated, "When art evolves, we evolve. It's a pursuit of truth."[148]

From his experience in the band, drummer Kenny Wollesen stated, "Butch changed my whole conception of music, what music could be. I realized that music did not have to be preconceived and fully written, nor did it have to be fully improvised. With his system, you could have a really tight arrangement of music in the moment, yet still incredibly spontaneous." Wollesen was also struck by what Morris drew out of the orchestra members:

> Butch was not interested in what you could already play, even if it was technically advanced, if it was not relevant or present. I had been taught, since I was young, that the drummer should lay down the beat and get into sync with the bass player. He wasn't interested in that; he wanted

to hear what was going on inside me at any given moment. He got me to see that rhythm and harmony can be much bigger, richer, and more complex than I had thought conventionally. He wanted to hear what a musician didn't know yet and to go beyond it. He wanted you to do what needed to happen right in the moment.[149]

Haffner echoed Wollesen's observations about Morris's impact on him:

He completely changed how I play music and how I hear music. Everything happened in the moment. We would create something that often surprised both of us. Butch's whole system of hand signals—the Conduction system—is really just the beginning of his concept of music. It was his way of exploring something other than a tune in a person's head, a tune on paper, or free improvisation. He would always encourage people to play something they had never played before or go to a place onstage that no one has ever gone to before. A feeling, a mood, it was about getting something new for the conductor, the musicians, and the audience.[150]

"Butch ruled that band with an iron fist," vibraphonist Bill Ware recalled, "like something out of another era. But he had the best ears of anyone I ever met. He heard everything that was happening in the music simultaneously."[151] Not everyone who was involved in the Morris orchestras felt the need for the level of control that he asserted; some saw it as micromanaging the music and stifling spontaneity. Some found it excessive or felt his methods were a bit draconian in achieving those ends. Some also felt that the method of control stifled individual contributions to the overall group sound. But as Kim explained, "He was at his best when he would take a couple of steps back and be present, in the moment, with what was happening, ride the group energy, and let the music flow. Then what was possible could be fully realized as we grew into a collective musical organism."[152] Brandon Ross added, "In the future, people will look back at Butch's orchestras and see them as the seed of the new American orchestra form."[153]

Many of the figures in Orchestra SLANG performances at Zebulon also worked with Morris in the Nublu Orchestra, which took its name from the club Nublu, where they played a weekly gig for an extended period and generated a significant body of work.[154] The Nublu Orchestra toured extensively in Europe, playing most of the major festivals in 2006–12, including the Saalfelden Festival in 2007 and the North Sea Jazz Festival in 2008, and after Morris's death, they played in Sardinia as a tribute band in 2016.[155]

In an obituary fellow trumpeter Taylor Ho Bynum wrote of Morris, "[Morris] became a virtuoso of nonverbal expression, gaining the ability to convey minute adjustments of articulation or dynamics with a twist of the wrist or an arched eyebrow. He performed around the world, leading orchestras and Brazilian drum choirs, groups of Japanese traditional instruments and Lower East Side poets, discovering he had invented a language universal in its implications, carrying the potential to unite musicians of any genre or culture in a musical experience unique to its participants."[156]

Music for the Streets:
The Kenny Wollesen Big Band

No band played more often or forged a more vibrant community around itself at Zebulon than the Kenny Wollesen Big Band, though it began the previous year as a protest marching band. Wollesen's band had the distinction of playing the very first concert at Zebulon. After the events of September 11, 2001, a collective depression hung over New York City, and the cultural atmosphere changed, which undermined the music and art scenes, as has been noted in earlier chapters. With the national push to invade Iraq, led by the administration of President George W. Bush, drummer Kenny Wollesen (b. 1966) wanted to form a band "that would change the whole feeling at the time."[157] He further explained, "I was going to a lot of protests then, and I wanted to create music for the streets. I wanted to turn the negative and often glum protests into something positive. Music is a healing force, and I felt it could serve to elevate people's spirits. That was the impetus of the big band."[158]

Wollesen gave an open invitation for people to join the band—professional musicians and amateurs—and formed a marching band, "but not like any high school, military, or New Orleans marching bands, just music of the moment, music for the streets."[159] The band gathered for the first time as part of one of the massive protests against the United States' escalation to war with Iraq in February 2003. "The attitude for the band was, if you have something to say about everything that was going on at that time, come and play with us," Jonathon Haffner remarked about the early days of the band.[160] "Kenny put a band together, and there were dozens of people involved, a kind of who's who of downtown jazz musicians, people from all different traditions all playing music together all with a focused purpose," trumpeter Michael Irwin explained. "It was an unforgettable day. It was beautiful."[161] On that day the band played continuously for approximately eight hours, and that level of energy and enthusiasm continued to pervade their performances in the years that followed.

One of the inspirations for the band came from Wollesen's involvement in puppet theater, such as the Boston-based organization Puppeteer Cooperative, which operated in the vein of Bread and Puppet, performing a kind of political street theater.[162] Wollesen worked with the Puppeteer Cooperative, which would often perform outside in parks and in the streets of New York during the summers, especially doing programs with children in underserved neighborhoods. This work inspired Wollesen to consider how art, performance, and music could be melded together for social effect. One particular performance, by an iteration of the band called Upper Planets, in collaboration with the Puppeteer Cooperative's production of *Godzilla*, has survived as a recording and displays an eclectic, yet playful side of the band. Sousaphone provides the sauntering pace of the music, and brass and reeds direct the main unison melody, while percussion, synthesizer, and organ create the flurry of activity happening on all sides of the main point of action, together illustrating a whole visual scene.[163] Of the early performances, Irwin noted, "Most of the gigs were not paid. It was about bringing an energy, bringing a presence to a place and to take part in life that way."[164]

Wollesen wanted to play original pieces with the band. The aim was to select pieces that were not overly complicated but to draw them from the world of creative music. Much of the band's early work focused on compositions by well-known downtown figures such as John Zorn, Bill Frisell, and Steven Bernstein, as well as band members Sarah Wilson and Jesse Harris, Brazilian samba-inspired pieces, and Wollesen's own tunes.[165] "I saw these as songs from the community, for the community," Wollesen observed.[166] The band also performed pieces from the Don Cherry corpus, such as "Until the Rain Comes," as well as pieces by Richard Marriott's Club Foot Orchestra, "African Marketplace" by Abdullah Ibrahim, and spirituals like "Down in the Valley to Pray."[167] They used head charts primarily, and Wollesen allowed each individual who was involved to find their own harmony within a piece. Wollesen had also worked with Butch Morris and adapted aspects of the Conduction system for the band, even inviting Morris to conduct the band at times. "The effect of Conduction was that it created instant arrangements on the spot," Wollesen observed. "If Butch was not available, either I or another member of the band would do the conductions." There was also a certain kind of conduction in Zorn's music, very different from that of Morris, that Wollesen also drew from at the time.[168]

Over time, a circle of musicians began to form the core of the big band. Saxophonist and clarinetist Jonathon Haffner, trumpeters Michael Irwin and Sarah Wilson, electric bassist and guitarist Tony Scherr, percussionist Jennifer Harris, and singer-songwriter Jesse Harris were all early members.[169] Wilson began composing for the band after seeing Wollesen perform at the 55Bar in 2003, after the war had started; she had penned her first piece for the group on her way home while still on the subway platform, "WSU Terrorist Theme" (WSU stood for Wollesen Street Unit).[170] The tune became one of the band's most popular pieces. Wilson also later wrote the piece "Himalayas" when the band had taken on that name while performing at Zebulon. She wrote four parts for the band: trumpet, saxophone, trombone, and bass/tuba, often favoring grooves and countermelodies of various kinds that could work with a large ensemble. She would bring charts when conditions were amenable or otherwise play each part for the assembled musicians to relay the ideas.

When the band included other instruments, as it often did, they would double on whichever parts made sense, while Wollesen laid down rhythms and directed whichever percussionists were a part of any given performance. Irwin consciously integrated New Orleans and Caribbean rhythms and aesthetics like vamps and repeated riffs that were not overly complicated so that they lent themselves to a marching band along with plenty of improvisation.[171] The band gradually developed a repertoire, though the pieces continued to evolve and grow organically over time.[172] "The theme was that 'all sounds are welcome,'" Irwin explained. "It was very inclusive."[173]

Wollesen also connected with an experimental music scene that surrounded Anthology Film Archives, which included a lot of Lithuanian musicians such as Dalius Naujokaitis and trumpeter Auguste Varkalis, who would gather at a basement studio at Anthology and have raucous jam sessions on an almost daily basis.[174] Wollesen would later bring this community to Zebulon. Moving indoors allowed additional kinds of instruments to join. In the band's earliest manifestations, it had mostly been brass, woodwinds, and percussion instruments, but performing in a venue allowed stringed instruments such as guitars, violins, banjos, and acoustic basses to join and electric instruments like synthesizers to be involved. Beat box performers and other vocals were also incorporated into the mix. Because of the open nature of the band, the same lineup never performed more than once, and for a time Wollesen gave each formation a new name. By 2005 he briefly settled on the name SLAM, and from 2006 onward, the band settled around the name Himalayas, though in more recent years the band has again adopted shifting monikers for each unique lineup.

Through the Anthology scene, Wollesen met avant-garde filmmaker, critic, and poet Jonas Mekas (1922–2019), who began contributing to the band and who had a significant impact on the scene at Zebulon.[175] Mekas was a Lithuanian-born filmmaker and poet who had been a founding figure in American avant-garde film in the 1960s. Mekas brought original poems that he would either perform in a kind of preacher style or occasionally sing if they seemed conducive to the music.[176] "His lyrics cut to the core of life, what was happening, what was important," Wollesen recounted. "There are no distractions in his words, nothing superfluous. Very direct and fundamental."[177] In some ways, Mekas's poetry translated to the musical setting quite naturally. As one writer observed of Mekas, "Everything he did had not only a certain rhythm, sometimes a swing, and sometimes something more lyrical, it also had a melody."[178] Mekas had been a self-taught musician from a young age, including violin, mandolin, *bayan* (Russian accordion), *daudytė* (1.5-meter-long Lithuanian wooden trumpet), and other instruments.[179] As one of Mekas's colleagues would later observe, Mekas "was truly musical, perhaps because he grew up surrounded by singing."[180] In his more than half a century of work in New York, he avidly consumed music whenever he had the opportunity and was in an arts circle that included Robert Frank, Philip Glass, La Monte Young, Patti Smith, Barbara Rubin, Harry Smith, Peter Kubelka, the Velvet Underground, and many others.[181]

As Wollesen's milieu expanded to include Mekas, it brought the latter's process of near-constant filming of everyday life into the fold at Zebulon. Mekas once famously stated, "I make movies, therefore I live."[182] Following Mekas's lead, Wollesen began making films, using a Super Eight (8 mm) camera, that he would project while the band was playing. The films typically depicted everyday life, often just three-minute takes. Then he would either string a number of them together or put them on a loop. "The whole point, coming from the philosophy of Mekas, was not to make films but to film life. Mekas's eye was the camera. His studio was the street. The point was not to create a story but to rather capture something on film throughout the day."[183] Sometimes Wollesen would employ an intervalometer in the camera so that, for instance, it would take one frame every minute, so one might be able to shoot a whole day of activity that is condensed down to three minutes. Wollesen also showed films by Mekas, Naujokaitis, and others from the Anthology scene, usually shot within a few weeks before a performance. Because he was nearly always filming when he was not performing himself, Mekas filmed extensive footage at Zebulon that became part of his 365 Day Project.

The big band released a single in tribute to Mekas, "Jonas Song," on the one-year anniversary of his death, January 23, 2020.[184] The memorial, which has the energy of a New Orleans send-off more than that of a typical funeral dirge, features multiple percussionists opening with frantic beats, from which brass and reeds eventually emerge as aesthetic counterpoint with unison lines that eventually give way to free improvisation that, in turn, surrenders back to the melodic lines gradually before finally ending with ascendant bright drones filled with light.[185]

To add to the visual effects of the performances at Zebulon, Wollesen designed his own light machines using a rotating disc that was filled with colored dye and oil, similar to a lava lamp, paired with three mirrors that would refract in three directions to project kaleidoscopic images or light effects throughout Zebulon. "It was more than just music, it was meant to be a full show, a deep sensory experience," Wollesen explained. "Kenny became liberated and became inhabited by a shamanistic kind of spirit," Wilson added, "like he was in another place mentally, wearing costumes, walking around with his bass drum within the band or around the club, performing from the tops of tables. He blossomed as an artist and as a bandleader. He was able to tap into different levels of how music connects with people. It was magical to experience, focused on creating a collective energy."[186] And then, in the midst of it all, they might stage a play or an opera with costumes, props, lighting, staging, and a chorus, though it relied on considerable spontaneity and improvisation to orchestrate.[187] Dancers also sometimes contributed to the performances with their own improvisations that reacted to the music and the light. "We didn't have to do anything to make the audio and visual connect. It was natural," Wollesen explained.[188] At times, the revelry compelled the band to march out onto Wythe Avenue outside the venue, which was possible in 2005 and 2006 before luxury condos were built in the neighborhood that drew a new demographic to the area that insisted—via calls to the police—that silence prevail.[189] The big-band performances were an all-encompassing sensory experience.

The big band was the first group ever to perform at Zebulon, for the preopening party to test the stage and system in mid-2004, and then again for the official opening.[190] From that point on, the band became a major fixture at the club, playing almost every Saturday night through late 2006, never repeating the same lineup twice (see figure 4.4).[191] One of their most concentrated periods was in February 2005, when the band was conducted

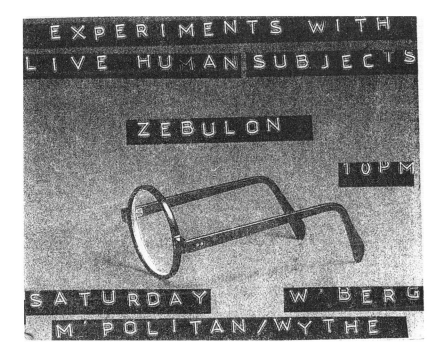

Figure 4.4 Experiments with Live Human Subjects poster (*designed by Kenny Wollesen*)

by Butch Morris as part of Black February. Morris's Conduction system worked well with the band to create grooves and to draw out the collective energy, which resulted in ecstatic live performances. "It was necessary to bring some shape and structure to the large performances," Irwin noted of Morris's Conduction. Even after Morris stopped performing with the group, "Different members of the band would fill the role, in a way, taking turns for ten or twenty minutes at a time, using Butch's symbols."[192] Or the band would look for cues from Wollesen, who would often "break it down" after a sustained period of building energy to make room for a solo instrumentalist or another kind of performer, such as a dancer or poet.[193] The solos were not decided in advance, so Wollesen would choose someone on the spot and give them full control over what they played or performed.

Most of the time, the band ranged from fifteen to twenty participants at any given performance.[194] "There was so much volume, so much energy, the music would reach a palpable feeling of catharsis by the end of the set, and we felt a strong connection with the audience," Irwin noted. "We were each a thread in a much bigger sonic tapestry," he added.[195] The stage was never big enough to hold the entire band, often just the percussionists or keyboardists, so the band naturally was in closer proximity to the audience than most. Zebulon recorded every live set, so there are many dozens of live recordings, amounting to hundreds of hours of live performances. The band was also included on the live compilation of Zebulon performances with their piece "Until the Rain Comes," which captured soprano saxophonist Sam Newsome with a superb solo accompanied by Mekas's poetry.[196] "The big band was at its most ecstatic with the most synergy during the long residency at Zebulon," Wilson commented.[197] The band was especially effective in the live setting but finally released its first studio recording in 2013.[198]

One of the organizers of the Willisau Jazz Festival in Switzerland happened to see the big band perform at Zebulon and invited them on the spot to perform; they closed out the festival there on September 2, 2007.[199] Afterward, the big band took their music-as-community-building efforts to Barcelona, where they played in parks until the local police evicted them, and then they spent a week playing on a beach near the city, where they drew large gatherings every afternoon.[200] They returned and played a few weeks later at the fifth annual Festival of New Trumpet Music in New York on September 19, where trumpeter and festival organizer Taylor Ho Bynum described the band's work as "jazz folk music" because of the way the community worked together and the feel of the music.[201] After their time at Zebulon passed, the big band found a new home at Spike Hill, also in Williamsburg, where they continued to draw audiences for their cathartic performances, though the residency did not have the same duration as their Zebulon run. The big band also played regularly at the Honk Festival in Somerville, Massachusetts, which was an annual gathering of activist marching bands each year in October. Though the band has been less active in recent years, it still performs and records occasionally.

Inventing the Sonic Medium: Ken Butler

For sculptor, multimedia artist, musician, and instrument inventor and designer Ken Butler (b. 1948), his performances at Zebulon were the culmination of a life's work. To understand their significance, we must go back to Butler's work all the way back in the 1970s. Butler is a singular artist, even on the experimental music scene, and his work is a successful and unique fusion of sculpture, invention, design, and music. Butler grew up in Portland, Oregon, studying viola, jazz piano, and blues guitar in his youth with a pianist mother who exposed him to classical music and jazz at an early age. But Butler was more drawn to visual art, and he trained with various media and especially worked as a sculptor. In 1978, when he was in the basement of his apartment, he happened to look at an old, rusted hatchet that had been used to split logs next to the fireplace. He picked it up, placing the blade under his chin with the handle sticking straight out like a violin.[202] He had been experimenting with ideas and media at the time, and after examining an X-ray image, he was struck with the idea that the human torso resembled a guitar.

So Butler began creating artworks that grew out of these early ideas and images of the head-neck-body configuration. He attached the fingerboard, the chin rest, and the tailpiece; drilled two holes for tuning picks; and tightened the two strings that he fitted for it, and using a contact microphone, he was able to begin playing the instrument with his amplifier within the hour. He called the piece "Homage to Buddy Guy"—Guy had been his most prominent inspiration in blues guitar—with reference to the latter's tune "Just Playing My Axe."[203]

Previously Butler's work had been two-dimensional collage, so the piece constituted his first sculpture. He exhibited the piece at the Portland Center for the Visual Arts in 1978, where, by chance, musician and performance artist Laurie Anderson (b. 1947) was presenting unrelated work in another part of the building.[204] Butler witnessed her work and "was blown away by her use of unusual or invented instruments, anecdotal quasi-narratives, elaborate projections, and a multimedia way of thinking. That completely changed my way of thinking. I wanted to find a way to integrate music and visual art together. It occurred to me that if I made my own instruments that were sculptural, that was a way to bridge disciplines."[205] Butler began to exhibit a growing body of work, including a briefcase guitar, a crutch cello, and smaller pieces that often showed some influence from pop art, Dadaism, and bricolage.[206] The cubist work of Pablo Picasso and Georges Braque from 1910–14 that depicted guitar, mandolin, and violin abstractions was also a significant source of visual inspiration, while Erik Satie's lyric "guitars made with old hats" from "La Réveil de la mariée" (Awakening of the Bride) in *Sports et divertissements* was also a creative spark.[207] Since his late 1970s breakthrough, Butler's source materials have generally been found on the street or repurposed from older materials for the purposes of reenvisioning their possibilities in the present.

Butler's performances at Zebulon were the result of more than twenty years of developing his invented instruments for the stage. Butler first performed with his instrument sculptures at the Portland Center for the Visual Arts in 1981. From that point on, he experimented with elaborate projections, moving screens, and various lighting effects while he continued to design additional pieces. In 1983 he made the K-Board, which was a keyboard with lightbulbs connected to a bicycle wheel strung with guitar picks.[208] He designed an instrument from two hockey sticks with cello strings between them (see figure 4.6), created mbira-like instruments, and made other pieces that projected images from photographic slides.[209] Altogether, over the decades, Butler created more than four hundred invented and handcrafted instruments (see figure 4.7).[210]

By the mid-1980s, before moving to New York City, he began to move toward some of the aesthetics of downtown-scene groups like Skeleton Crew, comprising guitarist Fred Frith, cellist Tom Cora, and harpist Zeena Parkins, who each played multiple instruments simultaneously onstage during live performances.[211] The instruments that Butler made were relatively light and thin, so he could stack as many as six of them in a guitar case. Each instrument had a different sound and timbre; for example, one had an Indian sitar sound, while another was closer to a Turkish or Middle Eastern stringed instrument, a third had a harsher bluesy guitar sound, while still another could be used to make sounds more in the sonic palette of funk.

Butler finally moved to the East Coast and settled in Williamsburg in September 1988, giving some of his first experimental performances at the Lizard's Tail, as mentioned in chapter 2.[212] He found a real home at the Knitting Factory, on the Lower East Side, where he performed regularly and continued to develop the project. The owner, Michael Dorf, even exhibited some of Butler's instruments on the wall at the club.[213] Butler also did a major exhibition of his work at Test-Site Gallery in Williamsburg in 1992 and toured as a solo artist in Europe in the years that followed. He also experimented with duo and trio formats, often with abstract improvising vocalist Dina Emerson, pairing that with a percussionist or electronicist such as Matt Kilmer or Herne Gadbois. The vocals were key because "there were no intonation issues and they could go wherever they wanted with the pitch" since the handcrafted instruments were not necessarily tuned to the same scales as standardized instruments.[214] With regard to Butler's early 1990s period of exploration, one critic commented, "Constructed of doorstops, saw blades, a vegetable slicer and more, Ken Butler's electricity-driven inventions bear a symbolic resemblance to the instruments of a string quartet, although one of them is held vertically on the thigh and largely plucked. The result is a synthesized sound, percussive and melodic, in all its bewildering variety."[215]

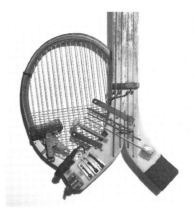

Figure 4.5 Ken Butler's cane racket viola, 1982 (*photo by Ken Butler*)
Figure 4.6 Ken Butler's double hockey racket cello, early 1990s (*photo by Ken Butler*)
Figure 4.7 Ken Butler in his studio with his many invented instruments, ca. 1990 (*private collection*)

Butler resisted requests to record his work in audio format, since the visual elements of what was being played mattered for the overall impact of his performances. He also took great care to orchestrate gestural effects, stage presence, and projections. But after being approached by John Zorn, who had seen his work exhibited at the Metropolitan Museum of Art, Butler eventually agreed to record for the Tzadik label; it remains the only purely audio recording of his career, though numerous videos have been made.[216]

By 1995 Butler's band had coalesced around some like-minded experimentalists who could work within his aesthetic. He hired Matt Darriau (b. 1960), who was a driving force behind the Pyramid Trio, a Bulgarian-inspired band. Darriau played a wide range of instruments including bagpipes, *kaval*, *shanai*, clarinet, saxophones, other reeds, and flutes. Butler also hired another member of the Pyramid Trio, the Roma *dumbek* and *tapan* player Seido Salifoski.[217] To round out the quartet, Butler hired electric bassist Stomu Takeishi (b. 1964), a figure who had risen to prominence playing with Henry Threadgill. Butler was attracted to Takeishi's sound because he used a fretless electric bass, which worked well with Butler's sculpted instruments, which were all fretless, allowing for the use of microtones in a more open manner.

One of Butler's favored instruments of the period that appeared on the record was a golf club that he fitted with cello strings, kind of like a sitar-tabla.[218] He could bow the top string and plucked the others in a way that resonated with Takeishi. Butler also used a bicycle wheel with spokes that were each tuned with four courses of two strings that aesthetically fell somewhere between an oud (a Persian short-necked lute), a *saz* (a Turkish long-necked lute), and a fretless guitar. Added to this, Butler also used an instrument crafted from an aluminum cane and a tennis racket with two tuned strings and a second cane with a wooden beach paddleboard as the body with the neck of a baritone ukulele. He could pluck both cane instruments simultaneously for a kind of short-scaled cello-bass sound or place one of the instruments under his chin and bow it like a giant viola with two strings. In addition, Butler used various other percussive inventions, a vegetable slicer, saw blades, an umbrella violin, and a sword violin, among others. The music that he arranged for the band drew from drones and non-Western scales, and they would often find grooves in the course of playing with space for improvisation.

Butler had moved out of the city to teach for a year in the art and design department at the University of Michigan and returned in the fall of 2004 to find Zebulon as the new magnet for the Williamsburg experimental music scene. Butler spoke French, and so he developed good relations with the Soubiran brothers quickly, and soon they were inviting him to play regularly at the club. Butler lived in the neighborhood, and it became the most conducive venue for his work. He presented his project Voices of Anxious Objects for the first time on March 10, 2005, and appeared again every other month into mid-2006. The regular gigs with the quartet at Zebulon showcased decades of work, and Butler was included on the Zebulon compilation record.[219]

Sonic Roleplay: Digital Primitives

Another band to emerge within the milieu of Zebulon in its early years was the collective trio Digital Primitives, comprising multi-instrumentalists Assif Tsahar and Cooper-Moore and drummer Chad Taylor. The band played its key early gigs at the club in 2006 and 2007, though its formation was the result of a few years of previous work by Tsahar and Cooper-Moore playing together. Cooper-Moore had been a visible figure on the loft scene at 501 Canal Street in the 1970s, had performed and recorded extensively with bassist William Parker in the 1990s and after, and had led or co-led a number of bands in the period.[220]

Cooper-Moore and Tsahar had met through the Improviser's Collective, a group of fifteen musicians, poets, painters, and other artists who had come together to coproduce and present their work, primarily at Context Studios on the Lower East Side. One of the caveats of the organization was that its members had to hire other members of the collective when they performed. "At first, I didn't like him," Cooper-Moore said of Tsahar, "but I didn't like that I didn't like him, so I hired him for my band." Tsahar, originally from Israel, had come to the city to study jazz at the New School. "I quickly discovered," Cooper-Moore added, "that he was a good person. Ethical, truthful, hardworking, and with high ideals."[221]

Tsahar and Cooper-Moore began playing together regularly as a duo in 2003 and recorded their early work at Tsahar's apartment.[222] The band became a staging ground for many of Cooper-Moore's handmade instruments, including bango, diddley-bow, mouth bow, twanger, and some unique instruments he invented that did not have names. The mouth bow, in a way, was played like a string instrument, as Cooper-Moore's mouth and throat formed the internal resonation chamber that produced each tone. By 2005 the two were eager to add a drummer to make the band a trio, and so they hired Chicago-based Hamid Drake and recorded *Lost Brother* in September of that year. They soon found it logistically difficult to work with Drake because of the latter's touring schedule, so they hired another drummer who had recently moved to New York from Chicago, Chad Taylor.[223] "I wanted someone who would put forward ideas, and at that time Chad really was developing as a player," Cooper-Moore recalled.[224] Taylor himself noted that "the early years of Digital Primitives were like finishing school for me. I thought of Cooper-Moore as a mentor."[225] Taylor brought a certain funk to the rhythms that propelled the band. The trio with Taylor played their first gig at Zebulon on December 4, 2005. One critic noted that the lineup with Taylor "expanded the sonic landscape" of the earlier trio "by removing a few of the typical saxophone trio tracks and replacing them with more in the way of fuzz, distortion and overmodulation."[226]

Digital Primitives' music always centered around storytelling. Each of the members of the trio would play a character or be part of a narrative embodied in the music. This method was something that Cooper-Moore and Taylor had developed with another trio, Triptych Myth, which also included bassist Tom Abbs. For example, for the latter band's piece "Frida K. the Beautiful," Abbs played the role of Diego Rivera, Taylor was Frida Kahlo, and Cooper-Moore was Kahlo's lesbian lover. Those dynamics guided their interactions as musicians in both composed and improvised sections. So, with Digital Primitives, they carried on a similar approach that featured conversations between individual members of the band or dealt with issues of jealousy and treachery through the music. "One secret about Cooper-Moore," Taylor noted, "is that he thrives on tension. He is brilliant at knowing how to use tension to create music. Sometimes he will create it just so he can get the music to where he wants it to be."[227] Cooper-Moore's many handcrafted instruments were critical to this work since they catered to the making of unique sounds, ideas, and characters. The mouth bow, for example, had "an ancient sound" and could be used to instill the feeling of history or something from long ago still alive in the music.[228] Onstage, Cooper-Moore generally directed the action of the music, and he was also the band's primary composer (see figure 4.8).[229]

Recording the music became a more detailed process as they attempted to get each piece and each layer of the musical narratives to fit together just right. While on tour in Spain, they rented a house in Málaga where they stayed for ten days, recording each day in an intricate process that allowed them to "construct the music."[230] One critic wrote of the music, "The amplified diddley-bow and backbeat of 'Human Interface'; the static, doings and whirs that encircle Tsahar's wheezing tenor on 'Electric Garden'; and the title track, with didgeridoo mumbling in the background and a distorted

Figure 4.8 Cooper-Moore with Digital Primitives (Assif Tsahar and Chad Taylor not pictured), Brecht Forum, 2003 (*photo by Peter Gannushkin*)

mouth bow crying like a saw, all allow dissonance to rise organically from the mix and embellish the established rhythms."[231] In 2006–7 the band played a number of concerts at Zebulon and the Tea Lounge in Park Slope. At one of the Zebulon shows, Cooper-Moore asked Taylor to begin the concert with a solo, saying that by the time he was sweating, they would join him onstage. But Cooper-Moore was being coy, and they let Taylor play for twenty or thirty minutes onstage by himself, the former's way of pushing Taylor to develop and dig deep within himself as a player.[232] Digital Primitives returned to the studio to record their second record, *Hum Crackle and Pop*, which they debuted at Zebulon on October 6, 2009.[233]

A New Spiritual Sound: Louis Belogenis

One band that played regularly at Zebulon that did not get a lot of critical attention at the time was saxophonist Louis Belogenis's Unbroken Trio with bassist Shanir Blumenkranz and drummer Kenny Wollesen. Belogenis (b. 1953) had played extensively with Rashied Ali in duos and trios as part of the latter's resurgence in the 1990s and in the octet Prima Materia with William Parker, John Zorn, and Wilber Morris, among others. Belogenis also recorded in a duo with Ali, as well as an expanded trio that included Wilber Morris.[234] Unfortunately, with the rise of Islamophobia after 9/11, Ali took some time away from touring because he found traveling so alienating. As a side effect, this provided an impetus for Belogenis to begin leading his own bands.[235]

The Unbroken Trio first came together in 2003. Belogenis had known Wollesen for many years but had just begun playing with Blumenkranz when the latter invited the unit to rehearse at his apartment at 125 Avenue D in the East Village (see figure 4.9). "I knew quickly that Kenny and Shanir are both beautiful people, totally dedicated to the music which requires people to rely on their instincts. They were very present," Belogenis explained. "Because this music requires people to put so much of themselves into it, you get a sense of who they are. Wherever we went, we supported each other in the music, and that led to new discoveries because we had a collective confidence."[236] The name for the trio referenced "a healthy spirit" generally but also Belogenis's devotion to Buddhism and to the teachings of Bokar Rinpoche, whom he studied with personally in India, and the lineage of teachings that Bokar represented, which stretched back to the tenth century.[237] The name also referred to the unbroken Zen circle. Belogenis had begun adopting Buddhist practices while still a teenager growing up in the Bronx, following a performance of Tibetan music that he attended at the Metropolitan Museum of Art in 1973.[238]

Through a stretch of regular sessions at Blumenkranz's apartment, they "took the warm, human connection and built a musical connection around mutual support and creativity to form a trio that embodied a soulful and inventive approach to playing free jazz."[239] Through playing together and generating ideas, the band would then take the most potent moments and codify them, whether such pieces were grooves, specific chord progressions, or plays on sonic space. Then, in live performances, the trio could touch on them and use them as springboards for further improvisational exploration as a form of composition in real time. Belogenis stated, "Shanir and Kenny, despite being experienced, were always still exploring with what Zen Buddhists call beginner's mind, one that is still rapt with curiosity about the possibilities and not fixed on some idea of their own greatness. The music is alive and open for them always."[240]

Zebulon became the primary home for the Unbroken Trio, where they played fairly regularly in 2005–10. The band's approach was to have a dialogue

Figure 4.9 Unbroken: Shanir Blumenkranz (*left*) and Louis Belogenis (Kenny Wollesen not pictured), Brecht Forum, 2007 (*photo by Peter Gannushkin*)

not only with each other but also with the audience as a collective fourth instrument. "I wanted to see the audience seeking, hearing, understanding, and processing what we had to say," Belogenis explained. "When we would do something unique onstage, something special in those moments, it was a metaphor for an audience member's own lives, how they can seek and find themselves, how they can explore and not rule out possibilities."[241]

After the first performance in the Unbroken Trio's Zebulon run of concerts, the band recorded tracks for their only record.[242] Most of the tracks were tributes to people Belogenis considered to be influences or inspirations, including musical and spiritual figures already mentioned such as Bokar, Ali, and Blumenkranz. One track, "Bells Canto," an adaptation of Albert Ayler's piece "Bells," was dedicated to the operatic soprano Maria Callas (1923–77).[243] Belogenis believed that the two musicians were not often thought to have a close connection but that "they were two artists deeply communing with their art form and their expressivity. When you think about it that way, their differences are not as great as their similarities in how deeply moving and touching the music is because they each transcend their respective idioms."[244] The connection between vocal music generally and the sound of the saxophone was deep for Belogenis. The record also contained tributes to Albert Ayler, Sonny Rollins, John Zorn, and poet Federico García Lorca.

Central Brooklyn Avant-Garde Meets the Downtown Scene: Andrew Lamb

One of the rare marks of how the downtown and the Central Brooklyn jazz scenes fused at Zebulon was a series of performances by saxophonist Andrew Lamb (b. 1958). He appeared there as a sideperson in ensembles led by drummer Warren Smith as well as leading his own trio. He had cultivated the Andrew Lamb Trio in restaurants and clubs in the vibrant Black cultural district that ran from southern Fort Greene to Bedford-Stuyvesant along Fulton Street as it evolved out of his earlier, interdisciplinary work.

The roots of Lamb's musical approach and associations may be traced back to when he attended the State University of New York College at Old Westbury in the late 1970s.[245] He encountered percussion instructor Andrei Strobert (1949–2006) there, and the two struck up a lifelong friendship. "Andrei was a completely different type of thinker on the drum set," Lamb observed. "For most drummers, the first beat is on the bass drum, but for Andrei it could be anywhere. His approach created a sound that surrounded the other players, full of life, different shapes, and filling the whole room without gaps. I never heard another person play like that."[246] Strobert played with a kind of rolling beat and use of the drum kit that one observer noted created the feeling of "a one-man marching band."[247]

Strobert maintained a low profile on the New York scene as a musician, recording sparsely, but he owned and ran Strobe Light Sound Studio, which engineered some critically important records by Reggie Workman, Roy Campbell Jr., William Parker, Mat Maneri, Frank Lowe, Billy Bang, Steve Swell, Warren Smith, Gunter Hampel, and other key figures on the downtown scene from 1993 until Strobert's death.[248] Lamb and Strobert began playing together more regularly in the 1990s in the circle of Warren Smith as Lamb began to get his bearings on the New York scene.

Andrew Lamb got a foothold in the scene at Joloff, a Senegalese restaurant that was, at that time, on the corner of St. James Place and Fulton Street in the heart of a Black cultural district in western Bedford-Stuyvesant, Brooklyn.[249] That part of Brooklyn had the longest history of jazz of any part of the borough, stretching back to the 1920s, and had also been a part of the 1980s–1990s Black arts wave, captured in some of the films of Spike Lee.

Seasoned clubs such as Jazz 966, the Jazz Spot, and Sistas' Place all presented musicians who often did not get attention from Manhattan-centric New York music critics.

Lamb began playing at Joloff in the late 1990s, after he convinced the owner to let him play solo saxophone there on a regular basis for a series of months. He also put together a large ensemble, the Moving Form, that included spoken-word artist Onaje Will Halsey (b. 1949, also known as Menshemsaqa Angaza) and live-action painter Jimmy James Greene. Lamb's association with Halsey dated back to them crossing paths as students at the College at Old Westbury. Halsey was a poet who had grown up in the Kingsborough housing projects in Crown Heights, Brooklyn, where as a teenager he was in the social milieu of Umar bin Hassan and other members of the Last Poets. Halsey attended his first poetry reading at the Pratt Institute in 1966 but also attended readings at local community centers, where he began to read the poems of Amiri Baraka and Edward Spriggs, the latter of whom mentored Halsey.[250] When he saw a reading by Yusuf Rahman, Spriggs, and the South African poet Keorapetse William Kgositsile (1938–2018, known commonly as Bra Willie) at a public school in Crown Heights around 1970, "the sky opened up for me," Halsey recalled.[251] His lyrics expressed themes of love, regardless of the range of topics, heavy in metaphor, which also covered a range of historical and political themes. Halsey recited well-known poems such as "Dream Deferred" by Langston Hughes and especially liked to perform Robert Hayden's poem "Runagate," depicting an enslaved person escaping northward:[252]

> Runs falls rises stumbles on from darkness into darkness
> and the darkness thicketed with shapes of terror
> and the hunters pursuing and the hounds pursuing
> and the night cold and the night long and the river
> to cross and the jack-muh-lanterns beckoning beckoning
> and blackness ahead and when shall I reach that somewhere
> morning and keep going and never turn back and keep on going[253]

The aesthetics of Halsey's poetry was rooted in the Black Arts Movement era, and he often modified poems on the spot, moving words around for placement or emphasis to enhance their impact in the live setting.[254] Thus, Halsey's work was improvisational, much like the other elements the group employed. Though Halsey did not consider his own work to be rap, others sometimes interpreted the "performance aspect of the poems" to be akin to rap.[255] "Working with musicians and a painter made me a better poet," Halsey remarked. "Most of the time poets work alone, so in the Moving Form, I had to pay attention to what the others were doing. It added a whole other dimension to it."[256]

Lamb and Halsey began performing together in 1985 in a protoversion of the group at drummer Jerome Cooper's arts-venue storefront in the East Village. But the Moving Form came together more fully with the addition of live figurative painter Jimmy James Greene in 1992. Greene had apprenticed as a mural painter in Detroit after high school and later studied formally at Rhode Island School of Design.[257] Greene typically painted live with his back to the audience so that they could see the canvas or paper as he created the images. "Everything we did was entirely improvised," Greene explained. "Sometimes I would visually pick up on something and do a picture of it, or I would listen to the poem that Will was reciting and do a response to that, and it also helped me to work quickly." Greene used some paints but often worked with water-soluble crayons as the base, then used a brush with water "to transform it into a painting."[258] Sometimes Greene would follow with pastels or acrylic paint to make the colors more intense or varied. Certain poems that Halsey recited regularly allowed Greene to deepen his visual representations of a particular idea. When painting for "Runagate Runagate," for instance, Greene might portray a lynching scene against a city backdrop.[259] At times, he would do portraits of Lamb, or do something to challenge perception by inverting the canvas midway through a performance before continuing or even creating three or four separate paintings throughout one performance and then selling them at the conclusion of the show.

The Moving Form took its name from a conversation between Halsey and Greene about cubism in which Greene stated, "Cubism shows objects in motion, you can see the same object from different points of view at the same time." From that, Halsey named the group. "But it wasn't really a band, it was a gathering of creative people doing their crafts together," Greene added. "If there is any historical precedent, it was the 'happenings' of the 1960s, where the event was as important as the by-product that came out of it."[260] While Lamb, Halsey, and Greene formed the core of the group, drummers Warren Smith and Andrei Strobert sometimes sat in with them, Tom Abbs often played bass, and Lamb invited many others to also join them, including numerous musicians, dancers, a juggler, and a magician. The band's only recorded output was a live set at Tillie's Café in Fort Greene, though the group performed in many different community centers, nightclubs, cafés, and other venues.[261] The work of the Moving Form was eclectic and covered a broad range of senses and media. "I was inspired by how Duke Ellington and Max Roach each said that they wanted to make music that was beyond category," Halsey noted. "We tried to be open to inspiration from everywhere."[262]

By 1999 Lamb formed a smaller unit out of the Moving Form that was oriented toward a free jazz trio with Abbs and Strobert, which refined its material playing at Joloff twice a month. Around the time that Joloff moved to Bedford Avenue and ceased having live music, Lamb found a new home at Zebulon, where he presented the trio at several dates in 2005. The focus was free improvisation "and getting to that place where the vibrations are just right," Lamb explained. "It was like an endless moment."[263] In live performances they would play free around the core of Lamb's compositions, relying on signals to enter and exit. "We relied on us being kindred spirits," Lamb remarked. "All of the pieces were organic, based on things I have lived, felt, and seen. It can happen anywhere. I might be at lunch and hear something and write the idea down on a napkin. You can go down the same road every day, but each day there is something different happening, different sounds, different birds, different people that you encounter. At other times, I might just be sitting with my horn, and it all comes out then and there. I always want to remain open."[264]

Toward a New Generation

Many dozens of other bands played at Zebulon during its first two and half years, most of which were drawn from the downtown scene. Some of them played only one or two concerts at the venue. Multi-instrumentalist Will Connell Jr.'s band Silverback, for example, played a two-night residency at Zebulon in August 2005.[265] The band did most of its definitive work at the club Niagara, which was located on the corner of East Seventh Street and Avenue A in the East Village, where the band played on Monday nights two to three times a month for about a year and a half.[266] Connell (1938–2016), who, like Butch Morris, had gotten his start playing in Horace Tapscott's Pan-Afrikan Peoples Arkestra in South Los Angeles, hired trombonist Ku-umba Frank Lacy (b. 1958); Butch's brother, bassist Wilber Morris; and longtime Henry Threadgill–affiliated drummer Newman Taylor Baker (b. 1943).[267] Connell played a number of instruments with the band, including flute, clarinet, bass clarinet, and alto, baritone, and tenor saxophone. Silverback began its stint at Niagara in 1999. The club eventually went out of business in the wave of closures that followed 9/11.[268]

Silverback is significant because Connell often worked in the background of the scene but in this instance stepped forward as a bandleader.[269] Connell's composition work was no doubt influenced by his decades of working as a copyist, though he wrote original pieces that were all his own.[270] The band played Connell's original compositions, and occasionally pieces by Lacy or Morris. Connell was a master of writing melodic counterpoint through the amalgamation of a variety of motifs.[271] "Each of the parts were very different from one another," Lacy explained, "but when they all came together, it was like spreading paint out on a much broader canvas. The pieces were much more than the sum of their parts. That was how he was innovative and what made his music at that time different from what everyone else was doing."[272] The Zebulon performances were the last concerts the band ever presented.

Around the end of 2006, Zebulon's music curation began to change. The club had become more popular, and the owners wanted to book music that had a broader appeal. This caused the venue to shift away from the raucous free jazz and big-band sets and toward smaller groups and, in many cases, Afro-beat and international music. They were able to book bigger-name bands with more mass appeal that pushed the venue a bit away from the New York arts crowd. Even within the improvised music that they booked, there was a distinct shift toward a younger generation of performers, many of whom lived in Brooklyn and especially Williamsburg.

CHAPTER FIVE

A New Generation Emerges

Zebulon, 2005–2012

Zebulon was beautifully bootleg.
—*Jason Merritt*

For a new generation of artists who now lived primarily in Williamsburg and Bushwick—whose artistic locus seemed to increasingly be positioned in Brooklyn—Zebulon became the prime staging ground, a public workshop for them to display their work. Much of the music was highly refined, but the owners were also open to works in progress, so Zebulon became one of the most dynamic music spaces in the city that catered to experimental music for a new generation.

Zebulon aimed to attract much of that scene to its doors in Williamsburg, and it was ultimately more successful in bridging the divide between Manhattan and Brooklyn than any other art space of its time in New York. Zebulon also reached out to younger musicians, and many key figures got their start at the club. Guitarist and record producer Dave Sitek (b. 1972) had his studio around the corner from the club, so the Zebulon stage was also a launching point for a host of indie rock bands, which included TV on the Radio, Grizzly Bear, Dirty Projectors, Sharon Van Etten, and many others.[1] On the weekends the club often featured danceable world music led by figures such as Vieux Farka Toure, Baye Kouyate, Janka Nabay, and others. The experimentalists continued to have a significant presence in the venue, however, and contributed to the overall aesthetic.

The new generation was increasingly conservatory trained and often seemed intent on furthering projects or intellectual pursuits that had begun in school. Others managed a more organic process. The musical avant-garde created by the new generation that appeared at Zebulon focused on a variety of things. Some were engaged in personal, spiritual, or historical storytelling, while challenging the mainstream or advocating for cultural transformation. Many of the conservatory-trained musicians of the era were either embracing or attempting to escape from the strictures of jazz, while mixing in new elements of classic or alternative rock, the mid-twentieth-century avant-garde, or a variety of international elements. How to regulate or control the action of improvised music, as inspired by Butch Morris and others, also became one of the puzzles that this new generation approached with fresh ideas.

Historical and Spiritual Dimensions
Matana Roberts

One of the key early figures of the new generation to emerge at Zebulon was saxophonist Matana Roberts. She was born and raised on Chicago's South Side and was one of a new wave of people who were mentored by the AACM. She had previously studied clarinet, but by the time she played professionally, her primary instrument was alto saxophone. She led or co-led groups at the Velvet Lounge in Chicago, including the collaborative trio Sticks and Stones with bassist Joshua Abrams and drummer Chad Taylor, but then pursued a master's degree from New England Conservatory and afterward settled in New York. She busked in the subways and published a zine, *Fat Ragged*, that documented her early years in the city. During those years she also played and toured with Greg Tate's band Burnt Sugar.

By 2004 she was leading her own quartet, which included trumpeter Taylor Ho Bynum, bassist Thomson Kneeland, and drummer Tomas Fujiwara. Their first gig was at CBGBs on the Bowery on October 17 of that year, but they began to play around at other clubs such as Barbès and the Jazz

Figure 5.1 Matana Roberts performing with Myra Melford Quartet (not pictured), Roulette, 2008 (*photo by Peter Gannushkin*)

Gallery before being offered an extended monthly residency at Zebulon from March to November 2005.

During the residency the Matana Roberts Quartet played her compositions, and she workshopped new material with the band.[2] Her pieces afforded the musicians ample room to improvise, either completely free or over a form with particular parameters. She also played pieces by musicians she admired, such as "My Man," written by Billie Holiday, and "We Travel the Spaceways," by Sun Ra, always with her own touches in the arrangements she contoured for the band. Some pieces of hers dealt explicitly with aspects of African American history, such as the Great Migration. Those critical sessions at Zebulon built her confidence as a composer and became the springboard for the genesis of new and bolder ideas. The musical relationships she forged there proved to be pivotal as she continued to develop her concept in the years that followed.

By 2006 Roberts had turned her attention to a visionary, monumental twelve-chapter project called Coin Coin, named both for an illustrious ancestor and for a related nickname given to her as a child by her maternal grandfather (see figure 5.1). She retained the personnel from her quartet and began expanding the band out for different iterations of the group. Music critic Nate Chinen described Coin Coin as "working with folklore, family archives, public records and other faded ephemera, she's creating her own patchwork monument to African-American history, a tale of harrowing struggle and brittle stoicism."[3] Roberts's work with Coin Coin is deeply personal, recounting tales from her family's past through stories, interviews, memories, histories, and myth. The name of the band is derived from Marie Thérèse Metoyer, known as "Coincoin" (1742–1816), an enslaved person born in central Louisiana during the colonial era.[4] Her parents had been brought from Africa. After her freedom was purchased by her longtime partner, she established herself as a prominent businesswoman—manufacturing medicine, planting tobacco, herding cattle, and trapping wild game. As her wealth grew, Coincoin set about buying freedom for at least three of her children and three grandchildren, eventually founding a prominent Creole community along the Cane River in Louisiana. She oversaw the construction of African House, "one of the earliest examples of African-influenced architecture in the United States."[5]

The musical concepts for Coin Coin began with Roberts's development of a unique system of notation that she initially called *panoramic sound quilting*.[6] "The full scores are a combination of the visual material and Western notation," Roberts explained, "and I collage them together in a way that makes sense to me and then I experiment with it on different musicians who I feel can handle it."[7] Roberts provided a key glossary and employed text, instructions, or words that the musicians were supposed to represent musically. For example, a lot of her cues for a new section were written as years, and she used the number of years for the musicians to play the intervallic relationships. So the transitions were rooted in the histories and stories she told and the organic sounds that grew out of them. Furthermore, different parts were sometimes connected to different characters from the stories themselves, and one might shift from character to character over the course of different concerts or tour dates. One of the band's earliest gigs was at the Moers Festival in Germany in 2006, showing that its advanced concepts quickly drew international attention.

Roberts based much of her work for the project on in-depth field research. Roberts often depicted parts of the graphic scores on the sleeves and covers of her Coin Coin records. They display a collage of photographs, writings, European musical notation, and other images. "I'm really interested in ephemera. It's about these traces of people, traces of stories, these things that we leave behind that seem to maybe not have any meaning, but to someone [they mean something]," Roberts explained. "I spend a lot of my free time in old junk shops just digging through stuff like that and I inherited a great deal of family ephemera which gives me an incredible amount of joy. It's just about the only thing of value I own outside of my saxophone."[8]

The collage work had been a part of Roberts's practice for over a decade by the time she began to develop it sonically:

I was painting my [instrument] cases and doing all of these collages, and I didn't understand yet that what I was trying to do with that was what I wanted to do with music. I just hadn't figured out a way to do it. I was talking to my maternal grandmother and she was telling me how her mother and father used to quilt; they were sharecroppers. She explained this system to me, taking all of these different pieces of worn-out clothing to create this whole other thing, which was a kind of living, breathing representation of the past. That's what I wanted to do with the scores and pieces [for Coin Coin].[9]

In the live setting, Roberts would also direct the action in the music. "I liberally use Butch Morris' system of conducting improvisers [Conduction], something that I learned a lot about from playing in Burnt Sugar. . . . It's a combination of visual cues and, depending on the mood and the music I'm trying to set, there will be certain things in the photographs or the collage that might be cues, or might be actual notes, or you can look in a photograph and see a certain story. . . . There's a lot of subtext in the ephemera. Sometimes I take actual data from the ephemera and turn it into sound."[10] For instance, Roberts might form music based on the rhythm in a sentence.

Certain performative elements also manifested in her live shows. "I also wanted to create a project so I could explore some other elements that I couldn't really explore in some of the other bands I've been in, in terms of dealing with theater and spectacle."[11] The climax of the first chapter of Coin Coin was a piece titled "Libation for Mr. Brown: Bid Em In," an adaptation of Oscar Brown Jr.'s "Bid 'Em High," from his debut record, *Sin and Soul* (1960).[12] Roberts contributed the vocals that had her performing in the role of a slave auctioneer, with Brown's pithy lyrics:

Don't you mind them tears
That's one of her tricks
She's healthy, she's strong, she's well-equipped
She makes a fine lady's maid when she's properly whipped.[13]

In the live setting, Roberts would often encourage the audience to sing along to the vocal parts of the piece, though sometimes she would inform them,

"This is a happy song, because if these people had not been bid in, I would not be here today enjoying my life."[14]

Roberts had an ability to establish an intimate relationship with the audience when performing live. In part, her work was so deeply personal that it naturally drew the audience into her world. "I want for us to be able to create a womb together," she later stated, describing the experience. "It's a spontaneous way of connecting with strangers who are not really strangers because we are all in this together." It was also a process of experiential learning for herself. "I want to know what pain feels like, I want to know what the depths of misery feel like. That's a hard way to live, but I just wanted to know. In those moments, there is a lot of joy, too, there's a level of living experience. I'm here, we are alive, let's celebrate what we do have."[15] Roberts's first Coin Coin record was released in 2011.[16] She has continued to develop and release subsequent chapters of the work in the years since.

Eye Contact

The band Eye Contact established itself at Zebulon in 2005–7. They played their first concert at Galapagos in October 2004, but after a gig at Zebulon the following February, the band soon played the club regularly, presenting material there ten times over the following two years (see figure 5.2).[17] Bassist Matthew Heyner, who had emerged to prominence with the band TEST around 1999, was joined by trumpeter and bass clarinetist Matt Lavelle and drummer Ryan Sawyer in a collaborative trio. By that time Heyner had developed into a lyrical player with a great amount of technical skill. Lavelle and Sawyer had previously played together for several years doing gigs at the Pink Pony and other venues, though they never recorded. Lavelle had also met Heyner by playing weekly sessions with Sabir Mateen at David Gould's basement on the Lower East Side for several years prior. Sawyer bartended at Galapagos at the time and set up their first gig; he soon arranged regular gigs at Zebulon.

"At that time," Lavelle recalled, "I wasn't doing melodies, just complete improvisation, and I was playing really hard. I was going for a late Coltrane, Albert Ayler, Pharoah [Sanders] kind of thing, but without saxophones. I could get closer with bass clarinet than trumpet, but Roy Campbell became more and more a reference point for me."[18] Sawyer's playing at the time was versatile and revealed knowledge of and vocabulary drawn from an eclectic array of sources, and he was an adept improviser. Heyner had gained considerable experience with TEST and brought that sensibility to

Figure 5.2 Eye Contact: (*from left*) Matt Lavelle, Ryan Sawyer, and Matthew Heyner, Tonic, 2006 (*photo by Peter Gannushkin*)

Eye Contact. Lavelle's personal life at the time pushed the music further into that ecstatic realm of free playing: his mother had to undergo brain surgery, and though she managed to recover, the initial prognosis had not been positive. "Eye Contact with God," the title track of the first record, "was meant as a reference point to her experience and illustrated the zone we were aiming for when we pushed forward in the music toward the edge," Lavelle revealed.[19] Or, as one critic noted, the music possessed "a spiritual imperative. The song travels the line between life and death." She added that the music evoked "a primordial trance state, exploring the edge where the ego gives way to something bigger."[20] In the live setting at Zebulon, the band sometimes played while screening films simultaneously, such as Maya Deren's depictions of Haitian voodoo.[21]

But Heyner also pushed them into new territory. He developed a kind of "free flamenco," where he established the setting on acoustic bass, Sawyer held down the beats, and Lavelle took on the role of the vocalist with his bass clarinet, while playing freely improvised sections.[22] His trumpet added a unique sound based on nondiatonic scales. "The band always had a primal pulse, no matter what we were doing," Lavelle observed.[23] In some ways,

A New Generation Emerges

A New Generation Emerges

195

they built on flamenco-influenced work that bassist Charles Mingus had done in the early 1960s, most notably *Black Saint and the Sinner Lady*, as well as some of the latter's final work in the late 1970s.[24]

Over time, however, Heyner got more and more interested in playing electric bass and began employing that at some gigs. Sawyer and Heyner then began to push the aesthetic of the band into punk rock and metal, pushing Lavelle out of his element, moving away from the spiritual free jazz that had informed the band's earlier work. The band's third record, *War Rug*, caught the band in the midst of their transition.[25] Proudly, the band recorded it without overdubbing, though it was inundated with atmospheric sounds including drones, distant-sounding hand drumming, and many other effects. The harder edges bristled with energy and force, such that one critic described the music as sounding "as if Roy Campbell were fronting the Minutemen."[26] The band did a Midwest tour from Chicago and Detroit to Pittsburgh in 2006, which was mismanaged and was not successful in the venues but included some well-attended house concerts. A fourth record recorded in Brooklyn in 2007 found the trio to have resolved some of their aesthetic differences, bringing harmony to their brand of electric free jazz, but because the band dissolved around that time, the record was never released.[27]

Edom

Several bands that emerged at Zebulon recorded work for John Zorn's record label, Tzadik, as part of the series Radical Jewish Culture. The most prominent of these was Edom. The series originated in the Festival for Radical Jewish Culture that Zorn organized in Munich, Germany, in 1992. One writer argued that the series "became an act of liberation and laid the foundation for new exploration of Jewish identity in music."[28] New experimental Jewish music came to form a major component of New York's downtown scene in the decade that followed. Zorn and many others made major contributions to creating music that was, as scholar Tamar Barzel stated, both "Jewishly identified and yet also in keeping with their other work—unconventional, experimentalist, and with wide-ranging musical influences."[29] Zebulon was the staging site for some of the second generation of this movement to present their work.

The roots of Edom may be traced to a meeting between guitarist Eyal Maoz and bassist Shanir Blumenkranz at Rimon School of Music in Israel in the mid-1990s.[30] In fact, the bassist had heard Maoz's exploratory approach, which convinced him to enroll at the school. Maoz was a secular Jew from Israel, while Blumenkranz had been born in Brooklyn and raised in Miami. They both attended Rimon School before deciding to study music in the United States.[31] Maoz attended Berklee College of Music in Boston in 1994–98, while Blumenkranz made a detour to Manhattan School of Music before leaving for Berklee, where they were reunited. Maoz and Blumenkranz formed a lifelong friendship and musical collaboration that eventually brought them to New York in 2000.

After a few years of situating themselves in New York, Maoz formed the band Edom and, after working on some material, approached John Zorn with a demo tape in 2005.[32] In its earliest manifestations, the band was an acoustic unit with violin and cello, but it soon took a turn toward jazz rock with the inclusion of organist John Medeski and drummer Ben Perowsky, in addition to Blumenkranz. Maoz considered his aesthetic influences to range from John Zorn's Electric Masada to Frank Zappa, Pat Matheny, and Marc Ribot.[33] "I don't really like most traditional Jewish music," Maoz observed, "but I consider what I do to be my own version of Jewish music."[34] Maoz's process usually began with a melody on guitar that he built out into broader pieces that he would work out with the band. By the summer of 2005, with Medeski and Perowsky busy with other work, Maoz decided to change personnel, looking for musicians who would be able to play and rehearse more regularly. So he evolved the band into a trio, retaining Blumenkranz and hiring drummer Yuval Leon, whom Blumenkranz described as "a master of groove and time."[35]

The music that Maoz wrote for the band was particularly inspired by his viewing of the documentary film *The Rise and Fall of the Third Reich*, based on the original book by William L. Shirer.[36] The piece "Hope and Destruction" in particular was permeated with ideas about the naivete of "false hope and the inability of people to see destruction coming." Maoz added, "The thing that struck me most powerfully was that people could see all of these historical processes happening, but they could still not see what might come out of it and escape in time. So, in writing the music, I wanted to address the human condition that made people refuse to see it and made such destruction possible."[37]

Maoz led the trio version of Edom at Zebulon beginning in July 2005, before the release of their first record. To further the jazz rock feel and to expand the harmonic possibilities, Maoz invited keyboardist Brian Marsella to join the band to make it a quartet in 2006, as they began workshopping and refining music for their second record. The music deepened the themes from the first record, bearing the title *Hope and Destruction* to signal that intensification.[38] The sonic aesthetic shifted dramatically, however, with the

Figure 5.3 Edom: (*from left*) Brian Marsella, Yuval Leon, Shanir Blumenkranz, and Eyal Maoz, Tea Lounge, 2011 (*photo by Peter Gannushkin*)

influx of new musicians and the ability to workshop material at Zebulon. It became very synthesizer based, instead of using organ, and more aggressive in its approach, but with aesthetic influences that could be traced to pop music. The music developed a harder edge, bearing influence from Joy Division and the Cure and even No Wave bands such as DNA, among many eclectic sources.[39] In the second record, Edom settled on the sound that the band has continued to explore and evolve in the years since.

"We played so much at Zebulon," Blumenkranz observed. "We forged our sound there, and the venue let us develop. I learned what we should and should not do. Joce and Jef Soubiran's love for the music and the musicians allowed that to happen." The band presented a string of concerts at Zebulon in 2007 and 2008 leading up to the release of *Hope and Destruction* in 2009 and then returned to the club in 2010 (see figure 5.3). "As we developed the pieces for the second record, I wanted to push everything we had done on the first one out," Blumenkranz recalled. "There is nothing more human than musicians interacting onstage with one another, so we wanted to keep that element while pairing it with machinelike music, as manifested in the bass and drum parts. Then we would switch those positions."[40]

Edom was eye-opening for Blumenkranz in his own personal development as a musician. He had begun a self-study of oud in the late 1990s because his mother was from Egypt but also had Moroccan roots, and he was exploring issues of his own identity. That led him to play the *gimbri*, an instrument of the Gnawa people of Morocco, who generally used it for rituals, trances, and healing ceremonies of various kinds. "But you can't learn the music unless you are eating the soup, you are there, you are surrounded by the culture," Blumenkranz stated. The quarter tones of Arab music, which did not exist in traditional European tabulation, as well as differing scales, further expanded the possibilities for Blumenkranz. "I was interested in learning music that had different rules and intentions, such as bebop jazz versus Japanese music versus rock music versus free jazz. Edom is where I began to understand the importance of exploring the different types of music and the possibilities of following or breaking those rules or even blending them together. The challenge became to move away from the jazz and blues sound and to focus on sounds made after 1975, 1980, or 1985."[41] The band's performances at Zebulon spoke to the venue's interest in experimental music with an international vision.

"Throughout Edom's music, though it may be difficult for some people to detect because it is not so obvious," Maoz noted, "I have chosen elements of Jewish music that I want to emphasize, things that others might not even place in that category. As a contributor to the Radical Jewish Culture movement, it is a sign that the culture is open not only to klezmer but also to new innovations. I am happy that the definition of modern Jewish music is being expanded to include mine."[42] "I grew up with Zorn's Masada as a kid," Blumenkranz recalled. "When I first heard those records, I felt like I was hearing the next step forward in Jewish music. I could feel and recognize the Jewishness of it, but yet it was new and exciting." Blumenkranz added, "Edom is Jewish music, so in a way it has that same element that John Coltrane put in *A Love Supreme*, a nonmusical ingredient that adds to the flavor of the mixture and puts it in a sacred place for me."[43]

Rashanim

Another band that recorded for the Radical Jewish Culture series on Tzadik was guitarist Jon Madof's band Rashanim. Moving from his hometown of Philadelphia, Madof had first gotten his bearings on the New York scene at the Knitting Factory around 2000, where he played some of his first gigs, and later at Tonic, once the scene shifted there. John Zorn's Masada, Dave

Douglas's Tiny Bell Trio, and evolving klezmer music like the Klezmatics and work by Andy Statman had been major sparks for Madof, and finding a way to bridge together Jewish music with experimental concepts and approaches became the drive behind many of his early projects. "John Zorn embodied the kind of cross-genre eclecticism that I loved," Madof recalled.[44]

Madof hired Shanir Blumenkranz and drummer Mathias Künzli for the project, both of whom were contemporaries and were just then emerging on the scene. The band played its earliest gigs at Makor, a Jewish cultural center near Lincoln Center in Manhattan, and also played a few times at the Knitting Factory and Cornelia Street Café. Madof then approached Zorn at Tonic one day and gave him a CD of demos that the band had recorded; they were soon after invited to record for Zorn's Tzadik label.[45] Recording on Tzadik quickly opened up opportunities to tour in Europe to gain wider exposure.

From around the time that Madof arrived in New York, he began composing for Rashanim, even though the band did not convene for the first time until 2002. Specific ideas compelled him to pursue the music. "I was emulating the way that Zorn would take a body of music or some sort of tradition and use it to inform his own music, but have it be about his own expression. But I was also inspired by the way that a band like Pachora carried explicit and strong influences from Balkan music into the jazz world," Madof explained.[46] In this grain, one of the first pieces the band recorded was the traditional Hasidic song "Der Khusid Geyt Tantsn," which Madof arranged with the melody over shifting time signatures that departed significantly from the original pushing into a kind of free noise.

Rashanim evolved rapidly and organically in the first few years of its existence. Though the original concept was to take klezmer and other Jewish music and bring it into Madof's own soundscape, the band evolved into a kind of "rock power trio that also incorporated the other influences. That was not my original intention, but it just came out of me because that is who I am," Madof explained.[47] "It felt great, it sounded great, so I didn't resist the band going in that direction." The critical transition came with their second record, *Masada Rock*, in 2005, which documented them playing Zorn's previously unreleased Masada music, but arranged by Madof with a rock sound.[48]

By 2006 Madof was developing more material, by then working with his own compositions that had grown out of his experience of playing Zorn's Masada works. On November 30 of that year, Rashanim presented the first of several concerts at Zebulon, with additional performances in 2008 and 2009. Madof used the opportunities to debut and workshop the latest material, a collection of songs that was much more focused than the band's earlier work.[49] "Yosefa" was the culmination of a number of years of Madof playing with shifting time signatures and other rhythmic experimentations finally coming to fruition. "Cracow Niggun," written by Rabbi Shlomo Carlebach, was another example of the maturing arrangements by Madof, drawing the piece into the rock realm again while playing on time. "Jacob and Esau" was a loud, brash, punk-inspired piece that exhibited those aspects of the band's aesthetic. Madof refined these pieces and others at Zebulon. The band's later concerts shifted to an acoustic exploration of the possibilities of the band's sound and concepts.[50]

Embracing/Escaping Jazz

One of the strongest preoccupations of the new generation at Zebulon was how they chose to relate to jazz, especially the way jazz was taught in music schools at the time. Because it was often dogmatic, many rejected it outright, even if they were heavily influenced by it. Many found its methods oppressive yet all-encompassing and therefore sought to find ways to move away from it, while some musicians managed a fusion between jazz and other forms of music through an organic process.

Eivind Opsvik's Overseas

One of the most enduring bands of the past two decades, Overseas, first really took off at Zebulon. The band was the work of Norwegian bassist Eivind Opsvik, who had moved to New York to pursue a master's degree at Manhattan School of Music in 1998. In 2002 he began to put a band together to workshop his growing list of musical ideas. His musical influences ranged from jazz and European classical music to rock, with bands like the first Miles Davis Quintet with bassist Paul Chambers, as well as Pink Floyd, Gustav Mahler, and the Norwegian guitar player Terje Rypdal permeating his thoughts.[51] Many of the early compositions were pieces that he had been working on since the mid-1990s. From the beginning he experimented with different lineups, with two groups eventually solidifying. The first involved friends from music school: saxophonist Loren Stillman, saxophonist and clarinetist Jason Rigby, pianist Wells Hanley, and drummer Jeff Davis. The second group involved more experienced players: tenor saxophonist Tony Malaby, pianist Craig Taborn, and drummer Gerald Cleaver. Pianist Jacob Sacks and percussionist Dan Weiss also joined the groups at different times.

The band's earliest gigs featured different lineups, but over the first few years, the two lineups began to meld together with Malaby becoming the regular saxophonist, Sacks becoming the regular pianist, and the drum chair oscillating between Cleaver, Davis, and Weiss. Stillman and Taborn occasionally doubled on their instruments. Their earliest public performances occurred in Manhattan at Nublu and 55Bar, but once Zebulon opened, it became the preferred venue for the band. After hearing Kenny Wollesen play at Tonic in 2004, Opsvik hired him on the spot as the drummer for the band, "because as soon as I heard him, I knew that his time feel and earthy, organic sense of the beat was what I had been looking for with Overseas."[52]

By the time Overseas began playing at Zebulon, they were performing the material they had recorded for their second record.[53] Opsvik's early compositions for the group ranged across a vast spectrum of tunes and were influenced by music such as the electric Miles Davis recordings (e.g., *In a Silent Way* or *Bitches Brew*), especially when Opsvik employed two electric keyboards, with Weiss on tabla.[54] "Italian Movie Theme" was broadly inspired by Ennio Morricone's score for the gangster drama *Once upon a Time in America*.[55] Opsvik found himself writing specifically for Malaby's lead melodic voice for the record. Overseas played at Zebulon every few months through 2005 and 2006.

By 2008 Opsvik was presenting work from his third record at Zebulon. He felt that some of the band's earlier work had been unnecessarily complicated, and he aimed to focus in on the concepts that were most emotionally engaging. The opening piece, "Neil," was an experiment in simple chord structures coupled with "melody sitting on the wrong notes," which was loosely a tribute to rock guitarist Neil Young.[56] To bring the vision into reality, Opsvik hired a pedal steel player for the record to enhance the "earthiness of the sound."[57]

The second piece they worked on was "Everseas," the band's attempt to make ambient music with live instruments, inspired by Brian Eno, particularly the latter's piece "Discreet Music."[58] Opsvik gave melodic lines to Malaby and Sacks with the idea that they could play them at any tempo, without having to listen to the other melodic voice, maintaining one static dynamic of overlapping and shimmering lines. When it came time to record the pieces, he did so entirely on analog recording equipment at the Hotel Edison on Times Square, which had an old recording studio inside that had operated at various locations since the 1940s for artists such as bebop pianist Thelonious Monk, among others.[59] No edits were made after the initial recordings, so it was an exercise in precision in the studio takes. The band

Figure 5.4 Eivind Opsvik
of Overseas, Shape-
shifter Lab, 2012 (*photo
by Peter Gannushkin*)

returned to Opsvik's native country of Norway to present their music at the
Molde Jazz Festival in 2009, near where he grew up. Opsvik and his father
had attended the festival with regularity in his youth.

In 2009 Overseas played three more concerts at Zebulon as Opsvik began
to explore new material again (see figure 5.4). He had never liked jazz guitar,
but after hearing meticulous, frantic, high-energy player Brandon Seabrook,
he felt he had finally found someone for the instrument in the band. So, at
first Seabrook subbed for Malaby when the latter was unavailable, but by
2010 the guitarist's inclusion in the band made it a quintet. "Seabrook's time
feel was transformative," Opsvik observed, "and he brought an increased
energy to the band, so it also grew louder, naturally. Layers of texture also
permeated everything we were doing, so he really expanded the sonic possibilities of the band."[60] As the band prepared to work toward the fourth
record, they also began to explore microtonal aspects of their sound through
a new set of compositions.[61]

With Seabrook sometimes now inhabiting the lead melodic voice, Opsvik gave Malaby greater license to shape his contributions to the band. For

example, with the piece "They Will Hear the Drums—And They Will Answer," he asked Malaby to play in the style of a castrato singer. For the piece "1786," he merely instructed Malaby to "solo like a punk singer."[62] But in other pieces Opsvik also composed sections for Malaby's saxophone parts to work more as an accompanying instrument or to play unison with his own arco bass, while Sacks or Seabrook played over the top, shifting the traditional roles of the instruments around within the ensemble pushing toward an organic sound.

The final element that emerged in Opsvik's fourth book of music for the band was a search for a new keyboard. With each record up to that point, he had used different keyboards including a grand piano, Hammond organ, celesta, and Wurlitzer. He turned to harpsichord for the fourth recording, though the unavailability of the instrument in New York performance spaces made it impossible to use it in front of a live audience. The baroque music included in the soundtrack for the film *Marie Antoinette*, directed by Sofia Coppola, brought him into the sound palette needed for the instrument, which he complemented by reading books such as Mark Twain's *Personal Recollections of Joan of Arc*.[63] Pairing harpsichord with electric guitar had few precedents and created a unique soundscape in which to navigate jazz compositions. Opsvik presented the music regularly at Zebulon between 2010 and when the venue closed in 2012.

Mike Pride

We last encountered drummer Mike Pride at the Right Bank Café and Newsonic Loft in chapter 3. By the mid-2000s, one of Pride's main collaborators was guitarist Charlie Looker, and for a time they had a band with Tyondai Braxton called Antenna Terra. Eventually Pride and Looker formed a duo called Period, named after the fifth book in the George Miles Cycle by writer Dennis Cooper.[64] Cooper's manner of "mining one idea deeply and completely for a hundred pages at a time" was an inspiration to Pride, and in a way, Pride and Looker adopted a similar approach to writing and improvising music together.[65]

Fittingly, Period's music was angular, dissonant, jagged music. One of them would start and often do something bold or unexpected, and the other would be forced to react, perhaps in a manner of countering the first statement or building it forward. Particular statements could go up or down in intensity, stop and start. Even from a rather simple rhythm, the duo often grew into an ecstatic frenzy. Pride and Looker discovered a shared aesthetic in these

Figure 5.5 Period: (*from left*) Chuck Bettis, Mike Pride, and Charlie Looker, Knitting Factory, 2008 (*photo by Peter Gannushkin*)

explosive moments that over time built sonic trajectories into a grander narrative arc. Their early work is documented on their debut record.[66]

After exploring this concept together, they began to invite additional musicians to join them who they thought would complement the band's aesthetic. By October 2007, for concerts at Zebulon and the Stone, the band had expanded to a quintet. The first person to join them was Chuck Bettis, a truly unique artist who blended electronics with guttural throat singing that meshed well with the spontaneous approach and sonic palette (see figure 5.5). Bettis made the music more aqueous and, at times, haunting. Adding saxophonists Darius Jones and Sam Hillmer expanded the possibilities immensely in terms of interaction and brought the explosive nature of the band to its fullest expression. The two horn players brought very different sounds, with Hillmer more of a fiery player and Jones having an extensive melodic voice. When onstage, they moved between duos, trios, and the full band, though always with Pride and Looker at the core, creating what Pride referred to as "sound slabs."[67]

Having established a relationship with the Soubirans and also begun to build a reputation for himself, Pride began to book his other bands at Zebulon.

One of the first of these was Whoopie Pie, which grew out of his friendship with keyboardist Jamie Saft. They invited saxophonist Bill McHenry to join them for a trio. Through a series of concerts at Zebulon in 2008 and 2009, the band developed its approach. Pride often brought heavier rock rhythms to the music that were both regimented and propulsive. Saft added a growling undertow with electric bass and organ, while McHenry provided shafts of light escaping the darkness beneath.[68]

The work with Whoopie Pie pushed Pride and Saft to consider trio possibilities with other musicians, and they eventually formed Angel OV Death with saxophonist Andrew D'Angelo.[69] The band played live in Brooklyn and generated some ideas to the point that they booked a date at a recording studio in February 2008 to lay down tracks. D'Angelo did not arrive at the scheduled time, and eventually mutual friend Oscar Noriega called Saft with the tragic news that D'Angelo had had a seizure; later it was discovered he had brain cancer. As Pride and Saft sat in the studio that day, they felt compelled to record a duo, at least partially dedicated to D'Angelo, in what became the band Kalashnikov, with a heavy-hitting, aggressive, percussive improvisatory sound that pushed the edges of noise, epic doom metal, and art metal music.[70] Saft played keyboards, electric bass, and guitar with Pride laying down beats, singing lyrics, and occasionally taking the place of the horn by screaming over the top with added whistles and other effects. From Kalashnikov, the band Spanish Donkey emerged, which was Saft's vision of improvised metal music with guitarist Joe Morris shredding over the top.[71] Angel OV Death, Kalashnikov, and Spanish Donkey all debuted their live work at Zebulon in May 2009.

While Pride participated in his various collaborative bands with Looker and Saft, he was also writing music for his own band, From Bacteria to Boys. The band had come together in the wake of MP3's breakup. It formed when Pride invited Darius Jones and bassist Evan Lipson to join him on an East Coast tour originally intended to be a series of solo events (see figure 5.6).[72] Pride began working on what he called "statement music," which was structured on loop-based material.[73] The central idea was to create repetitive motifs that band members could play for as long or as short as they wanted. For instance, Jones had a series of "cells of music," which were often melodic lines or rhythmic patterns with tempo indicated, that he moved through in order, staying with each one for as long as he wished. Lipson did the same, though the cells did not necessarily line up between players.

Over time, after playing together more extensively, the band members began to follow each other in the shifts from cell to cell, like cues, and the

Figure 5.6 From Bacteria to Boys: (*from left*) Darius Jones, Mike Pride, and Evan Lipson, late 2000s (*photo by Scott Friedlander*)

music became less free and more through-composed, though in a way that felt fluid and natural. "The goal was to create music where the combination of the voices created a sonic structure that in its totality was way more interesting than the individual parts," according to Pride.[74] The sonic structures were malleable and could shift in subtle ways when individual members moved from cell to cell. The other outcome was that it caused each of the musicians in the band to listen intently to the others in real time as the music was unfolding, to play an active, present role in shaping it.

From Bacteria to Boys evolved rather rapidly from that point forward. Pride retained Jones in the band and hired pianist Alexis Marcelo and bassist Peter Bitenc. With this set of musicians, Pride began to move more toward formal composition. Bitenc was a versatile player, and Marcelo brought a lively energy to keyboards that reshaped the overall mood of the music. Between 2006 and 2010, the band evolved from punk-informed angular and structural music toward more composed melodies with increasing amounts of dense jazz harmony. The band gained considerably more exposure after Pride was signed by the AUM Fidelity label, which had a reputation as one of the foremost free jazz labels of the time, having played an integral role in documenting some key figures of the downtown scene such as David S. Ware, William Parker, and Joe Morris.[75]

The series of concerts that From Bacteria to Boys played at Zebulon in 2011 and 2012 featured the band in a process of fine-tuning its abilities as Pride again adjusted the lineup. He had been playing duo with alto saxophonist Jon Irabagon, and he asked him to take Jones's place in the band. "In his first rehearsal," Pride recalled, "Jon learned the entire songbook, dozens of pages of music. It was incredible, so I knew I had the right person in the band."[76] Soon the band was deeply rooted in a common understanding, arrived at the breaks with precision, and transitioned from one part to the next effortlessly. Now they were prepared to work on what would be the music for the band's final record, *Birthing Days*.[77]

Many of the pieces were autobiographical, as they had been throughout the band's history. Much of the music was inspired by the time leading up to and after the birth of Pride's son in 2012. In reviewing a live performance at the time, I wrote, "By shifting from intense playing, to soloing, to sudden interludes of silence, Pride exhibits an incredible range of emotions through his music. The music carries a human resonance—an honesty about the beauty and the challenges, the unknown and the unexpected, the anxiety and satisfaction that one experiences in parenthood. Ecstatic exclamations, mild whimsies, sweet lullabies, and turbulent confessions are all present on the album and were brimming over in the live performance."[78]

Peter Evans and Collaborators

Perhaps no musician found more of a home for their music at Zebulon than trumpeter Peter Evans. He began leading his own bands soon after arriving in New York. His first critical attention came through his solo performances, but he soon also began putting together his own groups. One of his earliest projects was a duo with bassist Tom Blancarte called Sparks. The band had begun shortly after the two met and became friends while working together in a mail room in Manhattan in 2005. Blancarte's earliest musical interests had been sparked by Metallica and Black Sabbath, but he had later pursued interests in jazz, especially 1960s Miles Davis and Ornette Coleman, as well as the improvised, minimalist noise of the Japanese Onkyo movement, especially Sachiko M, Taku Sugimoto, and Yoshihide Otomo.[79] Seeing saxophonist Evan Parker perform solo while he was in college ignited Blancarte's imagination about what was possible in music. Pursuing jazz education in college, Blancarte experienced what he called "authoritarian and fascistic

Figure 5.7 Tom Blancarte performing with Sparks (Peter Evans not pictured), Zebulon, 2009 (*photo by Peter Gannushkin*)

ways of teaching music to people that was kind of traumatic," and by the time he arrived in New York, he was determined "not to play jazz."[80]

In a way, Sparks was modeled on the Evan Parker–Barry Guy Duo, which had been active from 1981 to 2003.[81] The duo rehearsed in Blancarte's living room in the East Village on a weekly basis through the first half of 2006 as the two developed a deep understanding of each other and a manner of anticipating what was to come through their improvisations (see figure 5.7).[82] "Evans's language was something I wasn't initially familiar with because he does a lot of stuff with polyrhythms," Blancarte reflected, "so that was a steep learning curve for me and had a big impact on how I make music, think about music, and really my own language." Part of Blancarte's developing language looked to destabilize and upset stasis in music "with elements of chaos to push it to the limits of what was possible rather than play safe. I always wanted to create situations where the outcome was not necessarily clear at the outset and to push it to the point where it was about to break."[83] Later that year, Evans released his first solo record on Psi, a label run by Evan Parker, and rather than tour solo, he invited Blancarte to join him. They played across Europe for two weeks, which was eye-opening for both musicians and helped Evans especially to establish himself on the international circuit. Back in New York, Sparks released their record in 2008 and presented the material at Zebulon through 2009.

Evans began a trio, originally as a side project, that flourished and recorded at Zebulon. The band included bassist John Hebert and drummer Kassa Overall, whom Evans described as "unacademic players." Hebert had gone to music school, but as Evans noted, "His strengths come from the fact that he has so much experience playing real-life music with real-life jazz musicians. I like his sound because he is super active and can play all over the bass. He has an amazing sense of time and can play in so many different settings from Andrew Hill to Fred Hersch." Evans had met Overall in music school at Oberlin College but was impressed by "how much his playing has evolved over time. He used to have an aggressive post–Tony Williams approach, but when we reconnected in New York years later, I could see his playing had opened up in all kinds of ways."[84] Overall often experimented with the kit setup itself, sometimes doubling up with two snare drums and two floor toms, for example, and tuning some of the drums down to create hushed tones. He would also include bongos in a manner that suggested some inspiration from Tony Oxley. "Overall's experiments have explored all kinds of colors and timbres in the music and reveal his own interests that range from hip-hop to jazz to the avant-garde," Evans observed.[85]

Evans's trio marked a new stage in his development. The trio's work focused on meeting and spontaneously improvising together. "I wanted to have a bass and drums group, but I was not sure how they would work together until we did it," Evans noted, "but it was a communal thing. It was as if we were all huddled around a fire, communing on the music, we were all going inward to something."[86] The trio began to play regularly at Zebulon in 2010, first in June and then a three-night stint in October. They returned the following September for three more nights and finally recorded live sets there on March 25–26, 2012.

Evans composed not more than a page of charts for each piece. For the piece "3625," he took a harmonic pattern often found at the end of standards, taking the final four bars and looping them, and started the piece with that instead. The piece built with intensity as the three musicians improvised over the loop for eighteen minutes and then ended with a complicated composed section. One example of this practice was Coltrane's recording of "But Not for Me," on *My Favorite Things*, which looped the final bars for over four minutes.[87] The music was, in many ways, Evans's most jazz-oriented group up to that time. The visibility of the trio at Zebulon led to the band being invited to play at the Bergamo Jazz Festival in Italy in 2013, where he was praised for "amazing technique, phrasing, intensity of dialog between musicians, and experimentation that was even more evident in the live festival set."[88]

Another significant project that Evans was a part of that came to fruition at Zebulon was a duo with fellow trumpeter Nate Wooley. The duo began playing publicly in 2007 with performances at Barbès and the Stone. By 2010 and 2011, they were performing at Zebulon and recorded their first record, *High Society*.[89] Their work together blew open the possibilities of the trumpet. Though they were individually very different players and had contrasting aesthetics, they complemented each other and over time developed a shared vocabulary. Wooley had previously worked a lot in drones in his solo work, and Evans's use of amplifier intensified his drones to the point of a piercing tone at times, though at other moments Evans's sound simmered so that Wooley could work around it deftly. Wooley's use of amplifier, discussed in chapter 3, allowed him to take on a percussive role that added structure and unpredictability to their collective sound. Both players had ways of working with feedback as well that created soundscapes that often trod on the palette of electric guitars and noise. "The goal, unattainable as it may be, is to be so fluent in your own language that you can simply exist within the music and build, change and obliterate statements quickly and beautifully," Wooley said of his improvisational approach. "Its purity exists in the attempt to make the gap from objective idea to expression of that idea as small as possible."[90] The duo continued to perform elsewhere and released additional records after Zebulon closed.

"The Soubiran brothers would let me do anything at Zebulon," Evans stated. "I experimented with a lot of different ideas, bands with two drummers, electronics, anything loud. We would play two sets a night and do multiple nights in a row. It was a rarity by the 2010s to have that opportunity anywhere in New York City."[91] More than any other space, Zebulon became the launching point for many of Evans's projects, its openness to experimental and sonically intense projects making it an ideal space for him to establish himself.

Jeremiah Cymerman

Clarinetist and electronicist Jeremiah Cymerman emerged with a few projects at Zebulon from early 2008 onward. Cymerman was more of a studio tinkerer and technician than he was a regular gigger, but when he finally brought projects to a live audience, they were usually well formed, more so

Figure 5.8 Jeremiah Cymerman, the Stone, 2007 (*photo by Peter Gannushkin*)

than those of a lot of musicians, who refined their projects on the stage. This practice may be traced back to his early adolescence, when he found music to be a sanctuary from what was otherwise a very challenging childhood.[92] Cymerman stated, "One of my favorite things about making records is following intuition through a practice to a final idea rather than trying to realize the original idea or form of something without letting it evolve. Studio technology allows you to play with color, shades, reverb, and so forth. I love playing live, but ultimately my biggest enjoyment is making records."[93]

Cymerman presented for the first time at Zebulon on January 22, 2008, material from his debut solo record, *In Memory of the Labyrinth System* (see figure 5.8).[94] Cymerman was particularly inspired by a record by composer Andre Popp (1924–2014), *Delirium in Hi-Fi*, released in 1958, that used creative studio techniques and recording tricks for a range of effects that Cymerman interpreted as "alien sounds."[95] Cymerman had also been inspired by debut solo records of two close friends, Nate Wooley's *Wrong Shape to Be a Storyteller* and Peter Evans's *More Is More*, both of which the clarinetist considered to be "extreme statements of solo trumpet music, totally different in their aesthetic.[96] I felt an imperative based on what they had done, so if I made a solo record, it had to be something that nobody had heard before. I wanted it to be almost unidentifiable when someone first put it on."[97] Cymerman had begun playing solo in 2005, and it was a gradual process of developing enough material. "At first," he recalled, "I only had five minutes of solo material. Then ten, and so on, I built it over the years. The goal was to have an hour of material to document and then to start over with the next hour."[98]

Cymerman had simultaneously developed two kinds of solo material. The first was creating a live sound environment through the public address system: "I wanted an ethereal quality and reverb," he explained. "And then I also worked on a recorded approach which was about really close mic sounds, rapid edits, and cut-ups."[99] The record itself ended up being a series of cut-ups, and the final piece, "Ending of Nerve in Recessus Utriculi," involved thousands of edits, almost like musique concrète, a type of musical composition that employs recorded sounds as raw material to form montages. He employed what he considered to be extended studio techniques, including "creative mic placement, hyper and micro editing, tape manipulation, cut and paste strategies, extreme mixes that take full advantage of the stereo field and various other approaches."[100]

"My fundamental aesthetic sense is dark," Cymerman wrote.

> I'm not interested in music being fun or entertaining. I'm not interested in things being precious and cute. My work is informed by profound personal experiences, dark and light. What I am most interested in is an artist's vulnerability. It took me a long time to accept and embrace that in my own music. Through the anger, the dark aesthetics, the feedback and distortion I think it is ultimately my goal . . . to expose that vulnerability and all else that lies beneath the surface, to convey the feelings of love and groundedness that I experience in the moment of creation.[101]

Still, *In Memory of the Labyrinth System* presented Cymerman with a kind of "existential crisis," in that what he produced in the studio and what he performed live were often quite different because of the possibilities in the two different settings. "I wanted the recorded music to breathe more and be more representative of what I did live, and I wanted what was happening live to have more of that articulate nature that the recording had."[102] One way to deal with this difference was to assemble a live ensemble unit that could bring to life more of the complexity of music that Cymerman had developed as a solo artist in the studio. Joined by saxophonists Matt Bauder and Josh Sinton in a group called Silence and Solitude, Cymerman played approximately ten concerts through 2008, including a June performance at Zebulon. The experience of playing with that ensemble informed some of his work of the late 2010s.[103]

Another record, *Fire Sign*, documented a range of compositional projects by Cymerman.[104] It began with the piece "Collapsed Eustachian," intended for two trumpets and performed by Wooley and Peter Evans. Cymerman had booked both of them for solo acoustic performances at a series that he ran at Ibeam in Brooklyn and had let recordings of those live performances play together using the software Pro Tools in his home studio.[105] After revealing this to the two trumpeters, they readily agreed to work with him to see the project fully realized. In a similar instance, Cymerman relistened to extended solos that Blancarte had made on alternative takes for pieces that Cymerman had composed on *Under a Blue Grey Sky*, and he again began taking bits and pieces of them from different sections and put together a solo piece.[106]

Then Cymerman relistened to a concert that he had played with a sextet at Roulette a year earlier and focused on a two-bar section that he then looped and began to pick apart.[107] At that point, he sent what he had to John Zorn at the Tzadik record label; the latter replied quickly, "One more piece and this is a record."[108] Cymerman thought about what had informed the other pieces and concluded they were "recordings by improvisers with some intentionality with me having some ultimate say how they fit together."[109] So for the final piece, he composed about thirty short spots of music for cellist Christopher Hoffman and drummer Brian Chase, sometimes with vague instructions or a prepared tonal center, each two to three minutes in length, and then Cymerman strung together a selection of the best segments. All together, *Fire Sign* represented a document of compositions drawing together some of his most important musical collaborators at the time, genuinely featured in their own voices.[110] *Fire Sign* was Cymerman's high-water mark as a composer up to that time.

Little Women

One of the bands that played a central role in establishing the Williamsburg aesthetic that came to prominence at Zebulon was Little Women. The origins of the band may be traced back to a meeting between saxophonists Darius Jones and Travis Laplante in 2005. Jones had just moved to the city after studying at Virginia Commonwealth University, and Laplante was completing the program in jazz studies at the New School. The two met for a session at Laplante's apartment for a duo improvisation that ended with them rolling on the floor, playing just through their mouthpieces and into their bells, and even crying. "We got into a space that neither of us had allowed ourselves to reach before that encounter," Laplante recounted. "After that, it became obvious that we had a deep musical connection."[111] "We got into a place then that we also reached in our early Little Women performances later, creatively, that made it clear that we should make music together," Jones stated. "Travis is a seeker. I love how relentless he is as an artist. The sounds he makes are sonically spectacular and provocative. He is one of the great tenor players of our generation."[112]

They set about organizing a band and soon invited drummer Jason Nazary, who had just moved to Brooklyn after graduating from New England Conservatory and who had been recommended by Jones's mentor, drummer Bob Moses (b. 1948). And they invited another New School graduate, Ben Greenberg, to join them as well. "We improvised together, and everything clicked," Jones recalled. "It became obvious that we should form a band together and work on our music."[113]

The members of Little Women began bringing ideas to the group to play that they workshopped in biweekly rehearsals through much of 2006, spending more than half a year refining their music before presenting it to a live audience. They generated their concepts in a democratic way, working together. The result was a collaboratively composed suite of music that they would perform in its entirety in live settings.[114] Laplante recounted how early work with the band resulted "in a number of veils being lifted for me and my relationship with music. I had been infatuated with jazz for many years, but studying the music in New York made me realize what I wanted and also what I did not want. The dogma of jazz had become constraining for me, and the band helped me sort that out. I think the other musicians were also working through something similar, though they might have ultimately reached different conclusions."[115] Nazary observed that "the members of the band all had an intense sound and an original approach to music."[116] Jones added, "We all worked like a team of archaeologists, digging, pushing the language of our instruments as far as we could as we looked for new discoveries."[117]

Little Women immediately connected to "the magical, underground music scene in Brooklyn that was high intensity, visceral, primal, but also sophisticated. There was a lot of fire in that music that I was not feeling in school," Laplante stated. "Little Women was our way of releasing all of our physical energy and putting our hearts and longings into the music without feeling we had to fit within a genre boundary or what some might define as jazz. In that journey, through some really loud, intense, dense music, we were able to have a connection and develop a deeper ability to listen and hear each other."[118]

Little Women's aesthetic was intense and loud, yet fully conscious and intentional. Though the focus in the making of the music was always on "being ourselves without feeling the need to conform to a particular standard," there were clearly lines of influence that could be traced back to rock music, noise, No Wave, and post-hardcore. "Some of our contemporaries were our greatest influences, however," Laplante noted. "I think in that moment we were inspiring each other."[119] Groups like Hank Shteamer's trio Stay Fucked, Hunter Hunt-Hendrix's hardcore and black metal groups Birthday Boyz and Liturgy, Patrick Higgins's project Animal, the quartet Human Feel, and Zs all made their mark on the group.[120] For Nazary, the bands Lightning Bolt, Zs, Arab on Radar, Deer Hoof, and U.S. Maple were primary influences on the aesthetic that he brought to Little Women.[121] Yet, as Jones noted, "We were also anti-influence. We were the kind of band that wanted to take everyone else out. Our massacre was a beautiful piece of art."[122]

Little Women's first public performance was at Pourhouse in mid-2006, and they soon after played at Aaron Ali Shaikh's loft in South Williamsburg. They shared a bill with Stay Fucked and People at Micheline's at Broadway and Myrtle Avenue on September 15, 2006, after which they began playing regularly at many lofts and other DIY venues in the Williamsburg underground scene throughout the following year.[123] They refined the material through a workmanlike ethic and released their first record while still circulating in the lofts. Also in that year, they made their first festival appearance, at the locally organized New Languages Festival at Rose Live Music. "When we played in Williamsburg or Bushwick, it was all love, people really got and appreciated what we were doing," Jones stated. "And our US shows got great reception in the underground improvised, experimental noise scene. When we went outside of that, sometimes people did not know how to react. We challenged audiences. It was confrontational and offensive to some people, even though we weren't necessarily aiming for that."[124]

Jones and Laplante often played ten or fifteen feet in front of the other two musicians, on the floor in front of the stage, engulfed in the audience to intensify the experience even more, while Nazary and Greenberg commanded the stage. To make it even more intimate, the saxophonists would get close to the audience members, reach out to them sometimes, while using all manner of extended techniques and blowing into the bells of their horns, sometimes causing a feeling of discomfort. Jones recalled audience members

Figure 5.9 Little Women: (*from left*) Darius Jones, Travis Laplante, Andrew Smiley, and Jason Nazary at Zebulon, 2012 (*photo by Peter Gannushkin*)

Figure 5.10 Little Women: (*from left*) Travis Laplante, Jason Nazary, Darius Jones, and Andrew Smiley at Zebulon, 2012 (*photo by Peter Gannushkin*)

at times recoiling from them, while in another instance bassist Trevor Dunn, who saw them play at Zebulon, broke into hysterical laughter because it was so intense. "We were aware that we were creating something, and we were serious about it," Jones explained. "We were trying to create something that was unique to us, a language that Little Women was speaking."[125]

With all of their success in Williamsburg, the band wanted to finally begin to tour outside of New York City. They had recorded their first record, *Teeth*, in one take at Excello Recording in Brooklyn in December 2006 and released it the following year. The music bore certain kinds of No Wave, lo-fi punk aesthetics and sounded quite raw, reflective of their live shows at the time.[126] A second record, intended to be titled *Swallow*, was recorded in 2008, but because there were technical issues during the recording and because it was recorded entirely to analog, the results were never released publicly. Nevertheless, *Swallow* documented a crucial next step for the group as they began to develop compositionally and the band's playing became tighter and more focused on song arc and melodic possibilities. The pieces were longer and improvised in ways that were quieter and more textural than the band's earlier material, anticipating some of the band's later work.

As the band moved toward the material that appeared on their second released record, *Throat*, they wanted something that was sonically richer.[127] Each member of the band would bring in material, and they would arrange it collectively in a way that Nazary described as "putting it through our blender," to calibrate it with the band's aesthetic, adding, "Intensity was the goal."[128] "Imagine going out and creating as much chaos as possible and surviving that to do it again and again," Jones added. "At the same time, we were really focused on how we did that. I think that is what made it so intense."[129]

Jones and Laplante also met by themselves to experiment to see what multiphonics or extended techniques resonated together and then bring those back to the band. Nazary laced the infrastructure of the music with intricate polyrhythms that "still groove in their own way" while creating a sound that was "stark and pummeling, trying to get away from the busy, flourishing jazz sound. I aimed for more of a rock sound, but with rhythms that were more complex."[130] Jones felt that *Teeth* had been more like four individuals improvising together, but by the time they were working on *Throat*, they were deeply into integrating each other's ideas, taking little seeds of ideas, cutting the pieces up, and shaping the music collectively.[131]

During their first US tour in the summer of 2008, Greenberg had to withdraw after a performance in Los Angeles, causing them to cancel the last half of the tour. So, in September of that year, Andrew Smiley became the new guitarist in the band. Smiley, who had been Laplante's roommate for a few years since arriving in New York, had followed the band closely in their previous years. "I liked that there was no limit in their aggressiveness but also a high level of musicianship without losing its edginess. The music was super tight, yet it always felt like it was about to fall apart, but never did. I had never heard another band with that combination of elements."[132] Like the others, Smiley had trained in jazz and had even played in the all-state jazz band in high school, but he found welcome relief in the scene that was growing around Little Women.

Smiley's arrival came at a propitious moment, because the band was just beginning to work on new material that would eventually appear on *Throat*. Smiley's approach was to find a way to cut through the saxophones without washing over them, while matching their intensity and connecting harmonically with the other musicians. He also consciously made sure to provide space to the other members of the band. "Simultaneously, I had to work with Nazary. His rhythmic sensibilities are advanced. His time feel was always extremely accurate but very complicated and abstract at the same time," Smiley stated. "It is not just that he employs polyrhythms but that he does so while staying right in the moment. It's not artificial."[133]

Nazary's long-form arc often structured the pieces, introducing ideas to which he would later return, or building layer on layer. Over time, Smiley and Nazary developed a language together, one where Smiley would listen and pick up on what Nazary was first laying down with the rhythms, while he leaped and burst off from that baseline. The four together were always attacking, but playing together and maintaining each singular voice, without melding together in an amorphous way. The quartet's work for *Throat*, which included composed sections by the three original members of the band, was eventually fused together to form a unified suite.

On September 17, 2009, they debuted their new work at Zebulon, which became their most frequented venue over the following three years, until its closure. "Playing at Zebulon was the closest relationship to home as a venue as I have ever had," Laplante remarked years later. "It was a magical place. I liked it because Joce and Jef Soubiran were extremely kind and genuinely supported our work and let us do what we wanted as artists. Curation was open. That is very rare for a venue."[134] Little Women was particularly dynamic in the live setting, and they waited until they had finely tuned every minute aspect of new pieces before presenting them to an audience. As Smiley observed, "I love the records the band did, but to experience the true power of the band, you had to hear us play live."[135] Many other musicians and audience members on the scene concurred.

Little Women signed with AUM Fidelity, one of the primary labels shedding light on New York's downtown scene, so the record *Throat* managed to receive far better distribution than *Teeth*. This enabled them to tour in Europe for the first time, playing in Amsterdam and at the Saalfelden Jazz Festival in 2009. It was a rather polarizing concert. For one, they were asked to present two sets, which they did not have at the time, so they elongated the set for *Throat* to last two hours, splitting it in two. The music involved high-intensity textures, and many people in the audience were not prepared for such music, causing the audience to dwindle to less than half by the conclusion of the first set. "It was like people were trying to escape the room," Jones recalled.[136] Nevertheless, this defining concert also garnered Little Women some dedicated fans and broadcast the aggressive improvised noise sound to an international audience.

For the final record, *Lung*, the band members did not contribute individually but rather worked on the music together in rehearsals in a more glacial approach that was a fully collaborative effort at forming one long piece that spanned more than forty minutes.[137] The band made greater use of space and unison rhythmic work while giving more attention to intricate sonic detail. The music had also become increasingly compositional, with every minute detail committed to memory. Even the improvised sections were not entirely free and were generally guided internally.[138] Each musician had their own vocabulary from which they drew their individual ideas, but the aim was not to do something new each time but rather to work with the collective language they had developed through rigorous rehearsing. And Little Women managed to make music that was always expansive and high energy. "I always tried to listen to what the others were saying through their sounds and think about what they meant by it. And, of course, doing that all in fast-paced real time," Smiley recalled.[139] The band debuted the work at the Stone in 2011 and presented it numerous times at Zebulon until the venue closed in 2012 (see figures 5.9 and 5.10).

The starting point for *Lung* was the four of them breathing together in sync to "center their breath and meditate before engaging in the music."[140] "We spent a lot of time improvising to find the sonic environments or spaces that felt the most alive and vibrant for us," Laplante explained. It took about six months of playing regularly together to settle on the length of the subsections of the long piece. "For instance, Darius and I would come up with something that we felt good about, and then we would spend hours honing in on the guitars and drums to find something that felt symbiotic between the four of us. It was a slow-moving process because it was a full-on collaboration without us composing on our own. It involved a deeper level of trust. The process of our music making for the final record was quite different than anything that we had done before as a group."[141] Little Women played the release show for their final record and one additional concert after that, and that was the end of the band.

By 2013 Jones wanted to begin working more on his own bands, and the group disbanded. "I think we became inactive just before a moment where we could have had an even greater breakthrough," Smiley observed. "It had been a struggle, even with the opportunities we had. I think if we had pushed through those frustrations, more opportunities might have come."[142] Europe seemed to just be opening up to them. Little Women was a seminal band in the development of the loud, aggressive improvised noise rock sound that became one of the defining features of the Williamsburg sound. No band did more to coalesce a Williamsburg avant-garde sound into an identifiable vocabulary at that time than Little Women, and they contributed significantly to the national aesthetic then developing around louder, unrestricted improvised music.

Structuring the Unknown and Unexpected
Kneebody

A band that drew from a multitude of influences as broad as Zebulon's booking was the progressive jazz collective quintet Kneebody. The band would come to epitomize a new trend in music school projects that continued to evolve in the live setting. Kneebody comprised trumpeter Shane Endsley, saxophonist Ben Wendel, keyboardist Adam Benjamin, bassist Kaveh Rastegar, and drummer Nate Wood. The band bore eclectic influences from jazz, classical, grunge, punk, indie rock, funk, electronic, and experimental hip-hop.[143] Critic Nate Chinen noted that Kneebody was "thoroughly acquainted with 1960s free-bop, 1970s jazz rock, 1990s hip-hop and postmillennial indie rock, along with classical postminimalism."[144] In an earlier article, the critic had commented, "Kneebody likes deep-pocket funk, shrewd dissonance and high dynamic contrast, often suggesting a brainy but visceral upgrade of fusion."[145] Endsley's work with saxophonist Steve Coleman also was an influence. The band first formed at Eastman School of Music in Rochester, New York, which they all attended at different times in the late

1990s. After finishing school, the musicians had all moved to the Los Angeles area by 2001, where they had a weekly residency at the Temple Bar in Santa Monica. There they developed a large repertoire of material that was later featured on their self-titled debut album.[146] They also toured the Southwest, visiting places like Phoenix and Denver.

Temple Bar was generally a rock and hip-hop club, so it was outfitted with a sound system that handled louder sounds, which immediately impacted how Kneebody performed live. All five of the musicians composed music for the band, and they made a point of memorizing their parts so that they did not have to read music while playing live. In the early years, they generally avoided long or dramatic solos and shredding, favoring collective improvisation that explored textures and motifs that bore a certain aesthetic influence from electronic dance music and hip-hop, though still with more complex rhythms.

One of the hallmarks of Kneebody's work was the development of a set of intricate cues that they embedded in the music itself to orchestrate a kind of live composition that allowed communication among the members of the quintet. The cues were integrated into the very function of the music. This began with a piece that Endsley had written for another band that also included Rastegar, "The Slip," which had A and B sections that were open-ended and employed a cue to direct the band. This later served as a collective point of genesis for Kneebody as they tried to develop their own vocabulary as a group. Cues gave the flow of the music elasticity by allowing sections to be elongated or improvisations to grow and develop, without having to worry about how to transition to another section or end a piece. As Chinen observed, "The striking thing is how fluidly this group weds advanced harmonic movement with instantly accessible groove and dynamics."[147]

Over time, Kneebody developed more than twenty cues that they were able to employ in the live setting. Many of their pieces were modular; to avoid giving them an arranged feel or having them follow the same pattern each time, the cues allowed for structural and compositional variation. Such cues might call for a section to be sustained or cut short, for a change of tempo or key, for certain combinations of players to contribute to certain sections, or for others to drop out.[148] Another feature, the looping cue, allowed them to create lines and to assign them to members as they were improvising or collectively composing in the moment. Such cues were a tight solution to melding improvised and composed sections of the music. Some pieces tended to be less cued, while others lent themselves to this method of orchestration.

Endsley moved to New York in 2003, which eventually pulled the band east for some gigs there. Kneebody played four concerts at Zebulon between June 2005 and February 2006, including a two-night stint there in September. These concerts helped establish the band in New York as they presented work that appeared on their debut record as well as on their second major release, *Low Electrical Worker*, which was released in 2007.[149] Some live tracks, such as "I'm Your General," recorded at Zebulon during that run, were preserved and appeared on a live record that displayed how their system worked in the heat of the moment.[150] This set them up to play around the city in places such as the Jazz Gallery, Nublu, Bleecker Street Theater, and Le Poisson Rouge.[151] The band rose to critical attention in 2012 and 2013 with appearances at New York–based annual events Winter Jazz Fest and Vision Festival, which opened more opportunities for touring in Europe and obtaining residencies and workshops at academic institutions in the United States.[152]

Mostly Other People Do the Killing

Another band that played often at Zebulon that developed a different kind of cued orchestration was Mostly Other People Do the Killing, led by bassist Moppa Elliott. The band was founded on the idea of drawing from the jazz tradition—from bebop to free jazz—and allowing the form, the pieces, and the trajectory of the music to take shape in real time through interaction among the band members themselves. The intention was to reference particular points of jazz history and to present material that expanded and challenged expectations, often with a touch of humor. The band took its name from a phrase that Elliott had spotted in an interview with Leon Theremin (1896–1993), the inventor of the instrument that bears his surname, who after being confined to a gulag in Soviet Russia and reemerging later in life was asked about Joseph Stalin and replied drily, "He wasn't that bad, mostly other people did the killing."[153] The term *killing* also had a second meaning in the jazz world: playing really well.

Moppa Elliott and trumpeter Peter Evans attended the conservatory at Oberlin College together, finishing in 2002 and 2003, respectively. They played together a bit in a number of different formations during their college years. Elliott moved to New York and met alto saxophonist Jon Irabagon, and by the time Evans arrived the following year, Elliott was ready to form the band Mostly Other People Do the Killing in the summer of 2003. Kevin Shea joined them on drums. "I selected the people for the band," Elliott explained, "because I wanted people who could work across the spectrum from the freest of free jazz to jazz that was regulated by chord changes. They had to be great improvisers and also be able to expertly work the changes and swing on it."[154] The most immediate influences were Ornette Coleman, John Zorn's Masada, and Steven Bernstein's Sex Mob.

Like many other bands trying to get their start in the early 2000s, they approached Will Connell Jr. for the band's first gig at Niagara, where they played a number of times. They were back across the river at Glasslands and lofts such as Chez Bushwick in Brooklyn in 2004 and 2005. The band managed to record at Vibromonk Studios in July 2004, laying out tracks for their self-titled debut record, which documented their early work.[155] It was more of a standard free jazz foray and did not feature the kind of material they would do in later years, but their cover of "Moanin'," the well-known piece composed by Bobby Timmons for Art Blakey and the Jazz Messengers, featured trumpeter Peter Evans playing Lee Morgan's solo note for note. This re-creation of famous jazz tunes became an obsession for the band and would propel them to recognition in the years that followed.

The years between their first release in 2004 and the band's sophomore record, *Shamokin!!!*, in 2007 were crucial in their conceptual development.[156] They began to make the forms in the music optional, and they began mining all of their various influences, while "going on wild tangents, cutting each other off, and having unaccompanied solo sections," which solidified the personality of the band.[157] For example, when the band performed live, they might be playing a piece composed by Elliott, but Irabagon would begin playing a piece by Charlie Parker, John Coltrane, or another figure. When the others heard him doing that, they might follow his lead, and suddenly they would all shift to playing that piece. Or it might be a classical concerto or a pop song. The band was not subtle about its influences, and the band became more explicit over time.

Mostly Other People Do the Killing straddled the line between playing typical jazz standards and playing key works from the free jazz canon, such as those of Cecil Taylor and William Parker. Elliott's own compositions that the band developed "might come out sounding like the Ornette Coleman Quartet or like Wynton Marsalis."[158] The repertoire was wide-ranging. At the same time, the other band members might choose not to follow the cue into a particular piece and instead form a kind of collage of multiple pieces together, depending on the mood in the moment.

Because such decisions were made in real time, live performances had an element of "game" as things unfolded. The musicians then worked either in collaboration, pushing the music in a particular direction, or in a subversive manner, in which one musician might try to obscure what one of the others was doing by going in a different direction. For example, the band often ended with the well-known standard "Night in Tunisia," by Dizzy Gillespie. But at one live performance, after beginning with one of Elliott's compositions, half the band proceeded on to "Night in Tunisia," while the other half elected to do "Hideaway," by David Sanborn, "for an uncomfortably long period of time."[159] Eventually the band agreed to play the melody for "Hideaway" and then finally proceeded to end with "Night in Tunisia," but not before an extended sonic standoff. "It is all a matter of negotiation," Elliott explained. "All of these options are on the table."[160] Elliott decided early on that they did not want to adopt signals like those of Butch Morris or other bandleaders and instead sort out the dynamics within the music itself.

By the time the band began to play at Zebulon in April 2008, they had a large body of work from which to draw. They had just recorded tracks for *This Is Our Moosic*, a reference to *This Is Our Music* by the Ornette Coleman Quartet, two months prior, which they debuted at the concert. From 2008 to 2011, the band played the venue at least eight times, refining work that would appear on the band's fourth record, *Forty Fort*.[161] "Zebulon was our home base in those years, just like other clubs were historically meeting points for musicians," Elliott recalled. "That was the same for us in how we connected with the community."[162] These were important performances for the band as they built an increasingly enthusiastic audience and attracted critical attention.

The band was gaining notoriety and in 2011 caught a couple of big breaks that propelled them onto the international touring circuit. They were invited to play at the Bimhuis, in Amsterdam, in July 2011 for a fiftieth-anniversary celebration of the Eric Dolphy–Booker Little concerts at the Five Spot, for which they decided they needed to add a piano player. Through the Zebulon run, pianist Ron Stabinsky began to attend the band's performances regularly, and after Peter Evans listened to a CD-R of the former's solo piano recordings, he urged Elliott to hire him for the band. Together they prepared a set of the Dolphy-Little tunes, adapted to their own aesthetic, debuting the work at their last concert at Zebulon on April 22, 2011. Thereafter, Stabinsky became an integral and permanent part of the band, joining them at the Bimhuis, the North Sea Jazz Festival, and later performances.

The band's other big break also came out of their series of performances at Zebulon. Toward the end of this run, George Wein, the organizer of the Newport Jazz Festival, went to the club in search of something up-and-coming and called Elliott after the gig to invite the band to play the festival in August 2011. The performance was recorded and rebroadcast on National Public Radio. They received such a positive response from the audience that they were invited back to perform and lead a workshop at Newport again in 2014.

As much as it encountered success, the band also had detractors. Some found the band's brand of jazz humor to be irreverent. This came to the fore with the recording of *Blue* in 2014, which intended to re-create Miles Davis's iconic *Kind of Blue* note for note.[163] Reactions to the record ranged from it appearing on best-of lists for the year to it being severely criticized in reviews and throughout the Brooklyn music community on Facebook and other social media. Some felt that it was disrespectful to the history of the music or appropriative for a band that included no African American musicians to draw material from iconic Black jazz records. Evans, whose solo career had really taken off, had already been thinking of leaving the band as early as 2013 and decided to make *Blue* his final recording with the band. Since then, Mostly Other People Do the Killing has continued to record and tour regularly, moving on to other projects as a quartet.

Closing

The bands analyzed here are those that maintained a consistent presence at Zebulon and owed a certain measure of their existence to the space, where they workshopped or refined their work on the club stage. In addition, a number of other groups, some previously discussed, performed at the club. Mary Halvorson and Jessica Pavone's duo played the club a number of times in 2008–9, and Pavone led some of her other ensembles there. Taylor Ho Bynum, another figure in the post–Wesleyan University milieu, also brought early versions of his sextet to Zebulon. Guitarist Brandon Seabrook often led his band Power Plant there, and Jim Hobbs developed music for his group Fully Celebrated Orchestra at the venue. Josh Sinton's Ideal Bread, a project focused on reimagining Steve Lacy's work, also appeared twice in 2008. Bassist Lisa Mezzacappa played the club when she was on tour in New York in 2009–11, and bassist Jason Ajemian also led some of his projects there. Drummer Weasel Walter appeared at the club in a number of different groups, though since he had more of a transformative presence at Death by Audio in the same period, his work is one of the foci of the following chapter.

"To this day, I still pine over the loss of Zebulon," one regular audience member stated in 2020, "because it was the one place I could go to enrich myself culturally and not have to think about it. There was something different happening there every night, and it opened my eyes to so many different things during the years it was in business."[164] Travis Laplante remarked, "What happened to Zebulon is the classic example of gentrification at its worst. People wanted to move near Zebulon, but soon people complained about the noise."[165] "Zebulon was one of the main reasons people wanted to live in that part of Williamsburg," Moppa Elliott recalled. "It was the magnet for so much that was happening. It made the neighborhood fun and inviting, and a lot of people moved there. Then the condos got built, and the people who lived there complained about the sound from the club."[166] The Williamsburg experimental music scene was not over yet, though no venue would ever again achieve the centrality, the eclecticism, and the atmosphere that Zebulon had established during its eight years of operation.

CHAPTER SIX

A Fractured Landscape

The Last Avant-Garde Music Spaces of Williamsburg,
2005–2014

> Death by Audio was like the CBGBs of our time period.
> —*Amnon Freidlin*

By the late 2000s, the musician community was already feeling severe pressure to move out of Williamsburg and relocate elsewhere. The immediate effect of the 2005 rezoning was that young artists, who had been bolstering the numbers in Williamsburg for nearly two decades, were almost universally unable to afford to live in the neighborhood. That meant that aspiring artists now had to move elsewhere or look for new community spaces. For the North Brooklyn community, it meant that young artists were now gravitating to Bushwick, where a smattering of postindustrial spaces along Broadway, in Morgantown, and scattered across postindustrial pockets throughout the neighborhood were the flash points for a new phase of music and the community.

For the existing community in Williamsburg, the 2005 rezoning meant that they would be subjected to variable rates of attrition. As artists had to renew their leases, many suddenly faced massive increases as the changes provided landlords with a clear financial incentive to displace them. For many people, rents doubled within a few years, or even tripled. This escalation in rental prices made the community no longer sustainable.

Simultaneously, the zoning of large swaths of North Williamsburg as residential allowed development companies to tear down derelict warehouses and factories. While some sections of the neighborhood saw the emergence of vibrant commercial districts, especially along Bedford Avenue, these were geared increasingly toward newcomers arriving in the area, who frequented the lavish restaurants, clothing boutiques, and hipster hotels. The biggest change, however, was the building of condominium towers and luxury rental units, which swiftly led to a significant demographic change. A new generation of wealthy professionals, many working in finance or law in Manhattan, jumped at the opportunity to live along the East River waterfront, paying Manhattan-like prices and contributing to the sudden and intense gentrification of not only the living spaces but also the commercial districts and the social scene along the waterfront.

Real estate developers made billions of dollars during the gentrification of Williamsburg. Musicians and artists, not to mention other residents of Williamsburg, had no effective means of turning back the tide, and the community rapidly disintegrated. Despite the economic forces that were set to dismember the community of artists in North Brooklyn, musicians did what they could to hold on to their living and performance spaces. Williamsburg had been the spatial center for many Brooklyn artists. As the situation grew direr, a few spaces held out against the wave. The late Williamsburg scene was increasingly fractured, but there were some dynamic spaces where considerable growth in the music occurred. Death by Audio was one of the most active venues of the period, catering to loud, amplified, and aggressive rock-influenced experimentalism. Connie Crothers's loft was a jazz-oriented space with an eye for pushing the boundaries. Monkeytown and a few other spaces also existed in these final years, serving distinctly different music communities. Together, they represented the last significant avant-garde music spaces in Williamsburg.

Death by Audio:
The Improvised Music–Rock–Punk–Metal–Noise Continuum

Death by Audio, located at 49 South Second Street, was the last great DIY venue of Williamsburg. It opened in the spring of 2007 and became the core of an underground scene that was a fertile site for experimentation as improvised music collided with rock, punk, metal, and noise. The club came directly out of the punk aesthetic, with every inch of the interior painted, graffitied, or covered in band stickers. At one end there was a makeshift stage in a room that could hold seventy-five people, with an adjoining room in the back for overflow that also had a speakeasy bar. Before the venue ran its own bar, people would often bring beer and keep it in a collective cooler; it was sold off the books for cheap. Once the "bar" was put in, it was just a table in front of a refrigerator, usually stocked with one type of beer and perhaps two types of liquor. The floors had black-and-white checkered tile that somehow gave the space an opulence, in contrast to the discolored ceiling tiles, some of which were decaying, hanging open, or missing entirely. Various paintings graced the wall behind the stage, but in the final years, a prominent one depicted the owner, Edan Wilber, amid other colorful abstractions.[1] Death by Audio was a subversive oasis in a neighborhood that was rapidly gentrifying and pushing artists out. It was the last vestige of a punk culture that had persisted in the neighborhood for over twenty years. Despite its humble appearance, Death by Audio was a venue of critical national importance as the epicenter of a scene focused on the improvised music–rock–punk–metal–noise continuum.

In its early days, Death by Audio pushed the limits of the DIY aesthetic. The sound system was low quality and certainly limited what was possible sonically. The organization was a bit chaotic, and shows often went until three or four in the morning, even on a Monday or Tuesday night, which made it difficult to attract an audience for the headlining bands. But Wilber was dedicated to improving things as time went on. They got better sound equipment in 2010, and Wilber learned how to run the system better. Complaints from the encroaching gentrifiers began to force him to end the nights by midnight or one o'clock, but that helped make the shows more cohesive, and they ended at a more reasonable time for attendees.

"For a lot of us," multi-instrumentalist Weasel Walter explained, "Death by Audio was a place where they understood what we were doing, and they welcomed us, whether we had a good night or not. We could do whatever we wanted, book whoever we wanted, and the sound was okay. They paid us if people showed up. That's what it takes for a scene to happen."[2] Vocalist Dominika Michalowska described it simply as "our home base."[3] "The magic of the space always made the music happen," drummer Marc Edwards remarked. "We were always treated with respect at Death by Audio and I felt like what we did mattered. What Edan Wilber had happening there was far superior to what was happening on the free jazz scene in Manhattan. The energy was way better as most of the musicians were much younger." Despite the perceived hard edge of the community that frequented the space, many musicians involved spoke of the strong community feel, with Edwards further commenting, "Death by Audio was such a beautiful space to come to and create art. It was such a nurturing environment, this alone made it stand out from other venues at the time."[4] When Death by Audio closed for the night, people would often drift back over to Zebulon, up until it closed in 2012, because it served drinks and sometimes had music until three or four in the morning.

Death by Audio was one of the most important venues for the development of a music that Walter had termed *brutal prog* back in 2000 to delineate bands that were more focused on dissonance and intensity than other forms of progressive rock. Incorporating elements of progressive rock, punk, postpunk, No Wave, free jazz, math rock, heavy metal, grindcore, and Japanese noise, brutal prog was loud, aggressive, and challenging to audiences. Walter's own band, the Flying Luttenbachers, founded in Chicago in 1992, was one of the forerunners of the music, though he coined the term in reference to the lineup that he assembled for the record *Infection and Decline* in 2001, which included Alex Perkolup and Jonathan Hischke on basses.[5] "I was trying to create a clear-cut distinction of what we were doing with progressive rock forms, minus the sort of 'flutes and fairies' elements I didn't like in prog," Walter stated. "The balladry and sensitivity were banished from our kingdom—asymmetry, dissonance, and speed ruled."[6]

Around the beginning of the new millennium, bands emerging in different parts of the United States were contributing to the growing brutal prog movement. The Sacramento-based band Hella, a guitar-drum duo, for example, played rapid, irregular rhythms in their music in a distinct, angular style. Upsilon Acrux, which originated in Los Angeles, also explored dissonant rhythms with a more ragged, acidic approach. Orthrelm, another guitar-drum duo, emerged in Washington, DC, around the same time and became known for their high-speed, complicated compositions and their exploration of repetition and nonrepetition. Cheer-Accident, an art rock band that had been around since the 1980s, also began to embrace the sound in their live performances.

From the mid-2000s, a broad movement emerged in the rock underground that embraced elements of noise, electronics, metal, postpunk, and occasionally free jazz, with Death by Audio as the epicenter for bands such as Chat Logs, Cloud Becomes Your Hand, the Dreebs, Liturgy, Sediment Club, White Suns, Xaddax, and Zevious. This sound extended to include bands elsewhere who played at Death by Audio when they toured through

New York, including Controlled Bleeding and Guerilla Toss (Boston), Micro-waves (Atlanta), and Tiger Hatchery (Chicago), among others. Videos that circulated on YouTube, especially those produced by the German filmmaker known as Unartig, helped develop a kind of mythical reputation for the venue that drew both fans and musicians to the city. Several musicians stated that Death by Audio was why they moved to Brooklyn. Death by Audio fostered some of New York's most prominent contributions to the movement, while also appealing directly to touring bands, which they supported with the majority of the door money.[7]

In addition to the more rock-oriented groups, many of the bands already discussed earlier in this book also had a presence at the club. This was partly because Death by Audio began hosting shows around the time that Tonic closed in Manhattan, and it managed to attract the younger elements of that scene. After Zebulon closed in 2012, it also drew the louder, more aggressive avant-garde to the venue. This included experimental indie rock bands like People or more sonically intense groups like Pulverize the Sound. Little Women often played the venue, finding that their intense sound fit well within the aesthetic of the place. Drummer Mike Pride also frequented Death by Audio with his bands Drummer's Corpse, From Bacteria to Boys, and others.

The Power of the Action:
Encounters between Marc Edwards and Weasel Walter

One of the main avant-garde bands to emerge at Death by Audio in its early years was the Marc Edwards–Weasel Walter Group. Edwards (b. 1949) was a generation older than Walter and had emerged in the 1970s, playing with eminent free jazz figures such as pianist Cecil Taylor and saxophonist David S. Ware, and later with Charles Gayle in the 1980s and 1990s.[8] Nevertheless, Edwards remained an underground figure, and what visibility he had attained had faded by the 2000s. Walter, also primarily a drummer, had emerged in the early 1990s on the Chicago improvised music scene with mutual interests in free jazz (such as the work of Albert Ayler, Cecil Taylor, and Archie Shepp) and punk rock.[9] "I was always equally into Albert Ayler and death metal," he later noted.[10] He founded the band the Flying Luttenbachers in 1992 and played with them for over a decade, releasing a series of groundbreaking records.[11] He later moved to San Francisco in 2003, where he reconstituted the band. His music blended elements of free jazz, No Wave, and art rock, glued together with a "punk energy" that gave a loud, aggressive edge to his sound. Walter was attracted to Edwards's work with

Taylor, in particular, and eventually sought him out because of Edwards's work as a "power free jazz drummer."[12]

"I never want music to be a sterile experience," Walter explained of his craft. "I also don't like the insularity of art. I make music to be part of the dialogue with or against society. I have always found myself fighting against the mainstream and the status quo. I was into free jazz as a teenager because I thought it was a way to articulate individuality and maybe aggression, which I also found in punk rock sometimes. This kind of music allows me to focus on the quality of the music and the relationships with the other musicians and the power of the action."[13]

"A lot of my inspirations in free jazz were people who did not fit into society," Walter stated.

> My inspirations mostly didn't go to expensive schools to get advanced degrees in improvisation. They are people who had a real urge to do something different and express themselves. I thought of people like Cecil Taylor, Albert Ayler, and Ornette Coleman as extreme iconoclasts. In a way, my mission has been to make iconoclastic music. I try to speak to other iconoclasts with this, in an era of conformity, to create a powerful experience. Then there are inspirations like [Iannis] Xenakis. He articulated the same kind of frenzy, aggression, and abstraction that I am interested in. People might say his music was very academic, but his music is warlike in demeanor because he got half of his face shot off fighting in the resistance against the Nazis.[14]

Edwards was surprised when he received a message from Walter via MySpace in early 2007 inviting him to join Walter for a gig at Tonic because Edwards had not had a presence on the New York scene since the early 1990s. The show at Tonic was their first encounter, and their shared ecstatic energy and intensity compelled them to consider working together again.[15] Walter described his performances as "irritainment: the nexus between irritating and entertainment."[16] His approach involved "high punk energy," which was matched by Edwards, who also played at high speeds and intensity, laying down a maelstrom of beats that created textures, even entire environments of sound, in which horns and other instruments could add color or try to push the energy even higher. Edwards's use of a double bass drum pedal transformed his sound and enabled him to elevate his rhythmic intensity to a level he had not had in earlier years as a jazz drummer.

Over the following six years, the band played often in New York, regularly shifting the lineups but co-led by the two drummers. At their first gig at

St. Vitus, a heavy metal club in Greenpoint, Walter "provided written instruction for how to set up the improvisations that," according to Edwards, "was similar to Cecil Taylor's approach, though without specific notes for musicians to play."[17] At times Walter would step away from drumming and engage in his own form of conduction to direct the horn players, especially when the band was in one of its larger formations, with the effect of "making the music even more intense" by creating room for solos or focusing on particular musical interactions within the band.[18]

In May 2008 Walter and Edwards invited a third drummer, Andrew Barker, to add to the high-energy rhythmic complexity, with a front line that included Ras Moshe and Mario Rechtern at the Lit Lounge.[19] "Barker meshed seamlessly with our drumming concepts," Edwards recalled of the encounter, though logistically it was difficult to accommodate three drummers in most venues, and they never attempted that lineup again.[20] They continued to experiment with lineups that included a range of figures such as trumpeter Peter Evans, saxophonists Paul Flaherty and Darius Jones, and bassist Tom Blancarte.

Then, in April 2009, they assembled a group at Otto's Shrunken Head in Manhattan that finally coalesced around the music. The band retained Darius Jones but added saxophonist Elliott Levin, trumpeter Forbes Graham, and bassist Adam Lane (see figure 6.1). The high level of musicianship in the band played a role in compelling Walter to move to New York later that year, and the band recorded in November, soon after his arrival. Edwards commented, "I had spent the year practicing for this session."[21] From that point on, the band began playing regularly around the city in clubs, a few remaining Williamsburg lofts, at Zebulon, at Silent Barn, and finally at Death by Audio in October 2010. "Edan Wilber did not like free jazz," Walter recalled, "but once he heard us, I think he thought of us as a noise band. After that, he always trusted us to bring something interesting to the club."[22]

"In a way, No Wave had been the harbinger of a type of fusion between abstract free jazz with improvisational aesthetics and punk rock" and served as a rallying cry for Walter as he contributed to the vision for the band.[23] For Walter, the music that he made with Edwards was "an attempt to get back to what I thought the point of the music was but not to do it in an old-fashioned way. At the same time, I thought there were some great older musicians that still had something to say, like Marc [Edwards] and Elliott Levin, but they would probably not have put it in a rock venue like Death by Audio. Presenting high-intensity free jazz at that club was my way of bringing it into a new place for a new audience and bring[ing] a current energy

Figure 6.1 Marc Edwards–Weasel Walter Group: (*from left*) Forbes Graham, Weasel Walter, Elliott Levin, Adam Lane, Darius Jones, and Marc Edwards, Otto's Shrunken Head, 2009 (*photo by Peter Gannushkin*)

to it." The racial and generational integration of the band seemed to be a conscious design for Walter, who stated, "Those kind of fusions are really exciting, possible in a place like New York."[24]

By June 2010 the band had condensed to a trio, which was more manageable and easier to sustain financially. The smaller lineup featured Marcus Cummins on soprano saxophone, and Walter shifted to electric bass, a formation they maintained for most of the remaining years that the band was together. They played at least monthly through 2010 and 2011, refining their concepts. For a performance in November 2011 at Freddy's Bar in South Brooklyn, they added tenor saxophonist Jeremy Viner to give it a more robust sound, and they recorded the live set and released the record on Walter's label, ugEXPLODE.[25] Later in the month, they performed at the Stone with free jazz luminaries Sabir Mateen and Roy Campbell Jr., though they returned to the trio and quartet formats generally at Death by Audio in 2012, with saxophonist Michael Foster guesting regularly in the lineup. The band played its final concert in June 2013. Walter had grown tired of playing innovative music without much of an audience beyond a few North

Brooklyn venues, and he turned his full attention to the band Cellular Chaos, which was exploring brutal prog a bit more directly.

Cellular Chaos

As the Marc Edwards–Weasel Walter Group began playing less, Walter asked Edwards to join his other band, Cellular Chaos, which had been playing since 2010. Originally the drummer had been Kevin Shea, but when Shea was unavailable for a gig because of another tour, Edwards filled the role and soon became a permanent fixture in the band. Walter played electric guitar in the band, and Ceci Moss played electric bass. Later Admiral Grey took on the role of vocals. Various other band members would come and go, eventually settling on bassist Shayna Dulberger.

Grey brought her experience as a dancer and actress to add to the theatrics that the band displayed at their live shows. Grey had studied many different forms of art, performance, philosophy, history, and other disciplines, which she considered to be "all part of the whole," and had engaged in both experimental music and theater in New York. But the "frustration with the hierarchy of theater and internships, and the closed, elitist world of academia in the 'fine' arts are what made me end up forming my first band," she explained, before eventually joining Cellular Chaos.[26]

Grey elevated the band's live concerts with high-energy performances that included visceral body movement, intense vocals, and screams. "My performances with Cellular Chaos were immediately a product of who I am and what I had wanted to do musically and express visually and physically," Grey explained. "It was more like a divining rod. It was meant to happen, we were looking for each other before we even knew it. I found Cellular Chaos and Cellular Chaos found me and then we exploded into a chaotic but highly calculated being" in live performances. "For me, there was no other way to express and perform that music and the challenging vocal parts I had written," she added. "Performing with Cellular Chaos was a trance-like, immediate, emotional, very physical lightning-rod-relationship streaking back and forth between the sound, the audience, and the performers in a kinetic and ecstatic expression of the extreme feelings of human existence and the universe."[27]

The music was loud and aggressive, with Edwards bringing down a maelstrom of beats while the guitar and bass played free, abrasive, dynamic melodies and riffs. The band displayed No Wave influence in its general aesthetic and drew fans that included trailblazing punk vocalist and writer Lydia

Lunch.[28] After releasing a demo tape in 2011, the band released a single in 2012 that included three tracks, including "Remake/Re-model," a cover of Roxy Music's 1972 art rock debut, which became one of Cellular Chaos's most popular songs. A full album drawn from the same recording session soon followed, along with a national tour that reached the Upper Midwest (including Chicago, Madison, and Minneapolis), as well as the Deep South (with stops in Pensacola, New Orleans, and a number of other cities) and then concluded at Death by Audio. Cellular Chaos was one of the defining sounds of aggressive experimental rock music at the time.

Slipstream Time Travel

Having been inspired by his collaborations with Weasel Walter, Marc Edwards turned his attention to leading his own band, Slipstream Time Travel, beginning in 2010. "From spending time with Weasel Walter," Edwards recounted, "I began to get into metal music. He introduced me to his musical world."[29] Edwards had already incorporated the double bass drum pedal into his playing as an explicit metal influence on his approach to the drum kit. With his new band, he continued to use blast beats, especially as a catalyst for improvisations. He also developed rock beats for Cellular Chaos that he carried over into the band. He considered Slipstream Time Travel's recording *Holographic Projection Holograms* to be a fusion of metal and free jazz, though there are perceptible influences from noise rock, punk, and electronic music as well.[30] Reflecting on the rebirth of his career, Edwards remarked, "I owe Weasel Walter a big thank you. Through working with Cellular Chaos and our other work, I was exposed to a much wider, younger audience. He rescued my career from obscurity."[31]

Edwards's inspiration for Slipstream Time Travel was rooted in his interest in science fiction, which may be traced back to visits he made to the Hayden Planetarium as a child. Beginning with his record *Time and Space*, volume 1 (1993), Edwards "wanted to maintain a connection to all the disciplines of science, math, astronomy, and science fiction" and began employing space-themed album covers on his records.[32] Authors Robert Heinlein, Isaac Asimov, Arthur C. Clarke, Allen Steele, Frederik Pohl, Octavia Butler, and Samuel R. Delaney were all monumental in building his vision and fantasy. The space imagery was also inspired by Sun Ra's album covers but also on a deeper level by the latter's focus "on the exploration of outer space in terms of philosophy, cosmology, and mysticism."[33] Edwards had been watching

Figure 6.2 Slipstream Time Travel: Marc Edwards (*left*) and Tor Snyder (Gene Janas not pictured), 2013 (*private collection*)

Gene Roddenberry's *Voyager* and *Andromeda* series and encountered the term *slipstream*, referring to travel that was faster than the speed of light.[34] It was also a reference to "a multi-dimensional space-time continuum. Each listener can determine what this means for themselves."[35]

The band originally began in 1996 but played off and on through the years with continuous variations in terms of personnel. Originally, it was more of a free jazz trio or quartet, but Edwards's work with Weasel Walter inspired him to solidify around new concepts around 2010 (see figure 6.2).[36] He primarily explored the use of electric sounds and eventually had as many as three guitarists, though the lineups shifted, at various times including Peter Mazzetti, Tor Snyder, Jeffrey Hayden Shurdut, Ernest Anderson III, Ed Chang, Takuma Kanaiwa, Karl Alfonso Evangelista, and Colin Sanderson. "We had found the 'slipstream' in our music," Edwards later wrote.[37] The band also included, at times, tenor saxophonists David Tamura and Ayumi Ishito, bicycle wheel electronicist Lawry Zilmrah, and electric bassist and guitarist Alex Lozupone.

Beyond the electric elements, there was some more obvious influence from jazz figures such as Miles Davis, Tony Williams, Rahsaan Roland Kirk, and Cecil Taylor, among many others. A blues undercurrent in the music manifested itself in ways that were less obvious. And numerous embellishments, motifs, and rhythmic and melodic elements were drawn from international sources that included Africa, China, Indonesia, Japan, and Tibet.[38]

The concept for the band was rather simple in that it focused on a melody and improvisations around that, though the intensity and number of electric guitars produced an unusual and unique sound. Most of the pieces were original compositions by Edwards, but occasionally they played works by other composers, though not pieces that audience members at Death by Audio were necessarily familiar with. For example, they played "Jupiter," one of the movements in English composer Gustav Holst's orchestral suite *The Planets*, with Kanaiwa playing the lead melody on electric guitar.[39]

The first concerts with the electric concept fully realized were at Zebulon and Goodbye Blue Monday, but the band found an even more welcoming home at Death by Audio, where they played with regularity because their aesthetic resonated with the scene there. From there, they began to play elsewhere in Brooklyn, including dates at Trans-Pecos, Silent Barn, the Legion, Spectrum, the Freedom Garden, and other DIY venues and bars. Slipstream Time Travel continues to make music and to evolve its sound up to the present time.

Grindcore Meets Free Jazz

The first show ever held in the space that became Death by Audio featured the experimental grindcore band Child Abuse on March 31, 2007. The band had started in 2004 but had originally been a duo of drummer Oran Canfield and keyboardist and vocalist Luke Calzonetti. Bassist Tim Dahl attended a show they had at the Cake Shop in Manhattan that was advertised as "Sun Ra meets Gorguts," which they had taken from a review of their work. The reference was not meant to be literal but to reflect the varied aesthetic and musical influences that the band exhibited.[40] Dahl was immediately impressed with what they did and soon joined the band.[41]

Dahl was originally from Chicago and had studied with Yusef Lateef and Archie Shepp at the University of Massachusetts Amherst, before moving to New York in 1998.[42] He spent his early years mostly in the free jazz scene but eventually wanted to move in the direction of experimental rock to work with people of his own generation.[43] Dahl had a transformative role in Child Abuse and soon began leading the band, booking gigs, and arranging tours in the northeastern United States and in Europe. Eventually, when Calzonetti left the band in 2011, Dahl also took over vocals for the group. The other musicians had formally studied music also but brought what Dahl termed "a folk art" to the music.[44]

Child Abuse generally created music that was entirely composed, even though everyone involved had some kind of improvisatory practice in their other work. Dahl described the other members of the band as "drawing from the oral tradition of music, not from an academic mindset or skill set. Our music is not notated, which allows it to mutate or to be malleable in ways that would not be possible in a more rigid system. Even when it is complicated and math-y, it grooves better than if we wrote it down." This meant that their compositional process did not come off of charts but rather was worked out in-person during rehearsals. "It can be a slow process," Dahl noted, "but it allows us to carefully work through each part and even argue through various versions of a piece collectively before we finalize it."[45] Dahl, Calzonetti, and keyboardist Eric Lau all used extended techniques that were outside of the typical range for the instruments, exploring timbre and the use of distortion in their sonic architecture.

In their early days, Child Abuse played a lot of shows, often booked by Todd P in Asterix, Dead Herring, Secret Project Robot, and other Williamsburg underground venues, splitting bills with everything from death metal bands to indie rock groups such as Parts and Labor, People, and Zs. From 2010 onward, they played on a bimonthly basis at Death by Audio. Child Abuse's music steadily evolved over time. Half of their self-titled debut record was rooted in grindcore, regimented by blast beats, which had been worked out by Canfield and Calzonetti before Dahl's arrival; he added bass parts to it after joining.[46] But the other half of the record, when the three of them composed collectively, was where the band began to establish its voice. When Lau replaced Calzonetti, "the music became more psychedelic and more experimental in form," Dahl explained.[47] By their third record, *Trouble in Paradise*, released in 2014, there was influence from German composer Karlheinz Stockhausen (1928–2007), especially the liberal use of glissandos in their playing.[48] Dahl's vocals were always written last and were "a kind of phonetic improv and vocalizations, not recognizable lyrics, though rooted in the death metal style."[49] Canfield's drumming provided the cohesion within the music and often the tangible tether that audiences recognized in what otherwise attempted to challenge expectations and conventions.

"Developing my own voice was a conscious decision," Dahl noted.

During my early days in New York, I played a lot of different gigs, even jazz brunch gigs. But at some point, I thought, that's not why I went into music, so I needed something different. I turned from double bass to electric bass and began exploring the timbres that were possible on the instrument. It became clear to me that there was a lot more I could do. It involves taking yourself out, being selfless, and being open to everything. I had to be honest with who I was, and then I began to discover myself, what I wanted to do as an artist. To create art, one has to develop their own voice, so I began to concentrate on that, focus on my interests, and use what I had learned in school and in various groups to do my own thing.[50]

Pulverize the Sound

Another sonically intense project that included Dahl was Pulverize the Sound, appropriately titled for the kinds of experiments they presented in the live setting. The band also included trumpeter Peter Evans and drummer Mike Pride and functioned as a composer's workshop with each member contributing pieces to the band.[51] Pulverize the Sound debuted their work at Death by Audio in 2010. The band was far removed from a jazz trumpet trio. The intensity, quite structured and tight in orchestration, nevertheless embraced distortion and deconstruction. Dahl often took on a role in the music "almost like a synthesizer player," in terms of tone and texture.[52] Dahl's contributions were the most abstract components, creating the imaginative interior of the musical sphere, or "countermelody," with Evans and Pride working on opposite poles, with more recognizable palettes that gave the music a tether.[53] Pride described the music as "really torturous in a good way; it is intense music without catharsis."[54]

As far out as they pushed the music, it never lost its cohesion, and the three managed to challenge audiences in the live setting, including a polarizing performance at the annual Vision Festival in 2011. As one critic described it, "The group's third number was jaw-dropping. To begin, Evans conjured a circular breathed muted drone, over which Dahl and Pride interjected a seemingly random sequence of furious outbursts of fuzz bass and crashing drums, though stopping and starting in perfect synchrony as if conducted or following a score, though none was in sight. All through it, Evans sustained his barely changing single tone. It was a startling juxtaposition of two kinds of amazing musicianship and elicited raucous affirmation from the rapt throng. But overall the raw volume and power divided the crowd."[55]

David Buddin

One composer who worked somewhat behind the scenes at Death by Audio was David Buddin. He composed music for Nebadon, which included vocalist Dominika Michalowska and drummer Kevin Shea, as well as his own work, such as the pieces that appeared on his record *Canticles for Electronic Music*, which appeared on Weasel Walter's ugEXPLODE label.[56] For the music, he built arrays based on hexachords that he drew from composer Milton Babbitt's serialist concepts with the aim "to extract from that array a harmonic language that may not always be dependent on the same number of pitch classes so that it is never at a loss for originality."[57] Buddin had first encountered

Babbitt's ideas and those of musicologist Allen Forte, which informed his own approach to composition, around the time he finished high school, and later he became particularly inspired by Igor Stravinsky and Charles Ives.[58] Over time, he developed many different ways to "do array routing to accomplish anything musically," as he experimented and tried out different versions of his scheme as he explored layers of homophony and polyphony.

Mick Barr and Orthrelm

One of the other bands on the first-ever show at Death by Audio in 2007 was guitarist Mick Barr's solo project, Ocrilim. Barr had originally established himself in Washington, DC, from 1996 onward with the short-lived post-hardcore band Crom-Tech, with drummer Malcolm McDuffie, and another duo, Orthrelm, with drummer Josh Blair. Ultimately, it was Orthrelm that brought Barr to New York. Blair had already moved north, and Barr followed him there, "spending months at a time couch surfing and practicing with him."[59] The latter band began to build a name for Barr, and fellow musician Weasel Walter referred to him in 2004 as "the most focused and uncompromising composer in the current rock underground."[60] Barr began another solo project, Octis, around the same time.

Orthrelm and Octis were innovative and exploratory, offering new sounds and structures to the rock music that was almost always through composed. Barr's early music was often marked by high-intensity, extremely fast playing. He stated, "I like the way it feels to play everything as fast as we can, and to play as much as we can. It's easier for me to do. The less going on in the music, the less comfortable I feel."[61]

As Weasel Walter observed of Orthrelm, "The instrumental duo's output is densely packed with musical information: with little or no structural repetition, discrete cells of notes are often frantically reconfigured into every possible permutation with staggering speed, revealing a fractal-like inner logic that is both chaotically asymmetrical and perfectly ordered at once."[62] Barr added, "The non-repetition is definitely deliberate," noting that in his conception of the music, "The things I tend to think of follow the cycle of the infinitely small and the infinitely large. The chaotic-ness reflects the chaotic-ness of the universe like the quantum jump of molecules. Insectoid speed. It stems from both science fiction and reality."[63]

Barr got involved in the underground experimental rock scene in Brooklyn that was welling up then and found a base at Death by Audio beginning the following year, while also playing at other venues around the city (see

Figure 6.3 Mick Barr
with I Don't Hear
Nothin' but the Blues
(Jon Irabagon and Mike
Pride not pictured), the
Stone, 2011 (*photo by
Peter Gannushkin*)

figure 6.3). In developing his own sound, Barr drew from things such as
hardcore, extreme metal such as Deicide's self-titled debut record, and free
jazz such as John Coltrane's *Interstellar Space* with drummer Rashied Ali.[64]
But he was most consciously inspired by the Turkish double-reed zurna,
Middle Eastern double-headed drum *davul*, and Berber Sufi trance music
of the Master Musicians of Jajouka, as well as "some general contrarianism"
in developing his unique voice on guitar.[65]

A few labels documented the scene at Death by Audio, each of which captured different elements of the music that occurred there. Weasel Walter's
ugEXPLODE captured some of the key improvised and experimental bands
that played there, including many of Walter's own bands, such as the Marc
Edwards–Weasel Walter Group, Cellular Chaos, and various ensembles that
he assembled under his own name. "At that time I wasn't necessarily looking
for records to put out on my label," Walter recalled. "At that time there was a
lot of good activity for the kind of aesthetics that I was into, so I just thought,
let's try to put that all under one banner. But I only put out music from bands
that met my own standard of rigor, experimentalism, and dissonance."[66]

"A lot of the bands that I find interesting are outliers because they are not part of any trend or movement, which is also why they are difficult to market. One of the first ones that I put out was by Orthrelm," Walter noted. "They are a singular band which I had followed ever since sharing a bill with them back in 2001 and feeling like they were brothers in the music. Mick Barr is one of the great outsider artists of my generation, and I value him immensely. I had always been a fan of Barr and enjoyed working with him when he was in the Flying Luttenbachers around 2005, so when he mentioned an Orthrelm anthology, I offered to put it out on the label."[67]

I Don't Hear Nothin' but the Blues

Barr would eventually collaborate with saxophonist Jon Irabagon and drummer Mike Pride in I Don't Hear Nothin' but the Blues, a band that emerged out of the scene at Death by Audio. At first, the band was a duo of just Irabagon and Pride, but the two became regular collaborators and bandmates through the years, often hiring each other or including each other on gigs they had, eventually forming a tight musical bond that is evident in their musical interactions. Commenting on Pride's vast knowledge and versatility, Irabagon stated, "He seems to know about every genre, from punk to the most experimental improvised music to electronic; he's always bursting with ideas. His music is unique because he exhibits all of these influences in his playing. He's also a family man, and one can hear that total responsibility in how he plays. We have fun together. That exuberance finds its way into the music, there is humor in the music, there is joking, but it is also serious. He is the perfect drummer foil for me."[68]

I Don't Hear Nothin' but the Blues grew out of duo sessions that Irabagon and Pride did at the latter's apartment in Windsor Terrace in 2006. "We really enjoyed playing together, sometimes just us, sometimes we would invite other people to join us," Irabagon described the process. "At times we would each bring compositions, while at other times we just played free. It was a workshop for us to bounce ideas off of each other and try new things."[69] As Pride was about to embark on a three-month world tour with another band in 2008, they finally went into the studio to record material for their self-titled debut record.[70]

The record exhibits a number of sonic ideas. Irabagon admitted that in the time leading up to the recording, he had been listening deeply to saxophonist Sonny Rollins. He was also exploring cellular improvisational ideas and motivic concepts. So Irabagon proposed that they play one long track and develop, on the fly, a resource bank of motivic ideas and rhythms that we can draw from as we go. The process was that we would each begin with one phrase or rhythm that we did not discuss beforehand, and then that phrase or rhythm would develop into another one, and so forth, each one introducing more material, but allowing one to go back to earlier phrases or rhythms as the piece developed. Nothing was preconceived. The motivic ideas had to develop organically out of where I started from, and, of course, I was interacting with another musician at the same time. I wanted the challenge that I encountered in those contexts because it made me play differently and challenged me to respond, grow, and reach for new ideas and concepts in the music.[71]

"I spent months of practice time working on this idea. It involved not just playing but also memory," Irabagon further described the process.

I had to learn to step aside of what I was doing, in the midst of the action, and take a snapshot whenever I crystallized an idea that became number two, number three, and so forth. It took many months practicing to be able to do this fluidly. It was the beginning of a mind-blowing process on how to do that in real time, a whole new way of thinking about music making for me. The process has had a deep impact on my other music, when I play straight-ahead jazz or pop, or other improvisational groups. It ended up being transformational.[72]

The music is "democratic," as Irabagon explained. "I may be the one that organizes gigs, tours, and recording dates, but I don't tell anyone what to do in the music. We figure that out together."[73] With the music emerging out of sessions and later in live gigs at Death by Audio and a few other venues, such as Goodbye Blue Monday and Zebulon, Irabagon began to get interested in adding a third musician to the concept. After performing at the Moers Festival with his trio on the same bill as Mick Barr's Orthrelm in 2011, Irabagon was immediately drawn to the former's playing and asked him to join the project. "I was mesmerized by Mick Barr's playing. I'd never seen anyone play live like that. I knew I wanted him to play with us immediately upon seeing him."[74]

Instead of asking Barr to do the cellular concept that the duo had developed, they just had Barr be "a free agent" within the music, freely playing and interacting with Irabagon and Pride as he wished while they played. "Barr's articulation on guitar has few parallels," Irabagon observed. "Sometimes he forms a kind of blanket with waves of sound that Mike and I could use to experiment off of, or sometimes he would play a section of crisp sixteenth notes played at the fastest possible pace that would push the energy about as high as I could imagine. His sound makes the band so much more versatile and expands the possibilities massively."[75] I Don't Hear Nothin' but the Blues with Barr was featured at the Moers Festival in 2012. Years later, they would add guitarist Ava Mendoza to further expand on the sound for their third record, edging louder, noisier, and "maximalist" as they evolved in their sound and aesthetic.

In reflecting on the centrality of Death by Audio to the development of the band, Irabagon stated, "As someone who comes from the jazzier side of things, Death by Audio was critically important for me and for a lot of creative musicians because it was something definitively different and was a rare intersection between improvised music and rock, punk, black metal, and noise. The venue was so important for musicians to feel comfortable to create and to work in this sonic zone where ticket sales were not an issue and we were given free rein. The most important thing was the community there that supported what we and others were doing."[76]

Normal Love

Another band situated on the improvised music–rock–punk–metal–noise continuum, with significant doses of noise, was Normal Love. The band had emerged first in the Philadelphia DIY music scene when bassist Evan Lipson, guitarist Amnon Freidlin, and drummer Eli Litwin all met while studying music at Temple University in 2005. Freidlin commented, "We came out of the 'noise bubble' that was really expanding then," during a period when "noise and fringe music" had growing cultural capital and noise bands could get guaranteed paid gigs on the college touring circuit.[77] Lipson began the band originally, but the band generally worked as a collective, with different members taking the lead creatively at different times. Lipson also knew violinist Carlos Santiago Jr. from high school and had met guitarist Alex Nagle on the Philadelphia scene and asked them to join the band. "The members of the band had diverse musical backgrounds but were all rigorous and formalized to some degree, had a high level of technical ability, and were interested by unusual or unknown music or sounds," Lipson observed.[78] The band drew its name from an unreleased film by Jack Smith from 1963 that stunned Freidlin with its "magnificent still shots."[79]

The early members exhibited influences that included classical chamber music, free jazz, "avant-garde industrial music" such as Test Dept., No Wave, noise, noise rock, black metal, death metal, atonal serialism, and various psychedelic manipulations of vocals and other elements. The band's unusual rhythmic concept drew from the polyrhythms of composer Steve Reich, various systems of African polyrhythms, and post-1960s avant-garde classical music.[80] Lipson drew considerable influence from mid-twentieth-century avant-garde composers such as Iannis Xenakis and Edgard Varèse, as well as the Japanese brutal prog band Ruins. Nagle was the other member who shaped the band in its early years, looking to the classical new complexity British composer Brian Ferneyhough, serial composer Milton Babbitt, and iconic No Wave bands such as Teenage Jesus and the Jerks as sources of inspiration.[81] One unifying factor was a mutual interest in free playing.

From the beginning, Normal Love developed difficult, complex rhythms and tight clusters of dark, edgy, and metallic sounds. Freidlin described the first piece he wrote for the band, titled "Ndugo," as a "freak in" rather than a freak-out, with identifiable elements that could be digested, but pushing the boundaries with that material in new ways. The band worked out their early material in weekly sessions at Jack Wright's Spring Garden Music House in West Philadelphia, which allowed them to work through difficult material over the course of a year before presenting it to the public.[82]

In 2007 Freidlin and Lipson moved to New York when Freidlin had the opportunity to house-sit an apartment for a family friend in Bensonhurst, Brooklyn, paying just $500 per month which he split with Lipson. "I come from a very modest background, my family was on food stamps through high school," Freidlin explained. "Getting a deal on rent was the only way to make it work for me financially, since by that point in the 2000s it had gotten really expensive, and most young people on the scene seemed to be upper middle class or wealthier, coming to the city, taking part in the music scene. I'm guessing 80 percent of the people at that time were getting subsidized by their families. Sometimes I was sending money home when I could, but I was able to live there for five years and make music."[83] Lipson stated, "We had this once-in-a-lifetime opportunity, which is how we were able to sustain living in New York for five years, but most other people who were there then had money some other way."[84]

Normal Love's first show in New York was at Death by Audio on a split bill with People in 2007 (see figure 6.4). "The venue was great from that point on. They would let a band try something new in front of a tiny audience on a Wednesday night or do something more refined on a weekend. It always had the same party atmosphere, people still smoked indoors, and maybe in some ways it was like the CBGBs of our time period. But in terms of cultural

Figure 6.4 Normal Love at Death by Audio (*from left*, Alex Nagle?, Evan Lipson, Eli Litwin, Carlos Santiago?, and Amnon Freidlin), 2012 (*private collection*)

norms, it felt like a safer space. I didn't feel like one generally had to worry about something racist or transphobic happening there. It felt like a punk house, it was a community."[85] Normal Love's presence at Death by Audio and at other New York venues enabled them to launch a tour in August and September 2007 that began in Baltimore, then came back through Philadelphia, New York, and New England, before turning west through Buffalo and Toronto, then south through Michigan and Ohio, and back through Pittsburgh and other towns in Pennsylvania.[86] A tour the following year retraced these steps and added additional stops in St. Louis and Lexington, as well as additional Canadian dates in Ottawa and Montreal.

After a break from touring and playing from late 2008 to early 2010, Normal Love reassembled with a new vision. The early material that the band developed still bore the heaviest influence from Lipson and Nagle, where "forms of new complexity meet extreme forms of metal and No Wave" with some experimentation with polyrhythms.[87] But soon they were workshopping material there that would later appear on *Survival Tricks*.[88] When Nagle left the band, one of Freidlin's aims was to hire a vocalist who would add the feel of punk or No Wave types of aesthetic and punk-apocalyptic lyricism, after splitting a bill with the band Whore Paint, fronted by Reba Mitchell.[89] Merissa Martigoni, from Philadelphia, embodied that sound, and she soon became integral to their aesthetic and stage presence.

Freidlin began to exert greater influence over the band; he was the principal architect of the band's later sound, as documented on *Peel/Kleinman* and *Survival Tricks*. "The sound I started to hear was a posthuman, polyrhythmic, postindustrial, posttonal contemporary chamber, raga-ish, female-fronted psychedelic future-punk vocalist thing."[90] In particular, he drew from an array of contemporary influences such as Lightning Bolt, Sightings, and Battles's guitar player, Tyondai Braxton. Christian Marclay's late 1980s polyrhythmic multiple-turntable recordings and performances were also foundational.[91] More established figures such as Sun Ra and Steve Reich, as well as electroacoustic innovator Louis Andriessen's piece "Hout," also had an impact on Freidlin, as well as general aesthetic influence from musique concrète and No Wave.[92] Lipson also felt that the sounds of bands such as Zs and Weasel Walter's the Flying Luttenbachers both had an impact on the later music of Normal Love.[93] Freidlin's use of a sampler, drawing from created, synthesizer, or unusual sounds, was central to creating electronic textures that added an additional dimension to the band's later music. Normal Love's structure became increasingly propulsive with simpler pitch-content, along with increased attention to textures, intricate or complex rhythms, noise elements, electronics, and aspects of sound design.[94]

By 2011 and 2012, the band was mostly workshopping pieces written by Freidlin, such as "Lend Some Treats" and "Grimy Super Soaker," both of which possessed a mix of industrial noise, surreal punk vocals, and mechanical polyrhythmic structures produced through extended techniques.[95] In particular, Freidlin used hocketing prominently, a feature he had encountered in his study of Renaissance music, in which each note in a phrase was played by a different musician to create an interlocking sonic effect. Another of his pieces, "Electrolytes in the Brine," also took from that world of sound, adding in a raga feel, and displayed his interest in electronics and homegrown sampling of unusual, instrumental, or noninstrumental sounds.[96] Some of the pieces, like "Cosmetic Rager" and "Cultural Uppercut," were collaboratively composed. The band performed regularly at Death by Audio in 2012 before embarking on a tour that took them through New England, Canada, and Wisconsin, southwest through the Great Plains, Arkansas, and Missouri, east through Chattanooga and Memphis, up through the Midwest via Chicago, and across upstate New York. After some additional shows in Brooklyn and a final performance at the Stone, the band became less active, though new material may be in preparation.

"Normal Love was another scene band that I thought was incredible," explained Weasel Walter, who put *Survival Tricks* out on his label, ugEX-PLODE. "I would classify them as brutal prog. They were trying to do the most complicated, bizarre, structured music that they could possibly come up with. I thought that the amount of work they put into that music was exemplary. They rehearsed so much. It is difficult because they put so much time and work into it, but so much of this music was not popular, so at times people feel it is futile. But that doesn't indicate anything about how interesting or groundbreaking music is."[97]

In hindsight, many musicians expressed amazement that Death by Audio lasted as long as it did in a neighborhood that was rapidly gentrifying and becoming hostile to musicians and music venues even during its early years. "Wilber's biggest contribution to the music scene was providing us all with a place to play," Marc Edwards commented. "It was similar to how ESP-Disk provided musicians with the means to express themselves through new music in the early days of free jazz. And how the Knitting Factory became the center of a whole scene in the 1980s and 1990s. Death by Audio served in a similar way for the underground experimental noise rock scene in the late 2000s and early 2010s."[98] Speaking in 2020, Weasel Walter commented, "Death by Audio was the best place to play in New York during the years that it was open. People are sentimental for it because Edan Wilber ran the venue the way it should be done. After Death by Audio came to an end, it was a really hard point for the scene. No one has stepped up to fill the void since."[99]

The Last Loft: Connie Crothers

Running parallel to the Zebulon and Death by Audio scenes, there was a loft scene that was almost a world to itself. Pianist Connie Crothers (1941–2016) moved to Williamsburg rather late in her career, in 2002, after many years of living elsewhere in the city. She rented a loft space at 475 Kent Avenue with a view of the East River and the Manhattan skyline. In some ways, she arrived at just the right time: the gentrifying push was to increase tenfold after 9/11, so she managed to secure a place just before it became financially impossible. By the 2000s the lack of commercial outlets for music was beginning to become acute in New York, so Crothers took it on herself to self-produce a series of concerts at her loft. She also brought with her a music scene that she had been cultivating since the 1970s as the protégé of pianist Lennie Tristano (1919–78).

Crothers grew up in San Jose, California, where the local music scene centered around jazz and blues singer Jimmy Witherspoon (1920–97) as well as rock and roll and blues dance halls. Having studied privately in her youth, she moved forty miles north to study composition at the University of California, Berkeley. Finding the program too focused on structure at the expense of expression, she encountered the recording "Requiem" by pianist

Lennie Tristano, which caused "an instantaneous personal revolution." She decided to relocate to New York City in 1962 to study with him.[100]

Over the next few years, Crothers thoroughly reconceived of her musical practice and learned to improvise. She later stated of the experience, "I sat down at my piano with the desire to improvise. I sat there for a half hour. I could not improvise one note. And in that moment, I became angry. I realized that as much as I had given, and as much as people had given me to learn, that this dimensional thing had been left out, and I was totally blocked. I was facing a wall, and I felt like I had been so deeply deprived of something that was so important."[101] Crothers felt comfortable studying with Tristano because she "would say that Lennie was a feminist" and was the only teacher she had ever had who had taken her seriously as a musician.[102] Beyond Tristano, Crothers drew inspiration from a range of pianists from Bud Powell to Cecil Taylor.[103]

Tristano's teaching method required his students to memorize key solos from the recorded output of Louis Armstrong, Lester Young, and Charlie Parker, at least in part owing to the fact that Tristano was born blind and had developed a system of self-study out of necessity. The approach was rooted in standard jazz education but was focused entirely on aural transmission of musical concepts. Tristano's students were also generally restricted in what chord progressions they could employ and were directed to learn "lines" that were composed and recorded by Tristano as well as the latter's colleagues, saxophonists Warne Marsh and Lee Konitz.[104] Saxophonist Richard Tabnik, a longtime student of Crothers, described lines as "an original melody with some altered harmony drawn from jazz standards that expresses something unique and is a springboard to improvising."[105] Lines had to be set into memory and refined through rigorous practicing. Tristano also encouraged his students to connect with the melody of a tune through singing it first before learning how to play it on an instrument.[106] Some students found the system confining, while others found it a useful springboard toward becoming skilled and original players themselves.

Crothers and Tristano formed a close relationship for many years, and Tristano arranged performances for Crothers, first at his apartment in Jamaica, Queens, where he regularly produced concerts, and later at Carnegie Hall for her sold-out debut public performance in 1974.[107] A future student of Crothers, pianist Carol Liebowitz, who was in attendance at the time, remarked, "She sounded original. I had never heard anything like it in my life."[108] Tristano stated, "Connie Crothers is the most original musician that I have ever had the privilege to work with."[109] She remained a pivotal figure within the community that revolved around Tristano until the latter's death in 1978, and she became the focal point for those who continued to be inspired by his legacy. The label that Crothers founded with drummer and life companion Max Roach in 1982, named New Artists Records, was organized as an artist collective and became one of the primary outlets for the post-Tristano community.[110] Crothers also began to develop her own community beyond Tristano, playing duo with saxophonist Richard Tabnik and leading a quartet with saxophonist Lenny Popkin, bassist Cameron Brown, and drummer Carol Tristano through the 1980s and 1990s.

One of the hallmarks of Crothers's music is that even in the 1980s, during the great divide between free playing and the return to bebop, she did not feel a need to go toward one end of the spectrum or the other. Throughout the early decades of her work, she navigated her own path between free improvisation and structure, always with an eye for spontaneity. Some of her students were drawn to her measured approach.[111] Whatever aspect of musicality piqued her interest, Crothers had a reputation for working tirelessly at it until she felt that she had mastered it and developed that aspect of her playing or concept to the fullest possible extent.

With the gentrification of the Lower East Side in full swing, Crothers's landlord decided to evict her in 2002.[112] With the help of her friend drummer John McCutcheon (b. 1956), Crothers found the loft space in Williamsburg on Kent Avenue, in what was a Hasidic neighborhood at the time, which was to become a vibrant space for her community.[113] Bassist Melvin Gibbs lived on the same floor and later attended and performed in the concert series that emerged in the space.

The space itself was approximately 1,600 square feet in a twenty-by-eighty-foot room with high ceilings. It was a typical raw former industrial space with a concrete floor and pipes running across the ceiling. One end of the space was completely covered in windows with a view of the city as the backdrop. The stage, in the middle of the space, held her piano, a magnificent 1922 Steinway A-3 made of mahogany.[114] Danish modern armchairs were scattered about along with other furniture where students or other audience members could sit. Lamps lit the periphery amid a few bookshelves and floor-to-ceiling metal shelving that contained all of the New Artists Records releases. A papier-mâché sculpture of saxophonist Lester Young graced the top of one of the bookshelves, illuminated in such a way that it projected a massive silhouette onto the wall. The space was open and airy with the focus entirely on the music. Crothers always cooked meals and offered fresh produce from the local farmer's market to anyone who attended a performance, presented on a fine oak table near the back of the space, surrounded by a set of Bank of England chairs.[115]

For the first few years of her residence on Kent Avenue, Crothers presented music at McCutcheon's loft, which was on the same floor in the building. Then, once McCutcheon was unable to continue to present music in his own space, Crothers decided to turn her loft space into a performance space.[116] McCutcheon, who was a carpenter, helped build a stage for her piano at the center of the space, and she began hosting occasional concerts in 2005. When public performances were not scheduled, Crothers still hosted jam sessions on a weekly basis.[117]

The Connie Crothers Quartet was the band that played most often in the space, drawing its origins from various lineups, generally involving saxophonist Richard Tabnik and drummer Roger Mancuso, that Crothers had organized in the 1990s and had solidified in 2001.[118] Tabnik had studied with her since 1980, and they had recorded and toured together as a duo.[119] Mancuso had an even longer history, having played with Crothers since the 1960s. Crothers and Tabnik's many years of practicing, performing, and composing lines together had them very refined by the time the quartet began to perform in earnest. Crothers's compositions were at times quite difficult, sometimes written above or even below the typical range of Tabnik's saxophone, so he had to develop techniques to extend his abilities to play the music.[120]

By their September 18, 2005, performance at the loft, the band had expanded to a quintet including poet Mark Weber and bassist Ratzo Harris.[121] Crothers employed many of the Tristano lines and composed some of her own, as well as performing a number of jazz standards; the band refined them with precision. Through this, however, Crothers developed "a highly personal and unique sound" influenced by Cecil Taylor, among others.[122] Harris and Tabnik had some disagreements, and Harris left the band, with Ken Filiano eventually replacing him (see figure 6.5).

In the early years of the loft venue, the most celebrated performance was at a benefit concert for bassist Sonny Dallas, the former bass player for Tristano, who was in failing health. Crothers organized a performance with Tabnik, drummer John McCutcheon, and bassist Jeremy Stratton. She called on a longtime friend, alto saxophonist Lee Konitz, to join the group, and they gave a sensational performance. They split the quintet up into duos and trios through the night. Crothers played densely, fully, with big, jam-packed, billowing chords and waves of energy. "But there was a solo performance of 'These Foolish Things,'" vocalist Andrea Wolper recalled,

Figure 6.5 Ken Filiano (*left*) and Connie Crothers at the loft, early 2010s (*photo by Michael Weintrob*)

"that was so intimate and quiet. It was extraordinary, a gorgeous single-note line, and every note communicated volumes. No matter how she approached a song, though, it was always very personal, there was nothing superficial, and what was most important was communicating feeling."[123]

At another particularly prescient moment at the concert, Konitz and Tabnik played "All of Me," originally composed by Gerald Marks and Seymour Simons in 1931 and performed by many jazz artists through the decades. Their version was a scatting duet that explored the boundaries of the piece. Despite the moments displayed onstage, there was tension between Konitz and some of the other performers on the bill, at least in part owing to underlying disagreements dating back decades, since many of the post-Tristano figures considered Konitz's work from the 1940s and 1950s to be more visionary than his later work. The fifty attendees packed the place to its limits.

The move to Williamsburg also marked some new frontiers in Crothers's playing, turning her a bit more toward free improvisation, though still rooted in the system of Tristano lines and by playing standards from the jazz tradition. Her music and the culture of the scene centered around a very specific vocabulary. As German pianist and writer Ursel Schlicht, who studied with Crothers in New York, noted, "Up to that time, Crothers faced the dilemma of being perceived as too free to be featured in jazz festivals and too bebop oriented to play at free jazz or improv festivals."[124] Her associations with saxophonist Jemeel Moondoc drew her further into free playing, and she gained visibility in front of new audiences at clubs such as the Stone. A quintet that included Moondoc, McCutcheon, trumpeter Nathan Breedlove, and bassist Adam Lane played Vision Festival in 2003. Crothers and Moondoc co-led the unit, and they worked abstractly but intuitively without forms in a music that possessed a lot of space and dynamics that came together through close listening by the players. The music was freely improvised but maintained Crothers's strong melodic style. The band never played again after the performance. Crothers and Moondoc did play duo for a few years, furthering their free improvisational approach, but they never recorded.[125]

Much like her teacher, Crothers built her music community by attracting many students. Some chose to study with her because they saw her as the living manifestation of the legacy of Lennie Tristano or Warne Marsh, while others found her approachable and found her teaching methods to be particularly effective. Pianist Harvey Diamond, for instance, had studied with Tristano in 1968–78 and then studied with Crothers in 1979–86. Whereas Tristano had been more systematic in his approach and generally focused on tunes, Crothers taught him how to freely improvise and how to extend the possibilities of the lower register of the instrument and both extremes of volume, loud and soft. "I realized that I could play anything," Diamond commented, "any combination of notes, and how to express what I felt in the moment at any given time."[126]

"I immediately found resolution," alto saxophonist Nick Lyons explained, "with the conundrum of how to integrate improvisation with all of the other elements in a way that was not clichéd straight-ahead jazz playing. I had never felt that jazz was meant to be boring or derivative, it was, as Tristano said, a feeling."[127] Musicians who studied with Crothers found that singing to records was a form of improvisation itself, a way of creating a more intimate and intuitive relationship with the music, drawing the student into dialogue with the great jazz artists of the past.[128] Crothers directed students to sing along with a number of records from the 1930s, 1940s, and 1950s, much like Tristano touching on Louis Armstrong, Lester Young, and Charlie Parker but also Roy Eldridge, Charlie Christian, Bud Powell, Fats Navarro, Lee

Konitz, and Warne Marsh.[129] "She had a way of making everything sound personal," as Carol Liebowitz characterized her teacher. "She had a natural feel for harmony and an adept ear for improvisation."[130]

Saxophonist Lorenzo Sanguedolce, who began studying with Crothers in 2004, recalled, "My heroes were Charlie Parker, Lester Young, and Warne Marsh, and when she said that was where she was coming from, I knew it was the perfect match for what I wanted to do. When we practiced and performed standards, we did it in a way that was not derivative. We were open to any approach available, such as straight swing, totally free, super slow or fast, or stretch it out with harmony to interpret even well-known tunes in a new way."[131] Pianist Ursel Schlicht regarded Crothers's approach, canon, and attention to bebop history as "a great foundation from which to enter into free playing." Schlicht also noted Crothers's idea that "if you play the melody with the left hand instead of the right, it sinks in differently. It's more emotional. Reversing that opened all kinds of possibilities. I learned a lot of unusual fingerings from her with her emphasis on making sure each finger possessed the same flexibility and strength. There was a conditioning process."[132]

In January 2011 Crothers decided to turn the occasional concert series into a more regular event. It began with concerts once a month, then every two weeks, and then, by May of that year, nearly every week. Crothers began to open it up to her students, collaborators, and friends to fill the bills with different bands for every event. The bills were a mixture of the post-Tristano community and many of her own students, some of whom had also studied with Tristano. Despite more than thirty years separating the concerts and Tristano's death, his legacy still had a significant place within the community. Pianists Kazzrie Jaxen and Harvey Diamond, who had studied with both Tristano and Crothers, were independently featured on several bills, for instance. Crothers's students who also appeared regularly included saxophonists Nick Lyons, Jessica Jones, and Lorenzo Sanguedolce; vocalists Andrea Wolper and Cheryl Richards; guitarist Adam Caine; and pianists Virg Dzurinko and Carol Liebowitz, among many others (see figure 6.6). From Vision Festival connections, musicians such as Henry Grimes and Michael Bisio also frequented the loft. Most of the sessions were recorded, though only a few have been released.[133] For many of the musicians who played, it was a launching point, but it was also a community, a place to nurture one's sound in a supportive environment.

The audience at Crothers's loft was primarily composed of her students, many of whom also performed in the concert series. Tristano devotees also

Figure 6.6 Connie Crothers (*left*) and Andrea Wolper at the loft, early 2010s (*private collection*)

regularly attended the events, some of whom had first seen Tristano live at the Half Note back in the 1960s.[134] Beyond that, a few other musicians and artists would frequent the space, especially younger and often female performers, in a room that could fit fifty to sixty people, though most of the time twenty-five to forty people attended. Crothers managed to maintain the loft series in the face of the constant threat of eviction.[135] In 2012, having grown tired of running the series, Crothers finally ceased hosting regular shows, though the loft remained a locus for many of the people in her community up until her death in 2016.

Other Venues
Monkeytown

Over the years, many other venues contributed to the Williamsburg music scene. Some venues had occasional shows over the span of years, while others hosted a short-lived regular series for a few months. Monkeytown was a venue that booked many different types of music, some of which was experimental, ranging from avant-jazz to avant-rock to avant-pop, not to mention indie rock bands like Dirty Projectors and singer-songwriter Sharon Van Etten, both of whom played some of their early shows at the venue.[136] Monkeytown had begun in a loft space at a different location in Williamsburg in 2003 but was transformed into a legitimate and legal venue by its owner, Montgomery Knott, in late 2005. At its second location, at 58 North Third Street, around the corner from Zebulon, the venue became a space for eclectic bills for over four years until it closed in early 2010. Zebulon remained the late-night community hangout for artists and other people who would drift over from Monkeytown and other places in the neighborhood.

To keep the business going, Knott tried to book shows that would draw at least thirty people for a space that had a capacity of fifty.[137] This meant that he often aimed at more popular acts, though he had an eye for bands that were pushing the envelope, trying to do something new or different, while still connecting with the general public. It was a natural fit for the music of the time, in which genre classifications were being blurred to the extreme; the bills of the venue reflected the eclectic nature of the scene. Originally, he had intended it to feature a lot of video art, but it quickly coalesced around music, which appeared there approximately 80 percent of the time.[138] Unlike many venues, Monkeytown was also a restaurant, and thus it provided opportunities for creative and artistic dining while patrons also engaged with live music.[139] By Knott's own estimates, the venue took about a year and a half to take off, but even after that, it was difficult to maintain through the late 2000s as rents escalated. "It was a miserable four years of trying to survive running a venue," Knott recalled. "I never made above minimum wage."[140]

The front dining room fit approximately thirty people at a dozen tables and also sported a bar. The twenty-foot ceilings gave the place a feeling of openness. Each of the bathrooms was home to a shifting set of sound installations by artists in the community. The performance space was in the back of the venue, the centerpiece of which was a cube where video images were broadcast. No matter where a person was in the space, they could see the videos. Underneath was the stage, so, again, all eyes were on the stage during live concerts, with the audience dispersed around the edges of the venue, focused inward.

In terms of the avant-garde, Monkeytown connected most with a musician community located primarily in South Brooklyn, in Park Slope, Kensington, and Ditmas Park. The scene there had gained a communal dynamism around the club Barbès in Park Slope from 2003, which hosted a music series organized by Michael Attias, though many of the musicians also played at Tonic and elsewhere in New York, as well as touring domestically and internationally. Within the eclectic mix of music, bandleaders such as drummer Harris Eisenstadt, with his quintet Canada Day, played the space. Violist Mat Maneri also led bands in numerous contexts. Multi-instrumentalist Matt Darriau brought music tinged with Balkan influences to the space with his band Paradox Trio. Bassist Mark Helias's band Open Loose presented music there at an advanced stage of their development after more than a decade of evolving and refining his concept and compositions. Monkeytown was a space where creative music, new music, and the jazz avant-garde collided occasionally, interspersed between many indie rock and avant-pop bands that held the day.

In spaces like Monkeytown, elements of improvised or experimental music sometimes took root in new forms. For instance, Knott's own band, Stars Like Fleas, which was a pop band, incorporated a lot of improvisation.[141] By Knott's own admission, the downfall of the venue was that it aimed too broadly in terms of audience. "I filled the calendar," he explained, "but it never had any focused vision." At a time when music was crossing a lot of boundaries, audiences were not necessarily ready for all of the transitions. "There was no audience for our eclectic programming."[142]

Spike Hill

A brief series was organized and booked by Harris Eisenstadt at Spike Hill, located at 184 Bedford Avenue, in the heart of Williamsburg, from September 2007 to January 2008. The music he booked was drawn from jazz and classical-informed improvised music played by people of his generation for what the venue owners called "a jazz night."[143] He themed the first month around drummer bandleaders, including Tomas Fujiwara, Aaron Siegel, Ches Smith, Michael Sarin, and himself. Occasionally, he booked older, well-known figures such as Wayne Horvitz, Barry Altschul, or Steve Swell to draw bigger crowds, though the audiences were always moderate to small. Trumpeter Nate Wooley and saxophonists Jason Mears and Matt Bauder all led bands at the venue, and Mary Halvorson and Jessica Pavone presented their duo. It also featured an early form of the innovative composers' collective the Thirteenth Assembly, which included Fujiwara, Halvorson, Pavone, and trumpeter Taylor Ho Bynum. "It was difficult to keep the series going," Eisenstadt commented, "so I had to decide how hard to fight for it in a place that did not seem into it. The money and the support wasn't there."[144] The series at Spike Hill was a weekly event over the span of four months, one of many such series through the years that gave a momentary foothold for figures such as Eisenstadt and the community of which he was a part.

Dissolution, Displacement, and Rebirth

In 2014 *Vice Magazine* bought the building that held Death by Audio and other DIY music venues. Ironically, a publication that claimed to be covering alternative culture displaced some of the most important venues in the city at the time for the presentation of new and challenging sounds, dealing a mortal blow to the Williamsburg avant-garde. The closing of Death by Audio formally ended the Williamsburg experimental music scene, pushing the fractured community south and east into Bushwick. In Bushwick a younger generation had been emerging since about 2005 and more so since 2011, which, together with the waves of displaced Williamsburg-based musicians and artists, would continue to bear the torch of the music going forward.[145]

As the Williamsburg music scene was displaced, the neighborhood of Bushwick inherited the community of artists. Located inland in a postindustrial corridor along the L train line, it was the next logical stop for artists who were interested in being a part of the community. Bushwick was geographically more complicated than Williamsburg, in some ways, with just one major zone of postindustrial decay in what became known as Morgantown, around the Morgan Avenue subway station. Many of the earliest avant-garde artist spaces appeared there or along Bushwick Avenue at the western border of Morgantown. The first significant club that catered to the music that appeared further south was Goodbye Blue Monday, on Broadway, which had an open curation policy allowing many then-unknown musicians to find an easy stage in a kind of open-mic type of atmosphere. Many artists who played there, such as Jon Irabagon, Peter Evans, Ras Moshe, Shayna Dulberger, Jeremiah Cymerman, Chris Welcome, and Yoni Kretzmer, all went on to have an impact on the scene.

Eventually, a new wave of loft DIY shows began to happen near Myrtle Avenue at places like the Freedom Garden, a series at 1012 Willoughby Avenue, the artist collective Silent Barn, and the Glove, which were some of the key germination points for an emerging Bushwick sound after 2010. I ran a series at my loft in the neighborhood, New Revolution Arts, in 2014–18, that was a part of that scene. Numerous other clubs, basements, lofts, pizza parlors, bars, and other spaces appeared in the years that followed and have continued to provide the community with spaces in which to develop new and experimental sounds.

Though Bushwick and ultimately Ridgewood, Queens, were the primary heirs to the Williamsburg avant-garde music scene, people also moved in many other directions. The South Brooklyn scene, originally centered in Park Slope but pushed south in a corresponding gentrification into South Slope, Kensington, and Ditmas Park, certainly became one place for displaced musicians from Williamsburg. Though the aesthetics of the South Brooklyn scene were related, there were also unique dynamics there that drew artists. Beyond New York City, there were many other destinations for artists who were a part of the scene. Some moved to nearby urban centers, hoping to remain connected to the increasingly diffuse community by situating themselves in Philadelphia or New Haven, or even more so in the artist corridor that can be traced through numerous towns on the Hudson River, with the greatest concentration in Beacon, New York. These reverberations continue to have effects as the alchemy of improvisation, creative composition, free jazz, rock, postpunk, electronic, and noise continues to evolve toward sounds yet unknown.

Afterword

Art, Experiment, and Capital

The Williamsburg avant-garde was witness to many musical explorations and innovations. Its particular aesthetic alchemy brought forces together that did not meet in the same way in other places in New York City or in any other location during the same period. In the early 1990s, postpunk elements mingled with the free jazz, electronic, and DJ scenes. By the late 1990s, noise became one of the primary aesthetic palettes that informed free jazz, indie rock, and a variety of cross-genre experimentations that even managed to seize unlicensed radio waves as a means of connecting with audiences. From the early 2000s, the scene became increasingly informed by creative compositional practices born in the academy, though they drew from a wide range of aesthetics. Even in the waning years of the Williamsburg scene, free jazz, postpunk, rock, and noise intermingled in new ways that produced some of the most innovative music of the period. Experimentation, improvisation, and the pursuit of newness were at the heart of these sonic discoveries. Pushed from warehouses to lofts to cafés to bars, the Williamsburg avant-garde remained a largely underground phenomenon despite the artists' massive output through the twenty-five years that the scene survived. Now, though the community has been displaced in various directions, many of the musical experiments continue in new sites and have led to further developments beyond the scope of this book.

The story of the Williamsburg avant-garde is that of the struggle between the forces of capital and cultural production, though the relationship between capital and the arts was complex. National and global flows of capital no doubt brought many artists to the neighborhood in the first place. Existing residents of nearby areas of Williamsburg were largely displaced by the corporate development that swept through the area. Most artists were swept out in the same or subsequent waves, while investors made billions of dollars in real estate ventures as property values skyrocketed. Though there were exceptions to the general trend, social class increasingly informed who participated in the music scene as it developed over time. Whereas artists from wealthier backgrounds were often reticent to talk about their position, working-class artists often spoke about their own struggles clearly and with conviction.

Williamsburg was the site of an eclectic yet dynamic community of cultural producers. This book has focused primarily on the experimental aspects of that community and the music that it produced. Many other vibrant communities and cultural outputs also came out of that milieu that deserve further study. It took capital less than a decade to find inroads into the area with an eye to exploiting the fragility of the financial position of most artists. In retrospect, it seems inevitable that billionaire investors, some of whom never set foot in Williamsburg, would ensnare such a place with their tentacles of power and transform it into a place accessible only to the economic elite. But the fact the hundreds of artists whom I spoke with in the course of this research so readily reminisce about Williamsburg during its years as an art center is living proof of its cultural dynamism and the utopian atmosphere it exhibited in those times.

Williamsburg is one example of a broader contest between capital and cultural production that has been transforming the United States rapidly since the 1990s and in some forms since the 1960s. The era of New York as a global cultural center, when its power and influence were particularly potent in 1965–95, was also a time when it suffered financially. Countless books have been written about these periods, and we still honor the cultural heroes who emerged in those times. When artists and other residents did not owe most of their money, time, and other resources to the matrix of capital forces that have since taken over the city, they were able to work more effectively as cultural workers. This book has tried to pull back the curtain on this process in more recent times by examining what strategies, solidarities, and communities artists formulated and what spaces they were able to occupy in times when it was possible.

Art, music, and other forms of cultural production have become increasingly difficult and costly. As artist Andrea Fraser articulated in 2005, "We're in the midst of the total corporatization and marketization of the artistic field and the historic loss of autonomy won through more than a century of struggle. The field of art and now only nominally public and non-profit institutions has been transformed into a highly competitive global market. The specifically artistic values and criteria that marked the relative autonomy of the artistic field have been overtaken by quantitative criteria . . . a popular and rich artist is almost invariably considered a good artist."[1] In other words, what Dave Beech refers to as "the capitalist drive to develop technologies of value production" has resulted in the value of art becoming equated to its monetary value, which is drawn from the matrix of global corporate interests that have little or no relation to aesthetics or innovation.[2] Equating commercial value with cultural value has pushed the United States into full cultural crisis.

For music, the value system has followed a similar pattern. Capital and digitization have devalued music as an art form, have elevated just a few "stars" who largely work in easily replicated and known forms, and have denigrated others who critique those who have received the endorsement of such marketing schemes. The symbiotic relationship between capital and a value system that is scaled to reflect capital interests has changed how we perceive and appreciate our sensory experiences. What we appreciate and what we disregard is informed by these scales of value.

Up until the early 2000s, it was still possible for musicians to make some income from the sale of records. But now music may be immediately replicated using digital technology, which has effectively caused most music to transition from what Beech refers to as *commodity* to *commons* but which is still set within an economic system that otherwise has not transitioned, thus robbing musicians of the products and financial benefits of their labor.[3] Streaming platforms make billions of dollars from an industry that provides little benefit to the vast majority of musicians.

To exacerbate the financial situation that most musicians face, since the 1990s, the formation of communities in urban settings, where music is most dynamically produced, has become less and less possible. This book itself charts how the Williamsburg artist community evolved from working class to middle class to upper middle class in just twenty-five years, though there were many exceptions to the general trend.[4] Largely because music making is based on a system of exploited labor, music itself has become grossly devalued through these years in terms of product, and class has been the prime determinant of who can participate in the process. As drummer Ryan Sawyer stated, "I want to live in a country that supports artists and the common person in general. When I was first making music in the early 2000s, there was a thin veil, but now the veil is off, and the system of capitalism is attacking us. The people in power want poor people to die, and if they sacrifice parts of the middle class, that's just collateral damage."[5] For an artist to move to Williamsburg today and engage in noncommercial art, they would have to be a millionaire.

Capital fractured the social landscape of Williamsburg in dramatic fashion. While gradual gentrification contributed to this process, it was suddenly accelerated and exacerbated by the 2005 rezoning implemented by the administration of Michael Bloomberg. This cut out significant pieces of a formerly culturally productive landscape, or, from a sensory standpoint, it cast an enforced silence across patches of Williamsburg where live music was no longer welcome or possible. Vibrant, colorful murals were also often removed when buildings were torn down, changing the visual palette of the neighborhood as well. A new generation of young professionals working in the finance sector took root in the luxury condos that resulted from new construction, while trust-fund hipsters who were there to live a faux-bohemian life found loopholes in the system and could afford to hire lawyers to exploit loft laws to take over former art spaces.[6] When loft buildings were taken over by developers, artists were sometimes evicted by the dozens or even hundreds. As these wealthy interests moved into the neighborhood, they did not intermingle with the existing social milieu; a luxury condo could not achieve its capital goal when situated next to a club where live music would disrupt the silence that was required. With the momentum on the side of capital, these zones of silence metastasized, imploding everything with which they came into contact. The manner by which the Williamsburg arts community was dismembered should serve as a warning to creative communities elsewhere in the United States.

Williamsburg was hardly the only part of Brooklyn that experienced destruction and displacement during the period covered in this book. Graham Avenue, for example, was the heart of the Puerto Rican community and has witnessed wide displacement of its population and sites of cultural production owing to escalating rental prices and the influx of wealthier residents. Fulton Street, running from southern Bedford-Stuyvesant to Fort Greene, was a particularly potent Black cultural district for many decades that has since been encroached on by developers flipping coveted brownstones; pushing out businesses, artists, and other residents; and moving people with higher incomes into the area. In southern Park Slope, an art scene that emerged in the late 1980s and peaked in the early 2000s has since been entirely displaced by capital forces: a brownstone that sold for $200,000 in the 1990s today is worth $4 million. And so on and on. All of these cultural zones, and numerous others even just within Brooklyn, are certainly deserving of study to uncover their unique cultural dynamics and the circumstances of their emergence and displacement.

Art space, and by extension community, is the cornerstone of cultural production, as outlined in this book. In other words, a music community cannot be culturally dynamic without space where artists are able to evolve existing cultural forms and forge new ones. New York's city government did not see the Williamsburg arts community (and many other cultural districts, including those just noted) as possessing real value. In fact, it seems that in some ways they did not see them at all. As urban ethnographer Jasmine Mahmoud has noted, the Bloomberg administration's official language of rezoning in Williamsburg characterized the neighborhood as "empty" and even saw artists as a necessary first wave to prime an area considered to be on the "frontier" so it could be made ready for profitable development.[7] Indeed, as one report from 2006 stated, the rezoning was aimed at "revitalizing underutilized land for economic development and expanding the city's property tax base."[8] In the takeover of Williamsburg, Brooklyn was colonized primarily by Manhattan capital, a process that has continued unabated on a broader scale up to the present time throughout the outer boroughs. Culture and community have been the casualties of capital.

Most cultural production is not commercially profitable and therefore cannot sustain itself. If any society is to have a thriving culture, it must invest in it; otherwise, culture will be left to starve. Even a scene like Williamsburg, overflowing with gifted individual artists, could not compete with the spatial displacement brought on by capital. This is purely because artists, especially those of the avant-garde, are dealing with the elemental forces of culture and rarely operate the mechanisms of power, taste, or value. Capital forces—the divergent interests embodied in capital—have little interest in cultural innovation and in fact are often threatened by it. Rather, the forces of capital are invested in existing cultural forms that already have a good degree of recognized value. Building since the 1960s, these forces have slowed the cultural evolution of the United States to a halt as the mechanisms of cultural reproduction (recasting the old as new) seek ever more frantically to market the past to people as progress or change. American cultural stagnation is the result of these manipulations and schemes.

The American cultural crisis is no less substantial than its present political crisis. The vast majority of the music illuminated in this book was created in illegal, unlicensed art spaces. The fact that such spaces were available in abundance in Williamsburg is the only reason the scene was able to take root there in the first place. Most of the venues were under constant threat of closure and fines throughout their existence and thus had to remain an underground cultural phenomenon. Though the tentacles of capital occasionally reach down to anoint cultural producers of whom they approve or for whom strategies of profit extraction may be formulated, most culture when first produced has little commercial value precisely because its newness gives it less cultural resonance than something that is already known and recognizable.

So most American artists across disciplines and genres face the monumental challenge of gaining access to space, without which community and creation are not possible. As one musician on the scene observed, for some, their entire existence and cultural practice were being criminalized. "I was an undocumented immigrant, working illegally as a bartender and waitress, and making music in an unlicensed venue. But those are the only kinds of spaces where America's culture is innovating."[9] After 2001 the federal government was also increasing the cost of artist visas and effectively requiring many artists to hire lawyers to navigate the process, making participation inaccessible to most noncitizens. The United States keeps its cultural visionaries at the margins.

Williamsburg art spaces were almost never in compliance with a wide range of safety codes. While this may have contributed to the allure of the scene at times, the nation witnessed the cataclysmic tragedy of the Ghost Ship arts collective burning in Oakland, California, in 2016, in which thirty-six people were trapped inside and died during an electronic music show.[10] While law enforcement focused on the surface-level circumstances by charging the tenant who rented the space, there has been no sustained mobilization against the United States' continued institutionalized divestment from its own culture. The circumstances of the Ghost Ship, even the physical layout, were remarkably similar to those of many Williamsburg DIY loft spaces covered in this book. Without any kind of substantial public commitment to funding art spaces throughout the United States that cater to the nonelite, similar tragedies will occur unabated as the country's creative class is kept at the margins by further capital takeover of cities and formerly vibrant cultural spaces.

The current grant system of funding for the arts is grossly inadequate as it is only a manifestation of trickle-down economics in the art world. On a functional scale, giving elite institutions the power to confer grants on a few "worthy" artists only exacerbates the economic disparities ever present in the world of music making. As many musicians noted, most people are left scraping by or have to spend many of their waking hours doing a day job that has nothing to do with their artistic practice, while just a few artists are given grants to do their work. A system in which even the most esteemed practitioners wait with the hope of winning a MacArthur "genius" grant or another lifetime-achievement grant, sometimes late in life, so that they can live with a measure of dignity is not a system that cultivates the exploration, growth, and creativity necessary to have a healthy culture of the arts. Rather, it resembles a lottery as the primary retirement plan—but only those who meet whatever the current cultural demand is and are not too offensive to sensitive tastes have any chance of winning. The grant system also pits people against one another in a contest that undermines the health of artist communities. The making of music and art is increasingly restricted to the upper class, or it is pushed to the margins of American society when produced by other people.

The Williamsburg musicians achieved many aesthetic triumphs. The space available in the early 1990s scene allowed people to explore the possibilities of sound in a variety of unique spaces. Visionaries were able to create sonic environments that inhabited those warehouses and lofts in ways that provided transformative experiences for those who frequented them. The technological innovations that were then spurring a generation of innovative DJs took root there, which allowed for key advancements.

Williamsburg's musicians reached their greatest critical mass from 1998 until about 2005, when the sheer number of people, the mixing of genres, and the addition of the noise palette spurred most of the innovations of the period. Experimentation had international connections and pushed much of the music out of its roots and into a transformative space where free jazz, rock, postpunk, and noise coalesced to allow for considerable innovation, growing in numerous directions and solidifying a North Brooklyn sound that has, in many ways, persisted to the present.

In the early years of the new millennium, with music schools becoming the primary training ground for most participants, many of whom had studied aspects of the twentieth-century classical avant-garde, the primary trend in the music was toward a variety of approaches to creative composition that both reimagined and rejected some of the jazz roots. Even as the

Williamsburg scene faded, free jazz, postpunk, rock, and noise intermingled in new ways that produced some of the most innovative music of the period. Expcrimentation, improvisation, and the pursuit of newness were at the heart of these sonic discoveries.

The Williamsburg avant-garde is but a snapshot of the possibilities of human artistic vision and imagination. When given the opportunity, as enabled by a unique set of socioeconomic factors outlined in this book, the artists involved in the scene managed a broad array of explorations, discoveries, and innovations. Sometimes pushing nigh to the verge of madness (the unthinkable), such perspectives peeled back the veil of the unknown. Ultimately, it is our senses that are tested in these moments when observing the avant-garde in action, as humanity glimpses something that moments before may have seemed impossible made suddenly visceral, conscious, and ecstatic. It is in the outer edges of sense that we encounter our most brilliant and startling discoveries.

Notes

Introduction

1   Rout, "Reflections on the Evolution," 158.

2   Jost, *Free Jazz*.

3   L. Jones, "Changing Same," 126.

4   Charles Gayle, in *Rising Tones Cross*, directed by Ebba Jahn (1985).

5   Heller, *Loft Jazz*, 34–61.

6   Lewis, "Experimental Music in Black and White," 80.

7   Tom Johnson, "The Kitchen Improvises," *Village Voice*, September 24, 1980, 72.

8   Tonic also drew inspiration from Alt Coffee, a small café on Avenue A, which was run by the same owners. Accordionist Ted Reichman curated both venues in the early years of their existence. Ted Reichman, interview by author, digital recording, June 24, 2019.

9   Russolo, *Art of Noises*, 23.

10   Cage, *Silence*, 3.

11   Whiteley, "'Kick Out the Jams,'" 13.

12   Spelman, "Recasting Noise," 24.

13   Mallinder, "Sounds Incorporated," 81.

14 Tham, "Noise as Music," 268.

15 Hegarty, *Noise/Music*, ix.

16 Hegarty, *Noise/Music*, 105.

17 Cogan, "'Do They Owe Us a Living?,'" 84–86.

18 The music of the initial festival was recorded and released: Various, *No New York* (Antilles, 1978); see M. Taylor, *Downtown Book*, 57; Court, *New York Noise*, 54–55; and Lawrence, "Pluralism, Minor Deviations, and Radical Change," 68–69.

19 Azerrad, *Our Band Could Be Your Life*, 231.

20 Reynolds, *Rip It Up and Start Again*, 140.

21 Traber, "Recentering the Listener in Deconstructive Music," 169. Simon Reynolds argued that No Wave bands found it most effective to "stag[e] their revolt against rock tradition using the standard rock instrumentation." Reynolds, *Rip It Up and Start Again*, 140.

22 Reynolds, *Rip It Up and Start Again*, 141.

23 Mereweather, *Art, Anti-art, Non-art*, 13, 16.

24 Hegarty, *Noise/Music*, 133–35; and Novak, *Japanoise*, 13–14.

25 Hegarty, *Noise/Music*, 133.

26 Hegarty, *Noise/Music*, 133.

27 Novak, *Japanoise*, 5.

28 Novak, *Japanoise*, 11.

29 Novak, *Japanoise*, 12.

30 Hermes, *Love Goes to Buildings on Fire*.

31 Attali, *Bruits*; and Barzel, "Praxis of Composition-Improvisation," 176.

32 Barzel, "Praxis of Composition-Improvisation," 176.

33 Russ Johnson, interview by author, digital recording, July 15, 2013.

34 Matt Pavolka, interview by author, digital recording, February 11, 2014.

35 Charles Waters, interview by author, digital recording, October 19, 2015.

36 Pavolka, interview.

37 Johnson, interview.

38 Mike Pride, interview by author, digital recording, August 31, 2013.

39 Waters, interview.

40 Waters, interview.

41 Angelica Sanchez, interview by author, digital recording, June 20, 2019.

42 Andy P. Smith, "Ten Years of Music in Williamsburg 2002–2012: An Oral History," *Medium*, March 4, 2015, https://medium.com/barns-kitchens-hotels -bodegas-and-stadiums/ten-years-of-music-in-williamsburg-2002-2012-an -oral-history-7fa2ac083470.

43 Stallabrass, *Internet Art*, 104; Rigi, "Foundations of a Marxist Theory"; Prey and Rigi, "Value, Rent," 398; and Beech, *Art and Postcapitalism*, 99.

44 Beech, *Art and Postcapitalism*, 100.

45 Sánchez Vásquez, *Art and Society*, 85.

Chapter 1. The Emergence of the Williamsburg Scene

1   "Institute for Young Jews," *New York Times*, July 16, 1903; and Manbeck, *Neighborhoods of Brooklyn*, 206.

2   Thomas W. Ennis, "Brooklyn Walkups Rehabilitated," *New York Times*, September 22, 1965; Miyares and Gowen, "Recreating Borders?," 35; and Duany, *Blurred Borders*, 52.

3   Lisa W. Foderaro, "A Metamorphosis for Old Williamsburg," *New York Times*, July 19, 1987; and Brad Gooch, "The New Bohemia," *New York Magazine*, June 22, 1992, 27. The Gooch article played a role in sparking real estate prospecting in the area, which almost immediately spurred the gentrification of the neighborhood.

4   In 1978 unemployment in Williamsburg generally was 12.1 percent, and among Puerto Rican communities it was even higher. Schneider, *Police Power and Race Riots*, 68.

5   The observer, Jose Ramos, grew up on South Fourth Street and Roebling Street, near the Williamsburg Bridge, in an area where his family had lived for four generations since emigrating from Puerto Rico in the 1950s. Obtaining a union job was his way of "moving into the middle class." Jose Ramos, interview by author, digital recording, August 10, 2020.

6   *Los Sures*, directed by Diego Echeverria (1984).

7   Lydia Cortés, "Lydia Cortés," 354; and Holton, "'Little Things Are Big,'" 16.

8   Gooch, "New Bohemia," 28.

9   Gooch, "New Bohemia," 28.

10 Peter Freiberg, "Artists' Escape to Williamsburg," *SoHo News*, April 30, 1980.

11 Freiberg, "Artists' Escape to Williamsburg."

12 Martin Gansberg, "Williamsburg Violence Reflects Tension in Area," *New York Times*, June 30, 1970; Edmund Newton, "Tension in Williamsburg—Housing for Whom?," *New York Daily Post Magazine*, December 22, 1976, 27; Foderaro, "Metamorphosis for Old Williamsburg"; and Margot Hornblower, "Cultures Clash," *Liberty*, March/April 1988, 23–25.

13 Freiberg, "Artists' Escape to Williamsburg."

14 Foderaro, "Metamorphosis for Old Williamsburg." A multifamily building cost about $150,000 at the time.

15 Richard Curtis, "Improbable Transformation," 1248; and Ric Curtis, "Negligible Role of Gangs," 45.

16 Curtis, "Improbable Transformation," 1249.

17 Brotherton and Barrios, *Almighty Latin King and Queen Nation*, 189–90.

18 Ethan Pettit, interview by author, digital recording, March 19, 2019.

19 In the early 1970s, a number of African American and Latinx artists moved into Williamsburg, before white artists from SoHo arrived around 1976. In 1978 an artist could get a 1,500-square-foot loft for $175 per month. Ann Standaert Bowden, "The Theft of SoHo," *ARTnews*, November 1979, 83; Freiberg, "Artists'

Escape to Williamsburg"; Ed McCormack, "Artists in Residence: Williamsburg's Latest Refugees," *Daily News Magazine*, May 26, 1985; David Samuels, "Local Arts Groups Find Real Estate Success in Brooklyn as Refugees from Manhattan's Notorious 'Space Chase,'" *Phoenix*, February 27, 1986, 17; and Baird Jones, "East Village Art, Brooklyn Artists," *Phoenix*, August 20, 1987.

20 Freiberg, "Artists' Escape to Williamsburg."

21 Freiberg, "Artists' Escape to Williamsburg"; and Foderaro, "Metamorphosis for Old Williamsburg."

22 The 1980 census indicates that approximately thirteen thousand full-time artists and performers lived in Brooklyn at that time. Freiberg, "Artists' Escape to Williamsburg"; and Amy Virshup, "The Newest Left Bank," *New York Magazine*, April 21, 1986.

23 McCormack, "Artists in Residence."

24 Minor Injury, press release, [1985?], Ethan Pettit private collection.

25 Association of Williamsburgh/Greenpoint Artists, press release, December 4, 1987, Brooklyn Museum Library.

26 Foderaro, "Metamorphosis for Old Williamsburg"; and B. Jones, "East Village Art."

27 Pettit, interview.

28 Michael X. Rose, interview by author, digital recording, May 12, 2019. Bruce Springsteen had some of his early shows at the Bottom Line in 1975.

29 Drummer Mike Bell first lived in squats on Thirteenth Street in the East Village and then moved to a warehouse squat at 397 Wythe Avenue between South Sixth Street and Broadway in Williamsburg in 1992. The building had originally been a munitions factory but had also served as an art gallery and performance space for other artists before his arrival. Bell was just one of a large group of people who was part of this move from the East Village to Williamsburg. Todd S. Purdum, "Melee in Tompkins Sq. Park: Violence and Its Provocation," *New York Times*, August 14, 1988; Lisa Napoli, "Police and Protestors Have Clashed Before in Tompkins Square; Gentrification's Price," *New York Times*, August 27, 1988; Dunn, "Never Mind the Bollocks," 194; Belkind, "Stealth Gentrification," 25; and Mike Bell, interview by author, digital recording, March 3, 2019.

30 Roberta Smith, "A Sprinkling of Exhibitions near Factories and the Water," *New York Times*, March 23, 1990.

31 R. Smith, "Sprinkling of Exhibitions." The consistent mislabeling of Newtown Creek as the Gowanus Canal is evidence of the critic's lack of familiarity with the neighborhood and failure to see beyond the arts community.

32 Sarah Ferguson, "Hello Kitty," *Village Voice*, October 30, 1990.

33 Gooch, "New Bohemia," 28.

34 Williamsburg's total population at the time was 115,000. Gooch, "New Bohemia," 27.

35 Heather Roslund, interview by author, digital recording, March 18, 2021.

36　Earwax Records originally opened in Greenpoint but moved to the Williamsburg location in 1990. Tom Schmitz, interview by author, email, January 13, 2021.

37　Hahn, "Cat's Head," 153; and Bell, interview, March 3, 2019.

38　Austin Scaggs, quoted in Goodman, *Meet Me in the Bathroom*, 93.

39　*Los Sures*; and Curtis, "Improbable Transformation," 1247–48.

40　Memorials often included crosses and bore the name of the deceased and the date of death. Nearly all of these, once numerous in the area, have since been covered up or removed. *Los Sures*; and Hahn, "Cat's Head," 154.

41　*Los Sures*.

42　Waters, interview, October 19, 2015; Bell, interview, March 3, 2019; and Sanchez, interview, June 20, 2019.

43　One notorious artist squat, at 529 East Fifth Street, eventually burned down, and Mayor Rudy Giuliani used it as propaganda to charge other artist squats with public endangerment. Waters, interview, October 19, 2015.

44　Bell, interview, March 3, 2019.

45　Waters, interview, October 19, 2015.

46　Gooch, "New Bohemia," 28; and Michael X. Rose, interview by author, digital recording, April 1, 2019.

47　Medea de Vyse, "Discours sur la Moutarde: The Evolution of Warehouse Events in Williamsburg," *Breukelen*, April 1993: 9.

48　Pettit, interview.

49　Pettit, interview. The term *immersive culture* to describe the Williamsburg warehouse movement was first coined in Suzan Wines, "Go with the Flow: Eight New York-Based Artists and Architects in the Digital Era," *Domus Magazine*, February 1998, 8.

50　Ebon Fisher, "You Sub Mod," Nerve Circle handout, 1988, Ebon Fisher private collection.

51　Ebon Fisher, email to author, November 3, 2021.

52　Brainard Carey, "Ebon Fisher," Museum of Non-visible Art: Interviews from Yale University Radio, Praxis, July 20, 2016, https://museumofnonvisibleart .com/interviews/ebon-fisher/; and Pettit, interview.

53　Hahn, "Cat's Head," 154.

54　Ethan Pettit, Ebon Fisher, and Susie Kahlich, "Immersionism, a Brief Introduction," Facebook, February 13, 2011 https://www.facebook.com/notes/ethan -pettit/immersionism/501003277687.

55　Pettit, interview.

56　Gregor Asch (DJ Olive), quoted in Laurent Fintoni, "Detuning the City: An Oral History of Illbient," *Red Bull Music Academy Daily*, August 18, 2014, https:// daily.redbullmusicacademy.com/2014/08/illbient-oral-history.

57　Dineen was a writer and a stand-up comedian who also worked in theater, basing some of her writing on her experience working as a waitress in Manhattan. Pottiez was a jack-of-all-trades who played music. Terry Dineen, interview by author, digital recording, October 11, 2020.

58 Hahn, "Cat's Head," 153–54; and Dineen, interview.

59 Peter Watrous, "Tomorrow's Stars Today in Brooklyn's Small Clubs," *New York Times*, March 23, 1990.

60 Dineen, interview.

61 Anna Hurwitz, interview by author, digital recording, April 17, 2019.

62 Watrous, "Tomorrow's Stars."

63 Like most DIY art spaces of the time, the bar operated without a license. Undercover police did come to the venue one evening, before one of the performances began, but they decided not to press charges against the proprietors because it was a small operation. Watrous, "Tomorrow's Stars"; and Hahn, "Cat's Head," 154.

64 Hurwitz, interview.

65 Hurwitz, interview.

66 Watrous, "Tomorrow's Stars."

67 Watrous, "Tomorrow's Stars."

68 Concert poster, Lizard's Tail, August 1989, Ethan Pettit private collection.

69 Jon Pareles, "Folk-Rock: The Fort in Series," *New York Times*, April 12, 1987.

70 Concert poster, Lizard's Tail, August 1989; concert poster, Lizard's Tail, September 21, 1990, Ethan Pettit private collection; and Brenda Kahn, *Goldfish Don't Talk Back* (Community 3, 1990).

71 Billy Syndrome played some of his early concerts at the Chameleon Club. He later formed a band named the Billy Syndrome. The Billy Syndrome, *Bootleg of My Choice* (Savage Smut, 1987); the Billy Syndrome, *The Power of Love* (Savage Smut, 1988); concert poster, Lizard's Tail, June 24, 1989, Ethan Pettit private collection; Jon Pareles, "270 Rock Bands to Perform at 10th New Music Seminar," *New York Times*, July 14, 1989; and Bell, interview, March 3, 2019.

72 Fly Ashtray gained some notoriety at the New Music Seminar in 1987. "Rebels to Revivalists: Who's Who at Seminar," *New York Times*, July 10, 1987; concert poster, Lizard's Tail, June 24, 1989; and concert poster, Lizard's Tail, August 1989, Ethan Pettit private collection.

73 Brian B., "Tina Fey Tapped for Curly Oxide and Vic Thrill," MovieWeb, August 26, 2004, https://movieweb.com/tina-fey-tapped-for-curly-oxide-and -vic-thrill/; and Ray Brazen, "Williamsburg, before It Was a Hipster Shithole," *Brazenblog!*, June 7, 2017, http://raybrazen.blogspot.com/2017/06 /williamsburg-before-it-was-hipster.html.

74 Brazen, "Williamsburg."

75 Ken Butler, interview by author, digital recording, September 13, 2016.

76 Butler, interview, September 13, 2016.

77 Concert poster, Lizard's Tail, August 1989, Ethan Pettit private collection.

78 Anthony Coleman, interview by author, digital recording, June 11, 2019.

79 Coleman also considered the early music by the Contortions, Suicide, and Gang of Four to have been influential. These influences, in turn, made their mark on the Knitting Factory scene with groups and figures such as electronic

experimentalists Odd Jobs, the work of harpist Zeena Parkins, and the early music of John Zorn's Naked City. A. Coleman, interview.

80 Playing with David Shea and Dave Douglas, who limited him to just producing loops and noise, compelled Coleman to work even harder to establish the sampler as an improvising instrument. A. Coleman, interview.

81 Early samplers were limited by memory space, but the ARS-10, which Coleman obtained in the early 1990s, was a major leap forward.

82 Coleman's recorded sampler tracks include, among others, "Trend Man," on Anthony Coleman, *Disco by Night*, Composers series (Avant, 1992), track 3; "Johnny Come Lately," on Roy Nathanson and Anthony Coleman, *Lobster and Friend* (Knitting Factory Works, 1993), track 6; "At the Rabbi's Table," on David Krakauer, *Klezmer Madness!*, Radical Jewish Culture, no. 1 (Tzadik, 1995), track 4; and "Ben," on Roy Nathanson and Anthony Coleman, *I Could've Been a Drum*, Radical Jewish Culture, no. 13 (Tzadik, 1997), track 9.

83 Happy Land Social Club had served the Honduran community of the East Tremont section of the Bronx as an after-hours dance club. The Bronx building had been in violation of numerous safety codes, and an arrest warrant for the owner, real estate tycoon Alexander DiLorenzo III, had never been enforced before the fire. At the time, the arson was the biggest mass murder in the history of the United States. James C. McKinley Jr., "Fire in the Bronx; Happy Land Reopened and Flourished after Being Shut as a Hazard," *New York Times*, March 26, 1990; Josh Barbanel, "Happy Land Arrest Order Ignored in 1989," *New York Times*, April 3, 1990; and Bromley, "Globalization and the Inner Periphery," 201–2.

84 It was estimated that approximately 1,220 such "social clubs" existed in New York City at the time; they were very popular. Don Terry, "Fire in the Bronx; Social Club Crackdown Is the Latest in a Series," *New York Times*, March 26, 1990; and James C. McKinley Jr., "Dinkins Reduces Task Force on Safety of Social Clubs," *New York Times*, June 30, 1990.

85 Hahn, "Cat's Head," 154.

86 Event flyer, Lizard's Tail, April 19–20, 1990, Ethan Pettit private collection.

87 Ebon Fisher, email to author, October 25, 2021; and Ebon Fisher, email to author, October 29, 2021.

88 Ebon Fisher, "The Sex Salon and the Web Jam: Rediscovering the Value of Social Ritual," *Utne Reader*, January/February 1995, 52.

89 Sam Binkley, "Learning from the Sex Salon (Was It Good for You Too?)," *Word of Mouth*, March 1990, 3.

90 Ebon Fisher, email to author, October 25, 2021.

91 Jean François Pottiez, quoted in Hahn, "Cat's Head," 153, 155. Since the mid-1980s, there had also been a counterculture reacting to the commodification of the New York art scene, manifesting first in the East Village but also seeming to take hold in Williamsburg. Gregor Asch (DJ Olive), interview by author, digital recording, April 7, 2019. Anna Hurwitz expressed similar sentiments. Hurwitz, interview.

92 A local staging company was going out of business at the time, so the organizers of the first Cat's Head event obtained a thousand-square-foot stage at low cost. The owners of the empty factory allowed them to use the space in exchange for "clearing debris and junk off an old roof." Hurwitz, interview; see also Dineen, interview.

93 Mike Cohen, "The Cat's Head and Sonic Youth and the Disco Inferno," *Word of Mouth*, August 1990, 1, 6.

94 Hahn, "Cat's Head," 153; see also Butler, interview, September 13, 2016.

95 Dineen, interview.

96 Hurwitz, quoted in Hahn, "Cat's Head," 155–56.

97 Hurwitz, interview.

98 Gooch, "New Bohemia," 29; and Hahn, "Cat's Head," 156.

99 Dineen, interview.

100 Hurwitz, interview.

101 Founded on the Bowery by Hilly Kristal, CBGBs was where punk bands such as Patti Smith and the Ramones played their first concerts, among many other seminal punk luminaries since the mid-1970s. Concert poster, the Cat's Head, July 14, 1990, Ethan Pettit private collection; John Rockwell, "Patti Smith Plans Album with Eyes on Stardom," *New York Times*, March 28, 1975; John Rockwell, "Speculations about Rock Spectacles," *New York Times*, May 16, 1975; and Cohen, "Cat's Head," 6.

102 Hurwitz, interview.

103 Hahn, "Cat's Head," 156.

104 Ferguson, "Hello Kitty."

105 Hurwitz, interview.

106 Hurwitz, interview; and Dineen, interview. Brooklyn Brewery sponsored the event.

107 Ferguson, "Hello Kitty."

108 Hurwitz, interview.

109 Ferguson, "Hello Kitty."

110 Cop Shoot Cop had emerged as an innovative new band on the punk–experimental–noise scene at CBGBs and the Knitting Factory in Manhattan by 1989. Cop Shoot Cop, *Live at CBGB* (Supernatural Organization, 1989); Peter Watrous, "The Pop Life," *New York Times*, September 18, 1991; event poster, the Cat's Head, October 6, 1990, Ethan Pettit private collection; and concert poster, the Cat's Head, October 6, 1990, Ethan Pettit private collection.

111 Michael J. Zwicky, interview by author, digital recording, April 3, 2019.

112 Zwicky, interview.

113 Moondoc was a central figure of the 1970s jazz loft era with Ensemble Muntu and has continued to lead bands up to the present. Bradley, *Universal Tonality*, 118–23. Borbetomagus, formed in 1979 by Don Dietrich and Jim Sauter, was on the forefront of the free jazz–noise–punk–rock innovations of the 1980s and after, and had a distinct impact on Japanese noise. Borbetomagus, *Live at In-Roads*

(Aeon, 1983). Sun Ra (1914–93) is too prolific to summarize easily but was one of the most influential and eclectic musicians of the twentieth century across a wide array of Black creative, avant-garde, jazz, and space music.

114 Zwicky, interview.

115 The only recording of the project was done at Nada Gallery on July 6–8, 1985. Scrap Metal Music, *Scrap Metal Music* (Screwgun Music, 1985).

116 Zwicky, interview.

117 Helena Mulkerns, "The Cat's Head II: On the Waterfront," *Downtown*, October 24, 1990, 32A–33A.

118 Gooch, "New Bohemia," 29.

119 Dineen, interview.

120 Dineen, interview.

121 Hurwitz, interview.

122 Lauren Szold emerged as an innovative sculptor and painter by the mid-1980s, working in feminist interpretations of the female body. Hahn, "Cat's Head," 158; Helen A. Harrison, "Not So Innocent 'Paper Dolls,'" *New York Times*, September 1, 1985; Lauren Szold, press release for *Medea's First Period*, June 5, 1991, Ethan Pettit private collection; event poster, Flytrap, June 15, 1991, Ethan Pettit private collection; event poster [2], Flytrap, June 15, 1991, Ethan Pettit private collection; Roberta Smith, "Art in Review," *New York Times*, June 26, 1992; Roberta Smith, "Art in Review," *New York Times*, December 4, 1992; Vivien Raynor, "Contemporary Artists Travel Two Paths in Hartford Shows," *New York Times*, April 4, 1993; and Roberta Smith, "Group Shows of Every Kind, Even Where the Show Itself Is an Art Form," *New York Times*, February 25, 1994.

123 Zwicky, interview.

124 No recording of the Flytrap performance survives, but there is a recording of a live radio performance from the same period. Fihi Ma Fihi, *Live at WKCR* (unreleased, n.d.).

125 At the time Pfahler was integral to the East Village artist community, where she resided in a squat for many years and was well known for her advocacy for victims of HIV-AIDS. Schulman, *Gentrification of the Mind*, 86.

126 Kembra Pfahler quoted in Bob Morris, "Karen Black on the Town," *New York Times*, January 16, 1994.

127 Ebon Fisher, Organism event poster, June 12, 1993, Ethan Pettit private collection.

128 Wines, "Go with the Flow," 90.

129 Kelly Webb, "A Bedtime Story," Organism catalog (June 1993), 58, Ebon Fisher, private collection.

130 Ebon Fisher, email to author, November 9, 2021.

131 Webb, "Bedtime Story," 57.

132 Wines, "Go with the Flow," 90.

133 Zachary Woolfe, "Williamsburg's Arcadian Past: Composer Billy Basinski Stars in Robert Wilson's Quasi-Opera *The Life and Death of Marina*

Abramovic," *Observer* (New York), November 1, 2011, https://observer.com
/2011/11/williamsburgs-arcadian-past-composer-billy-basinski-stars-in
-robert-wilsons-quasi-opera-the-life-and-death-of-marina-abramovic/; and
William Basinski, "William Basinski," *Flaunt,* December 1, 2013, http://www
.flaunt.com/content/art/william-basinski.

134 Mariano Airaldi, interview by author, digital recording, May 1, 2019.

135 Jeff Gompertz, interview by author, digital recording, May 17, 2019.

136 Jeff Gompertz and DJ Olive DJ'd the ground floor often. Gompertz obtained all
the interesting records he could find at Earwax for his selections, with the "cut-
and-paste" techniques of composer Christian Marclay as his inspiration. Gompertz, interview.

137 Gompertz had grown up listening to the WKCR and WFMU radio stations, and
he was committed to linking together different independent and underground
music scenes. Gompertz, interview.

138 Airaldi, interview.

139 Gompertz, interview.

140 Gooch, "New Bohemia," 26, 29.

141 Gabrielle Latessa Ortiz, interview by author, digital recording, April 18, 2019.

142 "Welcome to Lalalandia," *Paper Magazine,* Summer 1993, [1].

143 V. Owen Bush, "The Omnisensorialists 1991–1999" (unpublished essay, 2009,
posted to Immersionism Facebook discussion group, January 19, 2012), https://
www.facebook.com/notes/ethan-pettit/the-omnisensorialists-1991-1999
/10150489040717688.

144 Asch (DJ Olive), interview, April 7, 2019.

145 Latessa Ortiz, interview.

146 Airaldi, quoted in "Welcome to Lalalandia," [1].

147 Wines, "Go with the Flow," 6.

148 In some sense, omnisensorialism seems a precursor to later theories of immersionism. Asch (DJ Olive), interview, April 7, 2019; and Latessa Ortiz, interview.

149 Gregor Asch (DJ Olive), "Is That a Chicken in My Coat?," DJ Olive's website,
accessed April 8, 2019, http://www.djolive.com/lalalandia.html; Neil Strauss,
"At the Clubs, Murmurs and Ambient Music," *New York Times,* March 8, 1996.
Airaldi echoed these statements. Airaldi, interview.

150 Gregor Asch (DJ Olive), interview by author, digital recording, April 10, 2019.

151 Airaldi, interview.

152 Asch (DJ Olive), interview, April 10, 2019.

153 Asch was the son of two ethnographic filmmakers and had grown up living in a
number of different parts of the world, so his sense of a globally connected culture had been fostered from an early age. Asch (DJ Olive), interview, April 10,
2019.

154 Asch (DJ Olive), quoted in Fintoni, "Detuning the City."

155 Wines, "Go with the Flow," 6.

156 Comfort Zone Banquet was held at 232 Grand Street. Lalalandia Entertainment Research Corporation, flyer, n.d., Ethan Pettit private collection; and Asch, "Is That a Chicken in My Coat?"

157 Lalalandia Entertainment Research Corporation, flyer, n.d.; and Gooch, "New Bohemia," 31.

158 Emerson, quoted in Gooch, "New Bohemia," 31.

159 Airaldi, quoted in Gooch, "New Bohemia," 31.

160 Asch, "Is That a Chicken in My Coat?" The titles reference well-known lounge songs.

161 Bush, "Omnisensorialists."

162 Latessa Ortiz, interview.

163 Asch (DJ Olive), interview, April 10, 2019; and Lalalandia Entertainment Research Corporation, flyer, n.d.

164 Latessa Ortiz, interview.

165 Butler, interview, September 13, 2016; and Asch (DJ Olive), interview, April 10, 2019.

166 Asch, "Is That a Chicken in My Coat?"; see also Strauss, "At the Clubs"; and "Welcome to Lalalandia," [1].

167 Wines, "Go with the Flow," 7.

168 Neil Strauss, "The Cutting Edge," *New York Times*, January 3, 1997; Ben Ratliff, "At Vinyl, Fast-Paced Techno for Dancers Only," *New York Times*, January 6, 1997; Ethan Pettit, "The Inflatable Man: Dennis Del Zotto and the Williamsburg Scene," Ethan Pettit Gallery, June 7, 2006, https://ethanpettit.blogspot.com/2006/06/dennis-del-zotto-and-williamsburg-scene.html; and Asch (DJ Olive), interview, April 10, 2019.

169 Airaldi, interview.

170 Asch (DJ Olive), interview, April 7, 2019.

171 Latessa Ortiz, interview.

172 Asch (DJ Olive), interview, April 7, 2019; see also Bush, "Omnisensorialists"; and Asch (DJ Olive), interview, April 10, 2019.

173 Ethan Pettit, "Lalalandia," Facebook archive, November 10, 2014, accessed April 11, 2019.

174 Bush, "Omnisensorialists."

175 Asch (DJ Olive), interview, April 7, 2019.

176 Asch (DJ Olive), quoted in Fintoni, "Detuning the City."

177 Pettit, interview.

178 Airaldi focused on production, sound loops, and installations. Airaldi had begun experimenting with record loops as a child and had continued to work on ambient sound and soundscapes through his life. Butler, interview, September 13, 2016; Latessa Ortiz, interview; and Airaldi, interview.

179 Asch (DJ Olive), interview, April 7, 2019.

180 Fintoni, "Detuning the City."

181 Butler, interview, September 13, 2016.

182 Latessa, interview; see also Bush, "Omnisensorialists."

183 The early to mid-1990s saw galleries, music venues, and other unlicensed spaces closed on a mass scale. "36 Unsafe Social Clubs Chained and Locked," *New York Times*, April 5, 1990; James C. McKinley Jr., "New York Social Clubs Safer, but Problems Linger," *New York Times*, March 26, 1991; Jesse McKinley, "The Café Police Pop In for a Raid," *New York Times*, July 5, 1998; and Asch (DJ Olive), interview, April 7, 2019.

184 Developers had been eyeing the Williamsburg waterfront since the 1980s. Foderaro, "Metamorphosis for Old Williamsburg"; Marvine Howe, "Cabaret Law Would Aid Neighbors of Nightclubs," *New York Times*, July 26, 1992; and David M. Halbfinger, "For a Bar Not Used to Dancing around Issues, Dancing Is Now the Issue," *New York Times*, July 29, 1997.

185 Airaldi, interview.

186 The El Sensorium space became Rubulad in 1994, a rock music loft. Asch (DJ Olive), interview, April 7, 2019; and Latessa Ortiz, interview.

187 Lalalandia did several events in Manhattan venues as well as one at the High Museum of Art in Atlanta. Steve Dollar, "Event's Intent Is to Lose Yourself in Lala Land," *Atlanta Journal*, August 27, 1993; Asch (DJ Olive), interview, April 10, 2019; and Latessa Ortiz, interview.

188 Fintoni, "Detuning the City"; see also Strauss, "At the Clubs." Gregor Asch coined the term *illbient* to describe ambient music that was designed to make the audience ill at ease.

189 Bush, "Omnisensorialists."

190 Laurent Fintoni, "Illbient, Tension and the Brooklyn Immersionist Movement: DJ Olive in Conversation," *Medium*, October 14, 2014, https://medium.com /dancing-about-architecture/illbient-tension-and-the-brooklyn-immersionist -movement-dj-olive-in-conversation-6abdbe6c53d4; and Michaelangelo Matos, "The Bunker's Bryan Kasenic on the Berliniamsburg Era, Throwing Parties for Electronic-Music Nerds, and 'Amateur Night,'" *Village Voice*, January 6, 2012.

191 Rose resided in a back-lot shack at 291 Devoe Street, in what is now the Morgantown section of Bushwick. Rose, interview, April 1, 2019.

192 Greenpoint and Williamsburg communities eventually led a movement against Radiac, owing to the health risk to the neighborhood, and it closed in 1994. The movement was led by the Toxic Avengers of El Puente, a member organization of the National Congress of Puerto Rican Rights. Morales, "History and Recent Developments," 19; Soto-Lopez, "Environmental Justice for Puerto Ricans," 133; Allan R. Gold, "2 Brooklyn Areas Ask What Factories Are Doing to Them," *New York Times*, April 21, 1990; Gina Maranto, "The Big Dirty Apple," *New York Times*, August 26, 1990; Dennis Hevesi, "Protest Forms over Radioactive Waste in Brooklyn," *New York Times*, May 26, 1991; Kate Stone Lombardi, "Tons of Chemical Waste from Homes in County," *New York Times*, August 11, 1991; and Garry Pierre-Pierre, "Breathing Easier after the Last Shipment of Radioactive Waste," *New York Times*, June 12, 1994.

193 Brazen, "Williamsburg."

194 Michael X. Rose, untitled essay, *Waterfront Week*, July 29, 1992.

195 Rose, interview, April 1, 2019.

196 The name October Revolution had no relation to Bill Dixon's well-known 1964 October Revolution in Jazz, held at the Cellar Door, that sparked the Jazz Composers Guild. Rose, interview, April 1, 2019.

197 Jason Merritt, interview by author, digital recording, August 1, 2018. The shantytown included what is now North Fifth Street Pier and Park, East River State Park, Bushwick Inlet Park, and adjoining areas.

198 Merritt, interview.

199 Baker eventually went blind. Raphie Frank, "Ralph Baker, (Refusing to Be) Blind Photographer," *Gothamist*, September 10, 2005, http://gothamist.com /2005/09/10/ralph_baker_refusing_to_be_blind_photographer.php; and Matt Bua, interview by author, digital recording, March 18, 2019.

200 Bell, interview, March 3, 2019; and Rose, interview, April 1, 2019.

201 Michael X. Rose, concert flyer, October 12, 1991, Michael X. Rose private collection.

202 Michael X. Rose, concert flyer, October 12, 1991, Michael X. Rose private collection.

203 Bell, interview, March 3, 2019; Mikels, *The Astro-Zombies* (1968).

204 Michael X. Rose, quoted in David Grad, "The Astro Zombies," *Sound Views*, 11.

205 Rose, interview, April 1, 2019.

206 Lynyrd Skynyrd, *Second Helping* (MCA Records, 1974).

207 Michael X. Rose, interview, April 1, 2019.

208 Rose released a mixed tape of music by the bands featured on the bill for March 21, 1992. Liner notes, *October Revolution* (self-released, 1992).

209 Contrary to the information on the poster, the event did not happen at Dunham Place. Michael X. Rose, concert poster, July 4–5, 1992, Michael X. Rose private collection; and Rose, interview, April 1, 2019.

210 Mike Bell, interview by author, digital recording, August 27, 2019.

211 The Billy Syndrome, *Ill Mess* (Slutfish Recordings, 1995); and the Billy Syndrome, *The Billy Syndrome* (Slutfish Recordings, 1999).

212 Brazen, "Williamsburg."

213 Brazen, "Williamsburg."

214 Hahn, "Cat's Head," 154.

215 Gooch, "New Bohemia," 30; see also Butler, interview, September 13, 2016.

216 John Gallagher was the former lead singer of the Queens-based band Moving Violation. Gooch, "New Bohemia," 30; and Bell, interview, March 3, 2019.

217 Hideji Taninaka, interview by author, email, April 26, 2019.

218 Zwicky, interview; and Taninaka, interview.

219 Taninaka, interview.

220 Butler, interview, September 13, 2016.

221 Bonnie Kane, interview by author, digital recording, November 1, 2021.

222 Many of W.O.O.'s live recordings have been preserved and released, though no recordings of their gigs in Williamsburg have been released. W.O.O., *Should've, Might as Well: CS60, Live at CBGBs* (Sweet Stuff, 1989); and W.O.O., *W.O.O.topia: Live from Europe* (Funky Mushroom, 1994).

223 Kane, interview.

224 *Waterfront Week* was founded in 1991 and ran for nearly twelve years. It acquired a more formal editorial staff in 1994 and evolved from informal bulletin board into a community newsletter. Spike Vrusho, "Waterfront Week, R.I.P.," *New York Press*, July 16, 2002; and Pettit, interview.

225 Brazen, "Williamsburg."

226 Ando Arike, "Kerry Smith, Legendary Right Bank Café Owner, Dies at 67; Gala Memorial Planned for January," *Williamsburg Observer*, November 24, 2014, http://www.williamsburgobserver.org/2014/11/24/kerry-smith-dies-at-67/.

227 Reuben Radding, interview by author, digital recording, August 10, 2015.

228 Concert poster, Right Bank Café, November 18, 1994, Mike Bell private collection; Bell, interview, March 3, 2019; and Brazen, "Williamsburg."

229 Bell, interview, March 3, 2019.

230 Horak, *Saul Bass*, 193, 202, 261–64; and Bell, interview, March 3, 2019.

231 Brazen, "Williamsburg."

232 Brazen, "Williamsburg."

233 Radding, interview.

234 The drug was brought from the artist colony in Woodstock until the people involved got arrested by the police. Hurwitz, interview.

235 Malbon, *Clubbing*, 20; Reynolds, *Generation Ecstasy*, 139; and Takahashi and Olaveson, "Music, Dance and Raving Bodies," 80–83, 88.

236 Freiberg, "Artists' Escape to Williamsburg"; Peter Freiberg, "Loft Tenants Getting Their Act Together," *SoHo News*, May 7, 1980; and Jared McCallister, "Some Face Eviction from Loft Dwellings," *New York Daily News*, January 14, 1986.

237 Schmitz, interview, January 13, 2021.

238 The earliest proposals for large-scale transformations were not allowed owing to zoning laws, such as the one proposed by developer Morris Bailey in 1987 between North Fifth and North Eleventh Streets, which would have included 2,500 apartments and 120,000 square feet of light-industrial space. Other, less ambitious projects, however, began to chip away at the existing landscape of the area. Foderaro, "Metamorphosis for Old Williamsburg."

239 Between 2000 and 2010, the South Side witnessed a displacement of approximately 20 percent of its Latinx population. Foderaro, "Metamorphosis for Old Williamsburg"; Newman and Wyly, "Right to Stay Put," 47; and Ward Dennis, interview by author, digital recording, March 12, 2021.

240 Schmitz, interview, January 13, 2021.

241 The L Café on Bedford Avenue between North Sixth and North Seventh Streets was one of the first new coffee shops of the arts era and became a social hub for

artists, though it was also a clear mark of gentrification. Butler, interview, September 1, 3, 2016.

Chapter 2. Pirate Radio and Jumping the River

1 Steve Albini, "The Problem with Music," *Baffler*, no. 5 (December 1993), https://thebaffler.com/salvos/the-problem-with-music. By 2004 Albini had produced an estimated 1,500 records, mostly with bands that remained relatively unknown, though they also included prominent bands such as Nirvana, Godspeed You! Black Emperor, Cheap Trick, and Jimmy Page, among many others.

2 Hauser, *Boxing Scene*, 19; and Andrew Barker, interview by author, digital recording, June 18, 2015.

3 Even though Presidente was a Dominican beer, it had been imported into Puerto Rico for decades and was one of the preferred recreational beverages among the Puerto Rican community of South Williamsburg. Duany, *Blurred Borders*, 175–76; and Damian Catera, interview by author, digital recording, August 18, 2015.

4 Tunde Adebimpe, quoted in Goodman, *Meet Me in the Bathroom*, 95. The band TV on the Radio was formed in Brooklyn in 2001 and put out a self-released record before signing with Touch and Go Records and releasing the award-winning *Desperate Youth, Blood Thirsty Babes* in 2004.

5 Joseph-Hunter, "Transmission Arts," 34.

6 Roe was a co-owner of Blue Chair, a record store and alternative cultural center in Ybor City. Police SWAT teams closed down 87X on November 19, 1997, more than two years after Roe had moved to New York. Simpson, "Streets, Sidewalks, Stores, and Stories," 686, 690–701, 708; Dean Solov, "Feds Shut Down Pirate Radio Stations," *Tampa Tribune*, November 20, 1997; and Jim Cullen, "Pirate Radio Fights for Free Speech," *Progressive Populist*, April 1998, https://www.populist.com/98.4.pirate.html; Ray Roa, "Music Issue: Edwin Velez Opened His Doors to Misfits Galore," *Creative Loafing Tampa Bay*, July 13, 2017, https://www.cltampa.com/music/local/article/20867434/music-issue-edwin-velez-opened-his-doors-to-misfits-galore; and Matt Mikas, interview by author, digital recording, April 14, 2019.

7 Jason Merritt, interview by author, digital recording, August 1, 2018.

8 Merritt, interview.

9 Heller, *Loft Jazz*.

10 Montgomery Knott, interview by author, digital recording, August 6, 2020.

11 Tom Roe and Galen Joseph-Hunter, interview by author, digital recording, July 21, 2015.

12 Joseph-Hunter, "Transmission Arts," 34.

13 Roe and Joseph-Hunter, interview.

14 Ferrell, "Youth, Crime, and Cultural Space," 30; Zimmermann, *States of Emergency*, 156–57; and Brinson, "Liberation Frequency," 549.

15 Later, with support from both congressional Democrats and Senator John McCain, the US Congress passed laws giving micro radio stations broader rights.

16 Roe and Joseph-Hunter, interview.

17 John S. W. MacDonald, "free 103point9: Ten Years of Transmission Arts," *Brooklyn Rail*, July 6, 2007.

18 Singer-songwriter Edith Frost rented the apartment at 97 South Sixth Street in the interim, between the tenure of the Hells Angels and that of Roe.

19 Roe and Joseph-Hunter, interview.

20 Joseph-Hunter, "Transmission Arts," 34.

21 Roe and Joseph-Hunter, interview.

22 Catera, interview, August 18, 2015.

23 Brinson, "Liberation Frequency," 549, 556, 565n2; and Sassaman and Tridish, "Prometheus Radio Project," 183.

24 Dunifer and Sakolsky, *Seizing the Airwaves*; and Sassaman and Tridish, "Prometheus Radio Project," 183.

25 Mikas, interview.

26 MacDonald, "free 103point9"; and Mikas, interview.

27 MacDonald, "free 103point9."

28 Waters, interview, October 19, 2015.

29 Catera, interview, August 18, 2015.

30 Catera, interview, August 18, 2015.

31 Matt Mottel, interview by author, digital recording, November 24, 2015.

32 Roe and Joseph-Hunter, interview.

33 Gold Sparkle Band released seven records from 1994 to 2004, three of them appearing on the Squealer label and one on Waters's own label, Nu Records. They included Gold Sparkle Band, *Downsizing* (Nu Records, 1997); Gold Sparkle Band, *Nu-Soul Zodiac* (Squealer, 1999); and Gold Sparkle Band, *Fugues and Flowers* (Squealer, 2002).

34 Barker had also studied percussion at the school with Jack Bell. Roni Sarig, "Mr. Ruzow's Opus: The Gold Sparkler Who Stayed behind Builds Community with a Little Improvisation," *Vibes* (Atlanta), May 1–7, 2002, 86.

35 Sarig, "Mr. Ruzow's Opus," 86.

36 Barker credits multi-instrumentalist and improviser Daniel Carter as a major inspiration for moving to New York in the first place.

37 Tom Roe, "Gold Sparkle Band: Atlanta Transplants' Multifarious Orbits Converging," *Signal to Noise* 17 (May/June 2000): 13; and Charles Waters, interview by author, digital recording, March 6, 2019.

38 Roger Ruzow, quoted in Jon C. Morgan, "Gold Sparkle Band," *Copper Press* 5 (n.d.).

39 Waters, quoted in Roe, "Gold Sparkle Band," 13.

40 Waters, quoted in Roe, "Gold Sparkle Band," 13.

41 The band also occasionally played and recorded politically tinged songs written by other groups, such as "People's Republic" by Revolutionary Ensemble. Gold Sparkle Trio with Ken Vandermark, *Brooklyn Cantos* (Squealer, 2004), track 1.

42 Waters, quoted in J. Morgan, "Gold Sparkle Band."

43 Laurence Donohue-Greene, "New York @ Night," *All about Jazz—New York*, no. 38 (2005): 4.

44 Donohue-Greene, "New York @ Night," 4. Waters recalled listening to rap and hip-hop on WRFG—Radio Free Georgia as a kid. He also saw a lot of crossover shows at clubs like the MJQ, run by George Chang, and the Yin-Yang Café. Roe, "Gold Sparkle Band," 12; Ann Powers, "Tuning In the Brain Waves of the Wild Side of Jazz," *New York Times*, June 6, 2001; Christian Carey, review: *Brooklyn Cantos*, by Gold Sparkle Trio with Ken Vandermark, *Signal to Noise* 37 (2005): 57–58; and Waters, interview, March 6, 2019.

45 Roe, "Gold Sparkle Band," 13.

46 Roe, "Gold Sparkle Band," 13; and Waters, interview, March 6, 2019.

47 Charles Waters, quoted in Roe, "Gold Sparkle Band," 13.

48 Bill Meyer, review: *Fugues and Flowers*, by Gold Sparkle Band, *Signal to Noise* 25 (2002): 71. In addition to their own compositions, they also included a piece by bassist William Parker, "Holiday for Flowers," from his *Song Cycle* (Boxholder Records, 2001).

49 Meyer, review: *Fugues and Flowers*, 71.

50 Gold Sparkle Band, *Thunder Reminded Me* (Clean Feed Records, 2002).

51 Bill Meyer, review: *Thunder Reminded Me*, by Gold Sparkle Trio, *Signal to Noise* 31 (2003): 53.

52 Thom Jurek, review: *Thunder Reminded Me*, AllMusic, n.d., accessed March 13, 2019, https://www.allmusic.com/album/thunder-reminded-me -mw0000031767.

53 Jurek, review: *Thunder Reminded Me*.

54 Waters, interview, October 19, 2015. Vision Festival, founded by Patricia Nicholson Parker in 1996, is an annual event that features free jazz, primarily drawing from the downtown scene in Manhattan.

55 Jump Arts was founded in 1997. Jump Arts, press release, Jump Arts American Road Project, spring 2002, Tom Abbs private collection; and Kurt Gottschalk, review: *Jump Arts Orchestra Conducted by "Butch" Morris*, *All about Jazz— New York*, no. 3 (July 2002): 11.

56 One particularly ambitious tour in April and May 2002 involved approximately twenty musicians touring through the US South, with a show in Atlanta, among many other locations. *Not on Earth . . . in Your Soul!*, by Sabir Mateen, Daniel Carter, and Andrew Barker (Qbico, 2005), was recorded on this tour at the Eyedrum in Atlanta. Andrew Barker, interview by author, digital recording, July 22, 2015.

57 Tom Abbs, interview by author, digital recording, January 27, 2016.

58 Daniel Carter has been too prolific and difficult to categorize to summarize easily. Carter is the quintessential multi-instrumentalist, often playing seven or more instruments in a single performance. Carter has appeared on over sixty recordings, has led numerous sessions, and has collaborated on many more.

59 Peterson developed a reputation in the mid-1990s playing in the Joe Maneri Quartet and the Joe Maneri Trio, as well as playing with Maneri's son Mat, a violist, in several bands.

60 The Brecht Forum was an independent Marxist arts, cultural, and educational center that shifted between several Manhattan locations before moving to Brooklyn in 2012. It closed in 2014. Chris Iacono, "In Full Swing . . . ," *Signal to Noise* 7 (September/October 1998): 32; Gottschalk, review: *Jump Arts Orchestra*, 11; and Channing Joseph, "Where Marxists Pontificate, and Play," *New York Times*, November 4, 2010.

61 The performance was recorded live. Jump Arts Orchestra Conducted by Lawrence "Butch" Morris, *Conduction 117* (Jump Arts Records, 2003). See also Jump Arts, email to Rainbow Family/Rainbow Warriors, post no. 522, Yahoo! Groups, April 5, 2001 (no longer available online).

62 Ben Ratliff, "Butch Morris Dies at 65; Creator of 'Conduction,'" *New York Times*, January 29, 2013. Morris's concepts of conduction are discussed in more detail in chapter 4.

63 Lawrence D. Morris, "Butch Morris on the Art of 'Conduction,'" interview by Farai Chideya, *NPR*, February 18, 2008, https://www.npr.org/templates/story/story.php?storyId=19145728.

64 Butch Morris played at "Jumping in Context," at Context Studios on April 12, 2002, and at the Jump Arts Festival at the Brecht Forum on December 15, 2002. Jump Arts, email to Rainbow Family/Rainbow Warriors, post no. 969, Yahoo! Groups, April 11, 2002 (no longer available online); Jump Arts, "Jumping in Context," event poster, Context Studios, April 12–13, 2002, David Brandt private collection; and Jump Arts, email to Rainbow Family/Rainbow Warriors, post no. 1188, Yahoo! Groups, December 11, 2002 (no longer available online).

65 Jessica Pavone, interview by author, digital recording, March 19, 2019.

66 Chris Corsano, interview by author, email, May 2, 2019.

67 Abbs, interview, January 27, 2016.

68 Patrick Brennan, interview by author, email, May 5, 2019.

69 The band also played other spaces in Williamsburg, including the Sideshow Gallery on Bedford Avenue. Patrick Brennan, email to author, November 4, 2019.

70 TEST played several Jump Arts events, and its members played in other ensembles in the series as well. Jump Arts, email to Rainbow Family/Rainbow Warriors, post no. 1325, Yahoo! Groups, April 6, 2003 (no longer available online).

71 James Lindbloom, cited in Lopez, *William Parker Sessionography*, 8.

72 Scott Hreha, "Sax in the City," *Signal to Noise* 20 (2001): 32–37.

73 Carter had moved to New York in 1970, played regularly in the loft scene, and over the decades had honed his craft while playing in numerous ensembles. He

began playing on the streets and in the subways in 1978. Hreha, "Sax in the City," 32; and Scott Hreha, "Test: Mass Transit Appeal," *Signal to Noise* 13 (September/October 1999): 24–25.

74 Sabir Mateen, originally from Philadelphia, moved to New York in 1989. Hreha, "Sax in the City," 32.

75 Mateen, quoted in Hreha, "Test," 24.

76 Carter, quoted in Hreha, "Test," 24.

77 Despite TEST's success in the late 1990s and early 2000s, Mateen remained in poverty. He later moved to Italy.

78 Hreha, "Test," 24.

79 See, for example, TEST, *Live* (Eremite Records, 2000). Scott Hreha, review: *Live*, by TEST, *Signal to Noise* 15 (January/February 2000): 48.

80 Concert dates for the 2002 tour: April 29: Brooklyn, April 30: Philadelphia, May 1: Chapel Hill, May 2: Winston-Salem, May 3–4: Atlanta, May 6: New York. Sarig, "Mr. Ruzow's Opus," 85; and David Brandt, interview by author, email, June 25–August 30, 2019.

81 M. P. Landis, interview by author, email, May 29–June 5, 2019.

82 Steve Dalachinsky, interview by author, email, May 30, 2019.

83 Tom Abbs, interview by author, email, May 28, 2019.

84 Waters, quoted in Sarig, "Mr. Ruzow's Opus," 85.

85 Sarig, "Mr. Ruzow's Opus," 85.

86 Sarig, "Mr. Ruzow's Opus," 85.

87 The trio recorded at the Eyedrum in Atlanta on May 3, 2002. Mateen Carter, and Barker, *Not on Earth*.

88 The Transcendentalists, *Real Time Messengers*, Spirit Room Series, vol. 147 (CIMP, 2002). Abbs, interview, May 28, 2019.

89 M. P. Landis, interview by author, May 29–June 5, 2019.

90 The recording included "Promises of Democracy" and "Nelson Algren" by Gold Sparkle Band, "Shell" by Okkyung Lee, "The American Road" and "Transcendental Suspension" by the Transcendentalists, "Dichotomy" by Lee and Tom Abbs, and two poems by Steve Dalachinsky. Various, *Comin' at You: Jump Arts American Road Project* (Jump Arts Records, 2002). Landis, interview, May 29–June 5, 2019; and David Brandt, interview by author, June 25–August 30, 2019.

91 Schoolhouse Art Center, "Presents M. P. Landis, Paintings from the Jump Arts American Road Project Tour, 2002," event poster, Silas-Kenyon Gallery, July 12–24, 2002, David Brandt private collection.

92 Landis, interview, May 29–June 5, 2019.

93 He wrote "The Blowout (Officer Elmore's Trigger Finger)" on the road between North Carolina and Georgia on May 2, 2019, and he wrote "The Lynching" the next day in Roger Ruzow's backyard in Atlanta. Dalachinsky, interview.

94 Initially Andrew Barker booked shows at the Pink Pony, which was located at 176 Ludlow Street. After a few months, he handed the series off to drummer

Ryan Sawyer, who maintained it for over a year. They mostly booked younger, emerging figures of their own generation, but they also booked some more established players such as Roy Campbell Jr., Rashied Ali, Assif Tsahar, Joe Maneri, Mat Maneri, and Randy Peterson, who also presented their work there. Ryan Sawyer, interview by author, digital recording, June 11, 2020.

95 Roe and Joseph-Hunter, interview; and Mikas, interview.

96 Spacemen 3 was one of the primary bands to spark the shoegazer and drone-rock scenes in the United Kingdom in the 1980s, releasing nine records from 1986 to 1995. Nakatani, originally from Kobe, Japan, is a major percussion innovator. He was active in the Brooklyn scene of the 1990s and 2000s, releasing more than three dozen records under his own name as well as appearing as a sideperson on additional projects. Corsano is also a major figure, having released over fifty records, while working with Bill Nace, Bill Orcutt, Steve Baczkowski, Nate Wooley, and many others.

97 Free103point9, email to NYC-Improv, Yahoo! Groups, June 22, 2004 (no longer available online).

98 Eric Maurer, interview by author, email, July 16–September 23, 2015.

99 Chris Sienko, "The Triumphant Re-return of White Tapes," *Blastitude*, no. 5 (February 2001), http://www.blastitude.com/5/pg2.htm.

100 Russ Waterhouse, interview by author, email, July 16–24, 2015.

101 Fritz Welch, interview by author, email, April 22–25, 2019.

102 Welch considered Houston radio station KPFT, the Art Ensemble of Chicago, Skeleton Crew, the Neville Brothers, Culturcide, the Sun Ra Arkestra, and the Master Musicians of Jajouka all to be influences and sources of inspiration. F. Welch, interview, April 22–25, 2019.

103 The building was next to a brewery. Welch's first musical experiments came in the duo Wi77!N6 (pronounced "willing"). Fritz Welch, interview by author, digital recording, April 26, 2019.

104 F. Welch, interview, April 22–25, 2019.

105 *Heart Beat Ear Drum*, directed by Ellen Zweig (2018); and Jon Pareles, "Z'ev, Percussionist and Industrial Music Pioneer, Dies at 66," *New York Times*, December 26, 2017.

106 Hank Shteamer, "Fritz Welch," *Signal to Noise* 32 (2004): 11. Bennink (b. 1942) and Oxley (b. 1938) are two of the most influential early European drummers to work in free jazz and free improvisation, each leading dozens of recording sessions and appearing on more than a hundred records apiece.

107 F. Welch, interview, April 22–25, 2019.

108 Novak, *Japanoise*, 13. Caroliner Rainbow (alternatively just Caroliner) was active in 1983–2005. The Boredoms were a major Japanese noise band originally formed in Osaka; they released twenty records from 1986 to 2009. Their first US release was *Soul Discharge* (Selfish Records, 1989), distributed in North America beginning in 1990. Hisham Akira Bharoocha, "Boredoms," translated by Sawako Nakayasu, *BOMB*, no. 104 (2008): 52–58; and Ross Simonini, "Singing Bulls and Day-Glo Tapestry: The Spectacle of Caroliner Rainbow,"

SF Weekly, July 16, 2008, https://archives.sfweekly.com/sanfrancisco/singing
-bulls-and-day-glo-tapestry-the-spectacle-of-caroliner-rainbow/Content?oid
=2168463; Novak, *Japanoise*, 11; and F. Welch, interview, April 22–25, 2019.

109   Caroliner Rainbow and the Boredoms shared some aesthetic sensibilities and
even toured together in Japan in 1989. Novak, *Japanoise*, 79.

110   Free103point9, concert flyer, May 12, 2001, Wave Farm archive.

111   McClelland had been integral to the early math-rock band Craw, from Cleveland.

112   F. Welch, interview, April 22–25, 2019.

113   Shteamer, "Fritz Welch," 11.

114   Frith (b. 1949) and Zorn (b. 1953) are monumental figures in the downtown
scene and beyond, with discographies and influences too broad and deep to
summarize. Borbetomagus, comprising saxophonists Don Dietrich and Jim
Sauter and guitarist Donald Miller, was at the center of developing the aggressive extremes of loud improvised music. The band has released over two dozen
records since 1980. Barzel, *New York Noise*, 56–85.

115   Matt Bua, interview by author, digital recording, March 18, 2019.

116   Concert flyer, "free103point9 Turns Two," March 13, 1999, Wave Farm archive.

117   Matt Bua, Matt Mikas, and Tom Roe, *Of the Bridge* (Free103point9, 2001); Roe
and Joseph-Hunter, interview; Bua, interview; and Mikas, interview.

118   Bua, interview.

119   Bua bore influence from guitarist Elliott Sharp. Elliott Sharp/Carbon, *Larynx*
(SST Records, 1988). Bua, interview.

120   The Music Now! Festival on March 25, 2003, was organized in protest of the
United States' recent entry into the Second Gulf War.

121   Ras Moshe Burnett, interview by author, digital recording, March 22, 2021.

122   Burnett, interview.

123   Burnett, interview. *Umoja* is taken from the Swahili word for unity.

124   Burnett got the term *unit* from the Cecil Taylor Unit.

125   Burnett, interview.

126   Lavelle was Burnett's closest collaborator through the years, whom he considered
to be his "musical brother." For an example of the Music Now! Unit's live sound,
see Ras and the Music Now! Unit, *Live Spirits 2* (Utech Records, 2005), which
was recorded at the 2003 Improvised and Otherwise festival. Burnett, interview.

127   Merzbow is Masami Akita, founded in Tokyo in 1979, and has released hundreds of recordings in the years since. Graham, *Sounds of the Underground*,
203–4. The Blue Humans was improvising guitarist Rudolph Grey's unit in
which he experimented with figures such as reeds player Arthur Doyle, fellow
guitarist Alan Licht, drummers Beaver Harris and Tom Surgal, and tenor saxophonists Jim Sauter and Charles Gayle. The band first emerged in the postpunk New York art scene in 1980, bridging free jazz and downtown art noise.
Jim Sauter, "Jim Sauter Interview," interview by Jason Gross, *Perfect Sound
Forever*, July 1997, https://web.archive.org/web/20040409050541/http://www
.furious.com/perfect/borbetomagus.html.

128 David Nuss, interview by author, digital recording, December 11, 2015. The early DIY recordings of the No-Neck Blues Band were recorded in various buildings and on rooftops in Manhattan as well as other cities when they were on tour, such as the Boston area and Detroit: *Recorded in Public and Private* (Actuel, 1994), *Hoichoi* (Sound@One, 1994), *Letters from the Earth* (Sound@One, 1996), *The Circle Broken* (Sound@One, 1996), *A Tabu Two* (New World of Sound, 1997), *Letters from the Serth* (Sound@One, 1998), *The Birth of Both Worlds* (Sound@One, 1998), *Re: "Mr. A Fan…"* (self-released, 1999); *Sticks and Stones May Break My Bones but Names Will Never Hurt Me* (Revenant, 2001).

129 Peter Gershon, review: *Letters from the Serth*, *Soundboard* 6 (July/August 1998): 40.

130 Mike Zimbouski, review: *Sticks and Stones May Break My Bones but Names Will Never Hurt Me*, by No-Neck Blues Band, *Signal to Noise* 25 (2002): 60.

131 Zimbouski, review: *Sticks and Stones*, 60.

132 Sawyer, interview, June 11, 2020.

133 Sawyer, interview, June 11, 2020.

134 Sawyer, interview, June 11, 2020.

135 Ryan Sawyer, interview by author, digital recording, August 11, 2020.

136 Sawyer, interview, June 11, 2020.

137 Sawyer, interview, June 11, 2020.

138 Sawyer, interview, June 11, 2020.

139 Klotz is a fabricator, sculptor, and illustrator, and after feeling inspired by the Brooklyn Free Music Festival, he began to explore music in the indie rock band La Lus and the doom metal band Hallux (with Andrew Barker), among others.

140 Jake Klotz, interview by author, digital recording, March 20, 2019.

141 A listener-supported community radio station that broadcasts from Jersey City, New Jersey, WFMU has been central to a range of avant-garde music in New York since the 1980s. Terry Pristin, "WFMU in Fund-Raising Drive," *New York Times*, March 13, 1996; and Klotz, interview.

142 Tom Roe, email to Improv-NYC, Yahoo! Groups, May 13, 2002 (no longer available online).

143 Sari Rubinstein, interview by author, digital recording, March 28, 2019.

144 Klotz, interview; and Andrew Barker, interview by author, digital recording, April 4, 2019.

145 Steve Huey, "Fly Ashtray," AllMusic, n.d., accessed March 25, 2019, https://www.allmusic.com/artist/fly-ashtray-mn0000195050.

146 The Good/Bad Art Collective had been founded in Denton, Texas, in the 1990s but had moved to New York around 1999, before later returning to Denton. While in New York, they operated an unlicensed space on Grand Street near the Williamsburg Bridge. They were innovatively interdisciplinary, bringing together music, art exhibition, and performance art in events. F. Welch, interview, April 22–25, 2019.

147 David Simons, email to author, April 22, 2019.

148 Some of this material was later documented on David Simons, *Prismatic Hearing* (Tzadik, 2004).

149 Bat Eats Plastic began in 2000 and comprised drummer Hank Shteamer (also a well-known music critic), guitarist David McClelland, and bassist Adam Caine, alongside vocalist and guitarist Millie Benson. The band also collaborated with special guests like multi-instrumentalist Daniel Carter, who would add improvisational elements to the music. Millie Benson, interview by author, digital recording, March 23, 2019; and David McClelland and Millie Benson, interview by author, digital recording, April 20, 2019.

150 F. Welch, interview, April 22–25, 2019.

151 Chuck Eddy, "My Entire Pazz and Jop Comment Spiel," IlXor .com, February 10, 2004, 18:58 p.m., https://www.ilxor.com/ILX /ThreadSelectedControllerServlet?boardid=41&threadid=25858.

152 Gutierrez was influenced and inspired by Marina Abramović in testing the limits of the body as forms of protest. Fennelly and Gutierrez first began their work doing videos of detritus in their neighborhood in the fall of 2001 and soon involved performance art in relation to these impromptu street events. F. Welch, interview, April 22–25, 2019; and Jaime Fennelly, interview by author, digital recording, April 29, 2019.

153 After lending his bass amplifier to William Parker for the latter's performance in Washington, DC, Parker encouraged him to come to New York. Fennelly, interview.

154 Fennelly, interview.

155 *Freedom of Information* was performed at Gutierrez and Fennelly's loft at 249 Varet Street. The work was later presented to larger audiences at the Barn in Brooklyn in 2008 and at the Politics of Ecstasy Festival in Berlin in 2009.

156 "I Succumb" was one early piece that the Gutierrez-Fennelly duo developed that was a sort of code for "I Suck Cum." Gutierrez has since become a towering figure in the dance community, touring and presenting work in many of the premier dance and performance art festivals internationally. Fennelly, interview.

157 Miguel Gutierrez, "Sabotage @ Brooklyn Music Festival," Vimeo video, 40:44, uploaded April 15, 2016, https://vimeo.com/163034927; and Fennelly, interview.

158 F. Welch, interview, April 22–25, 2019; and Tamio Shiraishi, interview by author, email, October 6, 2019.

159 Fritz Welch, interview by author, email, September 24, 2019.

160 F. Welch, interview, September 24, 2019.

161 Chin Chin was formed in 2001 by keyboardist Wilder Zoby, drummer Torbitt Schwartz, and guitarist Jeremy Wilms, though they were often joined by a larger cast of musicians for both recordings and live performances, such as the one at the Brooklyn Free Music Festival. Jason Birchmeier, "Chin Chin," AllMusic, n.d., accessed March 26, 2019, https://www.allmusic.com/artist/chin-chin -mn0000991412/biography.

162   Barker, interview, April 4, 2019.

163   Barker, interview, April 4, 2019.

164   Ben Watson, "Randomness and Antagonism in Electric Guitar Stylings," *Signal to Noise* 14 (November/December 1999): 11; and Peter Gershon, review: *Kill Any/All SPIN Personnel*, by Thurston Moore et al., *Signal to Noise* 21 (2001): 49.

165   Charles Waters, interview by author, email, April 25, 2019.

166   Shiraishi, interview.

167   Shiraishi, interview.

168   In the 2000s, Shiraishi began to play in the New York subways with the train as an accompanying instrument. Some of these performances were documented by videographer and record label owner Kevin Reilly and appear on YouTube.

169   Mark Morgan, interview by author, digital recording, April 25, 2019.

170   Morgan moved from suburban Detroit to an apartment on Bedford Avenue and South Third Street in 1997. He worked at Kim's Music and Video on St. Mark's Place in the East Village until 2004, where he met many musicians and other artists. M. Morgan, interview.

171   The Birthday Party was an Australian postpunk band that had been active in 1978–83. Gang of Four is a postpunk band formed in Leeds, United Kingdom, in 1976 and has been active off and on since that time. Keiji Haino, *Execration That Accept to Acknowledge* (Forced Exposure, 1993).

172   Sightings played an important early concert on the same bill with Lightning Bolt and Oneida at the Polish National Home (which later became known as Warsaw). M. Morgan, interview; and Dan Friel, interview by author, email, October 2, 2019.

173   Sightings, *Michigan Haters* (Psych-O-Path Records, 2002); and Sightings, *Absolutes* (Riot Season, 2003).

174   Musicians pointing to the influence of Sightings on their work range from drummer Greg Fox to saxophonist Sam Weinberg. Sightings released records on the experimental and noise label Load Records, which was active from 1993 to 2017, and Dais Records, as well as a number of lesser-known labels, in addition to their self-released or live recordings. Sightings, *Sightings* (Load Records, 2002); Sightings, *Arrived in Gold* (Load Records, 2005); Sightings, *Through the Panama* (Load Records, 2007); and Sightings, *Terribly Well* (Dais Records, 2013).

175   Klotz, interview.

176   Klotz, interview.

177   Chris Jonas, interview by author, digital recording, May 22, 2019.

178   Barker, interview, June 18, 2015.

179   Catera, interview, August 18, 2015.

180   Mottel, interview, November 24, 2015.

181   Harry Rosenblum, interview by author, digital recording, July 13, 2015.

182   Friel, interview.

183   Friel, interview.

184 Academy Records has been a significant music vendor for decades. Kim's Music and Video was located at 124 First Avenue, just around the corner from St. Mark's Place, in the East Village, and was a hub for the punk, free jazz, and experimental music communities. Jim Farber, "Vinyl Mania Can't Save the Greenwich Village Record Stores," *New York Times*, June 10, 2016.

185 Rosenblum, interview; and Jon DeRosa, interview by author, digital recording, September 23, 2019.

186 DeRosa, interview.

187 Rosenblum, interview.

188 Friel, interview.

189 Friel, interview.

190 Amps for Christ was an experimental music project that combined a wide array of seemingly disparate sounds including punk, hardcore, and noise with more traditional music; they were especially prolific in 1995–2001, though they have continued to perform and record up to the present time.

191 Dan Friel, *Broken Man Going to Work* (self-released, 2001).

192 Parts and Labor, *Groundswell* (JMZ Records, 2003); and Friel, interview.

193 Friel, interview.

194 Joe Tangari, review: *Groundswell*, by Parts and Labor, Pitchfork, March 7, 2004: https://pitchfork.com/reviews/albums/6532-groundswell/.

195 Tyondai Braxton, interview by author, digital recording, October 30, 2019.

196 T. Braxton, interview.

197 Tyondai Braxton, "Tyondai Braxton," interview by Ben Vida, *BOMB*, no. 129 (October 1, 2014), https://bombmagazine.org/articles/tyondai-braxton/.

198 T. Braxton, interview.

199 T. Braxton, interview.

200 Braxton's first solo record documents the work that he presented at 220 Grand. Tyondai Braxton, *History That Has No Effect* (JMZ Records, 2002).

201 T. Braxton, interview.

202 T. Braxton, interview.

203 The early work of Battles bore this influence. Braxton left Battles in 2010. Battles, *Tras* (Cold Sweat Records, 2004); Battles, *B EP* (Dim Mak Records, 2004); Battles, *EP C* (Monitor Records, 2004); and Battles, *Mirrored* (Warp Records, 2007). With an evolved lineup, Battles continues to make music up to the present time.

204 DeRosa, interview.

205 This project was recorded over three sessions in 1999. Aarktica, *No Solace in Sleep* (Silber Records, 2000). DeRosa studied raga music with composer La Monte Young (b. 1935), one of the first American minimalists; vocalist Marian Zazeela (b. 1940), a key figure in the experimental music collective Theatre of Eternal Music in the 1960s; and composer and pianist Michael Harrison. Young's method involved teaching DeRosa how to split one ear into two to the extent possible. DeRosa also played with Stephin Merritt (b. 1965) of the

Magnetic Fields, through whom he became familiar with "the whole history of synth pop." DeRosa, interview.

206 DeRosa's first three records were solo projects, but he began working more with other performers with the band's fourth record, *Pure Tone Audiometry*. Aarktica, *Pure Tone Audiometry* (Silber Records, 2003).

207 DeRosa, interview; see also Aarktica, *Bleeding Light* (Darla Records, 2005).

208 Rosenblum, interview.

209 Rosenblum, interview.

210 Fennelly, interview.

211 Japanther is a postpunk band that formed at the Pratt Institute in Brooklyn in 2001. They were part of a wave of performance-oriented indie rock bands that came out of Pratt in the early 2000s that also included Matt and Kim and the band Swoon. A. Smith, "Ten Years of Music."

212 Concert flyer, seventh-anniversary free103point9 concert at Office Ops, March 20, 2004, Wave Farm archive.

213 Free103point9, email to NYC-Improv, Yahoo! Groups, March 9, 2004 (no longer available online). Nehil had been a founding member of Alial Straa with John Grzinich, who used handmade piano-wire instruments; they were later joined by Olivia Block. Nehil went on to work for the experimental arts magazine *ND* in 1996–2000; free103point9, concert flyer, March 20, 2004, Wave Farm archive.

214 Peeesseye's original name was psi (always spelled in lowercase letters), which was taken from Aum Shinrikyo, the Japanese apocalyptic cult that had a practice of selling their guru's blood as a sacrament called Perfect Salvation Initiation. Then it evolved to the peeesseye (incorrect versions abound). The band formed, practiced, and developed their early work in Welch's loft. Marc Masters, review: *Pestilence & Joy*, by Peeesseye, 2010, Pitchfork, July 26, 2010, https://pitchfork.com/reviews/albums/14487-pestilence-joy/; F. Welch, interview, April 22–25, 2019; F. Welch, interview, April 26, 2019; and Fennelly, interview.

215 Perlonex was a Berlin-based electroacoustic group comprising Ignaz Schick, Joerg Maria Zeger, and Burkhard Beins. Fagaschinski is a German noise artist who emerged in Berlin in the early 2000s. Dörner appeared on some of the key labels to document electroacoustic music, including Erstwhile Records, and has been incredibly prolific and influential on the entire generation of musicians to come after him. Hosokawa, "*Ongaku, Onkyō*/Music, Sound"; and Dan Warburton, review: Self-titled, by Axel Dörner and Kevin Drumm, *Signal to Noise* 23 (2001): 62.

216 Novak, "Playing Off Site," 36.

217 *Onkyō* spread quickly to New York, as evidenced by sold-out concerts there by 2005, though curious musicians had encountered it a few years earlier. Plourde, "Disciplined Listening in Tokyo"; Polaschegg, "Freiheit und Struktur," 40; Atton, "Listening to 'Difficult Albums,'" 351; and Anthony Tommasini, "Created on the Computer, but Pristine It Is Not," *New York Times*, April 4, 2005.

218 F. Welch, interview, April 26, 2019.

219 Fennelly, interview. Boar's Head had a distribution plant near Fennelly's Bushwick loft.

220 Fennelly, interview.

221 Sanfilippo and Valle, "Feedback Systems," 19. See also Toshimaru Nakamura, *No-Input Mixing Board* (Zero Gravity, 2000); "CD Companion Introduction," 79–80; Wilson, "Tabu oder Hohlform?," 38; and Gawthorp, "Film Noise Aesthetics," 59.

222 Shteamer, "Fritz Welch," 11.

223 F. Welch, interview, April 22–25, 2019.

224 F. Welch, interview, April 22–25, 2019.

225 Fennelly, interview. The peeesseye's studio recordings focused more on song and form. More than half of the records the band released documented their live performances. See psi, *Black American Flag* (Evolving Ear, 2004); psi, *Artificially Retarded Soul Care Operators* (Evolving Ear, 2005); peeesseye, *Commuting between the Surface and the Underworld* (Evolving Ear, 2006); peeesseye, *2008 Tour CDR (Teton Trout)* (Evolving Ear, 2008); peeesseye, *I Woke Up and Drank a Bottle of Cheap Kojak* (Golden Lab Records, 2009); and peeesseye, *Robust Commercial Fucking Scream*, 6 vols. (Digitalis Limited, 2009).

226 Peeesseye, *Pestilence & Joy* (Evolving Ear, 2010); peeesseye, *Sci Fi Death Mask* (humansacrifice, 2014).

227 Chris Forsyth, email to Jaime Fennelly, June 22, 2004, and shared with the author; and concert flyer, Free Jazz + Electronics presented by free103point9, Office Ops, June 26, 2004, Wave Farm archive.

228 Matthew Shipp and Guillermo E. Brown, *Telephone Popcorn* (Nu Bop Records, 2008).

229 Matthew Shipp, *Nu Bop*, the Blue Series (Thirsty Ear, 2002); Matthew Shipp, *Equilibrium*, the Blue Series (Thirsty Ear, 2003); and Matthew Shipp, interview by author, digital recording, January 14, 2021.

230 Shipp, interview.

231 Andrew Barker, interview by author, digital recording, January 13, 2016.

232 Matt Mikas, liner notes, *Interactive Audio Response Kit*, Audio Dispatch 18 (free103point9, 2004), [1].

233 Their first record, released in 2006, captured the band's live sound at two festivals: Experimental Intermedia: A Festival with No Fancy Name, New York, March 13, 2005; and Improvised and Otherwise festival, Brooklyn, May 7, 2005. Phantom Limb & Bison, *Phantom Limb & Bison* (Utech Records, 2006); and Phantom Limb & Bison, *Phantom Limb & Bison* (Evolving Ear, 2007).

234 Shawn Hansen, interview by author, digital recording, December 17, 2019.

235 *Le Jetée*, directed by Chris Marker (1962).

236 Northsix was later remodeled and became the Music Hall of Williamsburg.

237 Noise artist Emil Beaulieu of RR Records organized a noise festival at the Knitting Factory in 1998 that served as a precedent. Matt Mottel, interview by author, email, March 14, 2020.

238 Carlos Giffoni, interview by author, digital recording, February 12, 2021. Giffoni has an extensive discography. His first major solo release was *Welcome Home* (Important Records, 2005).

239 Mottel, interview, March 14, 2020. See Wolf Eyes, *Burned Mind* (Sub Pop, 2004).

240 Mottel, interview, March 14, 2020.

241 Giffoni, interview.

242 A label emerged from the festival, No Fun Productions, also run by Giffoni, that released sixty records from the scene between 2004 and 2011.

243 Ramos, interview. The vast majority of the Latinx communities were displaced between 1999 and the early 2010s, with small pockets surviving in areas around Havemayer Street and South Second and South Third Streets, as well as people living in public housing along Graham Avenue.

244 Seth Misterka, interview by author, email transcript, June 8–24, 2015.

245 Vrusho, "Waterfront Week, R.I.P."

246 Sabir Mateen, interview by author, email, June 11–19, 2015.

247 Figures like Twist and Obey were catapulted to stardom. Merritt, interview.

Chapter 3. Art Galleries, Clubs, and Bohemian Cafés

1 Kevin Walsh, "Bedford Avenue, Part 3," Forgotten New York, December 14, 2014, https://forgotten-ny.com/2014/12/bedford-avenue-part-3/; and Pavone, interview, March 19, 2019.

2 Dennis, interview.

3 Organizations such as the National Endowment for the Arts, Chamber Music America, and the Mid Atlantic Arts Foundation, along with state and local arts organizations, all gave significant support to this generation of artists.

4 Lee, in particular, has done much to illustrate this cultural milieu in his films, such as *She's Gotta Have It* (1986).

5 Mary Halvorson, interview by author, digital recording, September 10, 2012; Taylor Ho Bynum, interview by author, digital recording, November 22, 2013; and Brandon Evans, interview by author, digital recording, May 18, 2019.

6 Jason Cady, interview by author, email, May 23, 2019.

7 A. Braxton, quoted in Steve Koenig, "Anthony Braxton: Between the Quadrants," *All about Jazz—New York*, no. 2 (June 2002): 9.

8 A. Braxton, quoted in Koenig, "Anthony Braxton," 15. Braxton has also voiced this perspective elsewhere and faced criticism for it. Block, "Pitch-Class Transformation in Free Jazz"; Gagne, *Soundpieces 2*, 511; Radano, *New Musical Figurations*, 1; Borgo, "Negotiating Freedom," 173; Porter, *What Is This Thing Called Jazz?*, 241; Lewis, "Experimental Music in Black and White," 75–76, 78–79, 89–90; Lawrence, "Pluralism, Minor Deviations, and Radical Change," 72; and John Rockwell, "Jazz: Two Braxton Programs," *New York Times*, April 23, 1982.

9   A. Braxton, quoted in Koenig, "Anthony Braxton," 15.

10 Braxton's systems and vocabularies are immense and have been the focus of a
    number of scholarly studies. Lock, *Forces in Motion*; Lewis, "Singing Omar's
    Song," 77; Brown, *Noise Orders*, 119–24; Roelstraete, "Way Ahead," 117; and
    Jonas, interview.

11 Halvorson, interview, September 10, 2012; Bynum, interview; B. Evans,
    interview, May 18, 2019; and Brandon Evans, interview by author, email,
    June 20, 2019.

12 Matthew Welch, interview by author, digital recording, March 4, 2015.

13 Fei recorded most of his solo works while at Wesleyan. James Fei, *Solo Works*
    (Leo Records, 2000). Fei was less involved in the Brooklyn scene than most of
    his contemporaries because he was pursuing doctoral studies at Columbia Uni-
    versity in the early 2000s. Dan Warburton, review: *Solos and Duos*, by Jessica
    Pavone and Jackson Moore, *Signal to Noise* 25 (2002): 82; Koenig, "Anthony
    Braxton," 9, 15; and Kurt Gottschalk, "Parallactic Records," *All about Jazz—
    New York*, no. 16 (August 2003): 6, 21.

14 Evans lived in poverty at the time and obtained Braxton's books through the
    San Francisco Public Library. Before that, he had encountered Braxton's solo
    compositions on record. By his own estimations, Evans did not have the aca-
    demic credentials, nor the money, to study at Wesleyan, but Braxton invited
    him to work with him for free after he expressed an interest in studying Brax-
    ton's notated music in a series of phone conversations they had over a few
    months. Anthony Braxton, *19 (Solo) Compositions, 1988* (New Albion, 1988);
    B. Evans, interview, May 18, 2019; and B. Evans, interview, June 20, 2019.

15 The orchestra comprised a rotating cast of creative musicians that included
    Jenna Alden (tenor saxophone), Josh Blair (percussion), Marc Burns (key-
    boards), Taylor Ho Bynum (trumpet, flugelhorn), Peter Cafarella (accordion),
    Rafael Cohen (oboe, English horn), Josephina Conover (viola), Karen Correa
    (viola), Seth Dellinger (bass, electric guitar), Noelle Dorsey (voice), James Fei
    (bass clarinet), Jennifer Geller (violin), Dan Gilbert (electric guitar), Brian
    Glick (tenor saxophone), Van Green (bass), Anne Hege (flute, voice), Annie
    Hesslein (cello), Eli Hilbrun (tuba), Abigail Hurewitz (flute), Edward Kas-
    parek (percussion), Jesse Kudler (theremin, electric guitar), Allen Livermore
    (baritone saxophone), Chris Matthay (trumpet), Richard McGhee III (clarinet,
    saxophone), Seth Misterka (alto saxophone), Jackson Moore (alto saxophone),
    Deborah Netburn (oboe), Kevin Norton (vibraphone), David Novak (bassoon,
    melodica), Kevin O'Neil (guitar), Jessica Pavone (violin), Eric Ronick (me-
    lodica, piano), Ben Stanko (trombone), Phloyd Starpoli (trombone), Rachel
    Thompson (violin), Dortha Willets (dulcimer), Amanda Youngman (clarinet),
    and Jonathan Zorn (bass, viola).

16 Jessica Pavone, interview by author, digital recording, December 29, 2014.

17 Middletown Creative Orchestra, *10.6.97* (Newsonic Music, 1997); Brandon Evans
    and the Middletown Creative Orchestra, *Two Compositions for Chamber Orches-
    tra 1998* (Parallactic Recordings, 1998); Middletown Creative Orchestra, *4.11.98*

and 4.30.98 (Newsonic Music, 1998); Middletown Creative Orchestra, *Crystal Lake* (Newsonic Music, 1998); and Justin Yang and the Middletown Creative Orchestra, *Composition for Creative Orchestra no. 1* (Yang/Yin, 1999).

18 Jessica Pavone, interview by author, email, May 12, 2019.

19 Jonas had previously worked with Cecil Taylor and William Parker, having moved to New York in 1994. Jonas, interview.

20 B. Evans, interview, May 18, 2019.

21 A. Braxton, quoted in Koenig, "Anthony Braxton," 9.

22 Seth Misterka, interview by author, email, June 8–24, 2015.

23 Jackson Moore, interview by author, digital recording, June 12, 2015.

24 Pavone, interview, March 19, 2019.

25 Gottschalk, "Parallactic Records," 6.

26 Evans cofounded Parallactic Records with Hungarian saxophonist André Vida.

27 B. Evans, quoted in Gottschalk, "Parallactic Records," 6.

28 Newsonic Music released at least nineteen records, though their catalog numbering suggests that a number of additional sessions were considered but never pressed. The label documented some key live sessions from the scene at the Pink Pony, Tri-Centric Festival at Greenwich House Music School, Collective Unconscious, and unidentified locations in 1998–2001.

29 Peacock Recordings released ten records in 2001–9 and is especially important for understanding Pavone's early development.

30 Firehouse 12 has too extensive a catalog to summarize easily, having released major works by Bynum, Anthony Braxton, Bill Dixon, Peter Evans, Tomas Fujiwara, Mary Halvorson, Ingrid Laubrock, Myra Melford, Nicole Mitchell, Tyshawn Sorey, and Nate Wooley, among others.

31 Fei ran Organized Sound Recordings, which had two releases in 2001–4.

32 Gottschalk, "Parallactic Records," 6.

33 Mary Halvorson and Jessica Pavone, unreleased live recording at Sideshow Gallery, October 30, 2002, Jessica Pavone private collection.

34 P. Evans, quoted in Steve Dollar, "The Making of a Guitar Goddess," *New York Sun*, February 21, 2007, https://www.nysun.com/arts/making-of-a-guitar -goddess/48988/.

35 Halvorson, interview, September 10, 2012; Pavone, interview, December 29, 2014; and Pavone, interview, March 19, 2019. Halvorson and Pavone also played together in the band Jason Cady and the Artificials, which began around the same time. Cady led the band on synthesizers and drum machine, Halvorson played guitar, Pavone primarily played electric bass but also occasionally viola, and several different flute players joined them. The band played at many of the Brooklyn venues discussed in this chapter, including the Right Bank Café and Newsonic Loft. Cady, interview.

36 Steve Dollar, "Making of a Guitar Goddess."

37 Jessica Pavone, "Interview with Jessica Pavone," *El Intruso*, n.d.

38 Halvorson and Pavone, unreleased live recording at Sideshow Gallery.

39 Concert flyer, Read Café, December 6, 2002, Aaron Siegel private collection; Jessica Pavone, personal daily planner, Jessica Pavone private collection; Mary Halvorson and Jessica Pavone, *Prairies* (Lucky Kitchen, 2005); Mary Halvorson and Jessica Pavone, unreleased live recording at Zebulon, July 2, 2007, Jessica Pavone private collection; and Mary Halvorson and Jessica Pavone, unreleased live recording at Vision Fest 12, 2007, Jessica Pavone private collection.

40 Pavone, interview, March 19, 2019.

41 Pavone, personal daily planner.

42 Kurt Gottschalk, review: *Prairies*, by Mary Halvorson and Jessica Pavone, *Signal to Noise* 42 (2006): 63.

43 Elliott Sharp, quoted in Steve Dollar, "Pavone Brings Her Strings Back Home," *New York Sun*, March 11, 2008.

44 Peter Margasak, "Instincts Louder Than Words," *Chicago Reader*, July 10, 2007.

45 Shipp, quoted in Kurt Gottschalk, "It's in the Stars," *Signal to Noise* 53 (2009): 17.

46 Halvorson and Pavone, quoted in Philip Clark, review: *Prairies*, by Mary Halvorson and Jessica Pavone, *Wire*, May 2006.

47 Halvorson, "Invented Horizon Is Free," 104.

48 Mary Halvorson–Jessica Pavone Duo, concert flyer, January 12, 2006, Mary Halvorson private collection; and Pavone, personal daily planner.

49 Pavone, personal daily planner.

50 Mary Halvorson and Jessica Pavone, *On and Off* (Skirl Records, 2007); Mary Halvorson and Jessica Pavone, *Thin Air* (Thirsty Ear, 2009); and Mary Halvorson and Jessica Pavone, *Departure of Reason* (Thirsty Ear, 2011). In January 2007 they went on a West Coast tour through Los Angeles, Oakland, Portland, Seattle, and Sacramento; played the Vision Festival in June; and had a summer tour to Richmond, Greensboro, Lexington, Chicago, Detroit, Columbus, and Washington, DC, leading up to the release of *Off and On*. Good for Cows/Mary Halvorson–Jessica Pavone Duo, tour flyer, January 11–18, 2007, Mary Halvorson private collection; and Pavone, personal daily planner.

51 Halvorson and Pavone followed this with a Canadian tour in February 2010.

52 Experimental Arts Festival, program, April 10, 2010, Mary Halvorson private collection.

53 Troy Collins, "Mary Halvorson and Jessica Pavone: *On and Off*," All about Jazz, August 8, 2007, https://www.allaboutjazz.com/on-and-off-skirl-records-review -by-troy-collins.php.

54 Misterka, interview, June 8–24, 2015; and Seth Misterka, liner notes, *Compilation of Live Recordings from the AvantTuesdays@the Right Bank music series* (Newsonic Music 001, 2003), [1].

55 Radding, interview.

56 Nate Wooley, interview by author, email, December 3, 2012–May 20, 2014; and Jeff Arnal, interview by author, digital recording, May 14, 2015.

57 Radding, interview.

58   Dietrich Eichmann, liner notes, *Transit* (Clean Feed, 2005).

59   Dynamite Club, *The Legend of Tiger Mask* (Big Sleep Records, 2002); and Dynamite Club, *It's Deeper Than Most People Think . . .* (Funhole Records, 2004).

60   Pride, interview.

61   The MP3, *Sleep Cells* (Utech, 2006). The band was alternatively named the MPthree or the Mike Pride Trio.

62   Pride, interview.

63   Misterka, interview, June 8–24, 2015.

64   John Del Signore, "Williamsburg Mainstay Verb Café to Close," *Gothamist*, June 5, 2014, http://gothamist.com/2014/06/05/verb_williamsburg_closing .php; and John Del Signore, "New Chef at Williamsburg's Rabbithole Is Killing It," *Gothamist*, March 17, 2012, http://gothamist.com/2012/03/17/new_chef_at _williamsburgs_rabbithol.php.

65   Del Signore, "New Chef at Williamsburg's Rabbithole."

66   Aaron Siegel, interview by author, digital recording, June 19, 2015.

67   The *New York Press* emerged in 1988 as a rival to the *Village Voice* and listed art and music events until it was acquired by a corporate investment group in 2002 and stopped being culturally productive.

68   From December 14, 2000, to February 20, 2003, the series occurred regularly on Thursday nights. During the last three months of the series, from March 5 to May 28, 2003, the series shifted to Wednesday nights.

69   Aaron Siegel, interview by author, digital recording, June 19, 2015.

70   Siegel, interview, June 19, 2015.

71   Nate Wooley, interview by author, email, July 1–13, 2014.

72   Wooley, interview, July 1–13, 2014. Barnes is a prolific figure in New York's electroacoustic scene, and his label Quakebasket documented many of the key works from that scene after he founded it in 1999. Garcia is a well-documented Portuguese bassist who had a significant impact on lowercase music and is a significant composer and improviser, having worked with Thurston Moore, Loren Connors, and Manuel Mota, among many others. Bosetti (b. 1973) is an Italian saxophonist and composer who has explored the musical vocabulary of language and has also experimented with radio and text-sound projects. Wright (b. 1942) has been active since the 1960s and has extensively documented his work as a visionary improviser. See chapter 2 for a discussion of the peeesseye. Jon Dale, "Percussion Discussion," *Signal to Noise* 29 (2003): 15–19; Dan Warburton, "The Wright Stuff," *Signal to Noise* 27 (2002): 36–42; Dan Warburton, review: *Berlin Reeds*, by Alessandro Bosetti Gregor Hotz, Kai Fagaschinksi, and Rudi Mahall, *Signal to Noise* 31 (2003): 47–48; and Eric Weddle, review: *On Tour*, by Toshimaru Nakamura and Sean Meehan; *Loran*, by Margardia Garcia and Barry Weisblat, *Signal to Noise* 38 (2005): 68.

73   Wooley, interview, July 1–13, 2014.

74   Wooley, interview, July 1–13, 2014.

75   Nate Wooley, "Small, Still Voice," 75–76.

76 Nate Wooley, interview by author, email, December 14, 2015.

77 Swell emerged on the downtown scene in the 1980s, working with bassist William Parker, among others.

78 Bill Meyer, review: *13 Definitions of Truth*, by Peter Kowald and Tatsuya Nakatani, *Signal to Noise* 30 (2003): 50.

79 Derek Taylor, quoted in review: *Lovely Hazel*, December 19, 2005, http://www.publiceyesore.com/catalog/php?pg=3&pit=81 (accessed May 18. 2019).

80 Wooley, interview, December 14, 2015.

81 Jeff Arnal, interview by author, email, December 24, 2015.

82 Sean Fitzell, "Artist Feature: Steve Swell," *All about Jazz—New York*, no. 29 (September 2004): 7.

83 Derek Taylor, quoted in review: *Lovely Hazel*. Dixon (1925–2010) is well known for his October Revolution in Jazz in 1964, the first free jazz festival in New York, which led to the formation of the Jazz Composers Guild, an organization that advocated for jazz musicians of the time. Dixon was known for his minimalism and adept use of space in his music.

84 Aaron Siegel, interview by author, digital recording, August 14, 2015.

85 Matt Bauder, interview by author, email, July 20, 2015.

86 Siegel, interview, June 19, 2015.

87 Siegel, interview, August 14, 2015.

88 Siegel, interview, June 19, 2015.

89 Bauder, interview.

90 The Read Café survived the wave of gentrification until 2008, when it finally closed and was replaced by the coffee shop El Beit.

91 Siegel, interview, August 14, 2015.

92 In 2010 Siegel, together with Matthew Welch and Jason Cady, formed the company Experiments in Opera. All three had had their initial interest in opera sparked by Braxton. They have presented over eighty-five new works by approximately fifty-five composers to date.

93 Misterka, interview, June 8–24, 2015.

94 T. Braxton, interview.

95 BlackBook, "Brooklyn: The Borough That Never Sleeps," *BlackBook*, April 7, 2010, https://blackbookmag.com/archive/brooklyn-the-borough-that-never-sleeps/.

96 BlackBook, "Brooklyn."

97 Jenny Electrik, quoted in BlackBook, "Brooklyn."

98 BlackBook, "Brooklyn."

99 Misterka, interview, June 8–24, 2015.

100 Misterka, interview, June 8–24, 2015.

101 BlackBook, "Brooklyn." Close (b. 1940) is a photorealist painter.

102 Misterka, interview, June 8–24, 2015.

103 Nonsense NYC, email post, April 17, 2009 (no longer available online).

104 Nonsense NYC, email post, March 13, 2009 (no longer available online).

105 Misterka, interview, June 8–24, 2015.

106 Misterka, interview, June 8–24, 2015; see also Mike Pride, *Drummer's Corpse* (AUM Fidelity, 2013).

107 Nate Chinen, quoted in Jon Pareles, Ben Ratliff, and Nate Chinen, "Somber Tunes, Off-Kilter Beats," *New York Times*, May 20, 2013.

108 Blarvuster also played in Misterka's series at the Right Bank around 2003; at the Overground series at the Pourhouse on March 16, 2005; at the Issue Project Room on May 17, 2008; and thrice at Zebulon, on January 22, 2008, December 20, 2009, and December 8, 2010.

109 Matthew Welch, *Blarvuster* (Tzadik Records, 2010).

110 Vivien Schweitzer, "A Tent with Room for Sounds of All Kinds," *New York Times*, August 23, 2006.

111 Matthew Welch, "Music," Blarvuster.com, n.d., accessed May 28, 2019, blarvuster.com. See also Lara Pellegrinelli, "Sounds of Bali, Traditional yet Evolving," *New York Times*, December 10, 2010.

112 Schweitzer, "Tent with Room for Sounds."

113 Cady, interview.

114 Mary Halvorson, interview by author, email, June 24–30, 2015.

115 Halvorson, interview, September 10, 2012.

116 Kevin Shea, interview by author, digital recording, August 10, 2015.

117 Shea, interview.

118 The band benefited from having their records produced by Steve Albini and Jim O'Rourke. Williams later played bass in the band Battles. Storm and Stress, *Storm&Stress* (Touch and Go, 1997); Storm and Stress, *Under Thunder and Fluorescent Lights* (Touch and Go, 2000); and Shea, interview.

119 Shea, interview.

120 Talibam!, *Boogie in the Breeze Blocks* (ESP Disk, 2009); Peeesseye + Talibam!, *Peeesseye + Talibam!* (Invada Records, 2010); and Talibam! and Weasel Walter, *Polyp* (MNÓAD, 2014).

121 Shea, interview.

122 Halvorson, interview, September 10, 2012.

123 Luxx, concert flyer, May 11, [2003], Mary Halvorson private collection; Cake Shop, concert flyer, "From B to Z, Episode 3," February 12 [no year], Mary Halvorson private collection; and Shea, interview.

124 The personnel of Dynasty Electric changed considerably through the years. In its earliest manifestation, it was a trio with Misterka (guitar, saxophone), Electrik (voice, bass), and Edward Kasparek (drums). During a period when Kasparek moved out of New York, they used a drum machine, during which time it moved from being improvisation focused to more of a synth pop group. Then it was expanded to a sextet with a drummer and two synth players, including Jason Cady. It later returned to a trio once Kasparek moved back to New York. Cady, interview.

125 Cady, interview.

126 Misterka, interview, June 8–24, 2015.

127 Misterka, interview, June 8–24, 2015.

128 Misterka, interview, June 8–24, 2015.

129 Sam Hillmer, interview by author, digital recording, September 12, 2020.

130 Alex Mincek, interview by author, digital recording, January 31, 2021.

131 Hillmer, interview.

132 Numerous figures of the Washington, DC, punk scene had also moved to New York around that time, including members of Gang Gang Dance, Touchdown, the Metamatics, the ABCs, the Rapture, and Orthrelm.

133 Hillmer, interview.

134 Mincek, interview.

135 Hillmer, interview.

136 Guitarist Matthew Hough and trombonist Jacob Garchik were two early participants. One of the earliest compositions Mincek wrote for two saxophones, "Karate," appeared on an EP: Zs, *Karate Bump* (Planaria Recordings, 2005). Hillmer, interview.

137 Hillmer, interview.

138 Hillmer, interview.

139 Hillmer, quoted in Steve Dollar, "Same Name, New People and Sound," *Wall Street Journal*, February 1, 2013; see also Mincek, interview.

140 Hillmer, interview.

141 Mincek, interview.

142 Hillmer, interview.

143 Mincek, interview.

144 Hillmer, interview.

145 Mincek, interview. See Paul Motian, *Motian in Tokyo* (JMT, 1991).

146 Mincek, interview.

147 The first record was completed before the band grew to include guitarist Charlie Looker. The second record captured the sound of the double trio as the first full iteration of the band fully crystallized. Zs, *Zs*, Vothoc series (Troubleman Unlimited, 2003); and Zs, *Buck* (Folding Cassettes, 2006).

148 A. Smith, "Ten Years of Music."

149 Mincek, interview.

150 Hillmer, interview.

151 Mincek left the band to study composition with George Lewis at Columbia University. Mincek, interview.

152 Zs, *Arms* (Planaria Recordings, 2007).

153 Hillmer, interview.

154 Hillmer, interview.

155 Gooch, "New Bohemia," 29.

156 Estelle Woodward, interview by author, digital recording, July 1, 2015.

157 The Vision Festival in Manhattan and the Autumn Uprising, the latter modeled on Dixon's October Revolution of 1964, were also inspirations for the event. There was even a contingent of the Autumn Uprising performers on some of the Improvised and Otherwise bills, such as Nmperign with Bhob Rainey and Greg Kelley and the large ensemble the BSC. Jeff Arnal, interview by author, digital recording, March 5, 2021.

158 From 2003 to 2006, Improvised and Otherwise was funded by the Brooklyn Arts Council, which allowed them to pay artists a little more. Woodward, interview.

159 Gordon Beeferman, interview by author, digital recording, March 7, 2021.

160 Woodward, interview.

161 Ben Hall, interview by author, digital recording, March 13, 2021.

162 Beeferman, interview. Arnal's use of silence was drawn from the music of John Cage, new classical music, and his own listening practice.

163 Woodward, interview.

164 Arnal, interview, December 24, 2015.

165 Arnal, interview, December 24, 2015.

166 Bynum, interview.

167 Bynum, interview.

168 Bynum, interview.

169 Bynum, interview. See also A. Braxton, *Tri-Axium Writings*, 420; and Lewis, "Experimental Music in Black and White," 58.

170 Bynum, interview.

171 Bynum, interview.

172 Bynum, interview.

173 Bynum, interview.

174 Taylor Ho Bynum Sextet, *The Middle Picture* (Firehouse 12 Records, 2007).

175 Taylor Ho Bynum, liner notes, *The Middle Picture*, [1].

176 Bynum, liner notes, *The Middle Picture*, [1].

177 Bynum, interview.

178 Bynum, interview.

179 Bynum, interview.

180 Bynum, interview.

181 Bynum, interview.

182 Bynum, interview.

183 Taylor Ho Bynum Sextet, *Navigation (Possibility Abstract X and XI)* (Firehouse 12 Records, 2013).

184 Taylor Ho Bynum Sextet, *Asphalt Flowers Forking Paths* (Hat Hut Records, 2008).

185 Vision Festival, flyer, June 10, 2008, Taylor Ho Bynum private collection.

186 Tomas Fujiwara, interview by author, digital recording, October 1, 2013; Mary Halvorson, interview by author, digital recording, October 1, 2013; and Bynum, interview.

187 This lineup was featured on the band's third record. Taylor Ho Bynum Sextet, *Apparent Distance* (Firehouse 12 Records, 2011).

188 Bynum, interview.

189 Moore, interview.

190 Aaron Ali Shaikh, interview by author, digital recording, June 10, 2015; and Moore, interview.

191 Moore, interview.

192 Shaikh, interview, June 10, 2015; and Moore, interview.

193 For an example of Moore's music from that era, see Jackson Moore, *Trio of Eluctations* (self-released, 2007).

194 Moore, interview.

195 Moore, interview.

196 Moore, interview.

197 James Ilgenfritz, interview by author, digital recording, February 22, 2014; see also James Ilgenfritz, interview by author, email, January 19, 2021.

198 Ilgenfritz, interview, January 19, 2021.

199 Ilgenfritz was influenced by Balkan dance music as well as klezmer music, both of which were making their way into the Brooklyn repertoire in the 1990s and 2000s. Ilgenfritz, interview, January 19, 2021.

200 Ilgenfritz, interview, January 19, 2021.

201 Ilgenfritz, interview, January 19, 2021.

202 Moore, interview; see also Shaikh, interview, June 10, 2015.

203 One of Little Women's first shows occurred at one of Shaikh's house concerts. Brandon Evans also played a solo set there. Aaron Ali Shaikh, interview by author, email, September 12, 2016.

204 Shaikh, interview, June 10, 2015.

205 The festivals occurred annually from 2005 to 2009. The first festival occurred at Anthology Film Archives. In 2006–7 the festival was held at Rose Live, where Shaikh worked with the owner, Carlo Vutera, to get access to the space. In 2008 the festival was back in Manhattan at the Living Theatre. The final festival was at McCarren Hall in Williamsburg, partially sponsored by Lagunitas, as well as the beer distributor 12 Percent Imports. When Adam Schatz began organizing a series of annual Ecstatic Music Festivals, they stopped their festival series, and Shaikh left the scene that year to prepare for medical school. Nate Chinen, "New Languages Festival Makes Avant-Garde Inviting, If Not Compromising," *New York Times*, May 15, 2006; Shaikh, interview, June 10, 2015; and Moore, interview.

206 The 2008 festival coincided with the annual Vision Festival. Shaikh, interview, June 10, 2015.

207 Chinen, "New Languages Festival."

208 Chinen, "New Languages Festival."

209 Shaikh, interview, June 10, 2015.

210 Curran, "'From the Frying Pan to the Oven,'" 1435, 1437–38; and Dennis, interview.

211 Campo, *Accidental Playground*, 185–215.

212 Jane Jacobs, "Letter to Mayor Bloomberg and the City Council," *Brooklyn Rail*, May 2005, http://www.brooklynrail.org/2005/05/local/letter-to-mayor-bloomberg.

213 Campo, *Accidental Playground*, 260; and Larson, *"Building like Moses with Jacobs in Mind,"* 57.

214 Dennis, interview.

215 Dennis, interview.

216 Residential home values also increased dramatically. From just 2000 to 2006, average home values in Williamsburg and Greenpoint rose from $193,558 to $582,700. *Gentrification and Rezoning.*

Chapter 4. A Point of Confluence

1 It had formerly been an arts loft space run by costume designer Yvette Helin that presented performance art as well as music. The Blue Man Group performed at the Green Room before they were well known. Some artists were displaced when Zebulon's owners bought the building. Butler, interview, September 13, 2016; and Dennis, interview.

2 Jef Soubiran, quoted in Brian Lonergan, "Club Profile: Zebulon," *All about Jazz—New York*, no. 35 (March 2005): 6. The original television show was later adapted in the United Kingdom as *The Magic Roundabout*.

3 Lonergan, "Club Profile," 6. Boulevard Saint-Germain in Paris has been home to a well-known artist community at various times in its history, with numerous figures peopling its bohemian cafés over the past century, such as Gertrude Stein, Samuel Beckett, and countless others.

4 Lonergan, "Club Profile," 6.

5 Merritt, interview.

6 Lonergan, "Club Profile," 6.

7 Peter Evans, interview by author, digital recording, June 18, 2015.

8 Jules is still located at 65 St. Mark's Place. Casimir has since been sold, and the space, at 103 Avenue B, is now occupied by a different French bistro called Pardon My French.

9 Untitled, n.d., accessed June 22, 2015, https://www.zebuloncafeconcert.com (no longer available).

10 Jocelyn Soubiran, interview by author, email, July 10, 2015.

11 Louis Belogenis, interview by author, digital recording, May 14, 2020.

12 Butler, interview, September 13, 2016; Merritt, interview; and Travis Laplante, interview by author, digital recording, June 16, 2020.

13 Belogenis, interview.

14 P. Evans, interview.

15 Zebulon often recorded live sets, many of which were released either by the club or by one of the many independent labels that had an interest in the music scene at the time. The best early sampling of the music at the club is featured on a compilation that contains tracks by Butch Morris's Butchland Band, Charles Gayle Trio, Forro in the Dark, Kenny Wollesen's SLAM, Jim Hobbs's Full Celebrated Orchestra, Baye Kouyate, Yakouba Sissoko, and Ken Butler's Voices of Anxious Objects. Various, *This Is It: Live at Zebulon*, vol. 1 (Zebulon, 2005). Eye Contact, *Embracing the Tide/Making Eye Contact with God* (Utech Records, 2005); Matana Roberts Quartet, *The Calling* (Utech Records, 2006); Sonny Simmons Blaise Siwula, Daniel Carter, Adam Lane, Robyn Siwula, Mike Fortune, and Jeffrey Hayden Shurdut, *Live at Zebulon*, vol. 1 (self-released, 2006); and Sonny Simmons, Jeffrey Shurdut, Daniel Carter, Blaise Siwula, Adam Lane, Robyn Siwula, Mike Fortune, *Live at Zebulon*, vol. 2, *This Is the Music of Life* (Ayler Records, 2008).

16 Jocelyn Soubiran, interview.

17 Charles Gayle, *Repent* (Knitting Factory Works, 1992); and Charles Gayle Trio, *Live at Disobey* (Blast First, 1994).

18 Greene had arrived in New York City in 1986 and had a day job delivering mail from skyscraper to skyscraper for a bank. Greene, "Interview," 13–14.

19 Hilliard Greene, interview by author, digital recording, March 17, 2020.

20 Jon Pareles, "Jazz: Peter Kowald Quartet," *New York Times*, June 4, 1984.

21 H. Greene, interview. Greene is known for playing multiple styles of music, has performed and composed extensively in solo settings, and had an extended affiliation with vocalist Jimmy Scott, for whom he also worked as music director for well over a decade. H. Greene, "Interview: Hilliard Greene," 12–13, 15.

22 Charles Gayle, in *Rising Tones Cross*, at 0:10:12; see also Clifford Allen, "Charles Gayle," *New York City Jazz Record*, no. 146 (June 2014): 7.

23 Gayle, quoted in Davis, *Jazz and Its Discontents*, 171.

24 Gayle, in *Rising Tones Cross*, at 0:13:33.

25 Neidlinger, "Buell Neidlinger," 20.

26 Neidlinger, "Buell Neidlinger," 20; and Packer and Leach, *Gay Guerrilla*, 32. The only known recording of Gayle before 1987 is Buell Neidlinger, *Gayle Force* (K2B2, 2015).

27 Packer and Leach, *Gay Guerrilla*, 32.

28 Norman Salant, "Weather Report: Lack of Identity," *Spectrum* (Buffalo, NY), December 1, 1972.

29 Gayle inherited Charles Mingus's jazz course at the State University of New York at Buffalo in 1970 and taught there until 1973. Neidlinger had key associations with pianist Cecil Taylor in the 1970s and 1980s. Neidlinger, "Buell

Neidlinger," 20; Davis, *Jazz and Its Discontents*, 172; and Packer and Leach, *Gay Guerrilla*, 32.

30   Lynda Richardson, "Sparing a Dime, Whether They Agree or Not," *New York Times*, January 3, 1992; Davis, *Jazz and Its Discontents*, 168; and Brad Cohan, "Charles Gayle Embraces His Alter Ego," *Village Voice*, February 8, 2012.

31   Gayle, in *Rising Tones Cross*, at 1:14:46.

32   Gayle, quoted in Allen, "Charles Gayle," 7.

33   Gayle, in *Rising Tones Cross*, at 0:14:39.

34   Michael Wimberly, interview by author, digital recording, October 15, 2021.

35   Davis, *Jazz and Its Discontents*, 169.

36   Jon Pareles, "Jazz: Charles Gayle," *New York Times*, September 3, 1987. Pareles offered similar descriptions of a Knitting Factory performance in 1992. Jon Pareles, "Freedom and Physicality from Charles Gayle's Trio," *New York Times*, March 30, 1992.

37   Davis, *Jazz and Its Discontents*, 170. See Charles Gayle Trio, *Homeless* (Silkheart, 1989).

38   Gayle, in *Rising Tones Cross*, at 0:05:55.

39   Charles Gayle, "Charles Gayle: Interview by James Lindbloom," *Perfect Sound Forever*, March 2000, https://www.furious.com/perfect/charlesgayle.html.

40   Davis, *Jazz and Its Discontents*, 171.

41   H. Greene, interview.

42   H. Greene, "Interview: Hilliard Greene," 15.

43   H. Greene, interview.

44   H. Greene, "Interview: Hilliard Greene," 15.

45   H. Greene, interview.

46   Butler, interview, September 13, 2016.

47   Charles Gayle Trio, *Consider the Lilies . . .* (Clean Feed, 2006).

48   Charles Gayle, liner notes, *Consider the Lilies . . .*

49   Gayle, quoted in Davis, *Jazz and Its Discontents*, 172.

50   Kalaparusha Maurice McIntyre, interview by Jesse Dulman, digital recording, July 9, 2004, Jesse Dulman private collection.

51   Kalaparusha was originally sentenced to a span of sixty days to four years. He later claimed to have first started using heroin to deal with depression. At other times, saxophonists Sonny Rollins and Sonny Stitt, trumpeter Lee Morgan, drummer Elvin Jones, and numerous other artistic and literary figures, including Sammy Davis Jr., Ray Charles, and William S. Burroughs, served time in the same medical prison for using heroin or other narcotics in the 1950s and 1960s. Bobby Miller, who had been sentenced for a codeine addiction, later went to Chicago and played with Sonny Stitt and Gene Ammons, but died young of a heroin overdose. McIntyre, interview; Lewis, *Power Stronger Than Itself*, 139–40; Taylor Ho Bynum, "Postscript: Kalaparusha Maurice McIntyre, 1936–2013," *New Yorker*, November 14, 2013, http://taylorhobynum.com

/postscript-kalaparusha-maurice-mcintyre-1936-2013/; and Rebecca Gayle Howell, "The Lexington Cure," *Oxford American*, no. 99 (November 21, 2017).

52 McIntyre, quoted in Lewis, *Power Stronger Than Itself*, 139–40.

53 "All the Things You Are" was originally composed by Jerome Kern, with lyrics by Oscar Hammerstein II.

54 McIntyre, interview.

55 Kalaparusha worked in a print shop and sanitation during his time at the prison but eventually focused primarily on music. McIntyre, interview.

56 McIntyre, interview.

57 McIntyre, interview.

58 Eric Dolphy, *Out to Lunch!* (Blue Note, 1964).

59 McIntyre, interview.

60 Kalaparusha wrote the music for the record in the wake of the assassination of Dr. Martin Luther King Jr., which was a volatile time for the South Side of Chicago. Despite the record's success, Kalaparusha later quipped, "I was angry when I recorded that. [Delmark] had recorded the others but took so long to record me. I didn't have any humility! So, I don't think I was really ready when I did it. There is a lot of stuff on that record, I don't really care for." He was similarly critical of his second record, *Forces and Feelings*, feeling that the drummer, Wesley Tyus, had "gotten in my way. Fred Hopkins was the best player on that record." McIntyre, interview; see also "Jazz Musicians Group in Chicago Growing," *DownBeat*, July 28, 1966; Maurice McIntyre, *Humility in the Light of Creator* (Delmark Records, 1969); Lawrence Kart, "Maurice McIntyre," *DownBeat*, April 16, 1970; Kalaparusha Maurice McIntyre, *Forces and Feelings* (Delmark Records, 1972); and Lewis, *Power Stronger Than Itself*, 135.

61 Bynum, "Postscript: Kalaparusha Maurice McIntyre."

62 Kalaparusha, quoted in Lewis, *Power Stronger Than Itself*, 213.

63 Diphda (star) is an alternate spelling. The song "Difda Dance," composed by Henry Threadgill, was written as a tribute to Kalaparusha. New Air, *Live at the Montreal International Jazz Festival* (Black Saint, 1984); and Bynum, "Postscript: Kalaparusha Maurice McIntyre."

64 Kalaparusha received a $500 grant from the National Endowment for the Arts that facilitated the cross-country move. His most well-known students from his time at the Creative Music Studio were the sound engineer Jon Rosenberg and the bassist John Lindberg. McIntyre, interview; and Jon Rosenberg, "An Interview with Jon Rosenberg," interview by Beppe Colli, *CloudsandClocks*, April 2, 2017, http://www.cloudsandclocks.net/interviews/Rosenberg_interview.html.

65 McIntyre, interview; and Lewis, *Power Stronger Than Itself*, 333.

66 Lewis, *Power Stronger Than Itself*, 333.

67 Kalaparusha supposedly auditioned with Davis at a live concert in Chicago. He closed his eyes and was so focused on what he was doing that when he opened them, he was the only person left onstage. Davis supposedly remarked to him afterward, "It's a Disney Land world out there," and declined to hire him after

that. McIntyre, interview; see also Ravish Momin, interview by author, digital recording, April 20, 2020.

68 Lewis, *Power Stronger Than Itself,* 392–93, 396–400, 416.

69 Lewis, *Power Stronger Than Itself*, 440.

70 McIntyre, interview.

71 He had borrowed money from many of his friends in the AACM through the years, especially Lester Bowie. McIntyre, interview.

72 McIntyre, interview.

73 George Lewis, who won a MacArthur Foundation grant in 2002, reputedly gave Kalaparusha some money at the time to help him survive. Momin, interview.

74 "Kalaparusha Maurice McIntyre: 'That's Not a Horn, It's a Starvation Box,'" *Guardian*, September 13, 2010, https://www.theguardian.com/music/video /2010/sep/13/kalaparusha-maurice-mcintyre-horn-starvation-box.

75 Dulman had previously self-released a recording of his own quartet that included drummers Gary Fogel and Isaiah Cook, flutist Gamiel Lyons, and tenor saxophonist Mike Seropyan. Jesse Dulman Quartet, *Peace Psalm* (self-released, 1999). After many years of recording and playing as a sideperson with Kalaparusha, as well as brief stints with Burnt Sugar and Ravish Momin's Trio Tarana, Dulman reassembled the quartet in 2017, though with different personnel: saxophonists Dave Sewelson and Ras Moshe and drummer Leonid Galaganov.

76 Jesse Dulman, interview by author, digital recording, June 25, 2020.

77 McIntyre, interview.

78 Momin had previously studied North Indian classical music as well as jazz. The 1960s iteration of the band included drummer Jerome Cooper and pianist Amina Claudine Myers as part of a group that had a vocalist, trumpet, two saxophones, piano, two basses, and two drum kits that toured through the US South. McIntyre, interview; and Momin, interview.

79 Dulman, in *Jesse Dulman Documentary* (RR Gems Records, 2017), at 0:05:55.

80 Momin, interview.

81 McIntyre, interview. Songs such as "I Don't Have an Answer unless It's God" expressed his faith. Kalaparusha and the Light, *Morning Song* (Delmark Records, 2004), track 8.

82 Sam Rivers Tuba Trio/Earl Cross Sextet, *Jazz of the Seventies/Una Muy Bonita* (Circle Records, 1977); and Sam Rivers Quintet, *Zenith* (1977), Sam Rivers Archive Project, vol. 2 (NoBusiness Records, 2019).

83 John Chacona, "Seeing the Light," *Erie News Daily*, September 4, 2003; and David Vance, review: *Morning Song* by Kalaparusha and the Light (Delmark, 2004).

84 Momin, interview.

85 Kalaparusha and the Light, *South Eastern* (CIMP, 2002).

86 Tour dates: Hybrydy Club (Warsaw), March 4, 2003; Blue Note Club (Poznan), March 5, 2003; and Klub Collesium (Gdansk), March 6, 2003. Momin, interview.

87　McIntyre, interview.

88　Chacona, "Seeing the Light."

89　McIntyre, interview.

90　McIntyre, interview; and Momin, interview.

91　Momin, interview.

92　Dulman, in *Jesse Dulman Documentary*, at 0:08:33.

93　Momin introduced Kalaparusha to Lane. Momin, interview.

94　Kalaparusha was unhappy with his own performance on *The Moment* but was complimentary of his bandmates. Kalaparusha and the Light, *The Moment* (Entropy Stereo Recordings, 2003); Kalaparusha and the Light, *Morning Song*; and Kalaparusha and the Light, *Paths to Glory* (CIMP, 2004). McIntyre, interview.

95　McIntyre, interview.

96　Howard Reich, "Fearless Musical Experimenting Pays Dividends," *Chicago Tribune*, April 2, 2004.

97　Momin, interview.

98　Kalaparusha and the Light, *Moment*, track 1.

99　"Antoinette" appears in several versions in the band's recorded work, including two takes on their debut record, *South Eastern*, and a live version on *The Moment*. Kalaparusha and the Light, *South Eastern*, tracks 5–6; Kalaparusha and the Light, *Moment*, track 2; and Momin, interview.

100　Momin, interview.

101　Eyal Hareuveni, "Tel Aviv Jazz Festival 2006," All about Jazz, March 23, 2006, https://www.allaboutjazz.com/tel-aviv-jazz-festival-2006-by-eyal-hareuveni .php.

102　Dulman, interview.

103　Momin, interview. Dulman later recorded a tribute to Kalaparusha. Jesse Dulman Quartet, *Live at Downtown Music Gallery* (RR Gems, 2017), track 5. After Kalaparusha's band dissolved, Dulman cofounded a band called the Stumblebums that played dance music and was featured on *America's Got Talent*.

104　"Kalaparusha Maurice McIntyre."

105　Ha-Yang Kim, interview by author, digital recording, April 27, 2020.

106　Ken Butler, interview by author, digital recording, April 13, 2020.

107　Central Avenue had emerged by the early 1920s as the heart of the Black community in southern Los Angeles; despite restrictive real estate laws, hostile policing, and other racist political mechanisms, the corridor along Central Avenue became a dynamic cultural center for music by the 1940s. Eastman, "Central Avenue Blues"; Cox, "Evolution of Black Music," 249–73; Daniels, "Los Angeles Zoot," 99–100, 105; Flamming, *Bound for Freedom*, 92–125; Isoardi, *Dark Tree*, 18–19; and C. Smith, *Making Music in Los Angeles*, 170–71, 183–85.

108　Marmorstein, "Central Avenue Jazz"; Cox, "Evolution of Black Music," 259, 263, 265–67; Isoardi, *Dark Tree*, 19–20, 24–27; Alvarez, *Power of Zoot*, 115–16, 126–29, 133–35, 137, 140–41, 145; Dickerson, "Jazz in Los Angeles," 183–85; Meadows, "Clifford Brown in Los Angeles," 47; Gordon, "Dexter Gordon and

Melba Liston," 10–12; Gabbard, *Better Git It in Your Soul*, 27; and Gordon, *Sophisticated Giant*, 23–24, 26–27, 79–80, 100–101.

109 Even the musicians' union integrated in the early 1950s. Spellman, *Four Lives in the Bebop Business*, 104–25; Wilmer, *As Serious as Your Life*, 68–70; Litweiler, *Freedom Principle*, 33–40; Gioia, *West Coast Jazz*, 348–59; Tapscott, "Horace Tapscott," 299; Tapscott, *Songs of the Unsung*, 36–37, 42–50; and Isoardi, *Dark Tree*, 19, 30, 32–40.

110 The Watts Rebellion was the largest uprising of the civil rights era. Yang, "Thin Blue Line"; Yang, *California Polyphony*, 60–79; Stanley, "Butch Morris," 44–46; Camp, *Incarcerating the Crisis*, 21–23; and Rodriguez, *Yolqui*, 32–34.

111 Sharp, "Seeking John Carter and Bobby Bradford," 65–81; Tapscott, *Songs of the Unsung*, 101; and Isoardi, *Dark Tree*, 113.

112 Tapscott, *Songs of the Unsung*, 137–38.

113 Nicholls, "Changing the Subject," 31.

114 Isoardi, *Dark Tree*, 118.

115 Williams, quoted in Isoardi, *Dark Tree*, 267.

116 L. Morris, quoted in Isoardi, *Dark Tree*, 267.

117 Connell, who had a long career as a music copyist, got some of his first significant experience working in that capacity with the Pan-Afrikan Peoples Arkestra in the late 1960s.

118 Lawrence D. Morris, "First Curiosity," liner notes, *Testament: A Conduction Collection* (New World Records, 1995), 3.

119 L. Morris, quoted in Stanley, "Butch Morris," 53.

120 L. Morris, "First Curiosity," 3.

121 Robert Palmer, "Jazz: Rivbea," *New York Times*, June 27, 1977; Robert Palmer, "Newport Jazz," *New York Times*, June 28, 1978; Tapscott, *Songs of the Unsung*, 160; and Isoardi, *Dark Tree*, 144, 258.

122 L. Morris, "First Curiosity," 4.

123 L. Morris, "First Curiosity," 5.

124 L. Morris, "First Curiosity," 5.

125 David Henderson, "Butch Morris," *Bomb*, no. 55 (Winter 1996): 32.

126 Billy Bang, liner notes, *Outline No. 12* (Celluloid, 1983), [2].

127 L. Morris, "First Curiosity," 5; see also Lawrence D. Morris, "Theory and Contradiction," liner notes, *Testament*, 8.

128 The recording of the first official Conduction appears on *Current Trends in Racism in Modern America*, which featured an eclectic array of musicians that would exemplify Morris's wide-ranging approach in future years: Yasunao Tone (voice), John Zorn (alto saxophone, game calls), Frank Lowe (tenor saxophone), Tom Cora (cello), Brandon Ross (guitar), Curtis Clark (piano), Zeena Parkins (harp), Eli Fountain (vibraphone), Thurman Barker (percussion), and Christian Marclay (turntables). Lawrence D. "Butch" Morris, *Current Trends in Racism in Modern America* (Sound Aspects Records, 1985).

129 L. Morris, "First Curiosity," 5–6.

130 Greg Tate, in *Black February*, directed by Vipal Monga (2005), at 00:14:21.

131 Brandon Ross, in *Black February*, at 0:07:33.

132 Jon Pareles, "Morris Tests Limits of Improvisation," *New York Times*, July 26, 1985; and Jon Pareles, "Free Butch Morris Concerts," *New York Times*, November 16, 1989. Much of Morris's early work that followed appears together in the collection *Testament*. The box set documents performances in San Francisco in 1988 and New York in 1989 and 1993, as well as concerts around the world in Canada, Germany, Italy, Japan, the Netherlands, and Turkey in 1992–93. Lawrence D. "Butch" Morris, *Testament: A Conduction Collection*, 10 CDs (New World Records, 1995).

133 Lawrence D. Morris, "First Curiosity," liner notes, *Testament: A Conduction Collection* (New World Records, 1995), 3.

134 Lawrence D. Morris, "Another Jazz," *New York City Jazz Record*, no. 118 (February 2012): 11.

135 Morris quoted in Henderson, "Butch Morris," 33.

136 Jonathon Haffner, interview by author, digital recording, April 23, 2020.

137 Signals could include things like asking a guitarist to mimic a pianist, for example. Ben Ratliff, "A System of Conducting, or, Rather, 'Conduction,'" *New York Times*, April 3, 1998; Kim, interview; and Kenny Wollesen, interview by author, digital recording, April 28, 2020.

138 Kim, interview.

139 Morris, in *Black February*, at 0:04:26.

140 Ben Ratliff, "An Improvising Conductor Celebrates an Anniversary," *New York Times*, February 3, 2005.

141 Greg Tate, in *Black February*, at 0:08:02.

142 Morris, in *Black February*, at 0:10:44.

143 Mazz Swift, in *Black February*, at 0:12:17.

144 Morris, in *Black February*, at 0:21:11.

145 Orchestra SLANG, flyer for Zebulon residency, March 2006, Kenny Wollesen private collection.

146 Orchestra SLANG, flyer for Zebulon residency; Bill Ware, interview by author, digital recording, March 20, 2020; and Kim, interview.

147 Kim, interview.

148 Henry Threadgill, in *Black February*, at 0:37:53.

149 Wollesen, interview.

150 Haffner, interview.

151 Ware, interview.

152 Kim, interview.

153 Brandon Ross, in *Black February*, 0:41:09.

154 Nublu Orchestra, *Nublu Orchestra Conducted by Butch Morris* (Nublu Records, 2006).

155 Nublu Orchestra, *Live at Jazz Festival Saalfelden* (Nublu Records, 2010); and Haffner, interview.

156 Taylor Ho Bynum, "Postscript: Butch Morris (1947–2013)," *New Yorker*, January 30, 2013, https://www.newyorker.com/culture/culture-desk/postscript -butch-morris-1947-2013.

157 According to collaborator Sarah Wilson, Wollesen had been talking about starting a marching band since the mid-1990s, but the political events of 2001 and after necessitated its existence as a form of community response. Sarah Wilson, interview by author, digital recording, May 5, 2020.

158 Wollesen, interview.

159 Wollesen, interview.

160 Haffner, interview.

161 Michael Irwin, interview by author, digital recording, May 6, 2020.

162 "Spare Times," *New York Times*, August 7, 1998.

163 Upper Planets, *WSU Terrorist Theme* (Bandcamp, 2020). The piece, "WSU Terrorist Theme," was composed by Sarah Wilson. The lineup included Sarah Wilson (trumpet), Clark Gayton (sousaphone), Jonathon Haffner and Dave Binney (alto saxophones), Jessica Lurie (tenor saxophone), Briggan Krauss (clarinet), Michael and Frank London (trumpet), Art Baron (trombone), Tony Scherr and Matt McDonald (guitar), Jesse Harris (banjo), Brian Mitchell (B3 organ), Matt Mottel (synthesizer), Don Falzone (bass), Jennifer Harris (cymbals), Kenny Wollesen (bass drum), Dalius Naujokaitis (snare drum), and Baye Kouyate and Tim Keiper (percussion).

164 Irwin, interview.

165 Wollesen employed some of Zorn's Masada music that the latter was composing at the time.

166 Wollesen, interview.

167 The piece "Until the Rain Comes" was composed by saxophonist Peter Apfelbaum but popularized by Don Cherry, who recorded a version of it in 1990. Don Cherry, *Multikulti* (A&M Records, 1990); and Irwin, interview. "African Marketplace" is the title track from Ibrahim's Dollar Brand, *African Marketplace* (Elektra, 1994). "Down in the Valley to Pray" is a Black American spiritual.

168 Wollesen, interview.

169 Haffner had moved to Williamsburg from the West Coast in 1999, drawn by the music of Tim Berne, Jim Black, and John Zorn. Haffner's first residence was at 202 South Second Street between Driggs Street and Roebling Street in Williamsburg. He soon became a sub in Wollesen's band The Wollesens. Irwin, the son of jazz bassist Dennis Irwin, recorded extensively in many different formations from 2007 to 2016 with a lean toward Afrobeat music. He met Wollesen while practicing in a park in Manhattan and was asked to join the band. Scherr has recorded with Steven Bernstein, Brad Shepik, and many others since the late 1990s. Jesse Harris is best known for his song "Don't Know Why," performed by Norah Jones, for which he received a Grammy Award. Haffner, interview; and Irwin, interview.

170 Wilson, interview.

171 Irwin, interview.

172 Wilson, interview.

173 Irwin, interview.

174 Anthology Film Archives was founded in 1970 by avant-garde filmmakers Jonas Mekas, Stan Brakhage, Peter Kubelka, P. Adams Sitney, and Jerome Hill. Šumila, "New York Scenes and Echoes."

175 Mekas also began his own band around that time that played in art galleries throughout New York City, called the Jonas Mekas Now We Are Here Orchestra, which grew out of the same music scene. Haberski, *Freedom to Offend*; Šumila, "New York Scenes and Echoes"; and Haffner, interview.

176 Haffner, interview.

177 Wollesen, interview. For most of his life, Mekas wrote poetry entirely in the Lithuanian language, though later in life he composed in English. His earliest poems, a collection of over twenty idylls focused on his home village in Lithuania, were written in 1946 while he was living in a refugee camp in Germany and attending the University of Mainz. Mekas, "Interview with Jonas Mekas," 87, 93.

178 Šumila, "New York Scenes and Echoes."

179 References to Mekas's folk music roots appear in the film *Reminiscences of a Journey to Lithuania* (1972), featuring music by painter, composer, and writer Mikalojus Konstantinas Čiurlionis (1875–1911). The film chronicled his first return visit to his family in Semeniškiai, Lithuania, after fleeing the country with his brother Adolfas in the wake of World War II. *Reminiscences of a Journey to Lithuania*, directed by Jonas Mekas (1972).

180 Dalius Naujokaitis, quoted in Šumila, "New York Scenes and Echoes."

181 Šumila, "New York Scenes and Echoes."

182 Mekas, quoted in Šumila, "New York Scenes and Echoes." Mekas's career began in earnest in New York in 1953, when he first began organizing screenings and soon after was involved in the journal *Film Culture*.

183 Wollesen, interview.

184 JM Singers, *Jonas Song* (Bandcamp, 2020).

185 This lineup of the big band included Dalius Naujokaitis (snare drum, percussion, voice), Raha Raissnia (synthesizer), Jonathon Haffner (alto saxophone), Kirk Knuffke (cornet), Jessica Lurie (tenor saxophone), Jennifer Harris (cymbals, percussion), Matt Cole (baritone saxophone), Will Shore (vibraphone, glockenspiel, percussion), Panagiotis Mavridis (*atermon*), and Kenny Wollesen (bass drum, percussion). JM Singers, *Jonas Song*.

186 Wilson, interview.

187 The band performed operas by Julius Zizliauskas, such as *Contemplation on the Island of Freedom*, among others. Wollesen, interview.

188 Wollesen, interview.

189 Irwin, interview.

190 Haffner, interview; and Wollesen, interview.

191 Haffner, interview. Zebulon allowed Wollesen to store many of his percussion instruments in the basement, which made the performances much easier to carry out since he used so many drums, often large, in the live sets. Wollesen, interview.

192 Irwin, interview.

193 Irwin, interview.

194 Haffner, interview. Though no specific personnel are specified for some of the band's live recordings at Zebulon that have been released, a careful listening detects at least fifteen participants. Himalayas, *Ayeeta* (Bandcamp, 2020). The largest the band ever got was approximately seventy-five musicians, who performed at the Prospect Park Bandshell. Haffner, interview; Wollesen, interview; and Irwin, interview.

195 Irwin, interview.

196 Various, *This Is It*. The single was rereleased in 2020. SLAM, *Until the Rain Comes* (Bandcamp, 2020).

197 Wilson, interview.

198 Himalayas, *Shotgun Recordings* (Bandcamp, 2013).

199 In Willisau the band was able to rehearse every day, which was impossible in New York, and the live festival performance was recorded, though it remains unreleased.

200 Sarah Wilson, email to author, May 7, 2020.

201 Bynum, quoted in Wilson, interview. Photos of the concert are available from Scott Friedlander's Flickr page: https://www.flickr.com/photos/scottfriedlander/sets/72157714262517331/ (accessed April 24, 2021).

202 Butler, interview, April 13, 2020.

203 Buddy Guy (b. 1936) recorded the piece in 1968. Buddy Guy, *A Man and the Blues* (Vanguard, 1968).

204 Anderson recorded extensively for Warner Brothers Records in 1982–95 and since then has appeared on Nonesuch and other labels.

205 Butler, interview, April 13, 2020.

206 By *bricolage*, Butler meant "using what is at hand." Butler, interview, April 13, 2020. The term comes from Claude Lévi-Strauss, who used it to indicate the process of recontextualizing, repurposing, rethinking, and selecting the best parts of the old world to form a new one, to rebuild, without destroying the old parts. Lévi-Strauss, *Savage Mind*, 16–36.

207 Take, for example, Pablo Picasso's *Guitar and Violin* (1912), *Guitar, Sheet Music and Wine Glass* (1912), *Musical Instruments* (1912), *My Beautiful, Woman with Guitar* (1912), *Still Life with Violin and Fruits* (1912), two paintings titled *Violin* (1912), *Clarinet and Violin* (1913), *Geometrical Composition: The Guitar* (1913), *Guitar and Bottle* (1913), *Man with Guitar* (1913), *The Guitar* (1913), *Woman with Guitar* (1913), *Violin* (1913), and *Mandolin* (1914). And see Bracque's *Violin and Pipe* (1913). Mellers, "Erik Satie," 216; and James, "Duchamp's Silent Noise," 114.

208 Financial support from the Oregon Arts Commission and the National Endowment of the Arts helped spur Butler's work in 1983. Butler, interview, April 13, 2020.

209 The mbira, or *mbira dzavadzimu*, is a percussive, chimelike instrument originally developed by the Shona people of Zimbabwe, who often used them in religious ceremonies that involved spirit possession. Turino, "Mbira, Worldbeat," 85; and C. Jones, "Shona Women *Mbira* Players," 125.

210 Mark Dery, "Doing Your Own Thing by Making Your Own Thing," *New York Times*, August 19, 1990.

211 Skeleton Crew recorded two records that documented their groundbreaking work. Skeleton Crew, *Learn to Talk* (Recommended Music, 1984); and Skeleton Crew, *The Country of Blinds* (No Man's Land, 1986).

212 Butler, interview, April 13, 2020.

213 Dorf, *Knitting Music*, 2.

214 Butler, interview, April 13, 2020.

215 Bernard Holland, "Classical Music in Review," *New York Times*, December 7, 1992. The review described Butler's contributions to the Dave Soldier String Quartet at Merkin Concert Hall.

216 Ken Butler, *Voices of Anxious Objects* (Tzadik, 1997).

217 Salifoski has recorded widely as a sideperson, especially with Paradox Trio, Brad Shepik, and the Boston-based avant-garde big band Orange Then Blue. The *dumbek* is a kind of goblet drum, commonly used in the Middle East, North Africa, South Asia, and eastern Europe.

218 Lonergan, review: Various Artists, *This Is It: Live at Zebulon*, vol. 1, *All about Jazz—New York*, no. 44 (December 2005): 18.

219 Various, *This Is It*.

220 Cooper-Moore was a key figure in William Parker's band In Order to Survive and was also a member of the Little Huey Creative Music Orchestra, among other bands.

221 Cooper-Moore, interview by author, digital recording, March 19, 2020.

222 Cooper-Moore and Assif Tsahar, *America* (Hopscotch Records, 2003).

223 Assif Tsahar, Cooper-Moore, and Hamid Drake, *Lost Brother* (Hopscotch Records, 2005).

224 Cooper-Moore, interview.

225 Chad Taylor, interview by author, email, April 7, 2020.

226 Jeff Stockton, review: Digital Primitives, *Digital Primitives*, *All about Jazz—New York*, no. 64 (August 2007): 14.

227 C. Taylor, interview.

228 Cooper-Moore, interview.

229 During periods when Tsahar returned to Israel, alto saxophonist Darius Jones sat in with the band.

230 Cooper-Moore, interview.

231 Stockton, review: Digital Primitives, 14.

232 C. Taylor, interview.

233 Digital Primitives, *Hum Crackle and Pop* (Hopscotch Records, 2009).

234 Rashied Ali and Louis Belogenis, *Rings of Saturn* (Knitting Factory Records, 1999); and Rashied Ali, Louis Belogenis, and Wilber Morris, *Live at Tonic* (DIW, 2001).

235 Belogenis, interview.

236 Belogenis, interview.

237 Belogenis's teacher Bokar Rinpoche was from the Karma Ragyü and Shangpa Kagyü lineages of knowledge transmission, the former of which is the second largest of the Kagyü school, one of the four major schools of Tibetan Buddhism. Belogenis, interview.

238 Belogenis's initial Buddhist teachings came from Kalu Rinpoche (1905–89), who was the mentor of Bokar Rinpoche, at a Buddhist center in Manhattan. Belogenis, interview.

239 Belogenis, interview.

240 Belogenis, interview.

241 Belogenis, interview.

242 The band recorded in OMSS Studios, run by bassist Bill Laswell, in New Jersey on August 1, 2005. Unbroken Trio, *Unbroken* (Tick Tock, 2005).

243 "Bells" was a record-length piece that Ayler recorded at Town Hall in New York on May 1, 1965. Albert Ayler, *Bells* (ESP disk, 1965).

244 Belogenis, interview.

245 The State University of New York College at Old Westbury had one of the first African American music programs in the United States, founded by multi-instrumentalist Makanda Ken McIntyre (1931–2001).

246 Andrew Lamb, interview by author, digital recording, March 16, 2020.

247 Jimmy James Greene, interview by author, digital recording, February 9, 2021.

248 Strobert also owned and ran Ki-Ki Records. His brother was saxophonist and flutist Ricardo Strobert.

249 Joloff has since moved to 1168 Bedford Avenue, a few blocks to the east of the original location.

250 Halsey first encountered Spriggs in the *Journal of Black Poetry* around 1969.

251 Onaje Will Halsey, interview by author, digital recording, February 9, 2021.

252 J. J. Greene, interview.

253 Robert Hayden, *Collected Poems*, 33.

254 J. J. Greene, interview.

255 Lamb, interview.

256 Halsey, interview.

257 Greene had grown up in Xenia, Ohio, and apprenticed with muralist Jon Onye Lockard for three years in Detroit and Ann Arbor, Michigan, before attending art school. J. J. Greene, interview.

258 J. J. Greene, interview.

259 J. J. Greene, interview.

260 J. J. Greene, interview.

261 The set was recorded on November 21, 2003. The Moving Form, *Year of the Endless Moment* (Engine Studios, 2004). The videographer Chuck Moss also filmed some of their live performances at the Poet's Cafe. The group also performed at the Nuyorican Poets Café. J. J. Greene, interview.

262 Halsey, interview.

263 Lamb, interview.

264 Lamb, interview.

265 The band took its name from silverback gorillas. Frank Lacy, interview by author, digital recording, May 15, 2020.

266 Newman Taylor Baker, interview by author, digital recording, April 29, 2020.

267 Connell had known Morris for more than three decades from their roots in Los Angeles. Connell and Lacy had met in the David Murray Big Band. After Morris's death, Hilliard Greene joined Silverback on bass. Occasionally the band expanded to a quintet with Charles Eubanks on piano. Lacy, interview, May 15, 2020.

268 Baker, interview.

269 Connell was a key figure in the band Commitment with Jason Kao Hwang, Takeshi "Zen" Matsuura, and William Parker in 1979–84 and later played as a sideperson with Kalaparusha, trombonist Steve Swell, Parker's Little Huey Creative Music Orchestra, and bassist Alan Silva.

270 Connell got his earliest, substantive experience in copying charts with Horace Tapscott in Los Angeles but later worked for a variety of people in the jazz world and even figures like Michael Jackson. Momin, interview; and Baker, interview.

271 Connell also bears influence from Cecil Taylor, having worked as a sub for Jimmy Lyons in the former's band in the 1980s. Connell also absorbed some of Sun Ra's approach to composition. Lacy, interview.

272 Lacy, interview.

Chapter 5. A New Generation Emerges

1 Sitek is a musician, writer, and producer behind the band TV on the Radio and has also produced work by other indie rock bands such as Beady Eye, Celebration, Foals, Liars, Little Dragon, Weezer, and the Yeah Yeah Yeahs. All of the bands listed above are still based in Brooklyn; they constitute some of the major bands to emerge during Brooklyn's indie rock wave.

2 Some of the live material from the sessions was documented and released. Matana Roberts Quartet, *The Calling* (Utech Records, 2006).

3 Nate Chinen, review: *Coin Coin Chapter Three: River Run Thee*, by Matana Roberts, *New York Times*, February 2, 2015.

4   G. Mills, *Forgotten People*; Susan Dollar, "Red River Campaign, Natchitoches Parish, Louisiana," 413; Morgan, MacDonald, and Handley, "Economics and Authenticity," 44–59; Gikandi, *Slavery and the Culture of Taste*, 249–53; and E. Mills, "Demythicizing History," 404–14.

5   S. Morgan, "Clementine Hunter and Melrose Plantation," 26.

6   Peter Margasak, "Jazz Genealogy: Matana Roberts Releases the First Chapter of a 12-Part Epic That Traces African-American History Back across the Atlantic," *Chicago Reader*, May 5, 2011, https://www.chicagoreader.com/chicago/matana-roberts-jazz-african-american-history/Content?oid=3726878.

7   Matana Roberts, "Traces of People: An Interview with Matana Roberts," interview by Stewart Smith, *Quietus*, October 6, 2015, https://thequietus.com/articles/18937-matana-roberts-interview.

8   M. Roberts, "Traces of People."

9   M. Roberts, quoted in Margasak, "Jazz Genealogy."

10 M. Roberts, "Traces of People."

11 M. Roberts, quoted in Margasak, "Jazz Genealogy."

12 Oscar Brown Jr., *Sin and Soul* (Columbia, 1960).

13 Matana Roberts, *Coin Coin Chapter One: Gens de Couleur Libres* (Constellation, 2011), track 5.

14 "NewMusicBox Matana Roberts: Creative Defiance," New Music USA, January 4, 2013, YouTube video, 10:16, https://www.youtube.com/watch?v=XXI5pXB0_Ac.

15 "NewMusicBox Matana Roberts."

16 M. Roberts, *Coin Coin Chapter One*.

17 Their first record comprised live recordings from their first two concerts. Eye Contact, *Making Eye Contact with God* (Utech Records, 2005). The first record was soon after rereleased by the same label as a dual CD with other live performances that had been done at Zebulon the same year. Eye Contact, *Embracing the Tide/Making Eye Contact with God*.

18 Matt Lavelle, interview by author, digital recording, March 15, 2020.

19 Lavelle, interview.

20 Florence Wetzel, review: *Embracing the Tide/Making Eye Contact with God* by Eye Contact, *All about Jazz—New York*, no. 45 (January 2006): 13.

21 *Divine Horsemen: The Living Gods of Haiti*, directed by Maya Deren (1954); and Sawyer, interview, June 11, 2020.

22 Wetzel, review: *Embracing the Tide*, 13.

23 Lavelle, interview.

24 Charles Mingus, *Black Saint and the Sinner Lady* (Impulse!, 1963). See Robert Palmer, "Mingus Plays Flamenco with Azucena Dancers," *New York Times*, June 28, 1976; Connie Lauerman, "When Legendary Jazz Musician Charles Mingus Saw . . . ," *Chicago Tribune*, November 20, 1994; and Adam Schatz, "An Argument with Instruments: On Charles Mingus," *Nation*, September 17, 2013.

25 Eye Contact, *War Rug* (KMB Jazz, 2006).

26 Jeff Stockton, review: *War Rug*, by Eye Contact, All About Jazz, April 7, 2007, https://www.allaboutjazz.com/matt-lavelle-spiritual-power-and-war-rug-by -jeff-stockton.

27 Lavelle, interview.

28 Monika Hebbinghaus, "Radical Jewish Culture Movement Helped Musicians Uncover Identity," *DW*, April 20, 2011, https://www.dw.com/en/radical-jewish -culture-movement-helped-musicians-uncover-identity/a-15005319.

29 Barzel, *New York Noise*, 3.

30 Shanir Blumenkranz, interview by author, digital recording, March 26, 2020.

31 Blumenkranz and Maoz's first band was the Lemon Juice Quartet, with trumpeter Avishai Cohen and drummer Kevin Zubek, which began in Israel and reconvened in Boston and eventually moved to New York in 2000. Lemon Juice Quartet, *Republic* (Chant Records, 2001); and Lemon Juice Quartet, *Peasant Songs: The Music of Erik Satie and Bela Bartok* (Piadrum Records, 2002).

32 Eyal Maoz, *Edom*, Radical Jewish Culture, no. 105 (Tzadik, 2005).

33 Eyal Maoz, interview by author, digital recording, June 16, 2020.

34 Maoz, interview.

35 Blumenkranz, interview.

36 Shirer, *Rise and Fall of the Third Reich*.

37 Maoz, interview.

38 Eyal Maoz, *Hope and Destruction*, Radical Jewish Culture, no. 147 (Tzadik, 2009).

39 Blumenkranz, interview.

40 Blumenkranz, interview.

41 Blumenkranz, interview.

42 Maoz, interview.

43 Blumenkranz further explored many of these themes with the band Abraxas. Blumenkranz, interview. John Coltrane, *A Love Supreme* (Impulse!, 1965).

44 Jon Madof, interview by author, digital recording, March 22, 2020.

45 John Zorn/Rashanim, *Masada Rock* (Tzadik, 2005).

46 Madof, interview. Pachora, comprising Chris Speed, Brad Shepik, Skúli Sverrison, and Jim Black, was most active in 1997–2003 and was heavily influenced by eastern European, Mediterranean, and Middle Eastern folk music. Pachora, *Pachora* (Knitting Factory Works, 1997); Pachora, *Unn* (Knitting Factory Works, 1998); Pachora, *Ast* (Knitting Factory Works, 1999); and Pachora, *Astereotypical* (Winter and Winter, 2003).

47 Madof, interview. Madof's early rock influences were Jimi Hendrix, Led Zeppelin, and Pink Floyd, and later he encountered the Pixies, Jane's Addiction, and Fugazi.

48 The band had previously appeared on Tzadik's compilation *The Unknown Ma-sada*, with the piece "Olamim," which apparently impressed Zorn, which compelled him to work with Madof and Rashanim more in the years that followed. John Zorn, *The Unknown Masada* (Tzadik, 2003).

49 Rashanim, *Shalosh* (Tzadik, 2006).

50 Rashanim, *The Gathering* (Tzadik, 2009).

51 Eivind Opsvik, interview by author, digital recording, June 10, 2020. Rypdal (b. 1947) had come up on the Norwegian scene with saxophonist Jan Garbarek (b. 1947) and percussionist Jon Christensen (1943–2020).

52 Opsvik, interview.

53 Eivind Opsvik, *Overseas II* (Fresh Sound New Talent, 2005).

54 Opsvik, interview. See Miles Davis, *In a Silent Way* (Columbia, 1969); Miles Davis, *Bitches Brew* (Columbia, 1970).

55 *Once upon a Time in America*, directed by Sergio Leone (1984).

56 Opsvik, interview.

57 Opsvik, interview.

58 Opsvik, interview. See Brian Eno, *Discreet Music* (Obscure, 1975), track 1.

59 At the time of Opsvik's recording, Edison Studio was operated by Henry Hirsch, a longtime associate of singer-songwriter Lenny Kravitz. Opsvik, interview.

60 Opsvik, interview.

61 Opsvik, interview.

62 Opsvik, interview.

63 Opsvik, interview. Mark Twain, *Personal Reflections of Joan of Arc* (New York: Harper and Brothers, 1896); Sofia Coppola, dir., *Marie Antoinette* (2006).

64 Cooper was involved in a range of experimental arts himself, having connected with the early punk scene in England in 1976 and later collaborated with John Zorn, among many others.

65 Pride, interview.

66 Period, *Period* (Funhole, 2006).

67 Pride, interview.

68 Whoopie Pie, *Sweet* (Veal Records, 2007).

69 Out of respect for D'Angelo, the band's name was eventually changed to OV. Angel OV Death, *Live in Space and Time* (Veal Records, n.d.).

70 Kalashnikov, *Bang Bang* (Veal Records, 2008).

71 The Spanish Donkey, *XYX* (Northern Spy, 2011).

72 The band's debut record documented a live set in Philadelphia, which was the launch for the tour. From Bacteria to Boys, *Hang* (Funhole Records, 2006).

73 Pride, interview.

74 Pride, interview.

75 From Bacteria to Boys, *Betweenwhile* (AUM Fidelity, 2010).

76 Pride, interview.

77 Mike Pride, *Birthing Days* (AUM Fidelity, 2013).

78 Cisco Bradley, "Mike Pride's From Bacteria to Boys at Greenwich House Music School," Jazz Right Now, May 23, 2013, https://www.jazzrightnow.com/mike-prides-from-bacteria-to-boys-at-greenwich-house-music-school/.

79 See Toshimaru Nakamura and Sachiko M, *Do* (Erstwhile Records, 2001); and Yoshihide Otomo Keith Rowe, and Taku Sugimoto, *Ajar* (Alcohol, 2002).

80 Tom Blancarte, interview by author, digital recording, June 30, 2016.

81 Blancarte, interview.

82 Peter Evans and Tom Blancarte, *{Sparks}* (Creative Sources, 2008).

83 Blancarte, interview.

84 P. Evans, interview.

85 P. Evans, interview.

86 P. Evans, interview.

87 John Coltrane, *My Favorite Things* (Atlantic, 1961), track 4.

88 "Peter Evans: Zebulon," All about Jazz, May 6, 2013, https://www.allaboutjazz.com/zebulon-peter-evans-aire-sol-records-review-by-aaji-staff.

89 Peter Evans and Nate Wooley, *High Society* (Carrier Records, 2011).

90 Nate Wooley, "Point of Departure: Nate Wooley Interview," interview by Troy Collins, Clean Feed Records, March 10, 2016, https://cleanfeed-records.com/point-of-departure-nate-wooley-interview/.

91 P. Evans, interview.

92 Cymerman, "Life Preserver," 50–51.

93 Jeremiah Cymerman, interview by author, digital recording, June 10, 2020.

94 Jeremiah Cymerman, *In Memory of the Labyrinth System*, Composer Series (Tzadik, 2008).

95 Cymerman, interview, June 10, 2020. Popp's record was originally released under a different title: Elsa Popping and Her Dixieland Band, *Delirium in Hi-Fi* (Columbia, 1958).

96 Cymerman was also generally inspired by the solo music of Evan Parker and Ned Rothenberg.

97 Cymerman, interview, June 10, 2020.

98 Jeremiah Cymerman, interview by author, digital recording, April 2, 2017.

99 Cymerman, interview, April 2, 2017.

100 Cymerman, "Life Preserver," 54.

101 Cymerman, "Life Preserver," 53.

102 Cymerman, interview, April 2, 2017.

103 Silence and Solitude directly informed his later compositions for four clarinets and drums. Jeremiah Cymerman, *Systema Mundititius*, vol. 1 (self-released, 2020).

104 Jeremiah Cymerman, *Fire Sign*, Composer Series (Tzadik, 2011).

105 Cymerman, interview, June 10, 2020.

106 Jeremiah Cymerman, *Under a Blue Grey Sky* (Porter Records, 2010).

107 The sextet included Nate Wooley, Sam Kulik (trombone), Jeremiah Cymerman, Christopher Hoffman (cello), Tom Blancarte, and Harris Eisenstadt (drums).

108   Zorn, quoted in Cymerman, interview, June 10, 2020.

109   Cymerman, interview, June 10, 2020.

110   Cymerman, interview, June 10, 2020.

111   Laplante, interview.

112   Darius Jones, interview by author, digital recording, May 13, 2021.

113   D. Jones, interview.

114   Little Women, *Teeth* (Gilgongo Records, 2007).

115   Laplante, interview.

116   Jason Nazary, interview by author, digital recording, June 19, 2020.

117   D. Jones, interview.

118   Laplante, interview.

119   Laplante, interview.

120   Laplante, interview; and D. Jones, interview.

121   Nazary, interview.

122   D. Jones, interview.

123   UnartigNYC, "Little Women Live at Micheline's on September 15, 2006," YouTube video, 31:07, https://www.youtube.com/watch?v=F7moKZXGl1U.

124   D. Jones, interview.

125   D. Jones, interview.

126   Laplante, interview; and Nazary, interview.

127   Little Women, *Throat* (AUM Fidelity, 2010).

128   Nazary, interview.

129   D. Jones, interview.

130   Nazary, interview.

131   D. Jones, interview.

132   Andrew Smiley, interview by author, digital recording, June 18, 2020.

133   Smiley, interview.

134   Laplante, interview.

135   Smiley, interview.

136   D. Jones, interview.

137   Little Women, *Lung* (AUM Fidelity, 2013).

138   Smiley, interview.

139   Smiley, interview.

140   Nazary, interview.

141   Laplante, interview.

142   Smiley, interview.

143   Shane Endsley, interview by author, digital recording, March 17, 2020; Nate Chinen, "Tinges of Electro-Pop and Some Ives, Too," *New York Times*, February 18, 2010; Nate Chinen, "A Classicist of Rap, and a Crossover Crosses Back," *New York Times*, August 13, 2010; and Nate Chinen, "Jazz Intuition, American Roots and Double Hybrids," *New York Times*, December 16, 2015.

144 Nate Chinen, "Winter Jazzfest: A Happy Audience, for Whatever the Genre," *New York Times*, January 12, 2013.

145 Nate Chinen, "Jazz Acts, Blowing Superhot and Cool," *New York Times*, June 13, 2012.

146 Kneebody, *Kneebody* (Greenleaf Music, 2005); and Endsley, interview. At that time Temple Bar was located on Wilshire Boulevard near Eleventh Avenue, before moving to another location.

147 Chinen, "Winter Jazzfest."

148 Moody, "Musical Cueing of Kneebody," 11–53.

149 Kneebody, *Low Electrical Worker* (Jazz Engine, 2007).

150 Kneebody, *Live*, vol. 1 (self-released, 2006).

151 Chinen, "Tinges of Electro-Pop"; and Endsley, interview.

152 Chinen, "Jazz Acts"; and Chinen, "Winter Jazzfest."

153 Theremin, quoted in Moppa Elliott, interview by author, digital recording, April 8, 2020.

154 Elliott, interview.

155 Mostly Other People Do the Killing, *Mostly Other People Do the Killing* (Hot Cup Records, 2004).

156 Mostly Other People Do the Killing, *Shamokin!!!* (Hot Cup Records, 2007).

157 Elliott, interview.

158 Elliott, interview.

159 Mostly Other People Do the Killing, *Hannover* (Jazzwerkstatt, 2014), track 4.

160 Elliott, interview.

161 Ornette Coleman, *This Is Our Music* (Atlantic, 1961); Mostly Other People Do the Killing, *This Is Our Moosic* (Hot Cup Records, 2008); and Mostly Other People Do the Killing, *Forty Fort* (Hot Cup Records, 2009).

162 Elliott, interview.

163 Miles Davis, *Kind of Blue* (Columbia, 1959); and Mostly Other People Do the Killing, *Blue* (Hot Cup Records, 2014).

164 Merritt, interview.

165 Laplante, interview.

166 Elliott, interview.

Chapter 6. A Fractured Landscape

1 The producer Todd P originally found the space and booked the early shows at the venue with Edan Wilber as his assistant. Later Wilber took over the venue formally and ran it until it was forced to close in 2014. Tim Dahl, interview by author, digital recording, July 21, 2020.

2 Weasel Walter, interview by author, digital recording, May 9, 2016.

3 Dominika Michalowska, interview by author, digital recording, July 19, 2020.

4 Edwards, interview, November 24–December 24, 2015.

5 The Flying Luttenbachers, *Infection and Decline* (ugEXPLODE, 2002).

6 Walter, quoted in Marc Masters, "A Beginner's Guide to Brutal Prog," *Bandcamp Daily*, July 26, 2019, https://daily.bandcamp.com/lists/brutal-prog-guide.

7 Edwards, interview, November 24–December 24, 2015.

8 Cecil Taylor Unit, *Dark to Themselves* (Enja Records, 1976); David S. Ware, *Passage to Music* (Silkheart, 1988); and Charles Gayle Quartet, *More Live at the Knitting Factory February, 1993* (Knitting Factory Works, 1993).

9 Shepp's record *Three for a Quarter One for a Dime* (Impulse!/abc Records, 1969) was a particular inspiration.

10 Walter, interview, May 9, 2016.

11 The Flying Luttenbachers have had many different musicians involved over the years and continued to be active after Walter left Chicago. Their releases during the Chicago years include the Flying Luttenbachers, *Constructive Destruction* (ugEXPLODE, 1994); the Flying Luttenbachers, *Destroy All Music* (ugEXPLODE, 1995); the Flying Luttenbachers, *Revenge* (ugEXPLODE, 1996); the Flying Luttenbachers, *Gods of Chaos* (ugEXPLODE, 1997); the Flying Luttenbachers, *Trauma* (ugEXPLODE, 2001); and the Flying Luttenbachers, *Infection and Decline*.

12 Walter, interview, May 9, 2016.

13 Walter, interview, May 9, 2016.

14 Walter, interview, May 9, 2016. Xenakis fought against the Axis occupation of Greece, but his facial disfigurement actually came during the martial law imposed by British forces under Winston Churchill's orders, who were attempting to restore the Greek monarchy against the wishes of the Democratic Army of Greece. As a member of the communist student faction, Xenakis was wounded when shrapnel from tank fire struck his face and left eye, which was blinded in the incident.

15 Weasel Walter Quartet and Double Trio, *Firestorm* (ugEXPLODE, 2007).

16 Walter, interview, May 9, 2016.

17 Edwards, interview, November 24–December 24, 2015.

18 Edwards, interview, November 24–December 24, 2015.

19 Marc Edwards–Weasel Walter Group, *Mysteries beneath the Planet* (ugEXPLODE, 2009).

20 Edwards, interview, November 24–December 24, 2015.

21 Edwards, interview, November 24–December 24, 2015.

22 Walter, interview, May 9, 2016.

23 Walter, interview, May 9, 2016.

24 Walter, interview, May 9, 2016.

25 Marc Edwards–Weasel Walter Group, *Solar Emission* (ugEXPLODE, 2011).

26 Admiral Grey, interview by author, email, August 5, 2020.

27 Grey, interview.

28 Edwards, interview, November 24–December 24, 2015.

29 Edwards, interview, November 24–December 24, 2015.

30 Marc Edwards and Sonos Gravis, *Holographic Projection Holograms* (self-released, n.d.)

31 Edwards, interview, November 24–December 24, 2015.

32 Marc Edwards, "The History of Slipstream Time Travel," unpublished manuscript, [1], Marc Edwards private collection; and Marc Edwards, *Time and Space*, vol. 1 (Alpha Phonics, 1993).

33 Marc Edwards, interview by author, email, July 27, 2020.

34 Rick Berman, Michael Piller, and Jeri Taylor, *Star Trek: Voyager* (1995–2001); Gene Roddenberry, *Andromeda* (2000–2005).

35 Edwards, interview, July 27, 2020.

36 The early work is documented on Marc Edwards and Slipstream Time Travel, *Ion Storm* (Bandcamp, 2017).

37 A few of the band's live performances have since been recorded as well as one studio record. Edwards, "History of Slipstream Time Travel," [2]; Marc Edwards and Slipstream Time Travel, *Ode to a Dying Planet* (Bandcamp, 2008); and Marc Edwards and Slipstream Time Travel, *Planet X Just Blew Up!* (Amazon, 2013).

38 Edwards, interview, July 27, 2020.

39 Gustav Holst, *The Planets*, premiered in London, September 29, 1918.

40 Gorguts was a Quebec-based avant-death metal band that was active in 1989–2002.

41 Dahl, interview.

42 Lateef, in particular, was open to discussing Dahl's interests, including death metal. Dahl, interview.

43 Dahl, interview.

44 Dahl, interview.

45 Dahl, interview.

46 Child Abuse, *Child Abuse* (Lovepump Unlimited, 2007).

47 Dahl, interview.

48 Dahl, interview; and Child Abuse, *Trouble in Paradise* (Skin Graft Records, 2014).

49 Dahl, interview.

50 Dahl, interview.

51 Pride, interview.

52 Pride, interview.

53 Paul Acquaro, review: Pulverize the Sound—*Pulverize the Sound* (Relative Pitch, 2015), Free Jazz Collective: Reviews of Free Jazz and Improvised Music, June 13, 2015, https://www.freejazzblog.org/2015/06/pulverize-sound-st -relative-pitch-2015.html.

54 Pride, interview.

55 John Sharpe, "Vision Festival: Day 4, June 8, 2011," All about Jazz, July 14, 2011, https://www.allaboutjazz.com/vision-festival-day-4-june-8-2011-by -john-sharpe.php.

56 David Buddin, *Canticles for Electronic Music* (ugEXPLODE, 2012).

57 David Buddin, interview by author, digital recording, February 23, 2021.

58 Buddin encountered the writings of Babbitt and Forte in the Sumter County Library (South Carolina) near where he grew up. Forte, *Structure of Atonal Music*; and Babbitt, "Twelve-Tone Rhythmic Structure."

59 Mick Barr, interview by author, digital recording, August 25, 2020.

60 Weasel Walter, "Orthrelm," *Blastitude* 17 (November 2004).

61 Barr, quoted in Walter, "Orthrelm."

62 Walter, "Orthrelm."

63 Barr, quoted in Walter, "Orthrelm."

64 John Coltrane, *Interstellar Space* (abc Impulse!, 1974); and Mick Barr, interview by author, email, February 24, 2021.

65 Barr, quoted in Walter, "Orthrelm."

66 Weasel Walter, interview by author, digital recording, January 29, 2021.

67 Walter, interview, January 29, 2021.

68 Jon Irabagon, interview by author, digital recording, September 11, 2020.

69 Irabagon, interview.

70 Jon Irabagon and Mike Pride, *I Don't Hear Nothin' but the Blues* (Loyal Label, 2009); and Jon Irabagon with Mike Pride, *I Don't Hear Nothin' but the Blues*, vol. 2, *Appalachian Haze* (Irabbagast Records, 2012).

71 Irabagon, interview.

72 Irabagon, interview.

73 Irabagon, interview.

74 Irabagon, interview.

75 Irabagon, interview.

76 Irabagon, interview.

77 Amnon Freidlin, interview by author, digital recording, August 20, 2020.

78 Evan Lipson, interview by author, digital recording, November 6, 2020.

79 Freidlin, interview, August 20, 2020.

80 Freidlin, interview, August 20, 2020.

81 Freidlin, interview, August 20, 2020.

82 Their debut concert was presented by the Philadelphia Composers Society in a series called Something Else, at Broad Street Ministry, on May 5, 2006. The band performed monthly at various venues in Philadelphia until they moved to New York the following year. Freidlin, interview, August 20, 2020; and Lipson, interview.

83 Freidlin, interview, August 20, 2020.

84 Lipson, interview.

85 Freidlin, interview, August 20, 2020.

86 Freidlin, interview, August 20, 2020.

87 Freidlin, interview, August 20, 2020.

88 Normal Love, *Survival Tricks* (ugEXPLODE, 2012).

89 Freidlin, interview, August 20, 2020. The band later toured with Whore Paint and put out a split cassette with them. Whore Paint/Normal Love, *Whore Paint/Normal Love* (Linear B Tapes, 2010).

90 Freidlin, interview, August 20, 2020.

91 Amnon Freidlin, interview by author, email, January 28, 2021.

92 Originally composed in 1992, "Hout" has been recorded a number of times, by a variety of ensembles, the earliest being on Bang on a Can, *Industry* (Sony Classical, 1995), track 2.

93 Lipson, interview.

94 The earliest signs of this shift can be detected on the band's seven-inch release. Normal Love, *Peel/Kleinman* (High Two, 2009). Freidlin, interview, August 20, 2020; and Lipson, interview.

95 Freidlin, interview, August 20, 2020.

96 Freidlin, interview, August 20, 2020.

97 Walter, interview, January 29, 2021.

98 Edwards, interview, November 24–December 24, 2015.

99 Weasel Walter, interview by author, digital recording, October 8, 2020.

100 Lennie Tristano, *The New Tristano* (Atlantic, 1960), track 2; and Giovanni Russonello, "Connie Crothers, Jazz Pianist, Composer and Instructor, Dies at 75," *New York Times*, August 21, 2016.

101 Crothers, quoted in Ursel Schlicht, "Remembering Connie Crothers (1941–2016)," *NewMusicBox*, September 9, 2016, https://nmbx.newmusicusa.org /remembering-connie-crothers-1941-2016/.

102 Crothers, quoted in Schlicht, "Remembering Connie Crothers."

103 Ratzo Harris, interview by author, March 17, 2020; and Harvey Diamond, interview by author, digital recording, May 20, 2020.

104 Konitz was one of Tristano's first students in Chicago in the 1940s.

105 Richard Tabnik, interview by author, digital recording, April 21, 2020.

106 Tristano considered his technique of having his students sing with solos on records to be the "most important discovery of his teaching life." Crothers, quoted in Schlicht, "Remembering Connie Crothers."

107 Part of the strength of Tristano's community stemmed from his practice of hosting concerts in his home in Jamaica, Queens, which also served as a model for Crothers and others later. Tristano's students Liz Gorrill (now Kazzrie Jaxen) and Lenny Popkin played there, as well as Crothers's student Virg Dzurinko and Sal Mosca's students. Nick Lyons, interview by author, digital recording, March 16, 2020; Harris, interview; and Virg Dzurinko, interview by author, digital recording, April 9, 2020.

108 Carol Liebowitz, interview by author, digital recording, April 27, 2020.

109 Lennie Tristano, quoted in liner notes, Connie Crothers, *Perception* (Steeple-chase, 1975).

110 Dzurinko, interview.

111 Adam Caine, interview by author, digital recording, March 27, 2020.

112 Harris, interview.

113 John McCutcheon, interview by author, digital recording, April 14, 2020.

114 The model was discontinued in 1945, so they remain quite rare. Liebowitz, interview.

115 Lyons, interview.

116 Harris, interview.

117 Andrea Wolper, interview by author, email, March 29, 2020; and Lorenzo Sanguedolce, interview by author, digital recording, November 16, 2020.

118 Richard Tabnik, interview by author, email, March 23, 2020.

119 Connie Crothers and Richard Tabnik, *Duo Dimension* (New Artists Records, 1987).

120 Tabnik, interview, March 23, 2020.

121 The band released a record the following year and did a record release at the loft, though the recording was just a quartet without Weber. Connie Crothers Quartet, *Music Is a Place* (New Artists Records, 2006).

122 Harris, interview.

123 Wolper, interview.

124 Ursel Schlicht, interview by author, digital recording, November 6, 2020.

125 John McCutcheon, interview by author, digital recording, August 21, 2020.

126 Diamond, interview.

127 Lyons, interview. Lyons had been particularly inspired by Tristano's pieces "Line Up," "Requiem," and "Turkish Mambo," which were the first three tracks on the record *Lennie Tristano* (Atlantic Records, 1955). Ursel Schlicht made similar statements. Schlicht, interview.

128 Lyons, interview; and Caine, interview.

129 Caine, interview.

130 Liebowitz, interview.

131 Sanguedolce, interview.

132 Schlicht, interview.

133 Connie Crothers and Michael Bisio, *Session at 475 Kent* (Mutable Music, 2009); and Carol Liebowitz and Nick Lyons, *First Set* (Line Art Records, 2016).

134 Tabnik, interview, April 21, 2020.

135 Sanguedolce, interview.

136 Knott, interview.

137 Knott, interview.

138 Knott, interview.

139 At times, the venue would put on five- or ten-course meals that played on color themes, or evenings where the food connected somehow with the music or art that was being presented. Knott, interview.

140 Knott, interview.

141 Knott, interview.

142 Knott, interview.

143 Harris Eisenstadt, interview by author, digital recording, June 16, 2015.

144 Eisenstadt, interview.

145 Beck, "Urban Transitions," 346–47.

Afterword

1 Andrea Fraser, in "How Has Art Changed?," *Frieze*, no. 94 (October 2005).

2 Beech, *Art and Postcapitalism*, 13.

3 Beech, *Art and Postcapitalism*, 93.

4 A 2004 study by Pratt Institute analysts stated that the city's policy of attempting to attract artists "ignores opportunities to use development to benefit the city's working-class and middle- and low-income residents," which in many cases negatively impacted artists disproportionately. Lander and Wolf-Powers, *Remaking New York City*, 7; see also Indergaard, "What to Make of New York's New Economy?," 1080.

5 Sawyer, interview, August 11, 2020.

6 Roslund, interview.

7 Mahmoud, "Brooklyn's Experimental Frontiers," 101.

8 Sam Roberts, "Bloomberg Administration Is Developing Land Use Plan to Accommodate Future Populations," *New York Times*, November 26, 2006.

9 Musician (name withheld), interview by the author, 2020.

10 Thomas Fuller, Julie Turkewitz, Yamiche Alcindor, Conor Dougherty, and Serge F. Kovaleski, "Why the 'Ghost Ship' Was Invisible in Oakland, until 36 Died," *New York Times*, December 22, 2016; and Elizabeth Weil, "He Helped Build an Artists' Utopia, Now He Faces Trial for 36 Deaths There," *New York Times*, December 12, 2018.

Art Sources for the Williamsburg Avant-Garde

Music, Film, Painting, and Television

Music Recordings

Aarktica. *Bleeding Light*. Darla Records, 2005.

Aarktica. *No Solace in Sleep*. Silber Records, 2000.

Aarktica. *Pure Tone Audiometry*. Silber Records, 2003.

Ali, Rashied, Louis Belogenis, and Wilber Morris. *Live at Tonic*. DIW, 2001.

Ali, Rashied, and Louis Belogenis. *Rings of Saturn*. Knitting Factory Records, 1999.

Angel OV Death. *Live in Space and Time*. Veal Records, n.d.

Ayler, Albert. *Bells*. ESP-Disk, 1965.

Bang on a Can. *Industry*. Sony Classical, 1995.

Battles. *B EP*. Dim Mak Records, 2004.

Battles. *EP C*. Monitor Records, 2004.

Battles. *Mirrored*. Warp Records, 2007.

Battles. *Tras*. Cold Sweat Records, 2004.

Billy Syndrome, The. *The Billy Syndrome*. Slutfish Recordings, 1999.

Billy Syndrome, The. *Bootleg of My Choice*. Savage Smut, 1987.

Billy Syndrome, The. *Ill Mess*. Slutfish Recordings, 1995.

Billy Syndrome, The. *The Power of Love*. Savage Smut, 1988.

Borbetomagus. *Live at In-Roads*. Aeon, 1983.

Boredoms, The. *Soul Discharge*. Selfish Records, 1989.

Braxton, Anthony. *19 (Solo) Compositions, 1988*. New Albion, 1989.

Braxton, Tyondai. *History That Has No Effect*. JMZ Records, 2002.

Brown, Oscar, Jr. *Sin and Soul*. Columbia, 1960.

Bua, Matt, Matt Mikas, and Tom Roe. *Of the Bridge*. free103point9, 2001.

Buddin, David. *Canticles for Electronic Music*. ugEXPLODE, 2012.

Butler, Ken. *Voices of Anxious Objects*. Tzadik, 1997.

Bynum, Taylor Ho (sextet). *Apparent Distance*. Firehouse 12 Records, 2011.

Bynum, Taylor Ho (sextet). *Asphalt Flowers Forking Paths*. Hat Hut Records, 2008.

Bynum, Taylor Ho (sextet). *The Middle Picture*. Firehouse 12 Records, 2007.

Bynum, Taylor Ho (sextet). *Navigation (Possibility Abstracts X and XI)*. Firehouse 12 Records, 2013.

Cherry, Don. *Multikulti*. A&M Records, 1990.

Child Abuse. *Child Abuse*. Lovepump Unlimited, 2007.

Child Abuse. *Trouble in Paradise*. Skin Graft Records, 2014.

Coleman, Anthony. *Disco by Night*. Composers series. Avant, 1992.

Coleman, Ornette. *The Shape of Jazz to Come*. Atlantic, 1959.

Coleman, Ornette. *This Is Our Music*. Atlantic, 1961.

Coltrane, John. *Interstellar Space*. ABC Impulse!, 1974.

Coltrane, John. *A Love Supreme*. Impulse!, 1965.

Coltrane, John. *My Favorite Things*. Atlantic, 1961.

Cooper-Moore and Assif Tsahar. *America*. Hopscotch Records, 2003.

Cop Shoot Cop. *Live at CBGB*. Supernatural Organization, 1989.

Crothers, Connie (quartet). *Music Is a Place*. New Artists Records, 2006.

Crothers, Connie (quartet). *Perception*. Steeplechase, 1975.

Crothers, Connie, and Michael Bisio. *Session at 475 Kent*. Mutable Music, 2009.

Crothers, Connie, and Richard Tabnik. *Duo Dimension*. New Artists Records, 1987.

Cymerman, Jeremiah. *Fire Sign*. Composer Series. Tzadik, 2011.

Cymerman, Jeremiah. *In Memory of the Labyrinth System*. Composer Series. Tzadik, 2008.

Cymerman, Jeremiah. *Systema Mundititius*, vol. 1. Self-released, 2020.

Cymerman, Jeremiah. *Under a Blue Grey Sky*. Porter Records, 2010.

Davis, Miles. *Bitches Brew*. Columbia, 1970.

Davis, Miles. *In a Silent Way*. Columbia, 1969.

Davis, Miles. *Kind of Blue*. Columbia, 1959.

Dollar Brand. *African Marketplace*. Elektra, 1994.

Dolphy, Eric. *Out to Lunch!* Blue Note, 1964.

Dulman, Jesse (quartet). *Live at Downtown Music Gallery*. RR Gems, 2017.

Dulman, Jesse (quartet). *Peace Psalm*. Self-released, 1999.

Dynamite Club. *It's Deeper Than Most People Think . . .* Funhole Records, 2004.

Dynamite Club. *The Legend of Tiger Mask*. Big Sleep Records, 2002.

Edwards, Marc. *Time and Space*. Vol. 1. Alpha Phonics, 1993.

Edwards, Marc, and Slipstream Time Travel. *Ion Storm*. Bandcamp, 2017.

Edwards, Marc, and Slipstream Time Travel. *Ode to a Dying Planet*. Bandcamp, 2008.

Edwards, Marc, and Slipstream Time Travel. *Planet X Just Blew Up!* Amazon, 2013.

Eno, Brian. *Discreet Music*. Obscure, 1975.

Evans, Brandon, and the Middletown Creative Orchestra. *Two Compositions for Chamber Orchestra 1998*. Parallactic Records, 1998.

Evans, Peter. *More Is More*. Psi, 2006.

Evans, Peter, and Tom Blancarte. *{Sparks}*. Creative Sources, 2008.

Evans, Peter, and Nate Wooley. *High Society*. Carrier Records, 2011.

Eye Contact. *Embracing the Tide/Making Eye Contact with God*. Utech Records, 2005.

Eye Contact. *War Rug*. KMB Jazz, 2006.

Fei, James. *Solo Works*. Leo Records, 2000.

Fihi Ma Fihi. *Live at WKCR*. Unreleased recording, n.d.

Flying Luttenbachers, The. *Constructive Destruction*. ugEXPLODE, 1994.

Flying Luttenbachers, The. *Destroy All Music*. ugEXPLODE, 1995.

Flying Luttenbachers, The. *Gods of Chaos*. ugEXPLODE, 1997.

Flying Luttenbachers, The. *Infection and Decline*. ugEXPLODE, 2002.

Flying Luttenbachers, The. *Revenge*. ugEXPLODE, 1996.

Flying Luttenbachers, The. *Trauma*. ugEXPLODE, 2001.

Friel, Dan. *Broken Man Going to Work*. Self-released, 2001.

From Bacteria to Boys. *Betweenwhile*. AUM Fidelity, 2010.

From Bacteria to Boys. *Birthing Days*. AUM Fidelity, 2013.

From Bacteria to Boys. *Hang*. Funhole Records, 2006.

Gayle, Charles. *Repent*. Knitting Factory Works, 1992.

Gayle, Charles (quartet). *More Live at the Knitting Factory February, 1993*. Knitting Factory Works, 1993.

Gayle, Charles (trio). *Consider the Lilies* . . . Clean Feed, 2006.

Gayle, Charles (trio). *Homeless*. Silkheart, 1989.

Gayle, Charles (trio). *Live at Disobey*. Blast First, 1994.

Giffoni, Carlos. *Welcome Home*. Important Records, 2005.

Gold Sparkle Band. *Downsizing*. Nu Records, 1997.

Gold Sparkle Band. *Fugues and Flowers*. Squealer, 2002.

Gold Sparkle Band. *Nu-Soul Zodiac*. Squealer, 1999.

Gold Sparkle Band. *Thunder Reminded Me*. Clean Feed Records, 2002.

Gold Sparkle Trio with Ken Vandermark. *Brooklyn Cantos*. Squealer, 2004.

Guy, Buddy. *A Man and the Blues*. Vanguard, 1968.

Haino, Keiji. *Execration That Accept to Acknowledge*. Forced Exposure, 1993.

Halvorson, Mary, and Jessica Pavone. *Departure of Reason*. Thirsty Ear, 2011.

Halvorson, Mary, and Jessica Pavone. *On and Off*. Skirl Records, 2007.

Halvorson, Mary, and Jessica Pavone. *Prairies*. Lucky Kitchen, 2005.

Halvorson, Mary, and Jessica Pavone. *Thin Air*. Thirsty Ear, 2009.

Himalayas. *Ayeeta*. Bandcamp, 2020.

Himalayas. *Shotgun Recordings*. Bandcamp, 2013.

Holst, Gustav. *The Planets*. Premiered Queen's Hall, London, September 29, 1918; Adrian Boult, cond.

Irabagon, Jon, and Mike Pride. *I Don't Hear Nothin' but the Blues*. Loyal Label, 2009.

Irabagon, Jon, with Mike Pride and Mick Barr. *I Don't Hear Nothin' but the Blues*. Vol. 2, *Appalachian Haze*. Irabbagast Records, 2012.

JM Singers. *Jonas Song*. Bandcamp, 2020.

Jump Arts Orchestra Conducted by Lawrence "Butch" Morris. *Conduction 117*. Jump Arts Records, 2003.

Kahn, Brenda. *Goldfish Don't Talk Back*. Community 3, 1990.

Kalaparusha and the Light. *The Moment*. Entropy Stereo Recordings, 2003.

Kalaparusha and the Light. *Morning Song*. Delmark Records, 2004.

Kalaparusha and the Light. *Paths to Glory*. CIMP, 2004.

Kalaparusha and the Light. *South Eastern*. CIMP, 2002.

Kalashnikov. *Bang Bang*. Veal Records, 2008.

Kneebody. *Kneebody*. Greenleaf Music, 2005.

Kneebody. *Live*. Vol. 1. Self-released, 2006.

Kneebody. *Low Electrical Worker*. Jazz Engine, 2007.

Krakauer, David. *Klezmer Madness!* Radical Jewish Culture, no. 1. Tzadik, 1995.

Lemon Juice Quartet. *Peasant Songs: The Music of Erik Satie and Bela Bartok*. Piadrum Records, 2002.

Lemon Juice Quartet. *Republic*. Chant Records, 2001.

Liebowitz, Carol, and Nick Lyons. *First Set*. Line Art Records, 2016.

Little Women. *Lung*. AUM Fidelity, 2013.

Little Women. *Teeth*. Gilgongo Records, 2007.

Little Women. *Throat*. AUM Fidelity, 2010.

Lynyrd Skynyrd. *Second Helping*. MCA Records, 1974.

Maoz, Eyal. *Edom*. Radical Jewish Culture, no. 105. Tzadik, 2005.

Maoz, Eyal. *Hope and Destruction*. Radical Jewish Culture, no. 147. Tzadik, 2009.

Marc Edwards and Slipstream Time Travel. *Ion Storm*. Bandcamp, 2017.

Marc Edwards and Slipstream Time Travel. *Ode to a Dying Planet*. Bandcamp, 2008.

Marc Edwards and Slipstream Time Travel. *Planet X Just Blew Up!* Amazon, 2013.

Marc Edwards and Sonos Gravis. *Holographic Projection Holograms*. Self-released, n.d.

Marc Edwards–Weasel Walter Group. *Mysteries beneath the Planet*. ugEXPLODE, 2009.

Marc Edwards–Weasel Walter Group. *Solar Emission*. ugEXPLODE, 2011.

Mateen, Sabir, Daniel Carter, and Andrew Barker. *Not on Earth . . . in Your Soul!* Qbico, 2005.

Matthew Shipp. *Equilibrium*. The Blue Series. Thirsty Ear, 2002.

Matthew Shipp. *Nu Bop*. The Blue Series. Thirsty Ear, 2003.

McIntyre, Kalaparusha Maurice. *Forces and Feelings*. Delmark Records, 1972.

McIntyre, Kalaparusha Maurice. *Humility in the Light of Creator*. Delmark Records, 1969.

Middletown Creative Orchestra. *10.6.97*. Newsonic Music, 1997.

Middletown Creative Orchestra. *4.11.98 and 4.30.98*. Newsonic Music, 1998.

Middletown Creative Orchestra. *Crystal Lake*. Newsonic Music, 1998.

Mingus, Charles. *Black Saint and the Sinner Lady*. Impulse!, 1963.

Moore, Jackson. *Trio of Eluctations*. Self-released, 2007.

Morris, Lawrence D. "Butch." *Current Trends in Racism in Modern America*. Sound Aspects Records, 1985.

Morris, Lawrence D. "Butch." *Testament: A Conduction Collection*. 10 CDs. New World Records, 1995.

Mostly Other People Do the Killing. *Blue*. Hot Cup Records, 2014.

Mostly Other People Do the Killing. *Forty Fort*. Hot Cup Records, 2009.

Mostly Other People Do the Killing. *Hannover*. Jazzwerkstatt, 2014.

Mostly Other People Do the Killing. *Mostly Other People Do the Killing*. Hot Cup Records, 2004.

Mostly Other People Do the Killing. *Shamokin!!!* Hot Cup Records, 2007.

Mostly Other People Do the Killing. *This Is Our Moosic*. Hot Cup Records, 2008.

Motian, Paul, with Bill Frissell and Joe Lovano. *Motian in Tokyo*. JMT, 1991.

Moving Form, The. *Year of the Endless Moment*. Engine Studios, 2004.

MP3, The. *Sleep Cells*. Utech, 2006.

Nakamura, Toshimaru. *No-Input Mixing Board*. Zero Gravity, 2000.

Nakamura, Toshimaru, and Sachiko M. *Do*. Erstwhile Records, 2001.

Nathanson, Roy, and Anthony Coleman. *I Could've Been a Drum*. Radical Jewish Culture 13. Tzadik, 1997.

Nathanson, Roy, and Anthony Coleman. *Lobster and Friend*. Knitting Factory Works, 1993.

Neidlinger, Buell. *Gayle Force*. K2B2, 2015.

New Air. *Live at the Montreal International Jazz Festival*. Black Saint, 1984.

No-Neck Blues Band. *The Birth of Both Worlds*. Sound@One, 1998.

No-Neck Blues Band. *The Circle Broken*. Sound@One, 1996.

No-Neck Blues Band. *Hoichoi*. Sound@One, 1994.

No-Neck Blues Band. *Letters from the Earth*. Sound@One, 1996.

No-Neck Blues Band. *Letters from the Serth*. Sound@One, 1998.

No-Neck Blues Band. *Re: "Mr. A Fan . . ."* Self-released, 1999.

No-Neck Blues Band. *Recorded in Public and Private*. Actuel, 1994.

No-Neck Blues Band. *Sticks and Stones May Break My Bones but Names Will Never Hurt Me*. Revenant, 2001.

No-Neck Blues Band. *A Tabu Two*. New World of Sound, 1997.

Normal Love. *Peel/Kleinman*. High Two, 2009.

Normal Love. *Survival Tricks*. ugEXPLODE, 2012.

Nublu Orchestra. *Live at Jazz Festival Saalfelden*. Nublu Records, 2010.

Nublu Orchestra. *Nublu Orchestra Conducted by Butch Morris*. Nublu Records, 2006.

Opsvik, Eivind. *Overseas II*. Fresh Sound New Talent, 2005.

Otomo, Yoshihide, Keith Rowe, and Taku Sugimoto. *Ajar*. Alcohol, 2002.

Pachora. *Ast*. Knitting Factory Works, 1999.

Pachora. *Astereotypical*. Winter and Winter, 2003.

Pachora. *Pachora*. Knitting Factory Works, 1997.

Pachora. *Unn*. Knitting Factory Works, 1998.

Parker, William. *Song Cycle*. Boxholder Records, 2001.

Parts and Labor. *Groundswell*. JMZ Records, 2003.

peeessseye, the. *Commuting between the Surface and the Underworld*. Evolving Ear, 2006.

peeessseye, the. *I Woke Up and Drank a Bottle of Cheap Kojak*. Golden Lab Records, 2009.

peeessseye, the. *Pestilence and Joy*. Evolving Ear, 2010.

peeessseye, the. *Robust Commercial Fucking Scream*. 6 vols. Digitalis Limited, 2009.

peeesseye, the. *Sci Fi Death Mask*. humansacrifice, 2014.

peeesseye, the. *2008 Tour CDR (Teton Trout)*. Evolving Ear, 2008.

Peeesseye, and Talibam! *Peeesseye + Talibam!* Invada Records, 2010.

Period. *Period*. Funhole, 2006.

Phantom Limb and Bison. *Phantom Limb and Bison*. Utech Records, 2006.

Phantom Limb and Bison. *Phantom Limb and Bison*. Evolving Ear, 2007.

Pride, Mike. *Drummer's Corpse*. AUM Fidelity, 2013.

psi. *Artificially Retarded Soul Care Operators*. Evolving Ear, 2005.

psi. *Black American Flag*. Evolving Ear, 2004.

Ras and the Music Now! Unit. *Live Spirits 2*. Utech Records, 2005.

Rashanim. *The Gathering*. Tzadik, 2009.

Rashanim. *Shalosh*. Tzadik, 2006.

Reed, Lou. *Metal Machine Music*. RCA, 1975.

Rivers, Sam (quintet). *Zenith*. 1977. Sam Rivers Archive Project, vol. 2. NoBusiness Records, 2019.

Rivers, Sam (tuba trio), and Earl Cross (sextet). *Jazz of the Seventies/Una Muy Bonita*. Circle Records, 1977.

Roberts, Matana. *The Calling*. Utech Records, 2006.

Roberts, Matana. *Coin Coin Chapter One: Gens de Couleur Libres*. Constellation, 2011.

Scrap Metal Music. *Scrap Metal Music*. Screwgun Music, 1985.

Sharp, Elliott/Carbon. *Larynx*. SST Records, 1988.

Shepp, Archie. *Three for a Quarter One for a Dime*. Impulse!/ABC Records, 1969.

Shipp, Matthew. *Equilibrium*. The Blue Series. Thirsty Ear, 2003.

Shipp, Matthew. *Nu Bop*. The Blue Series. Thirsty Ear, 2002.

Shipp, Matthew, and Guillermo E. Brown. *Telephone Popcorn*. Nu Bop Records, 2008.

Sightings. *Absolutes*. Riot Season, 2003.

Sightings. *Arrived in Gold*. Load Records, 2005.

Sightings. *Michigan Haters*. Psych-O-Path Records, 2002.

Sightings. *Sightings*. Load Records, 2002.

Sightings. *Terribly Well*. Dais Records, 2013.

Sightings. *Through the Panama*. Load Records, 2007.

Simmons, Sonny, Blaise Siwula, Daniel Carter, Adam Lane, Robyn Siwula, Mike Fortune, and Jeffrey Hayden Shurdut. *Live at Zebulon*, vol. 1. Self-released, 2006.

Simmons, Sonny, Jeffrey Shurdut, Daniel Carter, Blaise Siwula, Adam Lane, Robyn Siwula, and Mike Fortune. *Live at Zebulon*. Vol. 2, *This Is the Music of Life*. Ayler Records, 2008.

Simons, David. *Prismatic Hearing*. Tzadik, 2004.

Skeleton Crew. *The Country of Blinds*. No Man's Land, 1986.

Skeleton Crew. *Learn to Talk*. Recommended Music, 1984.

SLAM. *Until the Rain Comes*. Bandcamp, 2020.

Spanish Donkey. *XYX*. Northern Spy, 2011.

Storm and Stress. *Storm and Stress*. Touch and Go, 1997.

Storm and Stress. *Under Thunder and Fluorescent Lights*. Touch and Go, 2000.

Talibam! *Boogie in the Breeze Blocks*. ESP-Disk, 2009.

Talibam! and Weasel Walter. *Polyp*. MNOAD, 2014.

Taylor, Cecil (Unit). *Dark to Themselves*. Enja Records, 1976.

TEST. *Live*. Eremite Records, 2000.

Transcendentalists, The. *Real Time Messengers*. Spirit Room Series, vol. 147. CIMP, 2002.

Tristano, Lennie. *Lennie Tristano*. Atlantic, 1955.

Tristano, Lennie. *The New Tristano*. Atlantic, 1960.

TV on the Radio. *Desperate Youth, Blood Thirsty Babes.* Touch and Go Records, 2004.

Unbroken Trio. *Unbroken*. Tick Tock, 2005.

Upper Planets. *WSU Terrorist Theme*. Bandcamp, 2020.

Various. *Comin' at You: Jump Arts American Road Project*. Jump Arts Records, 2002.

Various. *No New York*. Antilles, 1978.

Various. *This Is It: Live at Zebulon*, vol. 1. Zebulon, 2005.

Walter, Weasel (quartet and double trio). *Firestorm*. ugEXPLODE, 2007.

Ware, David S. *Passage to Music*. Silkheart, 1988.

Welch, Matthew. *Blarvuster*. Tzadik Records, 2010.

Whoopie Pie. *Sweet*. Veal Records, 2007.

Whore Paint/Normal Love. *Whore Paint/Normal Love*. Linear B Tapes, 2010.

Wolf Eyes. *Burned Mind*. Sub Pop, 2004.

W.O.O. *Should've, Might as Well: CS60, Live at CBGBs*. Sweet Stuff, 1989.

W.O.O. *W.O.O.topia: Live from Europe.* Funky Mushroom, 1994.

Wooley, Nate. *Wrong Shape to Be a Storyteller*. Creative Sources, 2005.

Yang, Justin, and the Middletown Creative Orchestra. *Composition for Creative Orchestra no. 1*. Yang/Yin, 1999.

Zorn, John. *The Unknown Masada*. Tzadik, 2003.

Zorn, John/Rashanim. *Masada Rock*. Tzadik, 2005.

Zs. *Arms*. Planaria Recordings, 2007.

Zs. *Buck*. Folding Cassettes, 2006.

Zs. *Karate Bump*. Planaria Recordings, 2005.

Zs. *Zs*. Vothoc series. Troubleman Unlimited, 2003.

Films

Burns, Ken, dir. *Jazz* (2001).

Coppola, Sofia, dir. *Marie Antoinette* (2006).

Deren, Maya, dir. *Divine Horsemen: The Living Gods of Haiti* (1954).

Jesse Dulman Documentary (RR Gems Records, 2017).

Echeverria, Diego, dir. *Los Sures* (1984).

Gutierrez, Miguel. "Sabotage @ Brooklyn Music Festival." 2002. Vimeo video, 40 minutes, 44 seconds, uploaded April 15, 2016. https://vimeo.com/163034927.

Jahn, Ebba, dir. *Rising Tones Cross* (1985).

Lee, Spike, dir. *She's Gotta Have It* (1986).

Leone, Sergio, dir. *Once upon a Time in America* (1984).

Marker, Chris, dir. *Le Jetée* (1962).

Mekas, Jonas, dir. *Reminiscences of a Journey to Lithuania* (1972).

Mikels, Ted V., dir. *The Astro-Zombies* (1968).

Monga, Vipal, dir. *Black February* (2005).

UnartigNYC. "Little Women Live at Micheline's on September 15, 2006." YouTube video, 31 minutes, 7 seconds. https://www.youtube.com/watch?v=F7moKZXGl1U.

Zweig, Ellen, dir. *Heart Beat Ear Drum* (2018).

Paintings

Braque, Georges. *Violin and Pipe* (1913).

Picasso, Pablo. *Clarinet and Violin* (1913).

Picasso, Pablo. *Geometrical Composition: The Guitar* (1913).

Picasso, Pablo. *The Guitar* (1913).

Picasso, Pablo. *Guitar and Bottle* (1913).

Picasso, Pablo. *Guitar and Violin* (1912).

Picasso, Pablo. *Guitar, Sheet Music and Wine Glass* (1912).

Picasso, Pablo. *Mandolin* (1914).

Picasso, Pablo. *Man with Guitar* (1913).

Picasso, Pablo. *Musical Instruments* (1912).

Picasso, Pablo. *My Beautiful, Woman with Guitar* (1912).

Picasso, Pablo. *Still Life with Violin and Fruits* (1912)

Picasso, Pablo. *Violin* (1912).

Picasso, Pablo. *Violin* (1913).

Picasso, Pablo. *Woman with Guitar* (1913).

Television

Berman, Rick, Michael Piller, and Jeri Taylor, creators (based on Gene Roddenberry's *Star Trek* series). *Star Trek: Voyager*. Aired 7 seasons (1995–2001), USA: Paramount Network Television.

Roddenberry, Gene, and Robert Hewitt Wolfe, creators. *Gene Roddenberry's Andromeda*. Aired 5 seasons (2000–2005), Canada/USA: Andromeda Productions/Fireworks Entertainment/MBR Productions.

Bibliography

Primary Sources
Public and Private Archives

Abbs, Tom. Private collection.
Barker, Andrew. Private collection.
Bell, Mike. Private collection.
Brandt, David. Private collection.
Brooklyn Museum Library.
Bynum, Taylor Ho. Private collection.
Edwards, Marc. Private collection.
Fisher, Ebon. Private collection.
Halvorson, Mary. Private collection.
Pavone, Jessica. Private collection.
Pettit, Ethan. Private collection.
Rose, Michael X. Private collection.
Siegel, Aaron. Private collection.
Wave Farm archive.
Wollesen, Kenny. Private collection.

Formal interviews conducted via email are listed as interviews, whereas "Email to author" indicates an email exchange that was not a formal interview.

Abbs, Tom. Interview by author. Digital recording. January 27, 2016.

Abbs, Tom. Interview by author. Email. May 28, 2019.

Admiral Grey. Interview by author. Email. August 5, 2020.

Airaldi, Mariano. Interview by author. Digital recording. May 1, 2019.

Arnal, Jeff. Interview by author. Digital recording. May 14, 2015.

Arnal, Jeff. Interview by author. Email. December 24, 2015.

Arnal, Jeff. Interview by author. Digital recording. March 5, 2021.

Asch, Gregor (DJ Olive). Interview by author. Digital recording. April 7, 2019.

Asch, Gregor (DJ Olive). Interview by author. Digital recording. April 10, 2019.

Baker, Newman Taylor. Interview by author. Digital recording. April 29, 2020.

Barker, Andrew. Interview by author. Digital recording. June 18, 2015.

Barker, Andrew. Interview by author. Digital recording. July 22, 2015.

Barker, Andrew. Interview by author. Digital recording. January 13, 2016.

Barker, Andrew. Interview by author. Digital recording. April 4, 2019.

Barr, Mick. Interview by author. Digital recording. August 25, 2020.

Barr, Mick. Interview by author. Email. February 24, 2021.

Bauder, Matt. Interview by author. Email. July 20, 2015.

Beeferman, Gordon. Interview by author. Digital recording. March 7, 2021.

Bell, Mike. Interview by author. Digital recording. March 3, 2019.

Bell, Mike. Interview by author. Digital recording. August 27, 2019.

Belogenis, Louis. Interview by author. Digital recording. May 14, 2020.

Benson, Millie. Interview by author. Digital recording. March 23, 2019.

Blancarte, Tom. Interview by author. Digital recording. June 30, 2016.

Blumenkranz, Shanir. Interview by author. Digital recording. March 26, 2020.

Brandt, David. Interview by author. Email. June 25–August 30, 2019.

Brandt, David. Interview by author. Digital recording. August 30, 2019.

Braxton, Tyondai. Interview by author. Digital recording. October 30, 2019.

Brennan, Patrick. Interview by author. Email. May 5, 2019.

Brennan, Patrick. Email to author. November 4, 2019.

Bua, Matt. Interview by author. Digital recording. March 18, 2019.

Buddin, David. Interview by author. Digital recording. February 23, 2021.

Burnett, Ras Moshe. Interview by author. Digital recording. March 22, 2021.

Butler, Ken. Interview by author. Digital recording. September 13, 2016.

Butler, Ken. Interview by author. Digital recording. April 13, 2020.

Bynum, Taylor Ho. Interview by author. Digital recording. November 22, 2013.

Cady, Jason. Interview by author. Email. May 23, 2019.

Caine, Adam. Interview by author. Digital recording. March 27, 2020.

Catera, Damian. Interview by author. Digital recording. August 18, 2015.

Catera, Damian. Interview by author. Digital recording. August 19, 2015.

Coleman, Anthony. Interview by author. Digital recording. June 11, 2019.

Cooper-Moore. Interview by author. March 19, 2020.

Corsano, Chris. Interview by author. Email. May 2, 2019.

Cymerman, Jeremiah. Interview by author. Digital recording. April 2, 2017.

Cymerman, Jeremiah. Interview by author. Digital recording. June 10, 2020.

Dahl, Tim. Interview by author. Digital recording. July 21, 2020.

Dalachinsky, Steve. Interview by author. Email. May 30, 2019.

Dennis, Ward. Interview by author. Digital recording. March 12, 2021.

DeRosa, Jon. Interview by author. Digital recording. September 23, 2019.

Diamond, Harvey. Interview by author. Digital recording. May 20, 2020.

Dineen, Terry. Interview by author. Digital recording. October 11, 2020.

Dulman, Jesse. Interview by author. Digital recording. June 25, 2020.

Dzurinko, Virg. Interview by author. Digital recording. April 9, 2020.

Edwards, Marc. Interview by author. Email. November 24–December 24, 2015.

Edwards, Marc. Interview by author. Email. July 27, 2020.

Eisenstadt, Harris. Interview by author. Digital recording. June 16, 2015.

Elliott, Moppa. Interview by author. Digital recording. April 8, 2020.

Endsley, Shane. Interview by author. Digital recording. March 17, 2020.

Evans, Brandon. Interview by author. Digital recording. May 18, 2019.

Evans, Brandon. Interview by author. Email. June 20, 2019.

Evans, Peter. Interview by author. Digital recording. June 18, 2015.

Fennelly, Jaime. Interview by author. Digital recording. April 29, 2019.

Fisher, Ebon. Email to author. October 25, 2021.

Fisher, Ebon. Email to author. October 29, 2021.

Fisher, Ebon. Email to author. November 3, 2021.

Fisher, Ebon. Email to author. November 9, 2021.

Freidlin, Amnon. Interview by author. Digital recording. August 20, 2020.

Freidlin, Amnon. Interview by author. Email. January 28, 2021.

Friel, Dan. Interview by author. Email. October 2, 2019.

Fujiwara, Tomas. Interview by author. Digital recording. October 1, 2013.

Giffoni, Carlos. Interview by author. Digital recording. February 12, 2021.

Gompertz, Jeff. Interview by author. Digital recording. May 17, 2019.

Greene, Hilliard. Interview by author. Digital recording. March 17, 2020.

Greene, Jimmy James. Interview by author. Digital recording. February 9, 2021.

Haffner, Jonathon. Interview by author. Digital recording. April 23, 2020.

Hall, Ben. Interview by author. Digital recording. March 13, 2021.

Halsey, Onaje Will. Interview by author. Digital recording. February 9, 2021.

Halvorson, Mary. Interview by author. Digital recording. September 10, 2012.

Halvorson, Mary. Interview by author. Digital recording. October 1, 2013.

Halvorson, Mary. Interview by author. Email. June 24–30, 2015.

Hansen, Shawn. Interview by author. Digital recording. December 17, 2019.

Harris, Ratzo. Interview by author. Digital recording. March 17, 2020.

Hillmer, Sam. Interview by author. Digital recording. September 12, 2020.

Hurwitz, Anna. Interview by author. Digital recording. April 17, 2019.

Ilgenfritz, James. Interview by author. Digital recording. February 22, 2014.

Ilgenfritz, James. Interview by author. Email. January 19, 2021.

Irabagon, Jon. Interview by author. Digital recording. September 11, 2020.

Irwin, Michael. Interview by author. Digital recording. May 6, 2020.

Johnson, Russ. Interview by author. Digital recording. July 15, 2013.

Jonas, Chris. Interview by author. Digital recording. May 22, 2019.

Jones, Darius. Interview by author. Digital recording. May 13, 2021.

Kane, Bonnie. Interview by author. Digital recording. November 1, 2021.

Kim, Ha-Yang. Interview by author. Digital recording. April 27, 2020.

Klotz, Jake. Interview by author. Digital recording. March 20, 2019.

Knott, Montgomery. Interview by author. Digital recording. August 6, 2020.

Lacy, Frank. Interview by author. Digital recording. May 15, 2020.

Lamb, Andrew. Interview by author. Digital recording. March 16, 2020.

Landis, M. P. Interview by author. Email. May 29–June 5, 2019.

Laplante, Travis. Interview by author. Digital recording. June 16, 2020.

Latessa Ortiz, Gabrielle. Interview by author. Digital recording. April 18, 2019.

Lavelle, Matt. Interview by author. Digital recording. March 15, 2020.

Liebowitz, Carol. Interview by author. Digital recording. April 27, 2020.

Lipson, Evan. Interview by author. Digital recording. November 6, 2020.

Lyons, Nick. Interview by author. Digital recording. March 16, 2020.

Madof, Jon. Interview by author. Digital recording. March 22, 2020.

Maoz, Eyal. Interview by author. Digital recording. June 16, 2020.

Mateen, Sabir. Interview by author. Email. June 11–19, 2015.

Maurer, Eric. Interview by author. Email. July 16–September 23, 2015.

McClelland, David, and Millie Benson. Interview by author. Digital recording. April 20, 2019.

McCutcheon, John. Interview by author. Digital recording. April 14, 2020.

McCutcheon, John. Interview by author. Digital recording. August 21, 2020.

McIntyre, Kalaparusha Maurice. Interview by Jesse Dulman. Digital recording. July 9, 2004.

Merritt, Jason. Interview by author. Digital recording. August 1, 2018.

Michalowska, Dominika. Interview by author. Digital recording. July 19, 2020.

Mikas, Matt. Interview by author. Digital recording. April 14, 2019.

Mincek, Alex. Interview by author. Digital recording. January 31, 2021.

Misterka, Seth. Interview by author. Email. June 8–24, 2015.

Momin, Ravish. Interview by author. Digital recording. April 20, 2020.

Moore, Jackson. Interview by author. Digital recording. June 12, 2015.

Morgan, Mark. Interview by author. Digital recording. April 25, 2019.

Mottel, Matt. Interview by author. Digital recording. November 24, 2015.

Mottel, Matt. Interview by author. Email. March 14, 2020.

Musician (name withheld). Interview by author. Digital recording. 2020

Nazary, Jason. Interview by author. Digital recording. June 19, 2020.

Nuss, David. Interview by author. Digital recording. December 11, 2015.

Opsvik, Eivind. Interview by author. Digital recording. June 10, 2020.

Pavolka, Matt. Interview by author. Digital recording. February 11, 2014.

Pavone, Jessica. Interview by author. Digital recording. December 29, 2014.

Pavone, Jessica. Interview by author. Digital recording. March 19, 2019.

Pavone, Jessica. Interview by author. Email. May 12, 2019.

Pettit, Ethan. Interview by author. Digital recording. March 19, 2019.

Pride, Mike. Interview by author. Digital recording. August 31, 2013.

Radding, Reuben. Interview by author. Digital recording. August 10, 2015.

Ramos, Jose. Interview by author. Digital recording. August 10, 2020.

Reichman, Ted. Interview by author. Digital recording. June 24, 2019.

Roe, Tom, and Galen Joseph-Hunter. Interview by author. Digital recording. July 21, 2015.

Rose, Michael X. Interview by author. Digital recording. April 1, 2019.

Rose, Michael X. Interview by author. Digital recording. May 12, 2019.

Rosenblum, Harry. Interview by author. Digital recording. July 13, 2015.

Roslund, Heather. Interview by author. Digital recording. March 18, 2021.

Rubinstein, Sari. Interview by author. Digital recording. March 28, 2019.

Sanchez, Angelica. Interview by author. Digital recording. June 20, 2019.

Sanguedolce, Lorenzo. Interview by author. Digital recording. November 16, 2020.

Sawyer, Ryan. Interview by author. Digital recording. June 11, 2020.

Sawyer, Ryan. Interview by author. Digital recording. August 11, 2020.

Schlicht, Ursel. Interview by author. Digital recording. November 6, 2020.

Schmitz, Tom. Interview by author. Email. January 13, 2021.

Shaikh, Aaron Ali. Interview by author. Digital recording. June 10, 2015.

Shaikh, Aaron Ali. Interview by author. Email. September 12, 2016.

Shea, Kevin. Interview by author. Digital recording. August 10, 2015.

Shipp, Matthew. Interview by author. Digital recording. January 14, 2021.

Shiraishi, Tamio. Interview by author. Email. October 6, 2019.

Siegel, Aaron. Interview by author. Digital recording. June 19, 2015.

Siegel, Aaron. Interview by author. Digital recording. August 14, 2015.

Simons, David. Email to author. April 22, 2019.

Smiley, Andrew. Interview by author. Digital recording. June 18, 2020.

Soubiran, Jocelyn. Interview by author. Email. July 10, 2015.

Tabnik, Richard. Interview by author. Email. March 23, 2020.

Tabnik, Richard. Interview by author. Digital recording. April 21, 2020.

Taninaka, Hideji. Interview by author. Email. April 26, 2019.

Taylor, Chad. Interview by author. Email. April 7, 2020.

Walter, Weasel. Interview by author. Digital recording. May 9, 2016.

Walter, Weasel. Interview by author. Digital recording. October 8, 2020.

Walter, Weasel. Interview by author. Digital recording. January 29, 2021.

Ware, Bill. Interview by author. Digital recording. March 20, 2020.

Waterhouse, Russ. Interview by author. Email. July 16–24, 2015.

Waters, Charles. Interview by author. Digital recording. October 19, 2015.

Waters, Charles. Interview by author. Digital recording. March 6, 2019.

Waters, Charles. Interview by author. Email. April 25, 2019.

Welch, Fritz. Interview by author. Email. April 22–25, 2019.

Welch, Fritz. Interview by author. Digital recording. April 26, 2019.

Welch, Fritz. Interview by author. Email. September 24, 2019.

Welch, Matthew. Interview by author. Digital recording. March 4, 2015.

Wilson, Sarah. Interview by author. Digital recording. May 5, 2020.

Wilson, Sarah. Email to author. May 7, 2020.

Wimberly, Michael. Interview by author. Digital recording. October 15, 2021.

Wollesen, Kenny. Interview by author. Digital recording. April 28, 2020.

Wolper, Andrea. Interview by author. Email. March 29, 2020.

Woodward, Estelle. Interview by author. Digital recording. July 1, 2015.

Wooley, Nate. Interview by author. Email. December 3, 2012–May 20, 2014.

Wooley, Nate. Interview by author. Email. July 1–13, 2014.

Wooley, Nate. Interview by author. Email. December 14, 2015.

Zwicky, Michael J. Interview by author. Digital recording. April 3, 2019.

Unpublished Documents

Association of Williamsburgh/Greenpoint Artists. Press release, December 4, 1987, Brooklyn Museum Library.

Edwards, Marc. "The History of Slipstream Time Travel." Unpublished manuscript, n.d.

Pavone, Jessica. Personal daily planner, 2003 calendar year. Jessica Pavone private collection.

Social Media and Email Lists

Bush, V. Owen. "The Omnisensorialists 1991–1999." Unpublished essay, 2009, posted to Immersionism Facebook discussion group, 2012. https://www.facebook.com/notes/ethan-pettit/the-omnisensorialists-1991-1999/10150489040717688.

Eddy, Chuck. "My Entire Pazz and Jop Comment Spiel." IlXor.com, February 10, 2004, 18:58 p.m. https://www.ilxor.com/ILX/ThreadSelectedControllerServlet?boardid=41&threadid=25858.

Pettit, Ethan. "Lalalandia." Facebook archive. November 10, 2014. Accessed April 11, 2019.

Pettit, Ethan, Ebon Fisher, and Susie Kahlich. "Immersionism, a Brief Introduction." Facebook, 2012. Accessed April 15, 2019. https://www.facebook.com/notes/ethan-pettit/immersionism/501003277687.

Published Primary Source

Braxton, Anthony. *Complete Tri-Axium Writings*. Lebanon, CT: Frog Peak Music, 2013.

Secondary Sources
Newspapers, Magazines, and Online Media

Acquaro, Paul. Review: Pulverize the Sound—Pulverize the Sound (Relative Pitch, 2015). Free Jazz Collective: Reviews of Free Jazz and Improvised Music, June 13, 2015, https://www.freejazzblog.org/2015/06/pulverize-sound-st-relative-pitch-2015.html.

Albini, Steve. "The Problem with Music." *Baffler*, no. 5 (December 1993). https://thebaffler.com/salvos/the-problem-with-music.

All about Jazz. "Peter Evans: Zebulon." May 6, 2013. https://www.allaboutjazz.com/zebulon-peter-evans-aire-sol-records-review-by-aaji-staff.

Allen, Clifford. "Charles Gayle." *New York City Jazz Record*, no. 146 (June 2014): 7.

Arike, Ando. "Kerry Smith, Legendary Right Bank Café Owner, Dies at 67; Gala Memorial Planned for January." *Williamsburg Observer*, November 24, 2014. http://www.williamsburgobserver.org/2014/11/24/kerry-smith-dies-at-67/.

Asch, Gregor (DJ Olive). "Is That a Chicken in My Coat?" DJ Olive website. Accessed April 8, 2019. http://www.djolive.com/.

Barbanel, Josh. "Happy Land Arrest Order Ignored in 1989." *New York Times*, April 3, 1990.

Basinski, William. "William Basinski." *Flaunt*, December 1, 2013. http://www.flaunt.com/content/art/william-basinski.

Bharoocha, Hisham Akira. "Boredoms." Translated by Sawako Nakayasu. *BOMB*, no. 104 (2008): 52–58.

Binkley, Sam. "Learning from the Sex Salon (Was It Good for You Too?)." *Word of Mouth*, March 1990: 1.

Birchmeier, Jason. "Chin Chin." AllMusic, n.d. Accessed March 26, 2019. https://www.allmusic.com/artist/chin-chin-mn0000991412/biography.

BlackBook. "Brooklyn: The Borough That Never Sleeps." *BlackBook*, April 7, 2010. https://blackbookmag.com/archive/brooklyn-the-borough-that-never-sleeps/.

Bowden, Ann Standaert. "The Theft of SoHo." *ARTnews*, November 1979, 82–86.

Bradley, Cisco. "Mike Pride's From Bacteria to Boys at Greenwich House Music School." Jazz Right Now, May 23, 2013.https://www.jazzrightnow.com/mike-prides-from-bacteria-to-boys-at-greenwich-house-music-school/.

Braxton, Tyondai. "Tyondai Braxton." Interview by Ben Vida. *BOMB*, no. 129 (October 1, 2014). https://bombmagazine.org/articles/tyondai-braxton/.

Brazen, Ray. "Williamsburg, before It Was a Hipster Shithole." *Brazenblog!*, June 7, 2017. http://raybrazen.blogspot.com/2017/06/williamsburg-before-it-was-hipster.html.

Brian B. "Tina Fey Tapped for Curly Oxide and Vic Thrill." MovieWeb, August 26, 2004. https://movieweb.com/tina-fey-tapped-for-curly-oxide-and-vic-thrill/.

Bynum, Taylor Ho. "Postscript: Butch Morris, 1947–2013." *New Yorker*, January 30, 2013. https://www.newyorker.com/culture/culture-desk/postscript-butch-morris-1947-2013.

Bynum, Taylor Ho. "Postscript: Kalaparusha Maurice McIntyre, 1936–2013." *New Yorker*, November 14, 2013. https://www.newyorker.com/culture/culture-desk/postscript-kalaparusha-maurice-mcintyre-1936-2013.

Carey, Brainard. "Ebon Fisher." Museum of Non-visible Art: Interviews from Yale University Radio, Praxis, July 20, 2016. https://museumofnonvisibleart.com /interviews/ebon-fisher/.

Carey, Christian. Review: *Brooklyn Cantos*, by Gold Sparkle Trio with Ken Vandermark. *Signal to Noise* 37 (2005): 57–58.

Chacona, John. "Seeing the Light." *Erie News Daily*, September 4, 2003.

Chinen, Nate. "A Classicist of Rap, and a Crossover Crosses Back." *New York Times*, August 13, 2010.

Chinen, Nate. "Jazz Acts, Blowing Superhot and Cool." *New York Times*, June 13, 2012.

Chinen, Nate. "Jazz Intuition, American Roots and Double Hybrids." *New York Times*, December 16, 2015.

Chinen, Nate. "New Languages Festival Makes Avant-Garde Inviting, If Not Compromising." *New York Times*, May 15, 2006.

Chinen, Nate. Review: *Coin Coin Chapter Three: River Run Thee*, by Matana Roberts. *New York Times*, February 2, 2015.

Chinen, Nate. "Tinges of Electro-Pop and Some Ives, Too." *New York Times*, February 18, 2010.

Chinen, Nate. "Winter Jazzfest: A Happy Audience, for Whatever the Genre." *New York Times*, January 12, 2013.

Clark, Philip. "Review: *Prairies*, by Mary Halvorson and Jessica Pavone." *Wire*, May 2006, 22.

Cohan, Brad. "Charles Gayle Embraces His Alter Ego." *Village Voice*, February 8, 2012.

Cohen, Mike. "The Cat's Head and Sonic Youth and the Disco Inferno." *Word of Mouth*, August 1990, 1, 3, 6.

Collins, Troy. "Mary Halvorson and Jessica Pavone: *On and Off*." All about Jazz, August 8, 2007. https://www.allaboutjazz.com/on-and-off-skirl-records-review-by -troy-collins.php.

Cullen, Jim. "Pirate Radio Fights for Free Speech." *Progressive Populist*, April 1998. https://www.populist.com/98.4.pirate.html.

Dale, Jon. "Percussion Discussion." *Signal to Noise* 29 (2003): 15–19.

Del Signore, John. "New Chef at Williamsburg's Rabbithole Is Killing It." *Gothamist*, March 17, 2012. http://gothamist.com/2012/03/17/new_chef_at_williamsburgs _rabbithol.php.

Del Signore, John. "Williamsburg Mainstay Verb Café to Close." *Gothamist*, June 5, 2014. http://gothamist.com/2014/06/05/verb_williamsburg_closing.php.

Dery, Mark. "Doing Your Own Thing by Making Your Own Thing." *New York Times*, August 19, 1990.

Dollar, Steve. "Event's Intent Is to Lose Yourself in Lala Land." *Atlanta Journal*, August 27, 1993.

Dollar, Steve. "The Making of a Guitar Goddess." *New York Sun*, February 21, 2007.

Dollar, Steve. "Pavone Brings Her Strings Back Home." *New York Sun*, March 11, 2008.

Dollar, Steve. "Same Name, New People and Sound." *Wall Street Journal*, February 1, 2013.

Donohue-Greene, Laurence. "New York @ Night." *All about Jazz—New York*, no. 38 (2005): 4.

Down Beat. "Jazz Musicians Group in Chicago Growing." July 28, 1966.

Ennis, Thomas W. "Brooklyn Walkups Rehabilitated." *New York Times*, September 22, 1965.

Farber, Jim. "Vinyl Mania Can't Save the Greenwich Village Record Stores." *New York Times*, June 10, 2016.

Ferguson, Sarah. "Hello Kitty." *Village Voice*, October 30, 1990.

Fintoni, Laurent. "Detuning the City: An Oral History of Illbient." *Red Bull Music Academy Daily*, August 18, 2014. https://daily.redbullmusicacademy.com/2014/08/illbient-oral-history.

Fintoni, Laurent. "Illbient, Tension and the Brooklyn Immersionist Movement: DJ Olive in Conversation." *Medium*, October 14, 2014. https://medium.com/dancing-about-architecture/illbient-tension-and-the-brooklyn-immersionist-movement-dj-olive-in-conversation-6abdbe6c53d4.

Fisher, Ebon. "The Sex Salon and the Web Jam: Rediscovering the Value of Social Ritual." *Utne Reader*, January/February 1995: 23.

Fitzell, Sean. "Artist Feature: Steve Swell." *All about Jazz—New York*, no. 29 (September 2004): 7.

Foderaro, Lisa W. "A Metamorphosis for Old Williamsburg." *New York Times*, July 19, 1987.

Frank, Raphie. "Ralph Baker, (Refusing to Be) Blind Photographer." *Gothamist*, September 10, 2005. http://gothamist.com/2005/09/10/ralph_baker_refusing_to_be_blind_photographer.php.

Freiberg, Peter. "Artists' Escape to Williamsburg." *Soho News*, April 30, 1980, 6–7, 60.

Freiberg, Peter. "Loft Tenants Getting Their Act Together." *Soho News*, May 7, 1980, 6.

Frieze. "How Has Art Changed?" No. 94 (October 2005): 13.

Fuller, Thomas, Julie Turkewitz, Yamiche Alcindor, Conor Dougherty, and Serge F. Kovaleski. "Why the 'Ghost Ship' Was Invisible in Oakland, until 36 Died." *New York Times*, December 22, 2016.

Gansberg, Martin. "Williamsburg Violence Reflects Tension in Area." *New York Times*, June 30, 1970.

Gayle, Charles. "Charles Gayle: Interview by James Lindbloom." *Perfect Sound Forever*, March 2000. https://www.furious.com/perfect/charlesgayle.html.

Gershon, Peter. Review: *Kill Any/All SPIN Personnel*, by Thurston Moore et al. *Signal to Noise* 21 (2001): 49.

Gershon, Peter. Review: *Letters from the Serth* by No-Neck Blues Band. *Soundboard* 6 (July/August 1998): 40.

Gold, Allan R. "2 Brooklyn Areas Ask What Factories Are Doing to Them." *New York Times*, April 21, 1990.

Gooch, Brad. "The New Bohemia." *New York Magazine*, June 22, 1992: 12–16.

Gottschalk, Kurt. "It's in the Stars." *Signal to Noise* 53 (2009): 12–17.

Gottschalk, Kurt. "Parallactic Records." *All about Jazz—New York*, no. 16 (August 2003): 6, 21.

Gottschalk, Kurt. Review: *Jump Arts Orchestra Conducted by "Butch" Morris. All about Jazz—New York*, no. 3 (July 2002): 11.

Gottschalk, Kurt. Review: *Prairies*, by Mary Halvorson and Jessica Pavone. *Signal to Noise* 42 (2006): 63.

Grad, David. "The Astro Zombies." *Sound Views* (July 1993): 11.

Halbfinger, David M. "For a Bar Not Used to Dancing around Issues, Dancing Is Now the Issue." *New York Times*, July 29, 1997.

Hareuveni, Eyal. "Tel Aviv Jazz Festival 2006." All about Jazz, March 23, 2006. https://www.allaboutjazz.com/tel-aviv-jazz-festival-2006-by-eyal-hareuveni.

Harrison, Helen A. "Not So Innocent 'Paper Dolls.'" *New York Times*, September 1, 1985.

Hebbinghaus, Monika. "Radical Jewish Culture Movement Helped Musicians Uncover Identity." *DW*, April 20, 2011. https://www.dw.com/en/radical-jewish-culture -movement-helped-musicians-uncover-identity/a-15005319.

Henderson, David. "Butch Morris." *BOMB*, no. 55 (Winter 1996): 32–36.

Hevesi, Dennis. "Protest Forms over Radioactive Waste in Brooklyn." *New York Times*, May 26, 1991.

Holland, Bernard. "Classical Music in Review." *New York Times*, December 7, 1992.

Hornblower, Margot. "Cultures Clash." *Liberty*, March/April 1988, 23–25.

Howe, Marvine. "Cabaret Law Would Aid Neighbors of Nightclubs." *New York Times*, July 26, 1992.

Howell, Rebecca Gayle. "The Lexington Cure." *Oxford American*, no. 99 (November 21, 2017).

Hreha, Scott. Review: *Live*, by TEST. *Signal to Noise* 15 (January/February 2000): 48.

Hreha, Scott. "Sax in the City." *Signal to Noise* 20 (2001): 32–37.

Hreha, Scott. "Test: Mass Transit Appeal." *Signal to Noise* 13 (September/October 1999): 24–26.

Huey, Steve. "Fly Ashtray." AllMusic, n.d. Accessed March 25, 2019. https://www .allmusic.com/artist/fly-ashtray-mn0000195050.

Iacono, Chris. "In Full Swing . . ." *Signal to Noise* 7 (September/October 1998): 32–33.

Jacobs, Jane. "Letter to Mayor Bloomberg and the City Council." *Brooklyn Rail*, May 2005. http://www.brooklynrail.org/2005/05/local/letter-to-mayor -bloomberg.

Johnson, Tom. "The Kitchen Improvises." *Village Voice*, September 24, 1980, 72.

Jones, Baird. "East Village Art, Brooklyn Artists." *Phoenix*, August 20, 1987: 2.

Joseph, Channing. "Where Marxists Pontificate, and Play." *New York Times*, November 4, 2010.

Jurek, Thom. Review: *Thunder Reminded Me*. AllMusic, n.d. Accessed March 13, 2019. https://www.allmusic.com/album/thunder-reminded-me-mw0000031767.

Kart, Lawrence. "Maurice McIntyre." *Down Beat*, April 16, 1970.

Koenig, Steve. "Anthony Braxton: Between the Quadrants." *All about Jazz—New York*, no. 2 (June 2002): 9, 15.

Lauerman, Connie. "When Legendary Jazz Musician Charles Mingus Saw . . ." *Chicago Tribune*, November 20, 1994.

Lombardi, Kate Stone. "Tons of Chemical Waste from Homes in County." *New York Times*, August 11, 1991.

Lonergan, Brian. "Club Profile: Zebulon." *All about Jazz—New York*, no. 35 (March 2005): 6.

Lonergan, Brian. Review: Various Artists, *This Is It: Live at Zebulon*, vol. 1. *All about Jazz—New York*, no. 44 (December 2005): 18.

MacDonald, John S. W. "free 103point9: Ten Years of Transmission Arts." *Brooklyn Rail*, July 6, 2007.

Maranto, Gina. "The Big Dirty Apple." *New York Times*, August 26, 1990.

Margasak, Peter. "Instincts Louder Than Words." *Chicago Reader*, July 10, 2007.

Margasak, Peter. "Jazz Genealogy: Matana Roberts Releases the First Chapter of a 12-Part Epic That Traces African-American History Back across the Atlantic." *Chicago Reader*, May 5, 2011. https://www.chicagoreader.com/chicago/matana-roberts-jazz-african-american-history/Content?oid=3726878.

Masters, Marc. "A Beginner's Guide to Brutal Prog." *Bandcamp Daily*, July 26, 2019. https://daily.bandcamp.com/lists/brutal-prog-guide.

Masters, Marc. Review: *Pestilence and Joy*, Peeesseye, 2010. Pitchfork, July 26, 2010. https://pitchfork.com/reviews/albums/14487-pestilence-joy/.

Matos, Michaelangelo. "The Bunker's Bryan Kasenic on the Berliniamsburg Era, Throwing Parties for Electronic-Music Nerds, and 'Amateur Night.'" *Village Voice*, January 6, 2012.

McCallister, Jared. "Some Face Eviction from Loft Dwellings." *New York Daily News*, January 14, 1986.

McCormack, Ed. "Artists in Residence: Williamsburg's Latest Refugees." *Daily News Magazine*, May 26, 1985.

McIntyre, Kalaparusha Maurice. "Kalaparusha Maurice McIntyre: 'That's Not a Horn, It's a Starvation Box.'" *Guardian*, September 13, 2010. https://www.theguardian.com/music/video/2010/sep/13/kalaparusha-maurice-mcintyre-horn-starvation-box.

McKinley, James C., Jr. "Dinkins Reduces Task Force on Safety of Social Clubs." *New York Times*, June 30, 1990.

McKinley, James C., Jr. "Fire in the Bronx; Happy Land Reopened and Flourished after Being Shut as a Hazard." *New York Times*, March 26, 1990.

McKinley, James C., Jr. "New York Social Clubs Safer, but Problems Linger." *New York Times*, March 26, 1991.

McKinley, Jesse. "The Café Police Pop In for a Raid." *New York Times*, July 5, 1998.

Meyer, Bill. Review: *Fugues and Flowers*, by Gold Sparkle Band. *Signal to Noise* 25 (2002): 71–72.

Meyer, Bill. Review: *13 Definitions of Truth*, by Peter Kowald and Tatsuya Nakatani. *Signal to Noise* 30 (2003): 49–50.

Meyer, Bill. Review: *Thunder Reminded Me*, by Gold Sparkle Trio. *Signal to Noise* 31 (2003): 53.

Morgan, Jon C. "Gold Sparkle Band." *Copper Press* 5 (n.d.).

Morris, Bob. "Karen Black on the Town." *New York Times*, January 16, 1994.

Morris, Lawrence D. "Another Jazz." *New York City Jazz Record*, no. 118 (February 2012): 11.

Morris, Lawrence D. "Butch Morris on the Art of 'Conduction.'" Interview by Farai Chideya. *NPR*, February 18, 2008. https://www.npr.org/templates/story/story.php ?storyId=19145728.

Mulkerns, Helena. "The Cat's Head II: On the Waterfront." *Downtown*, October 24, 1990, 32A–33A.

Napoli, Lisa. "Police and Protestors Have Clashed before in Tompkins Square; Gentrification's Price." *New York Times*, August 27, 1988.

Neidlinger, Buell. "Buell Neidlinger: Interview." Interview by Bob Rusch. *Cadence* 12, no. 6 (June 1986): 5–21, 66.

"NewMusicBox Matana Roberts: Creative Defiance." New Music USA, January 4, 2013, YouTube video, 10:16. https://www.youtube.com/watch?v=XXI5pXB0_Ac.

Newton, Edmund. "Tension in Williamsburg—Housing for Whom?" *New York Daily Post Magazine*, December 22, 1976, 27.

New York Times. "Institute for Young Jews." July 16, 1903.

New York Times. "Rebels to Revivalists: Who's Who at Seminar." July 10, 1987.

New York Times. "Spare Times." August 7, 1998.

New York Times. "36 Unsafe Social Clubs Chained and Locked." April 5, 1990.

Palmer, Robert. "Jazz: Rivbea." *New York Times*, June 27, 1977.

Palmer, Robert. "Mingus Plays Flamenco with Azucena Dancers." *New York Times*, June 28, 1976.

Palmer, Robert. "Newport Jazz." *New York Times*, June 28, 1978.

Paper Magazine. "Welcome to Lalalandia." Summer 1993, [1].

Pareles, Jon. "Folk-Rock: The Fort in Series." *New York Times*, July 14, 1989.

Pareles, Jon. "Free Butch Morris Concerts." *New York Times*, November 16, 1989.

Pareles, Jon. "Freedom and Physicality from Charles Gayle's Trio." *New York Times*, March 30, 1992.

Pareles, Jon. "Jazz: Charles Gayle." *New York Times*, September 3, 1987.

Pareles, Jon. "Jazz: Peter Kowald Quartet." *New York Times*, June 4, 1984.

Pareles, Jon. "Morris Tests Limits of Improvisation." *New York Times*, July 26, 1985.

Pareles, Jon. "270 Rock Bands to Perform at 10th New Music Seminar." *New York Times*, July 14, 1989.

Pareles, Jon. "Z'ev, Percussionist and Industrial Music Pioneer, Dies at 66." *New York Times*, December 26, 2017.

Pareles, Jon, Ben Ratliff, and Nate Chinen. "Somber Tunes, Off-Kilter Beats." *New York Times*, May 20, 2013.

Pavone, Jessica. "Interview with Jessica Pavone." *El intruso*, n.d. Jessica Pavone private collection.

Pellegrinelli, Lara. "Sounds of Bali, Traditional yet Evolving." *New York Times*, December 10, 2010.

Pettit, Ethan. "The Inflatable Man: Dennis Del Zotto and the Williamsburg Scene." Ethan Pettit Gallery, June 7, 2006. https://ethanpettit.blogspot.com/2006/06 /dennis-del-zotto-and-williamsburg-scene.html.

Pierre-Pierre, Garry. "Breathing Easier after the Last Shipment of Radioactive Waste." *New York Times*, June 12, 1994.

Powers, Ann. "Tuning In the Brain Waves to the Wild Side of Jazz." *New York Times*, June 6, 2001.

Pristin, Terry. "WFMU in Fund-Raising Drive." *New York Times*, March 13, 1996.

Purdum, Todd S. "Melee in Tompkins Sq. Park: Violence and Its Provocation." *New York Times*, August 14, 1988.

Ratliff, Ben. "At Vinyl, Fast-Paced Techno for Dancers Only." *New York Times*, January 6, 1997.

Ratliff, Ben. "Butch Morris Dies at 65; Creator of 'Conduction.'" *New York Times*, January 29, 2013.

Ratliff, Ben. "An Improvising Conductor Celebrates an Anniversary." *New York Times*, February 3, 2005.

Ratliff, Ben. "A System of Conducting, or, Rather, 'Conduction.'" *New York Times*, April 3, 1998.

Raynor, Vivien. "Contemporary Artists Travel Two Paths in Hartford Shows." *New York Times*, April 4, 1993.

Reich, Howard. "Fearless Musical Experimenting Pays Dividend." *Chicago Tribune*, April 5, 2004.

Richardson, Lynda. "Sparing a Dime, Whether They Agree or Not." *New York Times*, January 3, 1992.

Roa, Roy. "Music Issue: Edwin Velez Opened His Doors to Misfits Galore." *Creative Loafing Tampa Bay*, July 13, 2017. https://www.cltampa.com/music/local/article/20867434/music-issue-edwin-velez-opened-his-doors-to-misfits-galore.

Roberts, Matana. "Traces of People: An Interview with Matana Roberts." Interview by Stewart Smith. *Quietus*, October 6, 2015. https://thequietus.com/articles/18937-matana-roberts-interview.

Roberts, Sam. "Bloomberg Administration Is Developing Land Use Plan to Accommodate Future Populations." *New York Times*, November 26, 2006.

Rockwell, John. "Jazz: Two Braxton Programs." *New York Times*, April 23, 1982.

Rockwell, John. "Patti Smith Plans Album with Eyes on Stardom." *New York Times*, March 28, 1975.

Rockwell, John. "Speculations about Rock Spectacles." *New York Times*, May 16, 1975.

Roe, Tom. "Gold Sparkle Band: Atlanta Transplants' Multifarious Orbits Converging." *Signal to Noise* 17 (May/June 2000): 12–13.

Rose, Michael X. Untitled essay. *Waterfront Week*, July 29, 1992: 1.

Rosenberg, Jon. "An Interview with Jon Rosenberg." Interview by Beppe Colli. *CloudsandClocks*, April 2, 2017. http://www.cloudsandclocks.net/interviews/Rosenberg_interview.html.

Russonello, Giovanni. "Connie Crothers, Jazz Pianist, Composer and Instructor, Dies at 75." *New York Times*, August 21, 2016.

Salant, Norman. "Weather Report: Lack of Identity." *Spectrum* (Buffalo, NY), December 1, 1972.

Samuels, David. "Local Arts Groups Find Real Estate Success in Brooklyn as Refugees from Manhattan's Notorious 'Space Chase.'" *Phoenix*, February 27, 1986, 17–18.

Sarig, Roni. "Mr. Ruzow's Opus: The Gold Sparkler Who Stayed behind Builds Community with a Little Improvisation." *Vibes* (Atlanta), May 1–7, 2002, 85–87.

Sauter, Jim. "Jim Sauter Interview." Interview by Jason Gross. *Perfect Sound Forever*, July 1997. http://www.furious.com/perfect/borbetomagus.html.

Schatz, Adam. "An Argument with Instruments: On Charles Mingus." *Nation*, September 17, 2013.

Schlicht, Ursel. "Remembering Connie Crothers (1941–2016)." *NewMusicBox*, September 9, 2016. https://nmbx.newmusicusa.org/remembering-connie-crothers-1941 -2016/.

Schweitzer, Vivien. "A Tent with Room for Sounds of All Kinds." *New York Times*, August 23, 2006.

Sharpe, John. "Vision Festival: Day 4, June 8, 2011." All about Jazz, July 14, 2011. https://www.allaboutjazz.com/vision-festival-day-4-june-8-2011-by-john -sharpe.

Shteamer, Hank. "Fritz Welch." *Signal to Noise* 32 (2004): 11.

Sienko, Chris. "The Triumphant Re-return of White Tapes." *Blastitude*, no. 5 (February 2001). http://www.blastitude.com/5/pg2.htm.

Simonini, Ross. "Singing Bulls and Day-Glo Tapestry: The Spectacle of Caroliner Rainbow." *SF Weekly*, July 16, 2008. https://archives.sfweekly.com/sanfrancisco/singing -bulls-and-day-glo-tapestry-the-spectacle-of-caroliner-rainbow/Content?oid =2168463.

Smith, Andy P. "Ten Years of Music in Williamsburg 2002–2012: An Oral History." *Medium*, March 4, 2015. https://medium.com/barns-kitchens-hotels-bodegas -and-stadiums/ten-years-of-music-in-williamsburg-2002–2012-an-oral-history -7fa2ac083470.

Smith, Roberta. "Art in Review." *New York Times*, June 26, 1992.

Smith, Roberta. "Art in Review." *New York Times*, December 4, 1992.

Smith, Roberta. "Group Shows of Every Kind, Even Where the Show Itself Is an Art Form." *New York Times*, February 25, 1994.

Smith, Roberta. "A Sprinkling of Exhibitions near Factories and the Water." *New York Times*, March 23, 1990.

Solov, Dean. "Feds Shut Down Pirate Radio Stations." *Tampa Tribune*, November 20, 1997.

Stockton, Jeff. Review: Digital Primitives, *Digital Primitives*. *All about Jazz—New York*, no. 64 (August 2007): 14.

Stockton, Jeff. Review: *War Rug* by Eye Contact. All About Jazz, April 7, 2007. https://www.allaboutjazz.com/matt-lavelle-spiritual-power-and-war-rug-by-jeff -stockton.

Strauss, Neil. "At the Clubs, Murmurs and Ambient Music." *New York Times*, March 8, 1996.

Strauss, Neil. "The Cutting Edge." *New York Times*, January 3, 1997.

Šumila, Edvardas. "New York Scenes and Echoes from Lithuania: Jonas Mekas' Musical Milieu." Music Information Centre Lithuania, accessed May 5, 2020, https:// www.mic.lt/en/discourses/lithuanian-music-link/no22-january-december-2019 /edvardas-sumila-new-york-scenes-and-echoes-lithuania-jonas-mekas/.

Tangari, Joe. Review: *Groundswell* by Parts and Labor. Pitchfork, March 7, 2004. https://pitchfork.com/reviews/albums/6532-groundswell/.

Terry, Don. "Fire in the Bronx; Social Club Crackdown Is the Latest in a Series." *New York Times*, March 26, 1990.

Tommasini, Anthony. "Created on the Computer, but Pristine It Is Not." *New York Times*, April 4, 2005.

Vance, David. Review: *Morning Song* by Kalaparusha and the Light (Delmark, 2004).

Virshup, Amy. "The Newest Left Bank." *New York Magazine*, April 21, 1986.

Vrusho, Spike. "Waterfront Week, R.I.P." *New York Press*, July 16, 2002.

Vyse, Medea de. "Discours sur la Moutarde: The Evolution of Warehouse Events in Williamsburg." *Breukelen*, April 1993: 9.

Walsh, Kevin. "Bedford Avenue, Part 3." Forgotten New York, December 14, 2014. https://forgotten-ny.com/2014/12/bedford-avenue-part-3/.

Walter, Weasel. "Orthrelm." *Blastitude* 17 (November 2004). http://www.blastitude .com/17/ORTHRELM.htm.

Warburton, Dan. Review: *Berlin Reeds*, by Various. *Signal to Noise* 31 (2003): 47–48.

Warburton, Dan. Review: Self-titled, by Axel Dörner and Kevin Drumm. *Signal to Noise* 23 (2001): 62.

Warburton, Dan. Review: *Solos and Duos*, by Jessica Pavone and Jackson Moore. *Signal to Noise* 25 (2002): 82.

Warburton, Dan. "The Wright Stuff." *Signal to Noise* 27 (2002): 36–42.

Watrous, Peter. "The Pop Life." *New York Times*, September 18, 1991.

Watrous, Peter. "Tomorrow's Stars Today in Brooklyn's Small Clubs." *New York Times*, March 23, 1990.

Watson, Ben. "Randomness and Antagonism in Electric Guitar Stylings." *Signal to Noise* 14 (November/December 1999): 10–12.

Weddle, Eric. Review: *On Tour*, by Toshimaru Nakamura and Sean Meehan; *Loran*, by Margarida Garcia and Barry Weisblat. *Signal to Noise* 38 (2005): 68.

Weil, Elizabeth. "He Helped Build an Artists' Utopia, Now He Faces Trial for 36 Deaths There." *New York Times*, December 12, 2018.

Welch, Matthew. "Music." Blarvuster.com, n.d. Accessed May 28, 2019.

Wetzel, Florence. Review: *Embracing the Tide/Making Eye Contact with God* by Eye Contact. *All about Jazz—New York* 45 (January 2006): 13.

Wines, Suzan. "Go with the Flow: Eight New York–Based Artists and Architects in the Digital Era." *Domus Magazine*, February 1998, 1–10.

Wooley, Nate. "Point of Departure: Nate Wooley Interview." Interview by Troy Collins. Clean Feed Records, March 10, 2016. https://cleanfeed-records.com/point-of -departure-nate-wooley-interview/.

Woolfe, Zachary. "Williamsburg's Arcadian Past: Composer Billy Basinski Stars in Robert Wilson's Quasi-Opera *The Life and Death of Marina Abramovic*." *Observer* (Brooklyn), November 1, 2011. https://observer.com/2011/11/williamsburgs -arcadian-past-composer-billy-basinski-stars-in-robert-wilsons-quasi-opera-the -life-and-death-of-marina-abramovic/.

Zimbouski, Mike. Review: *Sticks and Stones May Break My Bones but Names Will Never Hurt Me*, by No-Neck Blues Band. *Signal to Noise* 25 (2002): 60.

Alvarez, Luis. *The Power of Zoot: Youth Culture and Resistance during World War II*. Berkeley: University of California Press, 2008.

Attali, Jacques. *Bruits: Essai sur l'économie politique de la musique*. 2nd ed. Paris: PUF/Fayard, 2001.

Atton, Chris. "Listening to 'Difficult Albums': Specialist Music Fans and the Popular Avant-Garde." *Popular Music* 31, no. 3 (2012): 347–61.

Azerrad, Michael. *Our Band Could Be Your Life: Scenes from the American Indie Underground, 1981–1991*. Boston: Back Bay, 2001.

Babbitt, Milton. "Twelve-Tone Rhythmic Structure and the Electronic Medium." In *Collected Essays of Milton Babbitt*, edited by Stephen Peles, 109–40. Princeton, NJ: Princeton University Press, 2003.

Barzel, Tamar. *New York Noise: Radical Jewish Music and the Downtown Scene*. Profiles in Popular Music. Bloomington: Indiana University Press, 2015.

Barzel, Tamar. "The Praxis of Composition-Improvisation and the Poetics of Creative Kinship." In *Jazz/Not Jazz: The Music and Its Boundaries*, edited by David Ake, Charles Hiroshi Garrett, and Daniel Goldmark, 171–89. Berkeley: University of California Press, 2012.

Beck, Sam. "Urban Transitions: Graffiti Transformations." In *Public Anthropology in a Borderless World*, edited by Sam Beck and Carl A. Maida, 314–50. New York: Berghahn Books, 2015.

Beech, Dave. *Art and Postcapitalism: Aesthetic Labour, Automation and Value Production*. London: Pluto, 2019.

Belkind, Lara. "Stealth Gentrification: Camouflage and Commerce on the Lower East Side." *Traditional Dwellings and Settlements Review* 21, no. 1 (2009): 21–36.

Block, Steven. "Pitch-Class Transformation in Free Jazz." *Music Theory Spectrum* 12, no. 2 (1990): 181–202.

Borgo, David. "Negotiating Freedom: Values and Perspectives in Contemporary Improvised Music." *Black Music Research Journal* 22, no. 2 (2002): 165–88.

Bradley, Cisco. *Universal Tonality: The Life and Music of William Parker*. Durham, NC: Duke University Press, 2021.

Brinson, Peter. "Liberation Frequency: The Free Radio Movement and Alternative Strategies of Media Relations." *Sociological Quarterly* 47, no. 4 (2006): 543–68.

Bromley, Ray. "Globalization and the Inner Periphery: A Mid-Bronx View." In "Globalization of the Changing U.S. City," special issue, *Annals of the American Academy of Political and Social Science* 551, no. 1 (1997): 191–207.

Brotherton, David C., and Luis Barrios. *The Almighty Latin King and Queen Nation: Street Politics and the Transformation of a New York City Gang*. New York: Columbia University Press, 2004.

Brown, David P. *Noise Orders: Jazz, Improvisation and Architecture*. Minneapolis: University of Minnesota Press, 2006.

Bryant, Clora, Buddy Collette, William Green, Steve Isoardi, and Marl Young, eds. *Central Avenue Sounds: Jazz in Los Angeles*. Berkeley: University of California Press, 1998.

Cage, John. *Silence: Lectures and Writings*. London: Marion Boyars, 1968.

Camp, Jordan T. *Incarcerating the Crisis: Freedom Struggles and the Rise of the Neoliberal State*. Berkeley: University of California Press, 2016.

Campo, Daniel. *The Accidental Playground: Brooklyn Waterfront Narratives of the Undesigned and Unplanned*. New York: Fordham University Press, 2013.

"CD Companion Introduction: Splitting Bits, Closing Loops: Sound on Sound." In "Groove, Pit and Wave: Recording, Transmission and Music," special issue, *Leonard Music Journal* 13 (2003): 79–81.

Cogan, Brian. "'Do They Owe Us a Living? Of Course They Do!': Crass, Throbbing Gristle, and Anarchy and Radicalism in Early English Punk Rock." *Journal for the Study of Radicalism* 1, no. 2 (2007): 77–90.

Cooper, Dennis. *Period*. New York: Grove, 2000.

Cortés, Lydia. "Lydia Cortés." In *Puerto Rican Poetry: An Anthology from Aboriginal to Contemporary Times*, edited by Roberto Márquez, 354–56. Amherst: University of Massachusetts Press, 2007.

Court, Paula. *New York Noise: Art and Music from the New York Underground, 1978–88*. London: Soul Jazz, 2007.

Cox, Bette Yarbrough. "The Evolution of Black Music in Los Angeles, 1890–1955." In *Seeking El Dorado: African Americans in California*, edited by Lawrence B. de Graaf, Kevin Mulroy, and Quintard Taylor, 249–78. Seattle: University of Washington Press, 2001.

Curran, Winifred. "'From the Frying Pan to the Oven': Gentrification and the Experience of Industrial Displacement in Williamsburg, Brooklyn." *Urban Studies* 44, no. 8 (2007): 1427–40.

Curtis, Ric. "The Negligible Role of Gangs in Drug Distribution in New York City in the 1990s." In *Gangs and Society: Alternative Perspectives*, edited by Louis Kontos, David Brotherton, and Luis Barrios, 78–97. New York: Columbia University Press, 2003.

Curtis, Richard. "The Improbable Transformation of Inner-City Neighborhoods: Crime, Violence, Drugs, and Youth in the 1990s." *Journal of Criminal Law and Criminology* 88, no. 4 (1998): 1233–76.

Cymerman, Jeremiah. "Life Preserver/In the Wilderness." In *Arcana VI: Musicians on Music*, edited by John Zorn, 50–59. New York: Hips Road, 2012.

Daniels, Douglas Henry. "Los Angeles Zoot: Race 'Riot,' the Pachuco, and Black Music Culture." In "The Past before Us," special issue, *Journal of African American History* 87, no. 1 (2002): 98–118.

Davis, Francis. *Jazz and Its Discontents: A Francis Davis Reader*. Boston: Da Capo, 2004.

Dickerson, Dwight. "Jazz in Los Angeles: The Black Experience." *Black Music Research Journal* 31, no. 1 (2011): 179–92.

Dollar, Susan E. "The Red River Campaign, Natchitoches Parish, Louisiana: A Case of Equal Opportunity Destruction." *Louisiana History: The Journal of the Louisiana Historical Association* 43, no. 4 (2002): 411–32.

Dorf, Michael. *Knitting Music: A Five-Year History of the Knitting Factory*. New York: Knitting Factory Works, 1992.

Duany, Jorge. *Blurred Borders: Transnational Migration between the Hispanic Caribbean and the United States*. Raleigh: University of North Carolina Press, 2011.

Dunifer, Stephen, and Ron Sakolsky, eds. *Seizing the Airwaves: A Free Radio Handbook*. Chico, CA: AK Press, 1998.

Dunn, Kevin C. "Never Mind the Bollocks: The Punk Rock Politics of Global Communication." In "Cultures and Politics of Global Communication," special issue, *Review of International Studies* 34 (2008): 193–210.

Eastman, Ralph. "Central Avenue Blues: The Making of Los Angeles Rhythm and Blues, 1942–1947." *Black Music Research Journal* 9, no. 1 (1989): 19–33.

Ferrell, Jeff. "Youth, Crime, and Cultural Space." In "Losing a Generation: Probing the Myths and Reality of Youth and Violence," special issue, *Social Justice* 24, no. 4 (1997): 21–38.

Flamming, Douglas. *Bound for Freedom: Black Los Angeles in Jim Crow America*. Berkeley: University of California Press, 2005.

Forte, Allen. *The Structure of Atonal Music*. New Haven, CT: Yale University Press, 1973.

Gabbard, Krin. *Better Git It in Your Soul: An Interpretive Biography of Charles Mingus*. Berkeley: University of California Press, 2016.

Gagne, Cole. *Soundpieces 2: Interviews with American Composers*. Metuchen, NJ: Scarecrow, 1993.

Gawthrop, Rob. "Film Noise Aesthetics." In *Experimental Film and Video: An Anthology*, edited by Jackie Hatfield, 53–60. Bloomington: Indiana University Press, 2015.

Gentrification and Rezoning in Williamsburg-Greenpoint. Newark, NJ: Edward Bloustein School of Planning and Public Policy, Rutgers University, 2007.

Gikandi, Simon. *Slavery and the Culture of Taste*. Princeton, NJ: Princeton University Press, 2011.

Gioia, Ted. *West Coast Jazz: Modern Jazz in California, 1945–1960*. New York: Oxford University Press, 1992.

Goodman, Lizzy. *Meet Me in the Bathroom: Rebirth and Rock and Roll in New York City, 2001–2011*. New York: Harper Collins, 2017.

Gordon, Maxine. "Dexter Gordon and Melba Liston: The 'Mischievous Lady' Session." *Black Music Research Journal* 34, no. 1 (2014): 9–26.

Gordon, Maxine. *Sophisticated Giant: The Life and Legacy of Dexter Gordon*. Berkeley: University of California Press, 2019.

Graham, Stephen. *Sounds of the Underground: A Cultural, Political and Aesthetic Mapping of Underground and Fringe Music*. Ann Arbor: University of Michigan Press, 2016.

Greene, Hilliard. "Interview: Hilliard Greene." Interview by Ludwig van Trikt. *Cadence* 32, no. 8 (August 2006): 12.

Haberski, Raymond J. *Freedom to Offend: How New York Remade Movie Culture*. Lexington: University Press of Kentucky, 2007.

Hahn, Melanie. "The Cat's Head: Constructing Utopia in Brooklyn and Dublin." *Drama Review* 37, no. 3 (1993): 153–65.

Halvorson, Mary. "The Invented Horizon Is Free." In *Arcana VI: Musicians on Music*, edited by John Zorn, 102–8. New York: Hips Road, 2012.

Hauser, Thomas. *The Boxing Scene*. Philadelphia: Temple University Press, 2009.

Hayden, Robert. *Collected Poems*. Edited by Frederick Glaysher. New York: Liveright, 1996.

Hegarty, Paul. *Noise/Music: A History*. New York: Bloomsbury, 2007.

Heller, Michael C. *Loft Jazz: Improvising New York in the 1970s*. Berkeley: University of California Press, 2017.

Hermes, Will. *Love Goes to Buildings on Fire: Five Years in New York That Changed Music Forever*. New York: Faber and Faber, 2011.

Holton, Adalaine. "'Little Things Are Big': Race and the Politics of Print Community in the Writings of Jesús Colón." In "New Perspectives on Puerto Rican, Latina/o, Chicana/o, and Caribbean American Literatures," special issue, *MELUS* 38, no. 2 (2013): 5–23.

Horak, Jan-Christopher. *Saul Bass: Anatomy of Film Design*. Lexington: University Press of Kentucky, 2014.

Hosokawa, Shuhei. "*Ongaku, Onkyō*/Music, Sound." In "Working Words: New Approaches to Japanese Studies," special issue, *Review of Japanese Culture and Society* 25 (December 2013): 9–20.

Indergaard, Michael. "What to Make of New York's New Economy? Politics and the Creative Field." In "Trajectories of the New Economy: Regeneration and Dislocation in the Inner City," special issue, *Urban Studies* 46, nos. 5–6 (2009): 1063–93.

Isoardi, Steven L. *The Dark Tree: Jazz and the Community Arts in Los Angeles*. Berkeley: University of California Press, 2006.

James, Carol P. "Duchamp's Silent Noise/Music for the Deaf." In *Marcel Duchamp: Artist of the Century*, edited by Rudolf E. Kuenzli and Francis M. Naumann, 106–26. Boston: MIT Press, 1989.

Jones, Claire. "Shona Women *Mbira* Players: Gender, Tradition and Nation in Zimbabwe." *Ethnomusicology Forum* 17, no. 1 (2008): 125–49.

Jones, Leroi. "The Changing Same (R&B and New Black Music)." In *The Black Aesthetic*, edited by Addison Gayle Jr., 118–31. Garden City, NY: Doubleday, 1971.

Joseph-Hunter, Galen. "Transmission Arts: The Air That Surrounds Us." *PAJ: A Journal of Performance and Art* 31, no. 3 (2009): 34–40.

Jost, Ekkehard. *Free Jazz*. New York: Da Capo, 1981.

Lander, B., and L. Wolf-Powers. *Remaking New York City*. New York: Pratt Institute, 2004.

Larson, Scott. *"Building like Moses with Jacobs in Mind": Contemporary Planning in New York City*. Urban Life, Landscape and Policy. Philadelphia: Temple University Press, 2013.

Lawrence, Tim. "Pluralism, Minor Deviations, and Radical Change: The Challenge to Experimental Music in Downtown New York, 1971–85." In *Tomorrow Is the Question: New Directions in Experimental Music Studies*, edited by Benjamin Piekut, 63–85. Ann Arbor: University of Michigan Press, 2014.

Lévi-Strauss, Claude. *The Savage Mind*. London: Weidenfeld and Nicolson, 1962.

Lewis, George E. "Experimental Music in Black and White: The AACM in New York, 1970–1985." In *Uptown Conversation: The New Jazz Studies*, edited by Robert G. O'Meally, Brent Hayes Edwards, and Farah Jasmine Griffin, 50–101. New York: Columbia University Press, 2004.

Lewis, George E. *A Power Stronger Than Itself: The AACM and American Experimental Music*. Chicago: University of Chicago Press, 2008.

Lewis, George E. "Singing Omar's Song: A (Re)Construction of Great Black Music." *Lenox Avenue: A Journal of Interarts Inquiry* 4 (1998): 69–92.

Litweiler, John. *The Freedom Principle: Jazz after 1958*. New York: Da Capo, 1984.

Lock, Graham. *Forces in Motion: The Music and Thoughts of Anthony Braxton*. New York: Da Capo, 1988.

Lopez, Rick. *William Parker Sessionography: Attempting a Complete Historical Arc*. New York: Centering, 2014.

Mahmoud, Jasmine. "Brooklyn's Experimental Frontiers: A Performance Geography." *TDR/The Drama Review* 58, no. 3 (2014): 97–123.

Malbon, Ben. *Clubbing: Dancing, Ecstasy, Vitality*. Critical Geographies. London: Routledge, 1999.

Mallinder, Stephen. "Sounds Incorporated: Dissonant Sorties into Popular Culture." In *Resonances: Noise and Contemporary Music*, edited by Michael Goddard, Benjamin Halligan, and Nicola Spelman, 81–94. New York: Bloomsbury, 2013.

Manbeck, John B., ed. *The Neighborhoods of Brooklyn*. 2nd ed. New Haven, CT: Yale University Press, 2004.

Marmorstein, Gary. "Central Avenue Jazz: Los Angeles Black Music in the Forties." *Southern California Quarterly* 70, no. 4 (1988): 415–26.

Meadows, Eddie S. "Clifford Brown in Los Angeles." *Black Music Research Journal* 31, no. 1 (2011): 45–63.

Mekas, Jonas. "Interview with Jonas Mekas." Interview by Scott MacDonald. *October* 29 (1984): 82–116.

Mellers, W. H. "Erik Satie and the 'Problem' of Contemporary Music." *Music and Letters* 23, no. 3 (1942): 210–27.

Mereweather, Charles. *Art, Anti-art, Non-art: Experimentations in the Public Sphere in Postwar Japan, 1950–1970*. Getty Trust Publications: Getty Research Institute for the History of Art and the Humanities. Los Angeles: Getty Research Institute, 2007.

Mills, Elizabeth Shown. "Demythicizing History: Marie Thérèse Coincoin, Tourism, and the National Historical Landmarks Program." *Louisiana History: The Journal of the Louisiana Historical Association* 53, no. 4 (2012): 402–37.

Mills, Gary. *The Forgotten People: Cane River's Creoles of Color*. Baton Rouge: Louisiana State University Press, 1977.

Miyares, Ines M., and Kenneth J. Gowen. "Recreating Borders? The Geography of Latin Americans in New York City." *Yearbook (Conference of Latin Americanist Geographers)* 24 (1998): 31–43.

Moody, Lewis. "The Musical Cueing of Kneebody." BA honors thesis, Edith Cowan University, 2012.

Morales, Jose. "History and Recent Developments in Puerto Rican Environmental Activism." In "Latinos and the Environment," special issue, *Race, Poverty and the Environment* 4, no. 3 (1993): 18–19.

Morgan, David W., Kevin C. MacDonald, and Fiona J. L. Handley. "Economics and Authenticity: A Collision of Interpretations in Cane River National Historical Area, Louisiana." *George Wright Forum* 23, no. 1 (2006): 44–61.

Morgan, Stacy. "Clementine Hunter and Melrose Plantation." *American Art* 19, no. 1 (2005): 25–28.

Newman, Kathe, and Elvin K. Wyly. "The Right to Stay Put: Gentrification and Resistance to Displacement in New York City." *Urban Studies* 43, no. 1 (2006): 23–57.

Nicholls, Tracey. "Changing the Subject: Making Democracy through Making Music." *CLR James Journal* 16, no. 1 (2016): 17–36.

Novak, David. *Japanoise: Music at the Edge of Circulation*. Durham, NC: Duke University Press, 2013.

Novak, David. "Playing Off Site: The Untranslation of *Onkyō*." *Asian Music* 41, no. 1 (2010): 36–59.

Packer, Renée Levine, and Mary Jane Leach, eds. *Gay Guerrilla: Julius Eastman and His Music*. Rochester, NY: University of Rochester Press, 2018.

Plourde, Lorraine. "Disciplined Listening in Tokyo: Onkyō and Non-intentional Sounds." *Ethnomusicology* 52, no. 2 (2008): 270–95.

Polaschegg, Nina. "Freiheit und Struktur: Regeln, Normen und Vorschriften in der improvisierten Musik." *Neue Zeitschrift für Musik* 169, no. 5 (2008): 38–41.

Porter, Eric. *What Is This Thing Called Jazz? African American Musicians as Artists, Critics, and Activists*. Berkeley: University of California Press, 2002.

Prey, Robert, and Jakob Rigi. "Value, Rent, and the Political Economy of Social Media." *Information Society* 31, no. 5 (2015): 392–406.

Radano, Ronald M. *New Musical Figurations: Anthony Braxton's Cultural Critique*. Chicago: University of Chicago Press, 1993.

Reynolds, Simon. *Generation Ecstasy: Into the World of Techno and Rave Culture*. London: Routledge, 1999.

Reynolds, Simon. *Rip It Up and Start Again: Postpunk, 1978–1984*. New York: Penguin Books, 2006.

Rigi, Jakob. "Foundations of a Marxist Theory of the Political Economy of Information: Trade Secrets and Intellectual Property, and the Production of Relative Surplus Value and the Extraction of Rent-Tribute." *Triple-C* 12, no. 2 (2014): 909–36.

Rodriguez, Roberto Cintli. *Yolqui, a Warrior Summoned from the Spirit World: Testimonios on Violence*. Tucson: University of Arizona Press, 2019.

Roelstraete, Dieter. "The Way Ahead: The Association for the Advancement of Creative Musicians and Chicago's Black Arts Revolution." *Afterall: A Journal of Art, Context and Enquiry*, no. 37 (2014): 112–19.

Rout, Leslie B., Jr. "Reflections on the Evolution of Post-war Jazz." In *The Black Aesthetic*, edited by Addison Gayle Jr., 150–60. Garden City, NY: Doubleday, 1971.

Russolo, Luigi. *The Art of Noises*. New York: Pendragon, 1986.

Sánchez Vásquez, Adolfo. *Art and Society: Essays in Marxist Aesthetics*. Translated by Mario Riofrancos. 1965. London: Merlin, 1973.

Sanfilippo, Dario, and Andrea Valle. "Feedback Systems: An Analytical Framework." *Computer Music Journal* 37, no. 2 (2013): 12–27.

Sassaman, Hannah, and Pete Tridish. "Prometheus Radio Project: The Battle over Low-Power FM in the United States." In *Strategies for Media Reform: International Perspectives*, edited by Des Freedman, Jonathan A. Obar, Cheryl Martens, and Robert W. McChesney, 182–89. Bronx, NY: Fordham University Press, 2016.

Schneider, Cathy Lisa. *Police Power and Race Riots: Urban Unrest in Paris and New York*. Philadelphia: University of Pennsylvania Press, 2014.

Schulman, Sarah. *The Gentrification of the Mind: Witness to a Lost Generation*. Berkeley: University of California Press, 2012.

Sharp, Charles. "Seeking John Carter and Bobby Bradford: Free Jazz and Community in Los Angeles." *Black Music Research Journal* 31, no. 1 (2011): 65–83.

Shirer, William L. *The Rise and Fall of the Third Reich: A History of Nazi Germany*. New York: Gallery Books, 1990.

Simpson, Timothy A. "Streets, Sidewalks, Stores, and Stories: Narrative and Uses of Urban Space." *Journal of Contemporary Ethnography* 29, no. 6 (2000): 682–716.

Smith, Catherine Parsons. *Making Music in Los Angeles: Transforming the Popular*. Berkeley: University of California Press, 2007.

Soto-Lopez, Ricardo. "Environmental Justice for Puerto Ricans in the Northeast: A Participant Observer's Assessment." In *Beyond Sun and Sand: Caribbean Environmentalisms*, edited by Sherrie L. Baver and Barbara Deutsch Lynch, 131–39. New Brunswick, NJ: Rutgers University Press, 2006.

Spellman, A. B. *Four Lives in the Bebop Business*. New York: Limelight, 1966.

Spelman, Nicola. "Recasting Noise: The Lives and Times of *Metal Machine Music*." In *Resonances: Noise and Contemporary Music*, edited by Michael Goddard, Benjamin Halligan, and Nicola Spelman, 24–36. New York: Bloomsbury, 2013.

Stallabrass, Julian. *Internet Art: The Online Clash of Culture and Commerce*. London: Tate Publishing, 2003.

Stanley, Thomas T. "Butch Morris and the Art of Conduction." PhD thesis, University of Maryland, 2009.

Takahashi, Melanie, and Tim Olaveson. "Music, Dance and Raving Bodies: Raving as Spirituality in the Central Canadian Rave Scene." *Journal of Ritual Studies* 17, no. 2 (2003): 72–96.

Tapscott, Horace. "Horace Tapscott." In *Central Avenue Sounds: Jazz in Los Angeles*, edited by Clora Bryant, Buddy Collette, William Green, Steve Isoardi, and Marl Young, 53. Berkeley: University of California Press, 1998.

Tapscott, Horace. *Songs of the Unsung: The Musical and Social Journey of Horace Tapscott*. Edited by Steven Isoardi. Durham, NC: Duke University Press, 2001.

Taylor, Marvin J., ed. *The Downtown Book: The New York Art Scene, 1974–1984*. Princeton, NJ: Princeton University Press, 2006.

Tham, Joseph. "Noise as Music: Is There a Historical Continuum? From Historical Roots to Industrial Music." In *Resonances: Noise and Contemporary Music*, edited by Michael Goddard, Benjamin Halligan, and Nicola Spelman, 257–72. New York: Bloomsbury, 2013.

Traber, Daniel S. "Recentering the Listener in Deconstructive Music." In "Hearings (Lending an Ear . . .)," special issue, *CR: The New Centennial Review* 7, no. 1 (2007): 165–80.

Turino, Thomas. "The Mbira, Worldbeat, and the International Imagination." *World of Music* 40, no. 2 (1998): 85–106.

Twain, Mark. *Personal Reflections of Joan of Arc*. New York: Harper and Brothers, 1896.

Whiteley, Sheila. "'Kick Out the Jams': Creative Anarchy and Noise in 1960s Rock." In *Resonances: Noise and Contemporary Music*, edited by Michael Goddard, Benjamin Halligan, and Nicola Spelman, 13–23. New York: Bloomsbury, 2013.

Wilmer, Valerie. *As Serious as Your Life: The Story of the New Jazz*. Westport, CT: Lawrence Hill, 1977.

Wilson, Peter Niklas. "Tabu oder Hohlform? Gedanken zur politischen Abstinenz der neuen elektronischen Musik." In "Musik und Politik," special issue, *Neue Zeitschrift für Musik* 164, no. 6 (2003): 36–41.

Wooley, Nate. "Small, Still Voice." In *Arcana VI: Musicians on Music*, edited by John Zorn, 275–80. New York: Hips Road, 2012.

Yang, Mina. *California Polyphony: Ethnic Voices, Musical Crossroads*. Champaign: University of Illinois Press, 2008.

Yang, Mina. "A Thin Blue Line down Central Avenue: The LAPD and the Demise of a Musical Hub." *Black Music Research Journal* 22, no. 2 (2002): 217–39.

Zimmermann, Patricia R. *States of Emergency: Documentaries, Wars, Democracies*. Minneapolis: University of Minnesota Press, 2000.

Index

anonymity, 40, 79

Antenna Terra, 204

Anthology Film Archives, 139, 170–71, 307n205, 317n174

Anthony Braxton Quartet, 132

antiauthoritarianism, 79. *See also* counter-culture; politics and protests

antifolk, 29, 49–50

Anti-Pop Consortium, 95

apocalypse, 11, 37, 45–46, 96, 248, 296n214

appropriation, 122, 226. *See also* white artists

aquatic, 42–44, 50, 90

Arab on Radar, 216

architecture, 38, 192

Arias, Ricardo, 97

Armstrong, Louis, 251

Arnal, Jeff, 108–9, 129, 306n162; Improvised and Otherwise, 126–29

arson, 277n83. *See also* fire; safety issues

artist earnings, 151; early avant-garde era, 32, 37, 40, 42, 50, 79; grant funding, 120; Kalaparusha, 156–158; late era (post-2005), 147, 230, 232, 258–59, 265–66; turn of the millennium, 101, 127, 137, 169, 246, 289n77, 306n158. *See also* capitalism; economy; poverty

artist lives, 26, 40, 43, 49–50, 72, 86–87, 89, 115, 154, 194, 252–53, 266, 333n4; community survival, 12–17, 30, 60, 85, 116, 126, 137, 174, 229, 248, 253

artists of color, 130–31

Artists Space, 11, 272n18

art rock, 231–32, 237

art theory, 127, 175, 186; bricolage, 242, 318n206; immersionism, 27–28, 31, 280n148; shared language, 127; web jams, 38. *See also* Butler, Ken

Asch, Gregor. *See* DJ Olive

Asimov, Isaac, 237

aspiring artists, 78; early avant-garde era, 25, 31–32, 36–37, 56, 58, 65, 91–92; Kala-parusha, 158–59; late era (post-2005), 147, 228, 260; turn of the millennium, 99, 133, 224, 333n4. *See also* artist lives

Assembled: Free Jazz + Electronics, 95–97

Association for the Advancement of Creative Musicians. *See* AACM

Association of Williamsburgh/Greenpoint Artists, 24

Astro-Zombies, 47–48, *48*, 52

Atlanta, 62–63, 68–69, 287n56

Attias, Michael, 259

attrition, 228–29

audience, challenges to, 119, 140, 166, 216, 231, 241; emotional effect, 153; engagement, 173, 193–94; immersion, 37–38, 42–44; interaction with, 38; response, 35–36, 98, 160, 164, 216, 220, 259

AUM Fidelity, 207–8, 220

autobiographical influence, 192–93, 195, 199, 208, 244

autonomy, 148, 173, 230, 240, 255; losses, 265

Ayler, Albert, 7, 50, 83, 137, 151, 183–84, 194, 232–33, 320n243

Babbitt, Milton, 247

bagpipes, 88, 103, 118

Bailey, Derek, 138

Baker, Chet, 154

Baker, Newman Taylor, 165, 187

Baker, Ralph, 46, 283n199

Balkan culture, 200, 259, 307n199

Baltimore, 52, 107

Bang, Billy, 146, 148, 164, 184

Baraka, Amiri, 8, 185

Barbès, 105, 109, 113, *132*, 139, 190, 211, 258

Barcelona, 174

bar culture, 28–29, 50–52, 79, 116, 127, 230. *See also* beer; unlicensed venues

Barker, Andrew, 13, 62–65, 68–69, 82–83, *83*, 85, 92, 95–96, 234, 287n56, 289n94

Barker, Thurman, 76

Barnes, Tim, 111

Baron, Art, 165

Baron, Joey, 76

Barr, Mick, 242–46

Bartók, Béla, 134

basements, 39, 120, 139, 170, 175, 194

bass, 96–97, 121, 132, 134, 170, 178, 196, 198, 206, 210, 236–37; arco bass, 204; experiments in, 11, 34, 137, 166, 178, 184, 195, 233, 240–41; lack of, 124; upright bass, 70, 80

Bat Eats Plastic, 80, 293n149

Battles, 88, 90, 119, 295n203

Bauder, Matt, 114, *132*, 132–34, 213–14, 259; in collaboration, 138, 213

Beacon, 261

demographics, 21–23; artists, 274n22; Williamsburg, 274n34. *See also* Black lives; displacement; gentrification; Puerto Rican lives

demolition, 45, 53, 128, 229, 266. *See also* real estate

Dempster, Loren, 118

Deren, Maya, 195

DeRosa, Jon, 86, 90–92, *91*, 295n205, 296n206

destruction of property, 110, 121

Diamond, Harvey, 255

Dichotomy, 69

didgeridoo, 70

Digital Primitives, 179–81, *181*

digital technology, 15, 71, 265. *See also* technology

Dilloway, Aaron, 98

Dineen, Terry, 28–32, 37, 275n57

Dinkins, David, 44

Dirty Projectors, 190, 258

disability, 90, 251, 283n199

displacement, 52–53, 130, 141, 229, 266–67, 284n239, 298n243, 308n1

dissonance, 11–12, 181, 204, 231

distortion, 94, 95, 116, 180, 213, 240, 241

Ditmas Park, 258, 261

Dixon, Bill, 74, 113, 126, 134, 283n196, 300n30, 303n83, 306n157

DIY: Bushwick, 260; Death by Audio, 229, 230, 260; decline, 141; ethos, 2–3, 16, 56; labels, 49, 104; Manhattan lofts, 9; as practice, 104; production, 89; punk, 10; radio, 58, 60, *61*;and safety, 268; space-building, 28–29, 32, *35*, 39–40, 45, 49, 60, 76, 111, 115, 229–30, 268, 276n63, 278n92, 269; Wesleyan scene, 104; Williamsburg lofts, 58, 99, 260; Zebulon, 148

DJing, 40, 43–44, 79, 84, 95, 269, 280n136

DJ Olive, 40, 41, 42–43, 45, 280n136, 280n153

DJ Spooky, 95

DJ Tom Roe. *See* Roe, Tom

DNA (band), 11, 30, 122, 198

documentaries, 197

documentation, 208, 300n28; as art, 192; lack thereof, 150, 153, 161, 194, 196; rare recordings, 148, 159, 169, 178, 183–84, 186, 279n115; research methods, 16; street performance, 294n168. *See also* recording

Dolphy, Eric, 149, 155, 161, 225

Dominican lives, 22

Dorf, Michael, 176

Dörner, Alex, 93

downtown scene, 12–14, 30, 64–65, 69, 83, 93, 95, 137, 148, 176, 184, 208, 219, 291n114

Downtown Music Gallery, *74*, *113*, 313n103

Doyle, Arthur, 83, 91–92, 291n127

Drake, Hamid, 179–80

Drew, Kenny, 154

drinking. *See* bar culture

driving riffs, 120

drone styles, 11, 70, 114, 118, 172, 178, 196, 211, 290n96

drug use, crack epidemic, 6; in Williamsburg, 22–25, 46, 52, 61, 86, 121, 154, 156, 158, 160, 310n51

drum pedals, 233, 237

Dufallo, Cornelius, 166

Dulberger, Shayna, 236, 260

Dulman, Jesse, 10, 81, 156–60, 312n75

dumbek, 178, 319n217

Dunifer, Stephen, 60

Dunn, Judith, 126

Dunn, Trevor, 218

Dynamite Club, 109–10

Dynasty Electric, 120, 128, 304n124

Dzurinko, Virg, 256

Earwax Records, 25, 39, 53, 86, 275n36, 280n136

Eastman School of Music, 221

East New York, 74

East River, 25–26, 49, 81, 115, 229, 250

East Side, 70

East Village, 8, 10, 24–25, 45, 53, 274n29, 277n91, 279n125; Jerome Cooper, 186; Kim's Music and Video, 294n170, 295n184; Lawrence "Butch" Morris, 161; vs. Williamsburg, 29, 99; and Williamsburg collaborations, 64–65. *See also* downtown scene; Manhattan

Eaton, Tony, 92

echo, 95

economy, 23, 46–47, 76, 133, 156, 162, 247, 264–69, 333n4. *See also* capitalism

ecstasy, 52
editing music, 202, 213–14
Edom, 196–97, *198*
Edwards, Marc, 230–38, *235*, 243, 250
education: Anthony Braxton, 101–3, 299n14;
  Connie Crothers, 250–51, 256; learning
  experiences, 78, 157, 193–94, 198–99;
  privilege of, 46, 150; vs. traditional
  methods, 77, 122–24, 208–10, 233,
  236, 240; Lennie Tristano, 331n106;
  university programs, 150, 184, 190,
  221, 269–70, 309n29, 320n245; in
  Williamsburg, 6, 24. *See also* mentors;
  self-study
Eggwolf Series, 110–11, 114
87X, 57
Eisenstadt, Harris, 118, 259–60
Eldridge, Roy, 255–56
Electrik, Jenny, 115, 120–21
electronic music, 45, 81, 88, 95, 96, 176, 196,
  238, 202, 241–42, 249; electroacoustic
  music, 123, 296n215, 302n72
elitism, 264, 269
Ellington, Duke, 134, 186–87
Elliot, Moppa, 223–27
El Sensorium, 12, 42–45
email lists, 116, 137
Emerson, Dina, 29, 42, 43, 176
Emerson, Ralph Waldo, 112
Endsley, Shane, 221, 222, 223
energy orchestras, 163
Eno, Brian, 202
ensemble, 67, 69, 73, 118, 123, 135, 164, 185,
  204, 213–14
environmental topics, 27, 45, 133, 282n192.
  See also found objects
ephemerality, 44
Epoché, 31
Etten, Sharon Van, 190, 258
Eubanks, Duane, 165
Europe, 13, 39, 45, 93, 163, 290n106; critical
  tours, 77, *94*, 174, 180, 192, 211,
  220
Evangelista, Karl Alfonso, 238
Evans, Brandon, 103–4, 122–23, 299n14,
  307n203
Evans, Michael, 50, 129
Evans, Peter, 105, 148, 208–14, 223–26, 234,
  241, 260

event planning, 79, 104, 117, 126, 127, 140,
  147–48, 219, 230, 243, 258, 259; future
  of, 265
eviction, 24, 53, 85, 126, 141, 252, 266;
  abroad, 174; threat of, 257. *See also*
  displacement
Evil Jim. *See* Sherry, Jim
Ex, the, 77
experiment: sonic, 38
experimental cooking, 41–42
experimental music, 2–4; early avant-garde era,
  26, 28, 34–35, 38, 41–45, 47, 70–73, 75,
  85, 92, 95; turn of the millennium, 107,
  109, 112–13, 118, 123, 127, 129–31, 135,
  137, 139, 140, 149, 151, 155–60, 166, 169,
  176, 178, 180, 188; late era (post-2005),
  166, 192, 200, 202, 204, 206, 212, 215,
  218, 231, 238, 242, 255; legacy of, 269.
  See also composition; improvisation
Eye Contact, 194–96, *195*, 322n17

factories, 32, 38, 93, 112, 115, 274n29,
  278n92; environmental harm, 45. *See*
  postindustrial; warehouse movement
Fagaschinski, Kai, 93
fame, 158, 265
Fat Ragged, 190
Favors, Malachi, 155
Federal Communications Commission, 59–61
Federation of Ongolia, 45
Federici, Nicole, 166
feedback: uses of, 93, 96, 211, 213
Fei, James, 103–4, 139, 299n13
Feldman, Morton, 122
Fennelly, Jaime, 80–81, 93–96, 128, 293n153,
  293nn155–56
Ferneyhough, Brian, 123, 247
Festival of New Trumpet Music, 175
55Bar, 170
Fihi Ma Fihi, 37
Filiano, Ken, *108*, 136, 253–54, *254*
film: Anthology Film Archives, 139, 170–71,
  307n205, 317n174; B-movies, 37;
  Sofia Coppola, 204; Maya Deren, 195;
  documentaries, 197, 232; French films,
  96; *Godzilla*, 169; Italian films, 202;
  Spike Lee, 101, 184; Jonas Mekas, 146,
  171–72, 317n179; scenes, 25, 31, 44,
  48; stills, 246

Gnawa people, 199
Godzilla, 169
Goitsuka, Ryo, 84
Gold, Jessie, 69
Gold Sparkle Band, 62–65, 68, 286n33; as a duo, *83*
Gompertz, Jeff, 39, 280nn136–37
Good/Bad Art Collective, 80
Goodbye Blue Monday, 260
Goodie Mob, 63
Gordon, Dexter, 161
Gould, David, 194
Gowanus Canal, 135
graffiti, 25, 30, 34, 53, 58, 86, 99, 230
Graham, Forbes, 234, *235*
Graham Avenue, 24, 53, 266, 298n243
Grand Street, 13, 53, 60, 85–92, 100, 125, 129, 292n146
grant funding, 269, 298n3, 306n158, 311n64, 319n208
Great Migration, the, 191
Greenberg, Ben, 125, 215–16, 218
Greene, Hilliard, 148–49, 152, *153*, 309n21
Greene, Jimmy James, 185, 186, 320n257
Greenpoint, 24–25, 233, 275n36, 282n192, 308n216
Grey, Admiral, 236–37
Grimes, Henry, 256
grindcore, 239–40
Grizzly Bear, 190
G train line, 101
Guidici, Maria Alejandra, 40
guitar, 29, 35, 49, 70, 84; experiments by: Mike Barr, 245–46; Matt Bua, 72–73; DJ Olive, 43; Mary Halvorson, 107, 119–20; Medea de Vice, 33; Eivind Opsvik, 203; the peeesseye, 93–94; Kentaro Saito, 109; Andrew Smiley, 219; 220 Grand, 86–87; The Zs, 124
Gutierrez, Miguel, 80–81, 128, 293n152, 293n155–56
Guy, Buddy, 175

Haden, Charlie, 154, 161
Haffner, Jonathon, 165–68, 170, 316n169
Hagglund, Steve, 34
Haino, Keiji, 11, 84
Hairston, Jackie, 163
Haitian culture, 195

Hall, Ben, 128
Halloween, 116
Halsey, Onaje Will, 185–86
Halvorson, Mary, 92, 103–9, *106*, 117–20, 128, *132*, 132–33, 135–36, 226, 259, 300n35
Hamlet, 44
Hampel, Gunter, 184
handmade instruments, 34, 47, 71–73, 80–81, 86; Cooper-Moore, 179–80; Ken Butler, 175–79; piano-wire, 296n213
Hanley, Wells, 201
Hansen, Shawn, 96
Happy Land Social Club, 30, 52, 277n83
hardcore scene, 48, 216
Harlem, 75
harmonium, 95
harmony, 106, 256: experiments in, 11, 165, 167, 169, 196, 222, 251
harpsichord, 204
Harris, Jennifer, 169–70
Harris, Jesse, 169, 316n169
Harris, Ratzo, 253
Hartford, University of, 103
Hasidic lives, 21–23, 115, 121, 200–201, 252. *See also* Jewish lives; Radical Jewish Art
Hassan, Umar bin, 185
Hat Hut Records, 135
Hayden, Robert, 185
hearing loss, 81, 90
Hebert, John, 210
Heinlein, Robert, 237
Helias, Mark, 259
Helin, Yvette, 37, 308n1
Hella, 231
Helms, Jesse (Senator), 33
Hendrix, Jimi, 50
Henry, Myk, 37, 38
heroin, 154, 156, 158, 160, 310n51
Hersch, Fred, 210
hexachords, 241
Heyner, Matthew, 67, 75, 77, 194–96
Higgins, Billy, 161
Higgins, Patrick, 216
Hill, Andrew, 210
Hillmer, Sam, 122–25, 205
Himalayas. *See* Kenny Wollesen's Big Band
Hint House, 75

63, 83; Mary Halvorson, 118–20; Spike Hill, influence on, 259; Kalaparusha, 158; Kneebody, 221; Travis Laplante, 215; Matt Lavelle, 194; Lawrence "Butch" Morris, 161, 163; Mostly Other People Do the Killing, 223–24; Eivind Opsvik, 201–4; Matana Roberts Quartet, 191; Ryan Sawyer, 76–77; Matthew Ship, 95; Slipstream Time Travel, 238; TEST, 67; Kenny Wollesen's Big Band, 168; The Zs, 122–23; Zebulon, 146, 184–85, 210

jazz folk, 174

Jazz Gallery, 133, 136, 190

Jazz 966, 185

Jazz Right Now, 16

jazz rock, 197

Jazz Spot, the, 185

Jersey City, 292n141

Jewish lives, 21–22, 115, 121; and experimental music, 196–200, 323n43

JMZ Records, 87

Johnson, Russ, 13, 129

Joloff, 184–87, 320n249

Jonas, Chris, 65, 103

Jones, Darius, 205–8, 214–21, 234, *235*, 319n229

Jones, Jessica, 256

Jones, Leroi, 8

Jones, Will, 140

Judd, Donald, 27

Judson Memorial Church, 9

Jump Arts Festivals, 64–69, 146

Jus Grew Orchestra, 34

Kahlo, Frida, 180

Kahn, Brenda, 29

Kalaparusha and the Light, 154–61, *160*, 310n51, 311n55, 311n60, 311nn63–64, 311n67, 312n71, 312n73, 313n94, 313n99

Kalashnikov, 206

Kalisz, Corrina, 128

Kanaiwa, Takuma, 238

Kane, Bonnie, 50–51

Keep Refrigerated, 12, 39–40

Kelley, Greg, 139

Kenny Wollesen's Big Band, 168–72, 318n194

Kensington, 258, 261

Kent Avenue, 33, 37, 45, 46, 51, 53, *73*, 88, *89*, 250, 252, 253

Kerouac, Jack, 62

keyboards, 197, 202, 204, 207; experiments in, 11, 88, 129, 176, 240. *See also* piano

Kgositsile, Keorapetse William, 185

Kilmer, Matt, 176

Kim, Ha-Yang, 165–67

Kitchen, the, 9

Kjos, Jessica, 69

klezmer, 199–200, 307n199

Klotz, Jake, 78–79, 82, 84, 292n139

Kneebody, 221–23

Kneeland, Thomson, 190

Knitting Factory, the, 9, 12–13, 29–30, 64–65, 150–51, 158, 176, *205*, 250, 276n79, 278n110, 297n237; closure, 105; influence of, 71, 83, 86, 119; vs. Williamsburg, 77. *See also* downtown scene

Knoche, Christof, 165–66

Knott, Montgomery, 258–59, 333n139

Knuffke, Kirk, 166

Konitz, Lee, 251, 253–56, 331n104

Kosuth, Joseph, 27

Kouyate, Baye, 190

Kowald, Peter, 150

Krall, Jackson, 75

Kravas, Heather, 69

Künzli, Mathias, 200

Kwanzaa, 75

labor, exploited, 265–66

Lacy, Kuumba Frank, 187–88

Lalalandia, 40–45

Lamb, Andrew, 184–87

Landis, M. P., 69

Lane, Adam, 159, 234, *235*, 255

Laplante, Travis, 214–20, *217*, 227

Lateef, Yusef, 239

Latessa, Gabriella, 40, 43

Latin Kings, 23

Latino lives, 24, 98, 273n19, 284n239, 298n243

Lavelle, Matt, 65–66, 75, 194–96, 291n126

laws. *See* police, regulation

layering, 135, 219

Lee, Okkyung, 65, 69

Lee, Spike, 101, 184, 298n4

Ngaza Saba, 75
Niagara, 187
Nice Undies, 49, 52
Nicholson, Patricia, 9, 66, 287n54
nigguns, 201
Night Owl Studios, 70
9/11, 14–15, 67, 92, 168, 170, 182, 187, 250, 316n157
No Fun Festival, 97–98
No Wave, 198, 232, 234, 236, 272n21; influence of, 30, 216, 218, 247–49; movement, 10–11, 13
No-Neck Blues Band, 75–76, 292n128
Noë, Sasha, 38
NoHo: relocation from, 24
noise complaints, 172, 227, 230, 266
noise music, 9–12, 269; early avant-garde era, 29–30, 36–37, 49, 71, 81, 83–84, 88, 93, 297n237; late era (post-2005), 206, 208, 211, 216, 221, 230–31, 246, 250; turn of the millennium, 97, 111
non-repetition, 242
noncitizens, 268
nondiatonic scales, 195
Noriega, Oscar, 65, 206
Normal Love, 246–50, 247, 331n89
North Eighth Street, 53, 110
North Eleventh Street, 37, 60, 284n238
North Fifth Street, 46, 88, 284n238
North Ninth Street, 53, 100
North Seventh Street, 45, 48, 53, 81, 101, 127, 284n241
North Sixth Street, 39, 45, 50, 97–98, 100, 284n241
North Tenth Street, 33, 45, 46, 53
Northsix, 13, 97–98, 120
Norwegian musicians, 201–4
notated music, 299n14
notation, 192; lack of, 239
N.R.A., 97
Nublu Orchestra, 167
nudity, 37, 109
NuZion, 63

O'Brien, Julie, 38
O'Reilly, Evan, 132
O'Rourke, Jim, 97
Oakland, 268
occupation, 32

Ocrilim, 242
Octis, 242
October Revolution (punk venue), 45–48, 283n196
October Revolution in Jazz, 74, 283n196, 303n83, 306n157
Office Ops, 13, 92–96, 96
Old Dutch Mustard Factory, 12, 38–39
Olson, John, 98
omnisensorialism, 45, 280n148
Once 11, 40, 45
Onkyo, 93, 208, 296n217
Open Loose, 259
open-mics, 29, 260
opera, 127, 183, 303n92, 317n187
Opsvik, Eivind, 140, 201–4, 203
Optimus Tribe, 121
Orange Bear, 73
orchestras, 103, 118, 239; Lawrence "Butch" Morris, 165–67
Orchestra SLANG, 166
organ, 206
Organism, 38–39
Orthrelm, 125, 231
Otomo, Yoshihide, 93, 208
Otto's Shrunken Head, 234–35, 235
oud, 199
outside art, 244
Overall, Kassa, 210
Overground Improvised Music Series, 136–38
Overseas, 201–4, 203
Oxley, Tony, 71, 210, 290n106

Pachora, 138, 200
Paleface, 49
Pan-Afrikan Peoples Arkestra, 67, 162, 314n117
Panciera, Rich, 45
panoramic sound quilting, 192
Parallactic Records, 104
Parker, Charlie, 224, 251, 255–56
Parker, Evan, 208–9
Parker, Jeff, 136
Parker, William, 8–9, 156, 179, 182, 184, 208, 293n153, 319n220, 321n269; influence of, 64, 76–77, 224; as a mentor, 67, 80. See also downtown scene; Nicholson, Patricia
Parkins, Zeena, 176, 276n79

Public Nuisance (band), 48
Puerto Rican lives, 21–22, 45, 53, 56–57, 266,
    273nn4–5, 282n192, 285n3
Pugilese, Jim, 30
Pulverize the Sound, 241
punk, 10, 24, 32, 34, 37, 46–47, 48, 52, 196,
    201, 278n101, 278n110; influence of,
    78, 80, 218, 230, 231
puppet theater, 169
Pyramid Trio, 178

Queens (borough), 251, 261
Quiet Village, 42

racial disparity, 150–51, 154, 185–86, 273n4.
    See Black lives; Puerto Rican lives
racial integration, 161, 248, 314n109
Raddant, Megan, 38
Radding, Reuben, 52, 108
Radiac, 45, 282n192. See also environmen-
    tal topics
Radical Jewish Art, 196, 199, 200
radio, 12. 17, 22, 79, 283, 302n72; Radio Free
    Berkeley, 59–60; Radio Moscow, 30;
    WFMU, 79, 280n137. See also
    free103point9; pirate radio
Radioactive Bodega, 12, 45–50
Rahman, Yusuf, 185
Rainbow, Caroliner, 290n108, 291n109
Rainey, Bhob, 139
Ranaldo, Lee, 97
rap, 38, 185, 287n44
Rashanim, 200, 324n48
Rastegar, Kaveh, 221, 222
raves, 32, 41, 52
Rawlings, Vic, 97
Read Cafe, 13, 105, 110–13, 114, 142, 303n90
real estate, 39, 44, 53–54, 98–99, 126, 128–
    29, 141, 264, 266, 267, 273n3, 277n83,
    282n184, 284n238. See also gentrifica-
    tion; Mayor Michael Bloomberg; rent;
    zoning
Rechtern, Mario, 234
record stores, 15, 39, 285n6. See also Earwax
    Records
recording, 49, 104, 151, 158, 164, 179, 200,
    214, 218; Eye Contact, 322n17; field
    sounds, 72, 80; Improvised and Other-
    wise, 291n126; Jump Arts Orches-

tra, 288n61; live music, 67, 75, 148,
    153, 174, 223, 235, 272n18, 287n56,
    292n128, 309n15; vs. live music, 213;
    Butch Morris, 315n132; The Mov-
    ing Form, 321n261; Eivind Opsvik,
    324n59; the peeesseye, 297n225; as
    practice, 95, 180, 202, 212, 214, 249;
    Slipstream Time Travel, 329n37;
    Unbroken Trio, 320n242; value, 15;
    Kenny Wollesen's Big Band, 318n194.
    See also documentation
Red Hook, 130, 132
Red Krayola, 79
Reed, Bradford, 38
Reed, Lou, 10
Regev, Reut, 65–66, 75
regulation, 5, 30–31, 33, 44, 52–54, 85, 98,
    126, 266, 267, 268; fires, 40; lack
    thereof, 14, 25–26, 57; protests of, 33;
    radio, 59, 286n15. See also economy;
    police; politics and protest; rent; wars;
    zoning
Reich, Steve, 249
relevancy, 125
religion, 162; influence of, 150–51
relocation, 23–25
R.E.M., 79
removal of: memorials, 275n40; visual art,
    266. See also demolition
rent, 4; early avant-garde era, 13–14, 25, 28,
    37, 42, 53, 56, 58, 64, 78, 86, 157, 267,
    273n14, 273n19; turn of the millen-
    nium, 98–99, 115, 133, 308n216; late
    era (post-2005), 130, 140–41, 228,
    247, 266–67
Rent Regulation Reform Act of 1997, the, 53
repetition, 206
Residents, the, 80
restaurants, 146, 184, 187, 258, 308n8
reverb, 213
Reverb Motherfuckers, 32
Ribot, Marc, 197
Richards, Cheryl, 256
Richardson, Alison, 128
Ridgewood, 101, 261
riff effects, 169
Rigby, Jason, 201
Right Bank Cafe, 12–13, 50–52, 91, 104–9,
    125, 142

Silverback, 187–88, 321n265, 321n267

Simmons, Sonny, 104

Simons, David, 80

Simons, Seymour, 254

Sistas's Place, 185

sitar, 176, 178

SLAM. *See* Kenny Wollesen's Big Band

slavery: influence of, 192–94

Slipstream Time Travel, 237–39, *238*

Slutfish Recordings, 49

small audiences, 86, 107, 110, 148, 174, 254, 259

Smiley, Andrew, *217*, 219–21

Smith, Ches, 259

Smith, Jack, 246

Smith, Kerry, 51–52, 110

Smith, Patti, 171, 278n101

Smith, Wadada Leo, 31, 131

Smith, Warren, 158, 184, 186

smoking, 116, 247

Snyder, Tor, 75, *238*

SoHo, 8, 24; vs. Williamsburg, 31, 40

Sonic Youth, 83, 88, 97

Sorvisto, Glenn, 51

Soubiran, Jef, 134, 145–48

Soubiran, Joce, 145–48

Soubiran brothers, 145–48, 159, 161, 179, 188–89, 198, 205, 211, 219

sound installations, 258

Soundscape, 9

Sound Unity Festival, 74

South Brooklyn, 129, 139, 235, 258, 261. *See also* Ditmas Park, Kensington, Park Slope

South Fifth Street, 42, 53, 72, 139

South Second Street, 23, 229, 298n243, 316n169

South Sixth Street, 53, 56, 59, 60, 100, 274n29

South Slope, 261

Soviet Russia, 223

Spacemen 3, 70

space themes, 237

Spanish Donkey, 206

Sparks, 208–10, *209*

Spike Hill, 14, 174, 259–60

spiritualism, 155, 157, 172, 195, 236, 319n209

spoken word, 185

spontaneity, 210, 224, 252

Spriggs, Edward, 185

Spring Garden Music House, 247

squatting, 23–26, 33, 36, 45–46, 49, 52–53, 77, 150, 274n29, 275n43, 279n125, 282n191. *See also* artist lives; rent

St. James Place, 184

St. Vitus, 234

Stabinsky, Ron, 225

Stars Like Fleas, 259

Star Trek, 238

State University of New York at Old Westbury, 184

Stay Fucked (band), 216

Steele, Allen, 237

Sticks and Stones, 190

Stillman, Loren, 201–2

Stockhausen, Karlheinz, 240

Stone, the, 9, 14, 133, *212*, 235, *243*

Storm and Stress, 119, 304n118

Stratton, Jeremy, 253

streaming, 265

street life: fights, 47, 56–57; music, 44, 67, 148–49, 150–51, 156–57, 160

string instruments, 166; experiments in, 179

Strobe Light Sound Studio, 184

Strobert, Andrei, 184, 320

Strokes, the, 88

Studio Rivbea, 156

Sub Pop, 97

Sufism, 243

Sugimoto, Taku, 208

Sun Ra, 34, 120, 191, 237, 239, 249, 279n113, 290n102, 321n271

Sun Ra Arkestra, 50, 146

surfer rock, 52

Swell, Steve, 65–66, 69, 75, 112, 113, 184, 259, 303n77

Swift, Mazz, 166

Syndrome, Billy, 29, 31, 34, 35, 48–49, *49*, 52, 276n71

synthesizers, 70, 96, 170, 198

Szold, Lauren, 37, 279n122

tabla, 202

Tabnik, Richard, 251–53

Taboo (band), 42

Taborn, Craig, 201–2

tabulation, 199

Taino community, 53

Takahashi, Michiko, 81–82, *82*